This Far by Faith

Edited by

DAVID R. CONTOSTA

This Far by Faith

Tradition and Change in the Episcopal Diocese of Pennsylvania

The Pennsylvania State University Press
University Park, Pennsylvania

This publication was made possible by a generous grant from the Episcopal Diocese of Pennsylvania.

Library of Congress Cataloging-in-Publication Data

This far by faith : tradition and change in the Episcopal Diocese of Pennsylvania / edited by David R. Contosta.
p. cm.
Summary: "A collection of essays tracing the history of the Episcopal Church in Pennsylvania, with emphasis on the greater Philadelphia area. Includes discussions of the diversity of practice and belief within the church, and between the church and the wider national culture"—Provided by publisher.
Includes bibliographical references and index.
ISBN 978-0-271-05244-1 (cloth : alk. paper)
ISBN 978-0-271-05245-8 (pbk. : alk. paper)
1. Episcopal Church. Diocese of Pennsylvania—History.
2. Episcopal Church—Pennsylvania—Philadelphia—History.
I. Contosta, David R.
BX5918.P4T45 2012
283'.748—DC23
2011047417

Printed in the United States of America
Published by The Pennsylvania State University Press, University Park, PA 16802-1003

The Pennsylvania State University Press is a member of the Association of American University Presses.

It is the policy of The Pennsylvania State University Press to use acid-free paper. Publications on uncoated stock satisfy the minimum requirements of American National Standard for Information Sciences—Permanence of Paper for Printed Library Material, ANSI Z39.48–1992.

In Memory of

the Reverend F. Lee Richards (1918–2011)

Historiographer of the Diocese of Pennsylvania (1977–2005)

And with Gratitude

to Glenn Colliver, Archivist of the Diocese of Pennsylvania

CONTENTS

FIGURES

Unless otherwise noted, all images are from the Archives of the Episcopal Diocese of Pennsylvania, Philadelphia.

TABLES

TABLES

ABBREVIATIONS

BCC	Bulletin Clippings Collection, Urban Archives, Temple University, Philadelphia
Diopa	Episcopal Diocese of Pennsylvania
DN	*Diocesan News*
HMPEC	*Historical Magazine of the Protestant Episcopal Church*
HSP	Historical Society of Pennsylvania, Philadelphia
JDC	*Journal of the Diocesan Convention*
PE	*Pennsylvania Episcopalian*
PMHB	*Pennsylvania Magazine of History and Biography*
SPG	Society for the Propagation of the Gospel in Foreign Parts
TCN	*The Church News*

Introduction

DAVID R. CONTOSTA

The Episcopal Diocese of Pennsylvania—and its precursor, the Church of England in colonial Pennsylvania—have been shaped by complex historical forces. These include the history of Christianity, especially during its first centuries, the foundations of the Church of England in the sixteenth century, patterns of colonial society, an evolving American culture, world events, and life in southeastern Pennsylvania, where the diocese has been centered.

Local Episcopalians have also been part of a national church that over the past two centuries has often been informed by dual impulses. Their church has seen itself as both Catholic and Protestant—a "reformed" church that claims apostolic succession for its bishops but allows for a large degree of decentralization and governance by the laity. Despite Episcopalians' strong roots in the Church of England, they eventually came to see themselves as the most American of all Christian denominations. This claim stemmed in large part from the disproportionate number of Episcopalians in national leadership positions. Of the forty-four presidents of the United States, eleven of them, or 25 percent, have been Episcopalians, although Episcopalians have never made up more than 3 percent of the U.S. population. The decision by the Episcopal Church in the early twentieth century to build the National Cathedral in Washington, D.C., often the setting for funerals and other services involving high-ranking officials, is a powerful symbol of its claim to be the national church of the United States.

Another duality has involved the Episcopal Church's emphasis on tradition, combined, in the best of times, with an openness to change as the wider culture presents new challenges. Tradition is grounded especially in the basic faith statement of the Nicene Creed and in the Book of Common Prayer. But respect for reason, as a divine gift and as an appropriate tool for reconciling tradition with present reality, has saved the denomination from rigid traditionalism. Episcopalians have approached the Bible in a similar spirit: different persons derive various meanings from scripture, and the Bible needs to be interpreted in the light of modern life. The Book of Common Prayer, which draws heavily on the Bible, also permits some latitude. While the words of the liturgy will be the same in every parish, actual worship practices might vary from Anglo-Catholic, at one end of the spectrum, to evangelical at the other.

This "latitudinarian" approach to faith and worship has been part of the Church of England (and of the larger Anglican Communion, of which the Episcopal Church is now a part) since Queen Elizabeth I embraced a middle way that came to be known as the Elizabethan Settlement. This middle way has been one of the glories of Anglicanism, but it has also opened the door to controversy in every era. Without an infallible pope or a belief in a literal and unchanging understanding of the Bible, Episcopalians have been free to disagree about both faith and action. Yet, as one historian of the Episcopal Church has written, "Controversy is unpleasant but it is often a sign of life. A peaceful church is one that is slowly dying."

In the end, the Church of England's middle way and conditions in colonial Pennsylvania meshed very well. Pennsylvania was the quintessential "middle colony" and then, following independence, "middle state." Quaker tolerance did not allow for an established church in Pennsylvania. The Quakers' belief in human equality, combined with their practice of toleration, also meant that immigrants were welcome from all over western Europe, making Pennsylvania a precursor of the religious and cultural diversity that would come to characterize the entire United States. Though members of the Church of England in colonial Pennsylvania were initially unhappy about their status as just one religious group among others, they eventually accommodated themselves to the situation.

Pennsylvania's middling position, geographically and culturally among the original states, made it the obvious place for founding the Episcopal Church after the American Revolution. William White, the rector of Christ Church, Philadelphia, and the Diocese of Pennsylvania's first bishop, was able to use his sense of a middle way and a genius for compromise to persuade southern members of the faith, long wedded to lay control of their church, to accept bishops, without which the New Englanders would not have joined the fold. Meeting at Christ Church in 1789, the same year that the new Constitution of the United States of America took effect, White presided over the birth of the national church. Just five years before, in 1784, he had coaxed the Diocese of Pennsylvania into being.

White's newly minted diocese became the "mother diocese" of the Episcopal Church, while his Christ Church became the mother church of the entire denomination.

This history of the Diocese of Pennsylvania, especially during its earlier years, is in many ways a history of the Episcopal Church at large. Even in more recent years, as it remains one of the largest and most influential dioceses in the national church, its story has paralleled and illustrated the challenges and accomplishments of the wider denomination.

In chapter 1 of this volume (1695–1775), Deborah Mathias Gough examines the difficulties and anomalies that members of the Church of England faced in colonial Pennsylvania. During their first few decades, they campaigned to have Pennsylvania made into a royal colony, which would have deprived the Penn family of its proprietorship. They also petitioned the Church of England to send them a bishop. They failed on both counts, and by 1715 they had reconciled themselves to accepting religious pluralism and recognizing other denominations as legitimate. The church succeeded in attracting the small numbers of Swedish Lutherans in southeastern Pennsylvania, but the more numerous German Lutherans resisted calls to join. Clergy shortages plagued the Church of England in Pennsylvania throughout the colonial period, as did the lack of a bishop to supervise clergy and enforce order within the church.

William Pencak, in chapter 2, looks at how the crisis of the American Revolution (1775–1790) affected members of the Church of England, whose liturgy required prayers for the British monarch and whose clergy had had to swear loyalty to the Crown. Because of this, clergymen were automatically suspect among supporters of the Revolution, whether or not they were loyal to Britain. Thanks to the common sense and leadership of William White, the Diocese of Pennsylvania and a separate Episcopal Church were established during this period. As such, the Episcopal Church became the first of many autonomous churches within what would later be called the Anglican Communion. In the spirit of the new American Republic, both the diocese and the national church mandated the election of bishops and a bicameral legislative body, with wide representation for lay members. Although centered in Philadelphia, the new Diocese of Pennsylvania covered the entire commonwealth until the diocese was subdivided many years later.

In chapter 3, Emma Jones Lapsansky-Werner examines the diocese during its first three decades (1790–1820). Although they had declared their independence from Great Britain, Episcopalians were still sometimes stigmatized because of their prior connections to the Church of England

and its now unpopular monarchy. As an urban-centered church, many of whose members were prosperous, the Diocese of Pennsylvania often had a hard time relating itself to the less prosperous rural population elsewhere in Pennsylvania. The diocese also had difficulty competing with other denominations, such as the Methodists, who preached a simple but often inspiring message without the need for a highly structured liturgy, or even a church building in which to preach. Many African Americans felt more comfortable with the informal ways of the Methodist clergy than they did with the more formal Episcopal Church. Indeed, it took Bishop White ten years to raise Absalom Jones, the leader of the all-black African Episcopal Church of St. Thomas, from deacon to full-fledged priest, and Jones was never seated at a diocesan convention, as were all white clergy. Racial prejudice and segregation would continue to plague the diocese in the years to come.

Charles D. Cashdollar tackles a period of growth and new challenges for the Pennsylvania diocese in chapter 4. During the twenty-year period 1820–1840, the number of parishes doubled, and Pennsylvania's population spilled out into the central and western counties of the commonwealth. But much of this growth took place in Philadelphia, as groups of men decided, all too often, to start a new parish within just a few blocks of another Episcopal church. The diocese adopted a laissez-faire approach to this development, a position that would come back to haunt future bishops, who would face a shrinking urban population and demographic changes unfavorable to membership in the Episcopal Church. During this same period, the high-church Oxford Movement began to attract many in the diocese, touching off a protracted struggle between them and low-church adherents.

While the diocese continued to be rent by disagreements over worship style, Philadelphia was rocked by racial and religious conflict, described by Marie Conn in chapter 5 (1840–1865). The diocese was not involved in the violence that too frequently accompanied this conflict, but it attempted to deal with some of the underlying causes of urban strife by creating a number of institutions to address contemporary problems and needs in an organized way.

Ann Norton Greene takes on an especially rich period in diocesan history (1865–1910) in chapter 6. Membership surged during the so-called Gilded Age, as newly rich men and women found the respectability and orderly worship of the Episcopal Church a fitting match for their rising social status. Quarrels continued between the high- and low-church factions, however, leading to the foundation of the Reformed Episcopal

Church in 1873, which a small number in the diocese left to join. Greene concludes her chapter with a discussion of the Social Gospel Movement, one of the central forces in the Progressive Era.

During the period 1910–1945, Thomas Rzeznik explains in chapter 7, new parishes were formed, and the diocese laid plans for a huge cathedral in Roxborough. Episcopalians reached the zenith of their influence in these decades, laying claim more than ever before to being the "nation's church." The building of the George Washington Memorial Chapel at Valley Forge was a physical manifestation of this attitude. At the same time, however, attempts to establish more central authority over the diocese were sometimes resented and even resisted at the parish level. The Great Depression and the two world wars, by contrast, fostered a strong sense of collective mission—though some clergy thought it wrong to glorify war or to politicize the work of the church, especially during World War II.

During that war and the postwar period (1942–1963), with its crusade against Communism, many Americans turned to religion. The Pennsylvania diocese saw significant growth, especially in the suburbs outside Philadelphia. Some critics lamented that the suburban churches were cut off from the city, content to ignore poverty, racial injustice, and other urban problems. The diocese and the national church were also slow to address questions of gender inequality. William Cutler explores these issues in chapter 8.

The period 1963–1979, addressed by Sheldon Hackney in chapter 9, was a study in contrasts. Bishop Robert DeWitt plunged into a fight for social, racial, and gender justice that alarmed many members of the diocese. There was particular anger over DeWitt's acceptance of the Black Manifesto, which demanded massive monetary reparations from the white churches for historic and ongoing discrimination against African Americans. DeWitt also participated in the first ordination of a woman priest, in defiance of tradition and without the blessing of the national church. A significant number of members were so angry with their bishop that they stopped making pledges or left the denomination altogether. At the very end of DeWitt's term as bishop, the Episcopal Church adopted and began using a new Book of Common Prayer.

The new prayer book, more thoroughly revised than any of its American predecessors, angered many Episcopalians in the Pennsylvania diocese and elsewhere. As David Contosta explains in chapter 10, this disaffection was one of several issues that created a "perfect storm" in the period 1979–2010. Continuing unhappiness over the ordination of women among a small but vocal minority, combined with the ordination of gay and lesbian priests in the diocese, led several parishes to withhold their contributions to the diocese. Some parishes attempted to leave the diocese altogether and to affiliate themselves with more conservative bishops in the United States or abroad. Dwindling membership in urban parishes had led the diocese to subsidize a number of these parishes. Decisions to close or merge such parishes, instead of continuing to support them with diocesan funds, led to considerable anger toward Bishop Charles Bennison. Despite this contention, Bennison and his predecessor, Allen Bartlett, succeeded in making the large Victorian Gothic Church of the Saviour into the diocese's first cathedral.

Just how the most recent controversies would be resolved was unclear as the diocese moved beyond its 225th anniversary. It can at least be said that such controversy is no stranger to the Diocese of Pennsylvania. In the end, a middle way, in the best tradition of the Episcopal Church, might well offer answers that will prove acceptable to the great majority in the long run.

1

The Colonial Church

Founding the Church, 1695–1775

DEBORAH MATHIAS GOUGH

In 1695, thirty-nine committed Anglicans banded together to found Christ Church, Philadelphia, the first Anglican church in what would become Pennsylvania and the church that would become known as the mother of the Episcopal Church in the United States. Christ Church joined Gloria Dei (Old Swedes') Lutheran Church, whose members had begun worshipping at its current site in 1677, another Swedish church on Tinicum Island, and Immanuel Church in what would become New Castle, Delaware, as the only non-Quaker places of worship in the colony. Within the next ten years, similar small groups of Anglicans founded Trinity Church in Oxford, St. James's in Perkiomen, St. Peter's in the Great Valley, St. David's in Radnor, St. Thomas's in Whitemarsh, St. Martin's in Marcus Hook, St. John's in Concord, and St. Paul's in Chester.

These small groups of Anglicans throughout Pennsylvania were determined to re-create the church and the society that they had left behind in England, no small task in a colony dominated by Quakers. The seventeenth- and eighteenth-century Church of England defined itself primarily by three characteristics: its status as a state church; its episcopal form of government; and its adherence to the Book of Common Prayer and the theology contained therein. Of these three, only the prayer book existed in the Quaker colony.

Almost all Englishmen at the time believed in the necessity of an established church. To allow freedom of religion inevitably would lead to freedom *from* religion, something an orderly society could not allow. By the eighteenth century many had rejected the belief that the Church of England was the only way to salvation, but Englishmen still believed that the state had to promote inward virtue, or religion, to assure outwardly good behavior. Being an established church had both benefits and liabilities. Financial support was assured—all Englishmen, even dissenters, paid

FIGURE 1.1 Gloria Dei (Old Swedes') Church, Philadelphia, erected 1700

tithes to support the Anglican Church. People accused of immoral behavior could be brought to the archdeacon's and bishop's courts. But this also meant that neither clergy nor Anglican congregations had much control over their church. Most rectors were chosen by government officials or by prominent laymen. "Select vestries," a group of leading men responsible for the care of the poor, auditing the church warden's accounts, and other minor duties, were often self-perpetuating; they had no control over the selection of or salary given to clergy.

The second crucial characteristic of the Church of England was its episcopal form of government. While not all Englishmen agreed with the high-church faction that apostolic succession was crucial for a true church, they did believe that the episcopate was necessary to keep order in the church and to maintain the proper relationship between church and state. Either the bishop or his assistant, the archdeacon, visited each parish annually, checking on the performance of the clergy, the condition of the church building and other property, and the morals of the people. Only clergymen ordained by a bishop were considered legitimate.

Even more important than the episcopate in defining the Church of England for its members was the Book of Common Prayer. To an Anglican, the prayer book was both the symbol and the reality of the national church. No matter what personal or theological controversies might rock the church, the prayers would remain the same, providing continuity with the past and a sense of oneness with Anglicans throughout the realm. Anglicans believed that the liturgy, which should be characterized by "uniformity, dignity, comprehensiveness, order and tradition," was the prayer of the whole church, not of the individual. This devotion to a set liturgy provided the main source of unity among Anglicans and distinguished them most clearly from dissenters.[1]

It would be difficult to find a religious group whose beliefs, worship style, and way of life were more different from those of the Anglicans than the Quakers, or Society of Friends. Founded in 1652 by George Fox, Quakerism, which can accurately be called a form of "group mysticism," espoused the belief that all people—not just Christians—had God within themselves. Because God spoke directly to everyone, there was no need for an ordained ministry or even preplanned worship; Quaker meetings were silent until someone was moved by God to speak. Quaker beliefs also led to a lifestyle that rejected most of what Anglicans believed—they refused to use titles of any kind, abjured oaths, rejected most kinds of recreation, and, most notably, were active pacifists. It is not surprising, therefore, that churchmen in England reserved a special degree of odium for the Quakers, even after many Anglicans had reluctantly accepted the presence of other dissenters. In fact, many Anglicans did not even consider Quakers Christians.[2]

One Quaker belief did, however, help the Anglicans in Pennsylvania. Because God resided in each person, Quakers rejected the idea that the government could tell anyone what to believe. Among the laws "Agreed Upon in England" by the Quaker proprietor William Penn and later ratified by the legislature in Pennsylvania was one that assured all people who believed in God that they would not be "molested or prejudiced for their Religious Persuasion or Practice" or forced to "frequent or maintain any Religious Worship, Place or Ministry whatever."[3] In the end, this law establishing religious freedom determined the future of Pennsylvania more than any other, for it doomed most other aspects of the Quakers' "Holy Experiment," ensuring that Quakers would quickly become a minority in their own colony. At the same time, it allowed the colony to become a true religious experiment, the results of which would greatly influence the Episcopal Church and make Pennsylvania a precursor of religious life in nineteenth-century America.

To Anglicans in Pennsylvania in the 1690s, the entire "Holy Experiment" seemed to turn the world upside down. King William, Queen Mary, and the Anglican parliament had been replaced by the proprietary rule of the Quaker William Penn and a colonial Assembly dominated by Quakers who often seemed to forget that they were under royal rule. The dangerous beliefs of a hated religious minority—including pacifism—were now law. Quaker judges refused to administer oaths. Most forms of entertainment—cards, dice, the theater—were outlawed. And Quakers owned most of the best land and dominated commercial life in the city.

Colonial Pennsylvania

The religious situation may have looked bleak, but the colony, particularly the city of Philadelphia, was thriving. While only about fifteen hundred people lived there in 1695, Philadelphia was already a thriving business center and had established itself as the Delaware River's chief port, serving Pennsylvania, West Jersey, and what is today Delaware. Andreas Rudman, the pastor of Gloria Dei, reported in 1700, "If anyone were to see Philadelphia who had not been there [before], he would be astonished beyond measure [to] learn that it was founded less than twenty years ago. Even Uppsala, etc. would have to yield place to it. All the houses are built of brick, three or four hundred of them, and in every house a shop, so that whatever one wants at any time he can have, for money."[4]

Taking their cue from Boston and New York, Philadelphia merchants made their money by transporting Pennsylvania's agricultural goods and forest products to the West Indies, obtaining bills of exchange or sugar, which they used to buy manufactured goods in England. By 1700 there were four shipyards in Philadelphia. These shipbuilders were joined by craftsmen of all varieties who served both the city and the countryside.

While Philadelphia prospered, its residents refused to abide by William Penn's initial plan for a "green country town" spread out between the Delaware and Schuylkill rivers. Instead, the population congregated along the Delaware River, subdividing lots and creating alleys between the streets Penn had laid out. By 1698 nine alleys had been cut through from Front to Second Street. Soon Philadelphia became one of the most congested cities in America, with few people living beyond Fourth Street. It would be the mid-nineteenth century before Philadelphia expanded as far west as Penn had envisioned.[5]

Outside the city of Philadelphia, Pennsylvanians, both the Swedes who had been there since the 1640s and more recent English settlers, were primarily subsistence farmers during the early years, trading grain and meat for needed supplies. But the Pennsylvania countryside quickly developed into a thriving agricultural region, and by the late colonial period it had become the "breadbasket" of the British Empire.

Both the strong economy and religious freedom attracted settlers from throughout Europe. By the 1740s Lutherans from Germany and Presbyterians from Scotland and Ireland had joined such religiously oppressed groups as Mennonites, Moravians, Amish, and Catholics. Even as early as 1699, the 947 Quakers living in Philadelphia were neighbors to approximately 550 Anglicans, 969 Baptists, Presbyterians and others.[6] Despite this diversity, the Quakers controlled the legislature and dominated society for much of the colonial period.

Early Anglican Crusades

While Anglicans would eventually come to accept this diversity and form alliances with Lutherans and Presbyterians, during the early years of the colony their focus was on making their new home as much like their old one as possible. This required three things: making Pennsylvania a royal colony; bringing a bishop to the colonies so that true episcopal government could be returned to their churches; and converting as many Quakers as they could from "heathenism" to Anglicanism.

From 1700 to 1711 the vestry and rectors of Christ Church, as well as prominent Anglican laymen, wrote to both ecclesiastical and secular authorities, imploring them to establish royal government in Pennsylvania. They railed against marriage laws that required justices of the peace to be present and the refusal of Quakers to administer oaths or defend the colony against pirates. Penn complained about the "heat of a few churchmen, headed by a Flanders camp parson, under the protection of the Bishop of London [who] enveigh against us and our government." To the churchmen's dismay, neither their crusades nor Penn's eventual decision to sell his colony to the Crown were successful; the deaths of both Penn and Queen Anne ended these efforts.[7]

At the same time that Anglicans were attempting to control the government, they were also working to establish some order in their churches by obtaining a bishop for the colonies. From the time of the founding of the colonies, American churches had been under the authority of the bishop of London. While earlier bishops had considered this only a nominal responsibility, Henry Compton, who became bishop in 1689, took his responsibilities seriously. Despite his efforts, however, the absence of a resident bishop created problems. Since clergy had to travel to England to be ordained, they remained in short supply through much of the colonial period. Parishioners could not be confirmed, and neither clergy nor laity could be disciplined. As one minister put it, without a bishop there was no one to "Rule and Govern, no Ecclesiastical Sword to Punish the unruly, reduce the erring and cut off the obstinate heretique."[8]

Without a bishop, controversies between ministers or between ministers and laity often erupted out of control. In 1715 Christ Church was torn apart by allegations that its temporary minister, Francis Phillips, had slandered three prominent women by boasting that he had slept with them. Although Phillips was convicted of slander, in the absence of a bishop to remove him from his post, he was able to continue in the pulpit for months before a letter of removal arrived from England. Moreover, clergymen protested, without a bishop it was easy for their enemies—both within and outside the church—to falsely accuse them. In 1705 fourteen clergymen met in Burlington, New Jersey, and sent a letter to the bishop of London, arguing that a bishop was needed to protect the clergy from "Seditious Men's Counsels," to "Cover us from the Malignant Effects of those misrepresentation that have been made by some persons, impower'd to admonish and inform against us, who indeed want admonition themselves." Despite sound reasons for needing a bishop, English politics kept the colonial Anglicans from achieving their goal.[9]

The third goal of the early Pennsylvania Anglicans was to convert Quakers. Evan Evans, the energetic Welsh clergyman who became rector of Christ Church in 1700, led this effort. Regularly traveling up to forty miles to preach, he baptized eight hundred people in seven years. His efforts were greatly aided by the establishment in 1701 of the Society for the Propagation of the Gospel in Foreign Parts, or SPG, a private missionary society in England. Having heard that many colonists lacked "the Administration of God's Word and Sacraments, and seem to be Abandoned to Atheism and Infidelity," prominent Anglicans joined together to ensure that "a sufficient Maintenance be provided for an Orthodox Clergy to live amongst" these colonists. This was the first time that members of the Church of England involved themselves in missionary work; ironically, their primary beneficiaries were Anglicans themselves.[10]

The first act of the SPG in 1702 was to send two virulently anti-Quaker clergymen to Pennsylvania and equip them with one thousand copies of the most extreme anti-Quaker tracts. One of them, George Keith, a former Quaker who had caused a split within the Pennsylvania Quaker community before converting to the Church of England, was known for his love of controversy and his hatred of Quakers. He was joined by John Talbot, who remained an SPG missionary in New Jersey until his death in 1725. Their arrival ushered in several years of often nasty confrontations between Anglicans and Quakers in meetinghouses and the press. While they spoke to huge crowds, energizing Anglicans, by Keith's own admission his efforts at conversion were largely unsuccessful.[11]

By 1715 all three prongs of Pennsylvania Anglicans' strategy to re-create the society they had known in England had failed. They were forced to accept that the colony would remain in the control of the Penn family, that Quakers were not going to convert in large numbers, that Anglicans would be a minority in a heterogeneous society with no established church, and that a bishop would not arrive in the colonies anytime soon. But while they had not achieved any of their original goals, Anglicans had founded eleven churches and, particularly in Philadelphia, had a thriving religious community. Christ Church, which had five hundred members by 1700, had already been enlarged twice before construction began in 1717 on the building that stands today. As a result of this success, Anglicans learned to accept religious freedom, to view other denominations as legitimate, and to realize that vigorous competition, combined at times with cooperation, was conducive to the health and prosperity of both the church and the colony.

These were lessons that other colonies took far longer to learn. In Massachusetts and Connecticut, where Anglicans were the dissenters from the Puritan establishment and where many churchmen had converted, Anglican-Calvinist hostility continued off and on throughout the colonial period. Many Anglican ministers considered controversy essential for the growth of the church. In southern states, where the Anglican Church was established and dissenters were few until later in the colonial period, controversy was muted, but in South Carolina, where dissenters were numerous, hostility toward the establishment only increased as the eighteenth century progressed. And in New York, where the church was established in the lower counties, anti-Anglican sentiment remained latent, surfacing in the 1750s over issues related to King's College.[12]

Ecclesiastical Structures in Colonial Pennsylvania

While the Pennsylvania church leaders adjusted rather quickly to their heterogeneous environment, their acceptance of the absence of ecclesiastical authority and state financial support was much slower and more painful. In England, authority structures were clear. At the local level, most rectors were chosen by private patrons, often the local manor lord or other gentry, or by government officials. Congregations and vestries had a say in the selection of the rector in less than 1 percent of parishes throughout England. Even when the local gentry did not control the living, clergy knew whom they had to please in order to make their lives livable. Once inducted, rectors could only be removed from a parish after being convicted of gross offenses by the bishop's court. While bishops did not appoint rectors, they did keep watch over the behavior of both clergy and laity. Any controversy that could not be handled by the local gentry was brought to the immediate attention of the bishop. In England and Wales the parish served as the unit of local government, so the churchwardens and other officials elected by the vestry had wide-ranging responsibilities, including maintenance of the roads and caring for the poor.[13]

Pennsylvania had neither the ecclesiastical nor the social structure in place to provide stability and quick resolution of conflicts. At the local level, churches throughout the colonies elected vestries, or parish councils, which gradually tried to increase their power. In Christ Church, members—defined as those who had received communion at least once during the previous year—elected this group of twenty men each year. The vestrymen were responsible for selecting a rector and making certain that the church building and other property was in good repair. In Pennsylvania, however, their efforts to exert control were often stymied by various prominent men who vied for the power that local gentry in England possessed. And as the colonial period unfolded, vestries also had to contend with factions within the congregation who would not sit idly by when their choice of a minister was not approved. With all of these groups competing for power, it is not surprising that rectors themselves often rebelled, feeling that their prerogatives were being infringed upon. While the bishop of London generally stayed out of colonial affairs unless controversies arose, conflicts within Pennsylvania churches required his repeated involvement. And because the SPG paid the salaries of most clergy in the country churches, as well as that of the schoolmaster at Christ Church, officials of that organization also often became involved in disputes.[14]

The situation in Pennsylvania was not unique. In the absence of a bishop, all colonial Anglican churches struggled to create authority structures. This process was easier, however, in colonies like Maryland and Virginia, where the church was established, at least some of the responsibilities of the vestry were established by law, and local gentry could be identified more easily than in Pennsylvania.[15]

Establishing a Normal Church Life

Pennsylvania churches also faced serious financial problems, which often exacerbated conflicts. Anglicans were not used to supporting their churches voluntarily, since taxes and endowments supported churches in England. The SPG provided stipends for all of the clergy in the rural churches, as well as for the schoolmaster at Christ Church, but this was far from enough for a church to survive. At Christ Church the vestry used collections, voluntary subscriptions, and burial fees to support the church. Pew rentals for people who did not buy their pews were first introduced in 1717, but since most people chose to buy rather than rent, this provided little help. The rector's salary was provided entirely by voluntary subscription. Even after Evan Evans left for a more secure parish in Maryland, after a year in which almost nothing had been raised for his salary, the vestry refused to guarantee their minister a yearly income.[16] Fortunately, sometime between Evans's departure and the 1740s, a yearly salary, paid for by pew rentals (no doubt increased with the new church building), was established for the minister. But Christ Church and its sister church, St. Peter's, the wealthiest Anglican churches in Pennsylvania, struggled financially throughout the colonial period. In 1774 the staff salaries of these two churches, plus a sum of only £50 for building repairs, left a deficit of more than £190. When the vestry reluctantly increased rents by 50 percent for three years, the congregation responded by voting fourteen of the twenty vestryman out of office.[17]

Despite financial problems, Christ Church had established a full complement of worship services as early as 1700. Morning and evening prayer services were held each Sunday, on all holy days, and on Wednesdays and Fridays. In addition, there was a lecture on the last Sunday of each month in preparation for the Communion service, which was held once a month. And while much of the colonial environment was starkly different from what Anglicans were used to in England, the worship service itself united Anglicans around the world. Since all services were taken from the Book of Common Prayer, Anglicans would have felt immediately at home and at one with others in their congregation, no matter where they came from. The typical Sunday morning service consisted of three parts: the morning prayer, the litany, and, on Sundays when Communion was not observed, antecommunion (the part of the communion service up to the exhortation and invitation to the table), along with a thirty- to forty-five-minute sermon. On Communion Sundays, those not taking Communion, which probably meant most of the congregation, left after the offering that followed the sermon. Evening prayer was actually said in the afternoon, often as early as 2:30, giving those who had attended the morning service time for little more than lunch.

Music would not have been the highlight of the service. Christ Church did not get an organ until 1766. The clerk recited any responses or psalms before the congregation sang them. Although the new version of the metric psalms by Nahum Tate and Nicholas Brady was approved by the bishop of London in 1696, and was probably used by Pennsylvania Anglicans by the early eighteenth century, the congregation probably sang them to only five or six tunes. And because the clerk's recitation of the psalms often broke them up into "disconnected fragments," it was not uncommon for a congregation to start out singing one tune and end up singing another.[18]

Services were first held in small, simple churches befitting the size and wealth of the congregations. The first church building in Philadelphia was a small brick structure. While travelers' accounts referred to it as a "very fine church" and a "great church," it could not have been very big; when it was enlarged in 1711 it still had only forty-two pews. Many of the rural churches, including St. James's, Perkiomen, St. Peter's in the Great Valley, St. Thomas's, Whitemarsh, and St. John's, Concord, began as log buildings. As these structures burned down or as congregations grew, they were replaced by stone buildings. It appears that only Trinity Church in Oxford still retains a section of its original building, which was stone.[19]

Congregations generally tried to provide for the education of their children. Christ Church employed a schoolmaster from at least 1700. While we do not have records specific to Pennsylvania, we do know that the SPG, which supported many of the colonial schoolmasters, defined its main goal

FIGURE 1.2 Trinity Church, Oxford, Philadelphia, erected 1711

as "instructing and disposing Children to believe and live as Christians." Children were taught reading and arithmetic as well as manners and morals. They were also expected to memorize and understand the meaning of the catechism and to attend church morning and afternoon on Sunday and on other days of worship.[20]

Establishing a stable church life in rural areas proved far more difficult. The preponderance of "dissenters" and the dearth of wealthy parishioners made it hard to attract or keep ministers. The inability of local men to be ordained decreased the potential pool of ministers. Missionaries were often required to serve three churches at once. And the lack of a bishop often caused disputes to spiral out of control. Despite these challenges, Anglicans established congregations and worked hard to sustain them. Fortunately, reliance on the prayer book and the peripheral role of Communion in the liturgy made it easier for lay readers to preside over services in country churches.

St. Paul's Church in Chester was typical. One of many congregations started by Evan Evans, this small community of Anglicans in a town dominated by Quakers was able to complete a church building in 1703, aided by the prominent merchant Jasper Yeates. The SPG sent Henry Nichols to serve this church, and by 1706 Evans reported 150 worshippers. But money problems plagued St. Paul's, since its leaders "were lo[a]th to venture the Loss of such as have but lately returned from Quakerism to our Communion by" asking them for money. By 1707 Nichols and his chief supporter were waging "war" over an accusation that Nichols had "too much familiarity with a Gentleman's wife." Church attendance decreased, and Nichols, like many Pennsylvania clergy, chose a more secure parish in Maryland. George Ross served St. Paul's from 1708 to 1714, when he was transferred, against his will and the desires of his parishioners, and replaced by John Humphreys, who was sent from Philadelphia despite his protest. In 1725 Humphreys accepted a parish in Maryland, and for a while St. Paul's was used by dissenters. When Richard Backhouse arrived in 1729, he found that his congregation had dispersed "like sheep without a shepherd." But later that year he reported that the church was in a "flourishing condition," and his reports throughout his twenty-one-year rectorship continued to be positive.[21]

The many Welsh Anglicans in colonial Pennsylvania presented a particular challenge. Both Trinity Church in Oxford and St. David's in Radnor had predominantly Welsh-speaking parishioners. Evan Evans loved to preach at these churches. When Nichols went to Chester, he was also assigned to preach at Radnor. He was upset that many Welsh had left the church and feared that they would become impatient while he learned the language. Interestingly, he reported that while he could do the liturgy in Welsh, he couldn't give the sermon, and "preaching is here looked Upon to be ye most necessary part of divine service." In 1714 Humphreys feared that a Welsh Presbyterian minister would draw Oxford Anglicans away, since John Clubb, Oxford's Welsh rector, came only twice a month. As late as 1725 Radnor was still asking for a Welsh-speaking missionary, pledging £40 pounds in support.[22]

The Church in Philadelphia

While rural Anglicans continued to struggle, the Anglican congregation in Philadelphia had entered a new, relatively stable phase in its history by the late 1720s. When the new rector, Archibald Cummings, arrived in 1726, he found a congregation, a city, and a colony that had begun to mature. And during his fifteen years as rector of Christ Church, the face of the colony and the congregation changed still further. The population of Philadelphia increased from 3,200 in 1700 to 7,500 in 1730, while the colony's population increased from 17,950 to 51,700. Between 1726 and 1755 approximately 40,000 Germans and 30,000 Scots-Irish settled in the colony. The number of black slaves also increased; by the 1740s approximately

10 percent of Philadelphia's population was black. By 1750 Philadelphia boasted 12,700 inhabitants, while the colony had almost 120,000 residents. Only 25 to 30 percent of the Pennsylvania population was English and Welsh, with Germans being the largest ethnic group.[23]

The first half of the eighteenth century was an era of real opportunity for many colonists. Philadelphians thrived by importing and making goods needed in rural areas and exporting products harvested or mined in the hinterland. The number of ships leaving Philadelphia quadrupled during the 1730s, and by the middle of the decade Philadelphia exports of breadstuffs approached £50,000 annually, joined by lumber, flaxseed, and iron as the major exports from the colony's interior. It was still possible for the poor to rise to middle-class status, while artisans like Benjamin Franklin, who arrived in Philadelphia in 1723 to work as a printer, could occasionally become wealthy. The average farm family in Chester and Lancaster counties owned 125 acres, on which they grew grain and raised livestock. Increasingly, however, the third of all immigrants who arrived as indentured servants found themselves without resources, joining the ranks of wage laborers in the countryside or the working poor in the city.[24]

Philadelphia was hardly the genteel colonial city that we sometimes like to remember. People jostled with animals that roamed the streets, which were piled high with garbage. Pickpockets roamed the city, which had the highest crime rate in the colonies; Philadelphia's murder rate exceeded London's. By 1752 there were 120 licensed taverns, not including many illicit establishments. Even the London Coffee House, where merchants gathered each noon, served liquor as its primary drink.[25]

But Philadelphia had also begun to establish the many voluntary organizations and intellectual establishments for which it became famous. The American Philosophical Society was founded by Benjamin Franklin and others in 1727, and the Library Company began in 1731. In 1729 the first of many ethnic societies, the Society of Ancient Britons (Welsh), was established, followed by the Society of the Sons of St. George for the English. The first Freemasons lodge was begun in the 1730s, as was the elite fishing club Colony in Schuylkill and the Dancing Assembly. The first fire company, which protected its members from theft as well as fire, was founded in 1736.[26]

Many of these organizations had Anglicans among their most ardent supporters. While Christ Church continued to attract members from all classes throughout the colonial period, it could boast some of the wealthiest and most influential citizens among its congregation, including former

Quakers such as Joseph Shippen, William Plumstead, Joseph Redman, and Phineas and Thomas Bond. Many Anglicans were active in politics. Merchants Thomas Tresse and Charles Read and physician John Kearsley served in the Pennsylvania Assembly, while lawyers Ralph Assheton and Thomas Hopkinson, physician Thomas Graeme, and merchant Thomas Lawrence served on the Provincial Council. Merchants Jacob Duché Sr., William Till, and Samuel Hassell served on the Corporation, the body that governed the city, while Joshua Maddox, a merchant, served on the Orphans' Court. Wealthy Anglican tradesmen included Charles Willing, who accumulated £20,000, James Bingham, a saddler and large landowner, Phillip Syng Sr. and Phillip Syng Jr., silversmiths, Gustavius Hesselius, the distinguished portrait painter, and, of course, Benjamin Franklin, who rented a pew at Christ Church despite his openly Deist beliefs.[27]

Not surprisingly, given the elite status of many Anglicans, when the congregation decided in 1727 to build a new church, it chose an architectural plan that would make a statement in this Quaker city. Purposely rejecting the Quaker preference for simplicity, they erected a building ornate both inside and out and added a steeple that would dominate the Philadelphia skyline for years to come. Construction of the new building took sixteen years, and the famous steeple another eleven, but when it was all done, Anglicans could be proud. The *Pennsylvania Packet* declared that Christ Church, "in point of elegance and taste, surpasses everything of the kind in America." Greatly influenced by the architecture of London after the Great Fire, particularly the churches of Christopher Wren, it is still recognized as one of the handsomest and most elaborate Palladian churches in America. The ornate Georgian exterior of the church today is very similar to its original appearance, laid in Flemish bond brick, with extensive wood and stone trim. The large Palladian window at the east end, believed to be the first such window in the colonies, allowed the rising sun to stream in, symbolizing the Resurrection. The original interior contained elaborate paintings, including trompe l'oeil decoration, a style of painting used to suggest three-dimensional work, and plush furnishings.[28]

Even before Philadelphia Anglicans had finished Christ Church, they had determined that they needed a second church within the city. In 1740 Christ Church was declared "too little by one half to hold the members." Both internal politics and financial considerations delayed the new building, but St. Peter's Church finally opened at Third and Pine streets in 1761. While larger than Christ Church, seating more than nine hundred people, its simple, two-story rectangular style, lacking a steeple, did not dominate its environment as did the mother church (the steeple was added

FIGURE 1.3 Christ Church, Philadelphia, built 1727–1744

in the nineteenth century). To prevent the churches from becoming competitors, the United Churches of Christ Church and St. Peter's were organizationally connected, and the same ministers supplied both, rather than having an assistant in charge of a "chapel," as was usually the case.[29]

The Philadelphia congregations continued to be a cross section of the city of Philadelphia. An analysis of the 1756 tax list indicates that while they were overrepresented in the top socioeconomic levels and underrepresented at the bottom, the 216 members who could be identified covered the spectrum of the population, with 30 percent of the members being assessed £16 or less, compared to 55 percent of the overall population.[30]

Philadelphia Anglicans tried to serve the needs of their poorer brethren. Christ Church maintained a Charity School for most of the colonial period and distributed the money donated at Communion services to the poor within its parish. The recipients, who were almost entirely women, ranged in number from ten to twenty-four a month.[31]

The most significant outreach toward the poor and outcast involved blacks, including slaves. While the original impetus for charity to black Philadelphians actually came from the fear that blacks, who had flocked to hear the evangelist George Whitefield, would join the more radical religious organizations, with their leveling tendencies, in the end only Anglicans reached out to blacks in Philadelphia on a continuing basis. The process started when Aeneas Ross, the SPG missionary from Delaware who had previously converted blacks in his Delaware parish, filled in for the dying Archibald Cummings in 1741. During his short tenure, twelve of the eighteen adults baptized were blacks, including nine who were baptized at one time, "the like sight never . . . seen before in . . . Philadelphia." Cummings's successor, Robert Jenney, who had also reached out to blacks while serving in New York, continued Ross's work, baptizing twenty-one blacks between 1741 and 1745. He reported that he never administered Communion without several black parishioners present.[32]

In 1746, after much urging, the SPG agreed to provide a stipend for an assistant minister at Christ Church who would serve as "catechist for the Negroes," a position accepted a year later by William Sturgeon, a young Yale graduate and convert from Congregationalism. By April 1749 he reported that fifty blacks were attending his Sunday evening services, and in 1752 he baptized twenty-eight blacks. In 1757 he expanded his work with black people beyond teaching the catechism when he persuaded the Bray Associates, an English organization, to allow him to open a school. The mistress in charge of the thirty-some blacks was instructed to "teach the boys to read, the girls to read, sew, knit and mark," to take them to church every Wednesday and Friday, and to make certain that "all her Endeavors [were] directed towards making them Christians." Between 1745 and 1776 more than 250 blacks, about one-fifth of them free, were baptized at Christ Church, and forty-five black couples were married there. Many black people might have preferred a worship style different from the Anglican, but the Church of England was the only denomination to open its doors to blacks in colonial Philadelphia.[33]

Ecclesiastical Controversies

While the Pennsylvania environment allowed the church to grow and in many ways to prosper, the lack of any clear ecclesiastical structure continued to create internal problems. In 1726 the bishop of London tried to establish some order, appointing Cummings to be his commissary. According to Bishop Gibson, Cummings was to visit each parish annually, communicating the bishop's directives and making certain that the churches and rectories were in good repair. He was to examine the licenses of all clergymen and keep an eye on their morals. Overall, he was to provide leadership for the Pennsylvania church. Unfortunately, while the bishop took the role seriously, the same could not be said of either the laity or the Pennsylvania clergy. Robert Jenney, who succeeded Cummings as both rector of Christ Church and commissary, reported that "the Laity laughed at [his commission], and the Clergy seemed to despise it." While Cummings and Jenney occasionally tried to exert their leadership, the commissary turned out to be just one more player in the continuing power struggles.[34]

* * * * *

Introducing Richard Peters

Richard Peters was one of the most influential Anglicans in colonial Philadelphia in both the political and ecclesiastical worlds. A young Englishman educated in Holland, he came to America in 1735 hoping to start a new life. Having unwittingly committed bigamy, he and his wife (if we believe his story) agreed to separate amicably. He chose Philadelphia because he was related by marriage (not his own) to Andrew Hamilton, the prominent politician and lawyer who is best remembered for his defense of John Peter Zenger. Peters immediately began associating with the most important people in Pennsylvania, including the proprietor, Thomas Penn, who had converted to Anglicanism and was living in the colony at the time. When his attempt to become assistant minister and then rector of Christ Church was thwarted, he began a long, powerful, and lucrative career in politics. In 1743 he was appointed secretary of the land office for the proprietary family, secretary of the province, and clerk of the Provincial Council, the upper house of the Pennsylvania legislature. In 1749 he was appointed to serve on the

Provincial Council. He was instrumental in founding the College of Philadelphia (which became the University of Pennsylvania in 1791) and served as the president of its board of trustees from 1756 to 1764. By 1762 he had amassed a sizeable fortune, and he retired from political life to become rector of the United Churches, a position he held without pay until 1775, a year before his death. Closely aligned in the 1760s and 1770s with William Smith, the controversial provost of the College of Philadelphia, Peters never strayed from his loyalty to the Penn family and fervently believed that it was in the church's best interest to follow his lead in this respect.

SOURCES: Hubertis Cummings, *Richard Peters, Provincial Secretary and Cleric, 1704–1776* (Philadelphia: University of Pennsylvania Press, 1944); Joseph Fairbanks, "Richard Peters (c. 1704–1776), Provincial Secretary of Pennsylvania" (PhD diss., University of Arizona, 1972).

* * * *

A perfect example of the struggles that consumed so much energy in the Philadelphia church was the controversy caused by attempts to appoint Richard Peters assistant minister of Christ Church in 1736 and then rector in 1741. Peters, a man who would eventually play a key role in both politics and religion in Pennsylvania, arrived in Philadelphia in 1735 and immediately was asked to preach at Christ Church. When Archibald Cummings became ill, he took over all duties of the parish, and in 1736 the vestry of Christ Church asked him to become the assistant rector. Unfortunately for Peters, Cummings disapproved of Peters and opposed the vestry's invitation. Cummings pointed to Peters's theology (which Cummings argued was Deist) and personal problems, but the controversy was as much about politics as it was about religion. While Anglicans had largely withdrawn from politics after the failure of their efforts to obtain royal government, they reemerged in the 1720s, when the political peace of the province was broken by a fierce battle over paper money and other economic measures. Many, if not most, Anglicans supported Governor William Keith in his effort to introduce paper money, a move opposed by the proprietor. Even after political peace returned to the province in the 1730s, Anglicans continued disproportionately to support the antiproprietary party.[35]

Once the conflict began, however, political and theological motives became intertwined with struggles for power. In England, the result would have been clear; since the rector had the right to approve his assistant,

Cummings's opposition would have settled the matter. But this was not the case in Pennsylvania. Even after Peters resigned, both sides continued to bombard the bishop with letters. The vestry went so far as to argue that they had the right of "patronage" because they had built and supported their church and could therefore choose their own minister. Individual members also felt that it was their right to contact the bishop. And because this controversy was as much about politics as it was about theology, it is not surprising that Jeremiah Langhorne, a prominent Bucks County Quaker, wrote the bishop (to whom he was related) in support of Peters, or that Ferdinando Paris, who would become Thomas Penn's London agent, wrote to the Presbyterian William Allen about his efforts on Peters's behalf.

While Peters did not support these efforts to undermine the rector's authority in 1737, he eagerly encouraged his supporters to try again in 1741, when Cummings died. At the same time that Peters was enlisting the aid of the proprietors, his opponents persuaded six local clergymen to write to the bishop opposing Peters, something the congregation of Christ Church resented deeply. The fight over the bishop's authority escalated when fifteen Peters supporters asked "gentlemen" in England to determine whether Pennsylvania was really annexed to the bishop of London's diocese, Peters and Ferdinando Paris suggesting that the right of licensing should lie with the proprietor! Even in Virginia, ministers had to be licensed by the bishop.

Ultimately, Peters's supporters did not prevail. The bishop agreed to approve a rector for Christ Church only after the vestry assured him that the congregation would "zealously" pursue measures likely to "promote true piety and virtue, secure the peace of this church . . . supported by a strict observance of the wholesome rules and canons of the church of England . . . always bearing a due regard to the rights and jurisdiction of our lordship." On that promise, the bishop sent Robert Jenney to Philadelphia to gain the vestry's approval. Unfortunately, the conflicts, fueled by politics, continued during Jenney's rectorship. In fact, Christ Church members and area clergymen spent far more time arguing among themselves from the 1730s through the 1750s than they did fighting other religious groups.[36]

Rural Churches

While the churches in Philadelphia confronted their many problems in the mid-eighteenth century within a stable environment, the same cannot be said of rural churches. As settlers moved west, Anglicans, a small minority among mostly Presbyterians and German Lutherans, continued to build churches. By the end of the colonial period, sixteen churches stood outside Philadelphia in what would become the Commonwealth of Pennsylvania. These churches faced enormous challenges, however. First and foremost was the shortage of ministers. In 1766 Richard Peters reported to the bishop of London that more than twenty missions in Pennsylvania and Delaware had no priest to serve them. And when a church did receive a missionary, congregations continued to be unable or unwilling to provide financial support. William Thomson reported, for example, that the congregation at Carlisle had contributed only £35 in one year and nine months, rather than the £75 that had been subscribed. Almost all missionaries served more than one parish, and with the expansion of the frontier the distances between churches increased; Thomas Barton, the missionary in Lancaster and one of the most dedicated colonial clergymen, served a mission that extended over two hundred miles and had three churches.[37]

Vacant parishes did their best to keep services going with lay leaders, but parishioners inevitably drifted to Presbyterian or Lutheran churches, making the job of the next missionary that much harder. At times parishes turned to whomever they could find, choosing less than desirable ministers. The shortage of clergy also led country churchmen to be swayed more easily by traveling preachers. As Thomas Barton put it, "A broken officer, an English Baker, a Dutch Shoemaker & a crazy planter, besides a number of strolling Methodists have all in their turns been followed & admired whilst national religion & common sense have been rejected & forsaken." Despite these problems, William Smith estimated that there were twenty-five thousand Anglicans in Pennsylvania in 1762, in a total population of 280,000. Throughout the colonial period they continued to build churches and to beseech England to send missionaries and money.[38]

Reactions to Evangelical Religion and Theological Diversity

While Anglicans dealt with internal problems, they also had to confront the evangelical movement that was sweeping the middle colonies. The arrival in Philadelphia in November 1739 of George Whitefield, the renowned English evangelist, brought Anglicans face to face with the Great Awakening, which had already swept through New England. Promising a close relationship with God to those who repented and were reborn and threatening eternal damnation to those who did not, Whitefield's tremendous oratorical ability, his charismatic personality, and his emotional brand of religion appealed to people from all denominations. The Philadelphia newspapers reported crowds of between six and fifteen thousand during his three visits, which included return trips in April and November 1740. Because he was an Anglican cleric, his fellow ministers initially welcomed him and invited him to preach in their churches. Once they heard his attacks on the clergy for "hypocrisy and false doctrine," however, they turned against him, closing their churches to him and preaching sermons opposing his doctrines. Alexander Howie, the missionary at Oxford, reported to the SPG that Whitefield "by his Indecent way of haranguing the Populace Seems to debase the Dignity of Religion, and by gathering together a Dirty Crowd in the Dark-night he acts the part of a Merrie-Andrew in things Sacred."[39]

It appears that, at least initially, the "Dirty Crowd" included large numbers of Anglicans. Richard Backhouse of Chester maintained that his congregation was unaffected, but all the other ministers in Pennsylvania complained of large defections. Cummings reported that while his sermons had exposed the irrationality of Whitefield's doctrine to the "sensible part of mankind among us," greater numbers were led astray by his appeal to their emotions. William Currie, the missionary at Radnor, best summarized the initial response of his parishioners. He asked the SPG if it knew "how much pains & Labors the Reverend Mr. Whitefield has lately spent among us to rob us of our characters & then of our hearers. . . . This strolling preacher, what by a Musical voice, by an agreeably [*sic*] delivery . . . has raised such a confusion among the people of this province as I believe will not be laid in haste & (which I am most troubled about) has made a very great rent in all the Congregations belonging to the Church of England."[40]

Fortunately for the church, the Anglican laity's support for Whitefield seems to have ended as suddenly as it began. By 1741, a year after his departure, most missionaries reported a sharp decrease in enthusiasm, and by 1742 most congregations were back to normal. Currie reported in 1741 that his parishioners "who were Smitten with Whitefield are again returned to their former principles," while William Becket at Lewes wrote in 1742, "the truth is, your Missionaries have conquered and convinced them, not so much by Opposition, as by Patience." Robert Jenney, the rector of Christ Church, told the SPG that "not above two or three of Character" had left, and the following year he reported that his congregation enjoyed perfect peace.[41] Whitefield's style may have been appealing at first, but his Calvinist theology of predestination would not have resonated with Anglicans as well as it did with Presbyterians and Congregationalists. Moreover, once Whitefield left, Anglicans would have had to go to a

Presbyterian, Moravian, or Baptist church to find a similar style of preaching. For most members of the Church of England, denominational loyalties were still too strong for that.

Whitefield's departure was not the end of the evangelical threat to the Church of England. From the late 1750s through the end of the colonial period, Philadelphia Anglicans confronted a series of evangelical preachers and movements. The response varied depending on the theological leanings of the clergy, the political situation, and, most important, whether these evangelical ministers were willing to adhere to the episcopal government and use the prayer book. The Anglican reaction can tell us a great deal about what defined "Anglicanism" in the late colonial period.

* * * * *

Introducing William Smith

William Smith was born in Aberdeen, Scotland, and first came to America to teach on Long Island. While he left the University of Aberdeen before receiving his degree, he was later awarded honorary doctorates by Oxford, Aberdeen, and Dublin.

His essay "A General Idea of the College of Mirania" impressed Benjamin Franklin so deeply that he was appointed to teach at the Academy of Philadelphia and in 1755 became provost of the College of Philadelphia, a position he held until 1779. Ordained an Anglican minister in 1754, Smith always looked out for the Anglicans' interests at the college. And although he never held a rectorship in Pennsylvania (he did serve briefly in Oxford as a missionary), he came to see himself as an unofficial commissary, reporting regularly to the bishop and others in England on the state of the church. Closely allied with Richard Peters, he was a fiery supporter of the proprietor, often seeming deliberately to provoke controversy with the Quakers. In 1758 he was jailed briefly by the Pennsylvania Assembly for his printed attacks on its military policy. Nor was Smith shy about using the church for his political purposes, never understanding why any Anglican would support the "Quaker party." In the early years of the revolutionary struggle, he supported the resistance, but later he openly opposed independence. With his enemies in power, he was arrested, but he was soon released and removed as provost of the college in 1779. He moved to a small parish in Maryland, where he founded Washington College and presided over the 1780 diocesan convention. Despite his problems with alcohol in later years, he was a crucial player in the founding of the Episcopal Church.

SOURCES: Albert F. Gegenheimer, *William Smith, Educator and Churchman, 1727–1803* (Philadelphia: University of Pennsylvania Press, 1943); Thomas Firth Jones, *A Pair of Lawn Sleeves: A Biography of William Smith* (Philadelphia: Chilton Book Co., 1972).

* * * * *

By the 1760s the Philadelphia clergy were themselves a theologically diverse group. Although little is known about the theology of Robert Jenney, rector of the United Churches from 1742 to 1762, and his assistant, William Sturgeon, who remained until 1766, it appears that they were traditional, anti-evangelical clerics committed to the Church of England's teachings, liturgy, and form of government. But by the early 1760s the churches had come under the control of ministers with very different styles and beliefs. Richard Peters, who finally became rector of the United Churches in 1762, had rejected the overly rational views of his youth to embrace the deeply personal, pietistic teachings of the German mystic Jakob Boehme and his English disciple, William Law. He was joined in his mystical (often, to the congregation, incomprehensible) views by Jacob Duché, his assistant. Both men were close friends with William Smith, the rational, fervently anti-evangelical head of the College of Philadelphia, who was a frequent preacher at Christ Church and St. Peter's and shared the leadership of the Anglican community with Peters. When the churches had to choose additional assistant ministers in 1771, they chose Thomas Coombe and William White. White, whose views are discussed more thoroughly elsewhere in this volume, has been accurately described as one of a group of men who "were disposed to emphasize, perhaps too much, the rational and intellectual side of Christianity," but who "never yielded its supernatural claims altogether in favor of mere rationalism." Coombe went one step further than White, rejecting systematic theology as well. He asserted that "orthodoxy seems to be a word without any determinate meaning; since that which is *orthodoxy* at Rome, is heterodoxy in England." He concluded that "he is the *best* Christian who conforms his life the nearest to the moral *precepts* of the gospel."[42] By the end of the colonial period both clergy and laity in the Philadelphia church had come to accept a broad range of theology. The Pennsylvania ministers focused on producing pious and moral parishioners and peace in the churches. Rather than uphold strict standards of orthodoxy, Philadelphia Anglicans asked only that a minister be properly ordained, use the Book of Common Prayer, and not cause divisions within the congregation.

It is in this context that we need to examine the various evangelical challenges the churches faced. The most serious threat to their harmony and well-being appeared in Philadelphia in 1759 in the person of William McClenachan. Born and raised in Ireland as a Scots-Irish Presbyterian, McClenachan had served as a Presbyterian missionary for twenty years before converting to the Church of England and becoming a missionary for the SPG. He stopped in Philadelphia in 1759 and, as was common practice, was asked to preach. Perhaps because the churches were short-staffed at the time, a group of parishioners asked him to stay. A member of the evangelical wing of the church, McClenachan adhered to a Calvinist theology stressing the fallen state of man and his dependence on God's grace and, much to William Smith's dismay, often preached and prayed extemporaneously "instead of modestly using any of the excellent forms provided in our Liturgy." Robert Jenney, who agreed with Smith on few other things, bitterly opposed McClenachan and, along with six other clergyman, asked the bishop not to give him a license.

The controversy surrounding this evangelical rector and his numerous supporters within the United Churches consumed the Anglican community for a year, involving issues of congregational rights as much as theology. Eventually the bishop of London sided with Jenney, but that did not stop Macclenachan's supporters. One hundred fourteen men signed the articles of agreement for St. Paul's Church on June 24, 1760. When completed, St. Paul's, whose architectural style was greatly influenced by St. Peter's, became the largest Anglican church in the colony, seating more than a thousand worshippers. And while the articles required that the building be used only for performing the "liturgy, rites, ceremonies, doctrines and true principles of the established church of England," and that only ordained Anglican priests officiate, it did not mention the bishop's license, requiring only that all ministers be chosen by the congregation. As William Smith put it, they wanted "an Independent Church of England—a strange sort of Church indeed."[43]

The history of St. Paul's for the following ten years is one of internal dissension and disarray. In 1768, after being without a rector for three years, things seemed to bottom out when the congregation welcomed William Stringer, a former cheese monger and itinerant Methodist minister whom even John Wesley had condemned for being irregularly ordained by

FIGURE 1.4 St. Paul's, Philadelphia, completed 1761

"Erasmus," who called himself a bishop from Greece. Yet five years later the wardens wrote a polite letter to the bishop indicating that St. Paul's was "sincerely desirous of being a regular Church in Christian Unity with other Episcopal Churches," and Smith, Duché, and Peters joined the New York clergy in asking that the bishop ordain and license Stringer. When the bishop agreed, the thirteen-year schism in the church in Philadelphia ended.[44]

Macclenachan was only one of the evangelical ministers with whom the Anglicans had to contend. George Whitefield, who by now was aligned with the Methodists, returned to Philadelphia in 1763, 1764, 1765, and 1770. This time, Anglican clergy took different positions regarding the evangelist. In 1763 Hugh Neill at Oxford complained bitterly that Philadelphia clergymen were following Whitefield around "from the Church to the Meeting houses . . . with a greater degree of veneration . . . than if his Grace of Canterbury was to condescend to pay them a visit." While Neill obviously exaggerated, Peters, at the request of the congregation, did allow Whitefield to preach in the United Churches. When chastised by the archbishop of Canterbury, he reversed his position in 1764 and 1765, but in 1770, probably because there was a new archbishop, Whitefield once again preached at St. Peter's. Peters's mystical beliefs made him more sympathetic to Whitefield than Jenney had been, but his main concern seems to have been maintaining unity within the congregation.[45]

Perhaps surprisingly, when it came to the Methodists, it was the city clergy who opposed them and the rural clergy who were more accepting. Methodist lay preachers were never allowed to speak in the United Churches or, as far as we know, at St. Paul's. Since the Methodists bought their own church building in 1769, there was little reason for conflict over this policy. In contrast, Joseph Pilmore reported preaching at Anglican churches in Whitemarsh and Chester, and Anglican missionaries Samuel Magaw and Hugh Neill are mentioned often in Francis Asbury's journal as preaching and attending meetings with Methodists.[46]

This conflict with evangelicals continued into the next century. At least within the colonial period, however, the damage done by the evangelical movement was minimal. The addition of St. Paul's served as an alternative for churchmen who wanted an evangelical experience, and the expansion of what was considered orthodox within the Church of England minimized conflict. In general, if a clergyman was willing to be ordained by an Anglican bishop and use the prayer book, Pennsylvania Anglicans did not quibble over theology.

Interdenominational Relations in the Colonial Period

At the same time that Pennsylvania Anglicans were choosing to accept diversity within their own ranks, they were learning how to coexist and at times cooperate with other denominations. By 1740 Pennsylvania had become the most religiously heterogeneous colony in the British Empire. Quakers, Anglicans, and Swedish Lutherans were joined by significant numbers of Scots-Irish Presbyterians, Catholics, Baptists, German Reformed, German Lutheran, and a variety of other German sects. By 1770 Quakers made up only 13 percent of Philadelphia's population. German denominations represented almost 25 percent, Presbyterians, 12 percent, and Anglicans, 18 percent.[47]

While Anglican clergy accepted that the Church of England would not be established and agreed that other denominations were legitimate, they still worked to make their church the most dominant in terms of power and numbers. True religious cooperation did occur at times, but competition, both friendly and not so friendly, was more common. Denominational relations in Pennsylvania were influenced by differences in theology and church polity but also by the size of the denomination and whether it was mutually beneficial to cooperate.

Relations between Quakers and Anglicans continued to improve throughout the colonial period. In the 1740s and 1750s the Quakers turned inward, disowning more members than they accepted. While Anglicans did not openly proselytize, they did welcome many ex-Quakers into their congregations; six of the men who served on the vestry of Christ Church in the 1750s and 1760s came from Quaker families.[48] But while individual Anglicans and Quakers cooperated on individual philanthropic projects, the two denominations continued to keep their distance.

Anglican relationships with Lutherans serve as a good example of how size and mutual benefit came into play in determining the level of cooperation between denominations. The one group with which Anglicans truly collaborated was the Swedish Lutherans, who had founded churches as early as 1642, when Sweden controlled the area. By 1735 Swedish Lutherans had five churches in Pennsylvania. As Andrew Rudman, one of the Swedish missionaries, commented, "We have always been counseled and instructed from Sweden to maintain friendship and unity with the English, so that we and the English Church shall not reckon each other as dissenters like the Presbyterians, Anabaptists, Quakers, &c., but as Sister Churches." Anglicans shared this attitude; Rudman, the Swedish minister, was actually appointed as an SPG missionary to Oxford and served Christ Church in Evans's absence. In 1721 the SPG set a policy giving £10 to any Swedish clergyman who preached at least twenty times a year in English churches. The Swedes were invited to attend all meetings of the English clergy. Cooperation was made easier because the Swedes, a small minority in the now English colony, assimilated quickly; by 1730 most spoke English and many no longer understood Swedish. As a result, Anglican clergy returned the favor of their earlier Swedish brethren, preaching in Swedish churches when they were without ministers. Their similar episcopal traditions, liturgically based services, latitudinarian theology, and status as state churches made cooperation easy. And from an English point of view, there was no downside; the Swedes represented a ready-made source of converts, while there was little chance of Anglicans joining the small Swedish churches, whose services were conducted in Swedish.[49]

When German Lutherans began emigrating to Pennsylvania in large numbers, Pennsylvania Anglican clergy hoped that they would follow the lead of their Swedish brethren. Ignoring the differing ecclesiastical structures—German Lutherans did not follow the apostolic succession—and the much larger numbers of German Lutherans than Swedes, Anglican clergy foresaw the day when all Lutherans and Anglicans in Pennsylvania would be united. There had been efforts in Europe to unite the two churches, first under Queen Anne, whose husband was a Danish Lutheran, and then again with the ascendancy of the German George III to the throne. So it is not surprising that in the 1750s Smith and Peters tried to use the German Society, a nonsectarian effort to provide educational and religious services for Pennsylvania Germans, to further their plan to assimilate Lutherans into the Church of England. In 1755 Smith reported to the archbishop that he could offer a scheme for uniting the Anglicans and the Germans, "which," he wrote, "I am sure would easily take effect," adding that the timing was not yet right. While the German Society did not achieve Smith's ends, a new generation of Germans who had been born in Pennsylvania gave Anglican ministers even more hope. In 1760 Thomas Barton, the zealous missionary at Lancaster, submitted that the only way his church would flourish was "by means of the Germans," many of whom "gladly embrace every opportunity to teach their children the Religion, Manners and Customes of England." In 1766 he wrote to the SPG that the Lutherans "frequently in their coetus propose a union with the Church of England." In the same year Smith informed the bishop of London that there was an "extremely good disposition among the Lutheran clergy here to be united to our Church."[50] Unfortunately for the Anglicans, there is no evidence that Germans ever seriously considered merging with the Anglicans. Individual Germans would convert, but the size of the German community and the refusal to accept an episcopal form of government made any such union only wishful thinking.

Lutherans may have been seen as a source of converts for the Anglican Church, but Anglicans soon realized that Presbyterians were their biggest competitor. In 1742 Richard Backhouse, the missionary to Chester, reported that the Anglican people were going to the Presbyterian churches because of a lack of missionaries.[51] Anglicans seem to have agreed not to engage in open conflict with Presbyterians. After the Presbyterians split in 1741 into Old Side (which stressed doctrinal orthodoxy) and New Side (which supported the personal religion and revivalism of the Great Awakening), Anglicans even occasionally cooperated with Old Side Presbyterians. Relations were generally tense, however, and conflict simmered just below the surface.

The best example of relations between these two groups, and a testament to the uniqueness of interdenominational relations in Pennsylvania, was the College of Philadelphia. Founded in 1749 as an academy, this brainchild of Benjamin Franklin was the only college in England or America that was not controlled by one denomination, although Anglican influence, if not domination, was evident from the start. Eighteen of the first twenty-four trustees were Anglicans, among them Richard Peters, who served as president. Franklin considered only Anglicans to head the school, first turning to David Martin and then, in 1753, to the young Anglican cleric William Smith. Despite this obvious bias, Old Side Presbyterians, who were weaker than their New Side brethren and often felt that they had more in common theologically with Anglicans, willingly cooperated for more than fifteen years. Francis Alison, an Old Side minister, headed the Latin school from 1752 until 1766. Each denomination had its own motives, however, and neither ever really trusted the other side. William Smith noted that while he believed the church "should be wide and Catholic," Presbyterians, if they gained a majority, "would not wish the same in return." The trustees wrote to the archbishop that they would not allow the "interest of the Church" to deteriorate. Francis Alison, on the other hand, noted that his taking the position with the Latin school would have "a very probable tendency, not only to promote the good of the public, but also of the church," since it was the only institution where Old Side ministers could be trained.[52]

Cooperation gave way to conflict in 1761. The reunification of the Presbyterians in 1758 had made cooperation with Anglicans not only unnecessary but of questionable value, since New Side Presbyterians actually rejected ministerial candidates trained at the college. A series of small disagreements over what prayers to use became an irreparable rift in 1766 when three Presbyterian graduates of the college sailed for England to take Anglican orders. Alison and his supporters decided to stop fighting, choosing rather to open their own school at Newark, Delaware. Thus ended the most successful interdenominational cooperation of the colonial period.

The Church and Politics in the Late Colonial Period

When Anglicans first entered politics in large numbers in the 1720s, they were, as we have seen, largely antiproprietary. By the 1740s, however, as churchmen gained more prominence in government, most supported the proprietor. Ten of the seventeen members of the Provincial Council, the body appointed by the proprietor to look out for his interest, were Anglicans in the 1740s, and these men, mostly merchants, also dominated the

Corporation of Philadelphia. Not all Anglicans were friends of the proprietor, however; Benjamin Franklin, who rented a pew at Christ Church but was never an active member, led the antiproprietary group in the 1750s, and Thomas Leech, Daniel Roberdeau, and John Hughes served as antiproprietary assemblymen.[53]

Anglican involvement on both sides of the political debate would have been considered normal in England, and it might not have been cause for concern in Pennsylvania except for the involvement of two Anglican clerics—Richard Peters and William Smith. Both men considered it the cleric's right—whether in or out of a rectorship—to persuade fellow Anglicans to support his cause. And since the 1750s was a particularly contentious time in Pennsylvania politics—with issues of the colonial defense becoming intertwined with proprietary rights and economic policy—the involvement of Peters and Smith inevitably had consequences for the Anglican community. Peters generally operated behind the scenes, but Smith became embroiled in one public controversy after another in the 1750s and '60s. At one point the vestry of Christ Church was drawn into the fray and, much to Smith's dismay, sided with their fellow vestryman, Daniel Roberdeau, against the Scottish cleric. In 1758–59 Smith so angered the Quaker-controlled Assembly with his writings that the legislators tried and convicted him of libel, sentencing him to jail during each of their sessions until he submitted to their authority. Smith eventually had to go to England, where the Privy Council took his side. Clergy outside Philadelphia reacted with alarm to "this severe stroke leveled at the interests of the Church of England thro' the person of Mr. Smith." However, both the rector of Christ Church, Robert Jenney, who tried to keep politics out of his church and resented the influence and interference of Smith and Peters, and his assistant, William Sturgeon, actually wrote to their superiors in England *against* Smith.[54]

After Jenney's death in 1762, Richard Peters became rector of the United Churches. While his rectorship saw the maturation of the church in Philadelphia in a number of ways, it also allowed Smith to use the churches even more openly in his political campaigns. In 1764 the issue of Pennsylvania's becoming a royal colony resurfaced, but this time it was the Quaker-dominated Assembly party that supported the idea and Anglicans and Presbyterian proprietary supporters who opposed it! Smith went so far as to hold a meeting of opponents of royal government in Christ Church.

Other missionaries found themselves in a difficult position. As Hugh Neill, the missionary in Oxford, put it, if they signed the petition for royal government, they would incur "the displeasure of our superiors in Philadelphia," but if they opposed it, they would affront "such of our parishioners who called themselves Loyal Patriots and run the risk of being charged with disloyalty to the Crown of Great Britain." So they chose to remain silent. Fortunately for the church in Pennsylvania, this controversy was short lived, and Pennsylvania politics became relatively peaceful until the start of the Revolution.[55]

The Bishopric Controversy

At the same time that relationships between Presbyterians and Anglicans in Pennsylvania were deteriorating, the northern Anglican clergy launched their well-known campaign for an American bishop. Because it corresponded with the furor over the Stamp Act, the bishopric controversy is often seen in the context of the revolutionary struggle. From the perspective of American Episcopalian history, however, this controversy demonstrates the clear differences of opinion within colonial Anglicanism over the importance of one of the defining principles of the Church of England—the episcopal form of government.

The campaign, led by Thomas Bradbury Chandler of Elizabethtown, New Jersey, began in earnest in 1765 with a letter from the New York and New Jersey clergymen to the archbishop. It entered its public phase in 1767, when Chandler published *An Appeal to the Public in Behalf of the Church of England in America*, an attempt to quiet the fears of dissenters that had precisely the opposite effect. Chandler's ill-timed publication created a firestorm throughout the colonies and polarized both laity and clergy within the Anglican Church. Clergy in New England joined their brethren in New Jersey and New York in demanding a bishop. Many of these clergy had converted to the Church of England primarily because of a deep-seated belief in the necessity of apostolic succession; they considered the episcopacy divinely ordained, not just a convenient form of church government. When they attempted to gain the support of their brethren to the south, however, they found few who agreed with them and widespread opposition from both clergy and laity. In southern colonies where the church was established, ecclesiastical authority rested almost entirely in the laity, in the form of both the vestry and the legislature; a bishop would clearly decrease lay power. Even clergy who in principle might have supported a bishop could not risk losing the support of the laity, particularly at a time when both anticlericalism and opposition to English government were high.[56]

The situation of Pennsylvania Anglicans differed from that of their brethren to both the north and the south. Because the Pennsylvania charter guaranteed freedom of religion and the colony was still under proprietary rule, there was no legitimate fear that a bishop would have any political power, as there was in the South. And the sometimes chaotic condition of the country churches clearly made Pennsylvania clergy and laity understand the benefits of a resident bishop. Pennsylvania clergy wrote repeatedly to the bishop complaining about unsuitable men obtaining orders without the recommendation of any local clergy. Hugh Neill, the missionary at Oxford, had a personal interest in a resident bishop; his nephew, Hugh Wilson, whom he had educated for the clergy, drowned at sea on his way to being ordained in England.[57]

However, while acknowledging the expediency of a bishop, Pennsylvania clergy, at least those who served in Philadelphia, did not believe that the episcopal form of government was divinely ordained; Smith had been willing to accept Lutheran clergy into the fold without their being ordained in the Church of England. And after some rocky years, the Philadelphia churches had developed an authority structure by the 1760s in which power was shared by clergy, vestry, and congregation, with only occasional need for episcopal intervention. Moreover, Pennsylvania Anglicans had long since accepted the legitimacy of other denominations, preferring either to collaborate or to compete with them quietly. These circumstances, combined with the political situation—opposition to the Quaker-led push for royal government, and the controversies surrounding the Stamp Act—led the politically savvy Pennsylvania clergy to oppose the virulent tone of Chandler and his colleagues.

Thus the Pennsylvania clergy chose compromise; they refused to support Chandler's efforts but quietly campaigned on their own for a bishop. In 1762 Smith wrote to Archbishop Drummond that if the burden of crossing the ocean for ordination were not removed, the "comparative number of Church People" would gradually diminish, leaving them "in a manner to be at length wholly swallowed up among the numerous surrounding Sects." In a 1760 letter to Archbishop Secker, the Pennsylvania Anglican clergy as a group bemoaned the terrible condition of the church in America, suggesting that his "Grace's Primacy in the Church Militant may be rendered eminently glorious by introducing the Episcopal Character to America." George Craig of Chester declared that without a bishop "our Church will ever be a Jumble of confusion especially in Pennsylvania," while Thomas Barton of Lancaster told the SPG that the "Church of England alone sits like a distressed, mourning child that has lost a tender Parent and will not be comforted."[58]

Despite their opposition to Chandler's ill-timed campaign, when Pennsylvania Presbyterians published a series of vituperative articles in the *Pennsylvania Journal*, written by Francis Alison and John Dickinson under the pen name "The Centinel," that attacked not just the idea of a bishop but the entire Church of England, William Smith and other Anglicans felt they had to respond. They penned a series of articles in the *Pennsylvania Gazette* under the pen name "Anatomist." In an apologetic tone that would have angered his northern colleagues, Smith told the bishop that although he "could have wished our side had not given any cause yet they must not be left unsupported." Once engaged in the fight, however, Smith used his polemical skills to both defend the church and go on the attack. He argued that it was the Presbyterians who were intolerant and wanted to dominate; their real cause for objecting to a bishop was that a bishop's presence would interfere with their desire to dominate. But despite the virulent tone of these essays, both sides ended them prematurely, citing the need to concentrate on the fight against Britain.[59]

Thus, as Pennsylvania entered the revolutionary period, the ecumenical cooperation that had set it apart from other colonies had temporarily ended. But the Church of England was prospering in Philadelphia, and while the country churches faced both financial obstacles and trouble finding ministers, their numbers were increasing. The Church of England in Pennsylvania looked very different from what the founders of the early congregations had envisioned; Evan Evans would, no doubt, have been appalled. But its adaptation to a heterogeneous environment, as well as its increasingly successful ability to allow multiple groups and individuals to share power within a sometimes chaotic authority structure, positioned it well for the future.

NOTES

1. Horton Davies, *Worship and Theology in England from Watts and Wesley to Maurice, 1690–1850* (Princeton: Princeton University Press, 1961), 29.

2. See Howard H. Brinton, *Friends for 300 Years* (Philadelphia: Pendle Hill, 1964) for a good overall discussion of Quakerism. For a general discussion of Quaker persecution and problems at this time, see William C. Braithwaite, *The Second Period of Quakerism* (London: Macmillan, 1919), 177–206.

3. "Laws agreed upon in England by the Governor and Divers of the Free-Men of Pennsylvania" attached to William Penn's "Frame of Government," *The Papers of William Penn*, vol. 2,

1680–1684, ed. Richard Dunn and Mary Maples Dunn (Philadelphia: University of Pennsylvania Press, 1982), 225. Similar wording was included in the "Charter of Privileges," the constitution agreed upon in 1701. See Susan E. Klepp, "Encounter and Experiment: The Colonial Period," in *Pennsylvania: A History of the Commonwealth*, ed. Randall M. Miller and William Pencak (University Park: Pennsylvania State University Press, 2002), 67.

4. Rudman quoted in Ruth L. Springer and Louise Wallman, "Two Swedish Pastors Describe Philadelphia, 1700 and 1702," *PMHB* 84 (1960): 207.

5. Mary Maples Dunn and Richard S. Dunn, "The Founding, 1681–1701," in *Philadelphia: A 300-Year History*, ed. Russell F. Weigley (New York: W. W. Norton, 1982), 1–16.

6. Klepp, "Encounter and Experiment," 83.

7. Gary B. Nash, *Quakers and Politics, Pennsylvania 1681–1726* (Princeton: Princeton University Press, 1968), 188–98, 241–47, 314–15; Deborah Mathias Gough, "Pluralism, Politics, and Power Struggles: The Church of England in Colonial Philadelphia, 1695–1789" (PhD diss., University of Pennsylvania, 1978), 31–39. Penn's statement is from Penn to Robert Harley, n.d., William Penn Papers, HSP.

8. See Arthur Cross, *The Anglican Episcopate and the American Colonies*, Harvard Historical Studies (New York: Longmans, Green, 1902), chapter 4, for a discussion of the early efforts to obtain a bishop. The quotation is from Jeremiah Bass to Secretary of SPG, September 2, 1709, SPG Papers, Lambeth Palace, London, series A, vol. 5, no. 43.

9. For a discussion of the Phillips controversy, see Deborah Mathias Gough, *Christ Church, Philadelphia: The Nation's Church in a Changing City* (Philadelphia: University of Pennsylvania Press, 1995), 31–35. For the clergy's letter, see "The Clergy of New York, New Jersey and Pennsylvania to the Lord Bishop of London," November 2, 1705, in George Hills, *History of the Church in Burlington, New Jersey*, 2d ed. (Trenton, N.J., 1885), 61–62.

10. For more information on Evans's work, see Gough, *Christ Church, Philadelphia*, 14–17; and Evan Evans, "The State of the Church in Pennsylvania, Most Humbly Offered to Ye Venerable Society for the Propagation of the Gospel in Foreign Parts," in William Stevens Perry, ed., *Historical Collections Relating to the American Colonial Church*, vol. 2, *Pennsylvania* (Hartford, Conn.: Church Press Co., 1871; reprint, New York: AMS Press, 1969), 32–39. The quotation is from the charter of the SPG, found in David Humphreys, *An Historical Account of the Incorporated Society for the Propagation of the Gospel in Foreign Parts* (London, 1730; reprint, New York: J. Downing, 1969), xvi.

11. For details of the Keithian controversy, see Nash, *Quakers and Politics*, 144–60. For the life of John Talbot, see Edgar Pennington, *Apostle of New Jersey: John Talbot, 1645–1725* (Philadelphia: Church Historical Society, 1935). For Keith's accounts of his travels, see George Keith, "A Journal of Travels from New Hampshire to Caratuck, on the Continent of North American," *HMPEC* 20 (1951): 373–479.

12. Gerald Goodwin, "The Anglican Middle Way in Early Eighteenth-Century America" (PhD diss., University of Wisconsin, 1967); Joseph Ellis, *The New England Mind in Transition: Samuel Johnson of Connecticut, 1696–1772* (New Haven: Yale University Press, 1973); Sidney Bolton, *Southern Anglicanism: The Church of England in Colonial South Carolina* (Westport, Conn.: Greenwood Press, 1982); Jean Paul Jordan, "The Anglican Establishment in Colonial New York, 1693–1783" (PhD diss., Columbia University, 1971).

13. Warne, *Church and Society in Eighteenth-Century Devon*, 11–21; Daniel Hirschberg, "A Social History of the Anglican Episcopate, 1660–1760" (PhD diss., University of Michigan, 1976); A. Tindal Hart, *The Eighteenth-Century Country Parson* (Shrewsbury: Wilding, 1955); Bordon Painter, "The Anglican Vestry in Colonial America" (PhD diss., Yale University, 1965), chapter 1; James B. Bell, *The Imperial Origins of the King's Church in Early America, 1607–1783* (New York: Palgrave Macmillan, 2004), chapter 9.

14. For examples of the many conflicts at Christ Church, see Gough, *Christ Church, Philadelphia*, 29–83.

15. John Woolverton, *Colonial Anglicanism in North America* (Detroit: Wayne State University Press, 1984); Bell, *Imperial Origins of the King's Church*, chapter 9; Painter, "Anglican Vestry in Colonial America"; Joan R. Gunderson, "The Myth of the Independent Virginia Vestry," *HMPEC* 94

(1975): 133–41; John K. Nelson, *Parishes, Parsons, and Parishioners in Anglican Virginia, 1690–1776* (Chapel Hill: University of North Carolina Press, 2002).

16. Gough, *Christ Church, Philadelphia*, 29–30.

17. Ibid., 48, 102.

18. Marion J. Hatchett, "A Sunday Service in 1776 or Thereabouts," *HMPEC* 45 (1976): 369–85; Herbert Boyce Satcher, "Music of the Episcopal Church in Pennsylvania in the Eighteenth Century," *HMPEC* 18 (1949): 373–74.

19. Benjamin Dorr, *A Historical Account of Christ Church Philadelphia* (Philadelphia: R. S. H. George, 1841), 7–14; J. Wesley Twelves, *A History of the Diocese of Pennsylvania of the Protestant Episcopal Church in the U.S.A., 1784–1968* (Philadelphia: Diocese of Pennsylvania, 1969), 104–13.

20. Clifton Hartwell Brewer, *A History of Religious Education in the Episcopal Church to 1835* (New Haven: Yale University Press, 1924; reprint, New York: Arno Press, 1969), 28–29.

21. Minister and Vestry of St. Paul's to SPG, n.d. (1704?), in Perry, *Historical Collections*, 2:22–24; Henry Nichols to Secretary of SPG, July 24, 1707, ibid., 2:30–31; Vestry of Chester to Secretary of SPG, September 1, 1709, ibid., 2:53–54; Richard Backhouse to Secretary of SPG, March 12, 1728, ibid., 2:161–62; Backhouse to Secretary of SPG, May 10, 1729, SPG Papers, series B, vol. 6, no. 245; Backhouse to Secretary of SPG, November 7, 1732, in Perry, *Historical Collections*, 2:181–82.

22. For Evans's account of the early Welsh congregations, see "The State of the Church in Pennsylvania, most humbly offered to ye Venerable Society for the Propogation of the Gospel in Foreign Parts," 1707, in Perry, *Historical Collections*, 2:35–36; Henry Nichols to Secretary of SPG, March 20, 1704, SPG Papers, series A, vol. 1, no. 184; John Humphreys to Secretary of SPG, October 12, 1714, in Perry, *Historical Collections*, 2:76–78; Robert Weyman to SPG, April 4, 1723, in Perry, *Historical Collections*, 2:129.

23. Klepp, "Encounter and Experiment," 61.

24. Ibid., 87–92; Edwin B. Bonner, "Village into Town, 1701–1746," in Weigley, *Philadelphia*, 35–40.

25. Carl Bridenbaugh, *Cities in the Wilderness: The First Century of Urban Life in America, 1625–1742* (New York: Knopf, 1938), 269, 439–41.

26. Ibid.

27. Gough, *Christ Church, Philadelphia*, 47–48.

28. Ibid., 48–51; Donald Friary, "The Architecture of the Anglican Churches in the Northern American Colonies: A Study of Religious, Social, and Cultural Expression" (PhD diss., University of Pennsylvania, 1974), 835–36; Bruce Gill, "Christ Church in Philadelphia: Furnishings, the Early Years," in *The Catalogue of the 1981 Antique Show: A Benefit for the Hospital of the University of Pennsylvania* (Philadelphia: Privately printed, 1981), 129–32.

29. Gough, *Christ Church, Philadelphia*, 75–77.

30. Karin Peterson, "Christ Church, Its Congregation Between 1750 and 1760" (seminar paper, University of Pennsylvania, 1975).

31. Christ Church journals, 1743, 1744, 1745, Christ Church Archives, Philadelphia.

32. Gary B. Nash, *Forging Freedom: The Formation of Philadelphia's Black Community, 1720–1840* (Cambridge: Harvard University Press, 1988), 17–19.

33. Richard Shelling, "The Reverend William Sturgeon, Catechist to the Negroes of Philadelphia and Assistant Rector of Christ Church, 1747–66," *HMPEC* 8 (1939): 388–41; John van Horne, ed., *Religious Philanthropy and Colonial Slavery: The American Correspondence of the Associates of Dr. Bray, 1717–1777* (Urbana: University of Illinois Press, 1985) (the quotation is from William Sturgeon to Rev. John Waring, November 9, 1758, 135–36); Edgar Pennington, "The Work of the Bray Associates in Pennsylvania," *PMHB* 58 (1934): 4–5.

34. Edmund Gibson, "Methodus procedendi contra clericos irregulares in plantationibus Americanis," in Cross, *Anglican Episcopate*, 294–309; Robert Jenney to Bishop Sherlock, May 23, 1751, Fulham Papers, Colonial Section, 42 vols., Lambeth Palace Library, London (microfilm, Van Pelt Library, University of Pennsylvania), 7:314–15 (hereafter Fulham Papers). For Cummings's notes on his first visitation, see his "Notes" in the Society Collection, HSP.

35. For a detailed discussion of this controversy, see Gough, "Politics, Pluralism, and Power Struggles," 135–58, 166–79. For more on the political situation in Pennsylvania during this period, see Nash, *Quakers and Politics*, 331–37.

36. Vestry minutes, March 29 and May 1, 1742, Christ Church Archives, Philadelphia; Vestry of Christ Church to Bishop of London, May 27, 1742, Fulham Papers, Pennsylvania, no. 10. For conflicts during Jenney's pastorate, see Gough, *Christ Church, Philadelphia*, chapter 4.

37. William Thomson to Secretary of SPG, March 10, 1762, in Perry, *Historical Collections*, 2:335; Peters to Bishop, November 14, 1766, ibid., 2:409; Thomas Barton to Secretary of SPG, November 16, 1764, ibid., 2:366–67.

38. Barton to Secretary of SPG, December 17, 1770, ibid., 2:448; William Smith, "State of the American Church presented to Archbishop Drummond, Bishop of London and others" (1762), copy in Christ Church Archives, Philadelphia.

39. The best work on the Great Awakening in the middle colonies is Martin Lodge, "The Great Awakening in the Middle Colonies" (PhD diss., University of California, Berkeley, 1964). See Cummings to Secretary of SPG, November 14, 1739, in Perry, *Historical Collections*, 2:210; Cummings, *Faith Absolutely Necessary but not Sufficient to Salvation Without . . . Good Works . . .* (Philadelphia, 1740); Alexander Howie to Bishop Gibson, November 19, 1739, Fulham Papers, 7:248.

40. Cummings to Secretary of SPG, July 31, 1740, in Perry, *Historical Collections*, 2:210–11; William Currie to Secretary of SPG, July 7, 1740, ibid., 2:208–9; Jenney to Bishop Gibson, June 24, 1743, Fulham Papers, 7:305–6.

41. Currie to Secretary of SPG, May 2, 1741, SPG Papers, series B, vol. 9, no. 110; William Becket to Secretary of SPG, September 26, 1742, ibid., vol. 10, no. 126; Jenney to Bishop Gibson, June 24, 1743, Fulham Papers, 7:305–6; Jenney to Secretary of SPG, January 26, 1744, in Perry, *Historical Collections*, 2:235.

42. See Gough, *Christ Church, Philadelphia*, 87–89, 100–103; James Taylor, "Memoir of Bishop White," ed. John D. Kilbourne, *PMHB* 92 (1968): 50; Thomas Coombe Jr. to Thomas Coombe Sr., October 1, 1771, Coombe Family Papers, folder 21, HSP.

43. For information on Macclenachan's background, see Frederick L. Weis, *The Colonial Churches and the Colonial Clergy of the Middle and Southern Colonies, 1607–1776* (Lancaster, Mass: Society of the Descendents of the Colonial Clergy, 1938). For information on his theological leanings, see "An Address of some Presbyterian Ministers to his Grace the Archbishop of Canterbury in behalf of Reverend Mr. Macclenaghan [*sic*]," May 23, 1760, Smith Manuscripts, Archives of the Protestant Episcopal Church, Austin, Texas, vol. 3, 38, reprinted in Perry, *Historical Collections*, 2:307–8; Smith to Bishop of London, November 13, 1766, in Perry, *Historical Collections*, 2:414; Norris S. Barratt, *Outline of the History of Old St. Paul's Church, Philadelphia, Pennsylvania* (Philadelphia: Colonial Society of Pennsylvania, 1917).

44. Gough, "Pluralism, Politics, and Power Struggles," 312–21; Wardens of St. Paul's to Bishop Terrick, December 3, 1772, Fulham Papers, 8:48–49.

45. Gough, "Pluralism, Politics, and Power Struggles," 349–52.

46. Ibid., 352–53; Joseph Pilmore, *The Journal of Joseph Pilmore*, ed. Frederick E. Maser and Howard T. Maag (Philadelphia: Historical Society of the Philadelphia Annual Conference of the Methodist Church, 1969), 27, 112; Francis Asbury, *The Journal and Letters of Francis Asbury*, ed. Elmer Clark, J. Manning Potts, and Jacob Payton, 3 vols. (Nashville: Abington Press, 1958), 1:299, 304, 308, 310, 314, 315, 319, 320, 339, 345.

47. Robert James Gough, "Toward a Theory of Class and Social Conflict: A Social History of Wealthy Philadelphians, 1775 and 1800" (PhD diss., University of Pennsylvania, 1977), 138.

48. For information about Quakers who became Anglicans, see, for example, ibid.; and Steven Brobeck, "Changes in Composition and Structure of Philadelphia Elite Groups, 1756–1790" (PhD diss., University of Pennsylvania, 1972).

49. Nelson Rightmeyer, "Swedish-English Relations in Northern Delaware," *Church History* 6 (1946): 101–15; William A. Bultman, "The Society for the Propagation of the Gospel in Foreign Parts and the Foreign Settlers in the American Colonies" (PhD diss., University of California, Los Angeles, 1951), chapter 1; Kim-Eric Williams, "Roses Among the Thorns: Colonial Swedes and Anglicans on the Delaware," *Journal of Anglican and Episcopal History* 74 (2005): 3–22.

50. For a brief general account of the German Society, see *The Papers of Benjamin Franklin*, vol. 5, ed. Leonard Labaree and Whitefield J. Bell (New Haven: Yale University Press, 1959), 203ff.; William Smith to Archbishop Secker, November 1, 1756, Smith Manuscripts, Archives of the Protestant Episcopal Church, Austin, Texas, vol. 1, p. 20; Barton to Secretary of SPG, December 6, 1760, and November 10, 1766, in Perry, *Historical Collections*, 2:293–95 and 2:406–9, respectively.

51. Backhouse to Secretary of SPG, June 14, 1742, in Perry, *Historical Collections*, 2:232–33.

52. Edward Potts Cheyney, *History of the University of Pennsylvania, 1740–1940* (Philadelphia: University of Pennsylvania Press, 1940); William L. Turner, "The College, Academy, and Charitable School of Philadelphia: The Development of a Colonial Institution of Learning, 1740–1779" (PhD diss., University of Pennsylvania, 1952); Melvin Buxbaum, *Benjamin Franklin and the Zealous Presbyterians* (University Park: Pennsylvania State University Press, 1975); Francis N. Thorpe, *Benjamin Franklin and the University of Pennsylvania* (Washington, D.C.: U.S. Government Printing Office, 1893). William Smith's statement is from Smith to Richard Peters, March 2, 1763, Smith Papers, vol. 2, no 120, HSP. Alison's statement is in *Records of the Presbyterian Church in the United States of America . . . 1706–1775* (Philadelphia, 1904), 206.

53. For a discussion of politics during this period, see James Hutson, *Pennsylvania Politics, 1746–70: The Movement for Royal Government and Its Consequences* (Princeton: Princeton University Press, 1972), chapter 1. See also Stephen Brobeck, "Revolutionary Change in Colonial Philadelphia: The Brief Life of the Proprietary Group," *William and Mary Quarterly*, 3rd ser., 33 (1976): 410–34.

54. For a detailed discussion of this episode, see William Ridell, "Libel on the Assembly: A Pre-Revolutionary Episode," *PMHB* 52 (1928): 176–92, 249–79, 342–60. For Smith's side of the story, see "A Brief Narrative of the Case of Reverend Mr. Smith"; for Jenney's objections, see Robert Jenney to Archbishop Secker, November 27, 1758; William Sturgeon to Archbishop Secker, November 29, 1758; the quotation is from Robert McKean to Secretary of SPG, February 5, 1758, all in Perry, *Historical Collections*, 2:267, 273–74, 269, and 270–73, respectively.

55. Hugh Neill to Secretary of SPG, October 18, 1764, in Perry, *Historical Collections*, 2:363–66. For a general discussion of the royal government controversy, see Hutson, *Pennsylvania Politics*.

56. For a discussion of the New England clergy's attitude toward the episcopate, see Ellis, *New England Mind in Transition*. For a good discussion of this phase of the bishopric struggle, see Carl Bridenbaugh, *Mitre and Sceptre: Transatlantic Faiths, Ideas, Personalities, and Politics, 1689–1775* (New York: Oxford University Press, 1962); and Frederick V. Mills, *Bishops by Ballot: An Eighteenth-Century Ecclesiastical Revolution* (New York: Oxford University Press, 1978), 35–71.

57. For examples of complaints about men of ill repute being ordained, see Smith to Bishop, October 13, 1773, in Perry, *Historical Collections*, 2:461–62; Smith to Secretary of SPG, May 2, 1774, ibid., 2:466.

58. Peters to Bishop Terrick, November 14, 1766, ibid., 2:409; "To the Most Reverend His Grace Thomas, Lord Archbishop of Canterbury. . . . The Humble Address of the Missionaries and other Clergy of the Church of England residing in and near the Province of Pennsylvania, May, 1760," ibid., 2:317–19; Barton to Secretary of SPG, November 10, 1766, ibid., 2:408; Craig to Secretary of SPG, July 27, 1760, ibid., 2:293.

59. The Presbyterian articles appeared under the names "The Centinel," "Remonstrat," and "The North Briton" in the *Pennsylvania Journal* during the period March 24–July 28, 1768. Pieces signed "The Anatomist" appeared in the *Pennsylvania Gazette* from September 1768 through January 1769. William Smith to Bishop of London, May 6, 1768, in Perry, *Historical Collections*, 2:49. For a general discussion of these articles, see Gough, "Pluralism, Politics, and Power Struggles," 491–502.

2

From Anglicans to Episcopalians

The Revolutionary Years, 1775–1790

WILLIAM PENCAK

The Church on the Eve of Revolution

In 1780 the Marquis de Chastellux, third in command of the force led by French general Jean-Baptiste Rochambeau to assist the Americans in winning their revolution, visited Philadelphia. In his memoirs, he reviewed the service the Reverend William White had conducted at either Christ Church or St. Peter's, the "United Churches" belonging to the same parish that he served as rector:

> It appears to me a sort of opera, both because of the music and the scenery: a handsome pulpit placed before a handsome organ, a handsome minister in that pulpit, reading, speaking, and singing with truly theatrical grace; a number of young women responding melodiously from the pit and the boxes (for the two side galleries are much like boxes); soft and agreeable singing, alternating with excellent sonatas played on the organ; all this compared to the Quakers, Anabaptists, the Presbyterians, etc. appeared to me more like a little paradise in itself than as the road to it.[1]

Yet the aesthetic beauty of the service masked the desperate condition of what was once the Anglican but not yet the Episcopal Church in the United States. "Our ministry [was] gradually approaching annihilation," White later wrote. On the eve of the American Revolution, eleven Anglican clergymen ministered to thirteen congregations in Pennsylvania: between 1778 and 1781, only one priest performed his duties publicly—White himself.[2]

In 1775 Anglicanism, although not exactly flourishing in Pennsylvania outside Philadelphia, was certainly a presence. Congregations obtained missionary priests from the Society for the Propagation of the Gospel, headquartered in London, because of a special clause in Pennsylvania's charter, in which any twenty Anglican families who requested a clergyman would receive one. Outside the metropolis, which had six clergymen of its own on the eve of the Revolution, seven missionaries and college vice provost William Smith served from one to three churches each, usually visiting each at least once a month. Churches dotted the landscape of Chester, Philadelphia, and Bucks counties. Further west, Reading, Lancaster, Pequa, Caernevon, and the Swedish congregation at Mulatton (Douglassville) were joined by York, which built a church in 1768, Carlisle, and Huntington. In 1772 the bishop of London licensed Traugott Friedrich Illing, a Lutheran minister, to preach in the Juniata Valley. He also served the congregation at St. John's, Pequa.[3]

Beyond the City of Brotherly Love and its environs, Anglicans were usually small minorities surrounded by "all sorts of Presbyterians, even Covenanters, all sorts of Baptists, Moravians, Mennonites, Duncars [*sic*], and Quakers, besides those who are of no sectary," as the Reverend George Craig informed the SPG, not to mention the German Reformed and Lutherans, who made up nearly a third of the colony's population. Craig's estimate that "not six in one thousand belong to our church" in a population of about 250,000 suggests that nineteen congregations accommodating about fifteen hundred people is as good a guess as any of the state of the Anglican church outside Philadelphia in Pennsylvania in the early 1770s.[4]

In Philadelphia, however, Anglicans were at least as numerous as any other denomination. Historian Robert Gough has calculated that by the 1770s about 17.8 percent of the city's population, which he estimates at thirty-two thousand—some six thousand families, or approximately one thousand adult males—were Anglicans. Only Lutherans, Deborah Gough estimates, could muster a comparable number, which she puts at 15 to 20 percent of the population, Quakers having fallen to some 14 percent by the 1770s. The number makes sense given the combined seating capacity at the United Churches of Christ and St. Peter's (which shared governance and clergy in this period) of about fifteen hundred, with another thousand at St. Paul's Church. These last two churches opened in 1761, St. Peter's having been built to handle overcrowding at Christ Church.[5]

Anglicanism has traditionally been regarded as an elite church. This was only partially true of revolutionary Philadelphia. Robert Gough's study of Philadelphia's leading inhabitants shows that, to be sure, 31 percent of the members of the elite (or 153 members, measured as men assessed more than £150 in taxes, plus those prominent for other reasons) in 1775 were

FIGURE 2.1 St. Peter's, Philadelphia, built ca. 1758–1764

Anglicans. Of that 31 percent, however, nearly all (28 percent) belonged to the United Churches and only 3 percent to St. Paul's.[6]

But St. Paul's was not, as the city's other Anglicans claimed during an initial period of hostility that had passed by the late 1760s, founded mostly by the lower sort. Seventy-three of its 114 founders previously had belonged to the United Churches, and the average wealth of the members of the two churches was almost exactly equal—£42.1 and £41.2, respectively, on the 1756 tax list—as opposed to £27.4 for all taxpayers. The

United Churches, however, included many more people of below-average wealth (fifty-five below £12 as opposed to six at St. Paul's) as well as above average (seventeen above £100 versus three at St. Paul's). St. Paul's was a middle-class church, whereas the United Churches appealed more to the entire social spectrum, but especially to the rich and poor. That black Philadelphians preferred the United Churches before 1794, when the African Episcopal Church of St. Thomas, and "Mother Bethel," the first African Methodist Episcopal Church, were founded, accounts to some extent for this class distribution.[7]

On the eve of the Revolution, the United Churches of Christ and St. Peter's in Philadelphia were served by Rector Richard Peters (who died in 1776), his successor, Jacob Duché, and assistant rectors Thomas Coombe and William White. Dr. William Smith, vice provost of the College of Philadelphia, intermittently served several suburban Philadelphia congregations. With the exception of William Stringer, rector of St. Paul's, Philadelphia's clergy were at the top of the city's social ladder. Coombe, Duché, and White all came from wealthy Philadelphia merchant families. Although born in England, Peters had served as secretary of the province and was one of the Penn family's closest advisors; Smith had emigrated to Pennsylvania from Scotland and had mingled with the elite since coming to teach at the college in 1753.

Wealthy and prominent parishioners and pewholders abounded at the United Churches. They included Benjamin Franklin, Robert Morris, George Washington (when he was in town), George Clymer, James Wilson, and Francis Hopkinson, just to name signers of the Declaration of Independence and members of the national Constitutional Convention. Betsy Ross, artist Charles Willson Peale, Pennsylvania chief justices Benjamin Chew and Edward Shippen, and Thomas Willing, William Bingham, and Samuel Powel, three of the nation's wealthiest men, joined them. By the time the Revolution began, Anglicanism had become the preferred religion of the genteel elite. The Powels, Shippens, Penns, and some Pembertons had abandoned the Quaker meetinghouse.[8]

* * * * *

Burials at Christ Church and St. Peter's

Besides Benjamin Franklin, six other signers of the Declaration of Independence are buried in Christ Church's graveyard. James Wilson, Francis Hopkinson, Benjamin Rush (who lived next door to

Bishop White at 3rd and Walnut streets and whom White helped convert), and Robert Morris were members of the congregation. George Ross and Joseph Hewes died in Philadelphia while serving in Congress from Lancaster, Pennsylvania, and North Carolina, respectively. Hopkinson's grave was unmarked until 1930, when his remains were finally identified. Franklin, Morris, and Wilson also signed the Constitution, as did Pierce Butler of South Carolina. Bishop White buried David Franks, a Jew, in the yard in 1793: the Jews would not inter him because he married a Christian woman.

At St. Peter's, those interred include Lieutenant Colonel John Nixon, a founder of the church who gave the first public reading of the Declaration of Independence on July 8, 1776; George Mifflin Dallas, vice president of the United States from 1845 to 1849 (Texas was annexed while he held this office, and the city of Dallas is named for him); Charles Willson Peale, a prominent artist and revolutionary leader who founded the nation's first museum and painted portraits of many of the Revolution's prominent leaders (including Bishop White); Commodore Stephen Decatur, hero of the battle of Tripoli (1804), who was killed in a duel fought in Philadelphia; and eight Indian chiefs, who died of smallpox while visiting President Washington in 1793.

* * * * *

Surprisingly, for a congregation that included some of the wealthiest men in America, St. Peter's and Christ Church, like their country cousins, were frequently strapped for funds. (The rural missionaries complained repeatedly that they were poorly supported by their congregations and subsisted mainly on funds provided by the SPG.) If funding for 1789 (after the revolutionary troubles had ended and Philadelphia had returned to prosperity) was typical, the United Churches were £1,860 in debt and took in only £152 more than the amount required to pay clerical salaries. When he was appointed assistant rector in 1772, William White accepted a salary of £150 (£100 less than Thomas Coombe) because there was no more money to pay him. That women—who accounted for 191 of the 285 people White confirmed between 1787 (the first year he could perform this rite as bishop) and 1800—displayed a disproportionate dedication to the church (as has generally been the case throughout American history for nearly all denominations) may explain some of the financial hardship in a parish that included some of the wealthiest people in America.[9]

For most of the upper strata, in fact, Anglicanism represented a socially British, aristocratic way of life rather than a profound religious commitment. Most members of the elite were not interesting in actively participating in church affairs. In 1775 only three out of twenty vestry members at the United Churches, and the same number at St Paul's, were taxpayers assessed at £150 per year or more, giving credence to Pennsylvania chief justice William Allen's remark to Benjamin Chew in 1763 about Rector Richard Peters, who became a priest in his fifties and grew more devout as he aged. He had "laughed and joked as much as any of us"—that is, leading provincials—before "quitting us and herding with vestry men, old women, and other devotees" who took their religion seriously. More than three decades later, a clergyman complained that "the churches of other denominations were well attended by the great of their communions, whereas to the reproach of the Episcopal churches, those persons seldom or ever attended at all."[10]

During the revolutionary crisis, Philadelphia's population was divided into loyalists, neutrals, moderate revolutionaries, patriots who favored radical change in Pennsylvania's own government, and patriots who did not. Similar divisions and fluctuations characterized the Anglican clergy and community. Six Anglican merchants who can be identified on a 1769 list favored nonimportation from Britain to oppose the Townshend Acts; three were opposed. Twenty Anglican candidates who in 1774 ran for the Philadelphia Committee of Inspection supported the boycott of English goods to protest the Coercive Acts against Boston; they were elected, while fourteen Anglicans who opposed the boycott were defeated. Of 291 Christ Church pew owners in 1778, 49 percent were patriots and 41 percent were loyalists; of church members who belonged to the socioeconomic elite in 1775, 29 percent became patriots, 23 percent loyalists, and the rest were neutral or of unknown allegiance. Some changed their stance over time. Christ Church member and financier Robert Morris and his business partner Thomas Willing initially opposed independence but became ardent patriots. They opposed the 1776 state constitution, whereas pewholder Benjamin Franklin served as the president of the convention that approved it. Another Christ Church parishioner, William Adcock, headed Philadelphia's Committee of Privates, the most radical group in the state, which demanded the redistribution of wealth through taxation and the expropriation of "war profiteers." Franklin, like Charles Willson Peale and Francis Hopkinson, Duché's brother-in-law and the principal music director at the United Churches, ultimately repudiated the 1776 state constitution. When Franklin emerged as the elder statesman at the federal Constitutional Convention eleven years later, his own transformation from supporter of royal government, to leader of the radicals, to ardent nationalist embodied both a church and a state that reflected the entire spectrum of the new nation's political loyalties.[11]

The Church in the Revolution

With the exception of William Smith—a strong controversialist in matters of politics, education, and religion since he had arrived in the province—who served on numerous committees to resist British policy in the 1760s and early 1770s, the Pennsylvania Anglican clergy in both Philadelphia and the hinterland refrained initially from playing any political role in the severely divided province. But on September 7, 1774, when the first Continental Congress met in Philadelphia, Samuel Adams, the arch-Puritan from Massachusetts, suggested that the Anglican Jacob Duché open the session with a prayer. This "prudent" move Adams deliberately made—and boasted of in the *Boston Gazette*—to court some of the Revolution's "warmest friends," the Anglican delegates, most of whom were from the South. Pennsylvania's Joseph Reed, like Adams, a virulent patriot, bragged, "we were never guilty of a more masterly stroke of polity." Duché's reputation as a fine speaker preceded the prayer—because he was so nearsighted, he preached and prayed without notes. The other Massachusetts Adams, John, reported to his wife, Abigail, that Duché's prayer was "as pertinent, as affectionate, as sublime, as devout as ever I heard offered up to Heaven." He described Duché himself as "one of the most ingenious men and best characters and greatest orators in the Episcopalian order upon this continent; yet a zealous friend to the liberty of the country." Congress appointed Duché its chaplain.[12]

Shortly after war broke out the following spring, Philadelphia's other Anglican clergy, with one exception, spoke on behalf of the patriot cause. The exception, ironically, was the young William White, who in the end turned out to be the only priest to remain true to the Revolution to the end. White told Timothy Matlack, one of Philadelphia's most ardent revolutionaries, that although he shared his sentiments, he "would never beat the ecclesiastical drum," his objection being "the making of the ministry instrumental to the war." Only after he took the oath of allegiance to the new nation, which he thought "was exposing [his] neck to great danger . . . on account of [his] being a clergyman of the church of England" (having violated his oath, he might have been executed by the British), did he preach for the cause and thereafter remain faithful to it.[13]

The other three ministers—the aged Peters retired in 1775 and died in 1776—had no qualms about supporting resistance to Britain, although they were careful to tell the bishop of London that they entered the fray reluctantly. William Smith wrote to the Society for the Propagation of the Gospel that "our people have all taken up Arms. . . . We see nothing in our churches but men in their uniforms." Revolutionaries were "everywhere requesting occasional sermons on the present situation of things." Smith noted that Philadelphia's military associators demanded such sermons to win recruits and inspire resistance, if possible—and if not, then to force disloyal Anglican priests to show their true colors. All six Philadelphia clergymen justified their resistance activities in a letter to the bishop of London, while also praying that "the unhappy controversy between the Parent Country and these Colonies might be terminated upon Principles honorable and advantageous to both." They argued that if they did not support their "congregations [in which] people of all ranks have associated themselves, determined never to submit to the Parliamentary claim of taxing them at pleasure," they might "irritate the tempers of the people." "Our principles would be misrepresented," they wrote, "and even our religious usefulness destroyed."[14]

Although they had tried to advocate both spirited resistance and the restoration of harmony, the Anglican clergy had to make their choice once independence was proclaimed. They faced a unique problem. Aside from naturalized immigrants from outside the British Empire, they were the only people in the colonies who had to take a loyalty oath to their sovereign. Moreover, they swore to pray for the king, maintained that "it is unlawful upon any pretence whatever to take up arms against the king," and promised to "abhor that traitorous position."[15] At the United Churches, the new rector, Jacob Duché, called a meeting of the vestry on July 4, 1776, two days after Congress had voted for independence, and asked the vestrymen whether it was best "for the peace and welfare of the congregation, to shut up the churches or to continue the service, without using the prayers for the royal family." The vestry responded that "for the peace and well being of the churches" the prayers should be omitted. Duché continued to hold services.[16]

Yet only William White remained faithful to the patriot cause. William Smith was arrested twice by the patriots before he left Pennsylvania for Maryland, although he returned in the 1780s. The revolutionaries were about to send Thomas Coombe, along with other loyalists and neutrals, to Winchester, Virginia, as the British approached Philadelphia, but William White interceded on Coombe's behalf; Coombe remained in the city during the British occupation in 1777 and 1778 and departed with the British troops. Duché, on the other hand, was arrested by the British when they entered the city and threatened with prosecution for treason unless he recanted. He complied, making a futile effort to convince George Washington that the rebellion was lost and that he should sidestep Congress to negotiate a peace. Duché went to England, where he remained until 1793 (he died in Philadelphia five years later). St. Paul's rector William Stringer's turning point also came when the British troops occupied Philadelphia. He had previously been acceptable to the revolutionaries, but the Sunday after the redcoats arrived, in October 1777, Stringer preached a sermon on Ezekiel 20:38: "I will purge out the rebels from among you and those that transgress." The overwhelmingly revolutionary congregation at St Paul's, angered by the obvious reference to them, compelled him to shut his church. He too left with the British army the following year. That year, the congregation chose a new rector, Samuel Magaw, but he did not arrive until 1781.[17]

Furthermore, the churches underwent an internal revolution. Until 1779, the year after the British left, the vestry of the United Churches had included neutrals and loyalist sympathizers who protested the arrest of Thomas Coombe and the departure of Jacob Duché. That year, it was transformed. Fourteen of the twenty vestrymen were new, all of them revolutionaries, the loyalists having for the most part left with the British or been exiled to Virginia by the patriots. William Adcock, leader of the town's radical committee, was in; loyalists Tench Coxe and Charles Stedman were out. St. Paul's also boasted several notable revolutionaries. Blair McClenachan, brother of the Reverend William McClenachan (who had earlier been the church's rector), was a founder of the Bank of North America, leader of the Pennsylvania Anti-Federalists, and president of the Democratic Society of Philadelphia, inaugurated in 1793. Colonel Thomas Proctor, the Continental army's chief of artillery, also belonged. Stephen Girard, although not a communicant, attended St. Paul's and was married there in 1777.[18]

The church also lost control of the College of Philadelphia after the head of the state's radical constitutionalist government, President Joseph Reed, criticized Anglican domination. On November 28, 1779, the state legislature passed an act dissolving the college's board of trustees and faculty on the grounds that the institution had "departed from the plan of the original founders, and narrowed the foundation of said institution"—meaning that it was dominated by Anglicans who were either loyalists or moderate revolutionaries opposed to the new Pennsylvania constitution.

The revolutionary government waited until 1779 to enforce the act, both because the British occupied the city in 1777 and 1778 and also because the college's principal founder, Benjamin Franklin, was in France. Franklin had packed the board of trustees with Anglicans, as he believed that only they could guarantee a liberal education free from religious bigotry. William Smith—who was hired as the college's vice provost and had raised more money and interested himself more in the college's governance and welfare over the past quarter-century than anyone—was tainted by loyalism and left Pennsylvania for Maryland early in 1780. There he founded a college the following year, which he named after General Washington in an attempt to mend his fences with the new nation.[19]

Outside Philadelphia and Chester and Bucks counties, Anglican clergy found themselves nearly alone in a sea of ardent revolutionaries. Prominent Anglican revolutionary leaders were Anthony Wayne at St. David's in Chester County, attorney Edward Biddle and ironmasters John Patton and Mark Bird in Berks, and several men at St. James's in Lancaster: George Ross, a signer of the Declaration of Independence; Edward Shippen, head of Lancaster's committee of correspondence; William Henry, a manufacturer of the Pennsylvania rifle; and Edward Hand, adjutant general of the Continental army.[20]

The hinterland British-born and SPG-supported clergy were all loyalists, with the exception of the Lutheran reverend Traugott Illing on the Juniata frontier, who alone continued to serve Anglican/Episcopal congregations during the war and afterward. While the Reverend Thomas Barton of Lancaster was perhaps exaggerating when he wrote that the Anglican "missionaries suffered beyond experience or beyond the records in any of history in this time of trial," he was not off the mark when he mourned that "most of them have lost their all. . . . Many of them are in a melancholy state of pilgrimage and poverty."[21]

Rev. William Currie, who had preached since 1737 at St. David's in Radnor, St. Peter's in the Great Valley, and St. James's in Perkiomen, and George Craig, who since 1758 had served at St. Paul's in Chester County, St. John's in Concord, and St. Martin's in Marcus Hook, suffered the least, although Currie's home near Valley Forge was looted (by loyalist raiders), perhaps because his sons joined the revolutionary army, and several members of his family died of smallpox during the Valley Forge winter. Both priests refused to officiate without praying for the king, and resigned their posts in 1776. They ministered privately to the faithful for the duration of the war, during which visiting preachers of various denominations filled their pulpits. After hostilities ended, the aged Currie resumed his post briefly. In 1784 he attended the organizational meeting of the Episcopal Church in Philadelphia, and retired the following year; Currie died in 1793. Neither man was replaced until 1788, Currie by Slator Clay and Craig by James Connor.[22]

Clay was especially interesting for incorporating novel ideas into the ministry. Born in Newcastle, Delaware, in 1754, he had been a lawyer, was captured by the British on a voyage to the West Indies in 1780, was recaptured by the Americans, and was shipwrecked in Bermuda, where he discovered his religious calling. He was ordained in England and returned to Newcastle before being chosen by Currie's three former parishes. He was noted for rushing through the liturgy to concentrate on his extemporaneous and lively sermons. He supported the newly formed temperance movement, which began in the late 1780s, and would not officiate at funerals where liquor was served. Finally, he omitted "serve and obey" from the wedding service on the grounds that he "did not want to make the woman tell lies."[23]

Two of Pennsylvania's other Anglican clergy were more militant and were forced to leave the country. The rector at St. James's, Bristol, the famous loyalist satirist Rev. Jonathan Odell, was based primarily in Burlington, New Jersey, across the Delaware River, although William Smith and Jacob Duché also preached at times in Bristol. The son-in-law of Jonathan Dickinson who was a president of the Presbyterian College of New Jersey (later Princeton), Odell converted to Anglicanism after serving as a chaplain in the British army in the French and Indian War. A fervent loyalist, he wrote numerous satires criticizing the American cause, fled to British lines, spent the war in Philadelphia and New York, served as an intermediary between Benedict Arnold and John André when the former was planning treason, and was rewarded for his services to the Crown with an appointment as provincial secretary of New Brunswick, Canada. Located in heavily loyalist and neutral Quaker Bucks County, St. James's suffered destruction by the revolutionaries, who quartered their soldiers there. The building was reconstructed only in 1808, when services finally resumed.[24]

Unlike their colleagues, who ministered in heavily neutral and loyalist Philadelphia, Chester, and Bucks counties, Daniel Batwell of York, Thomas Barton, and Alexander Murray of Reading found themselves in the midst of one of the most fervently revolutionary areas in America.[25] Batwell's principal parish was St. John's in York, but he also officiated at St. John's in Carlisle and the church in Huntington near what is now York Springs. A new arrival in 1774, Batwell was thrown out of York in September 1776 when he refused to cease praying for the king. He took refuge

FIGURE 2.2 St. James's, Lancaster, as it appeared in 1925

in Huntington but was discovered trying to sneak back into town the following February by ethnically German revolutionaries. They pelted him with sticks and stones, dragged him from his horse, which they claimed he had stolen, and "with more than savage cruelty" led him to the river that flowed through the town, where "they soused him several times." Batwell responded that summer by joining an unsuccessful conspiracy to destroy the revolutionaries' arsenals at Carlisle, York, and Lancaster, vital to the Continental army's supply of rifles, cannon, and ammunition. Arrested on

September 30, 1777, he was released in February 1778, placed in a wagon with his family, and sent to British lines in Philadelphia over ice-covered roads, a journey that left him "well nigh blind" and unable to walk because of "the severity with which he ha[d] been treated." Batwell returned to England, where the Loyalists' Claims Commissions denied his request for £1,250 in compensation; he continued to be supported by the SPG.[26]

With Batwell removed, York enjoyed the services of Philadelphia's William White, one of the two chaplains of Congress, who fled Philadelphia along with that body in 1777–78. White's genial personality and religious toleration appeared in the fact that at first he lived with Rev. Kurtz, pastor of the town's Lutheran Church. St. John's only regained a permanent rector, the Reverend John Campbell, in 1784. Campbell served for twenty years, during which time he lost many of the congregation to the Presbyterian Church, forcing the Episcopal academy formed in York in 1787 to be taken over by the state of Pennsylvania.[27]

Except for the absence of physical violence, Thomas Barton fared no better than Batwell. A scientist, writer, and member of the American Philosophical Society, Barton was married to the sister of the astronomer and revolutionary leader David Rittenhouse.[28] Although his main parish was St. James's in Lancaster—his other charges being St. John's in Pequa and the church in Caernarvon (now Churchtown) before Rev. John Andrews took over both churches in 1769—Barton had also handled the churches in York and Carlisle. Removed from his pulpit in 1776 by the town of Lancaster because he insisted on praying for the king, in 1779 the Pennsylvania Supreme Executive Council credited Barton with being "very instrumental in poisoning the minds of his parishioners who are generally very disaffected disciples as to the present contest." It is interesting that Barton would receive such a backhanded credit, as by this time disaffection throughout the state with the constitutionalist government was rampant. The authorities were probably searching for scapegoats, as Barton did not preach publicly after 1776, and even earlier he had claimed that he had "not intermeddled with any matters inconsistent with our callings and functions." Deported to British lines, Barton died in New York in 1780 as he prepared to return to England.[29]

St. James's remained closed for five years, until 1781, after which preachers of other denominations visited from time to time. In 1784 the Reverend Joseph Hutchins became the church's first rector in eight years. That year he met at Philadelphia with other clergy and laymen and helped to form the Episcopal Church, but he is remembered chiefly for his vigorous defense of the English language as the only suitable tongue for Americans.

Hutchins managed to offend most of the population of Lancaster County, which was ethnically German, by insisting that "whatever impediments you throw in the course of spreading this language in its true pronunciation and elegance among your children, will be so many obstructions to their future interest in private and public life . . . to their future eminence in the public councils of America . . . and to that national union with their fellow citizens of the United States. . . . English . . . is the national language of the United States." Hutchins made these deliberately provocative remarks at a German Lutheran church to celebrate the beginning of the Franklin Academy (later Franklin and Marshall College) in 1787, which had both a German and an English curriculum. Not surprisingly, he became a professor of English language and literature there after he stepped down from the pulpit in 1788. Elisha Rigg, ordained in Philadelphia by Bishop White in 1788, succeeded him as rector and served from 1789 to 1796.[30]

Alexander Murray did double duty at St. Mary's Church in Reading (now Christ Church, not the current St. Mary's in that city) and St. Gabriel's in Morlattan, now Douglassville, at a Swedish Lutheran Church that had joined the Anglican Communion, as it could not pay a minister of its own. Born in 1727 and a graduate of the University of Aberdeen in Scotland, Murray found that his entire congregation in Reading (about forty-five families), with one exception, supported the Revolution. Murray had previously been a successful preacher. Between his arrival in 1763 and the Revolution, his flock had increased from six or seven families and included English-speaking Quakers, Baptists, and Presbyterians—who were bereft of clergy in this overwhelmingly German-speaking area. When he refused to encourage resistance to Britain by praying, on June 20, 1775, for the Continental army as required by Congress, the community's response was to boycott Murray's church, which was completely vacant the following Sunday. Murray continued to preach to his congregation of former Swedish Lutherans at Morlattan (Douglassville) until 1778, when a mob attacked his house, destroyed his furniture, books, and papers, and threatened to tar and feather him. The Reading Vigilance Committee, however, permitted him to escape to British lines, from which he went to England. Anglican services ceased in Reading until 1826. Murray returned to Philadelphia in 1790 and served his still-faithful Morlattan Swedes. He died in the yellow fever epidemic of 1793.[31]

In varying degrees, the Episcopal priests outside Philadelphia were loyalists. Currie, Barton, and Murray took no steps to further the loyalist cause or dissuade patriots from their course but wished to continue services with the proper loyalty to the Crown expressed even in an independent,

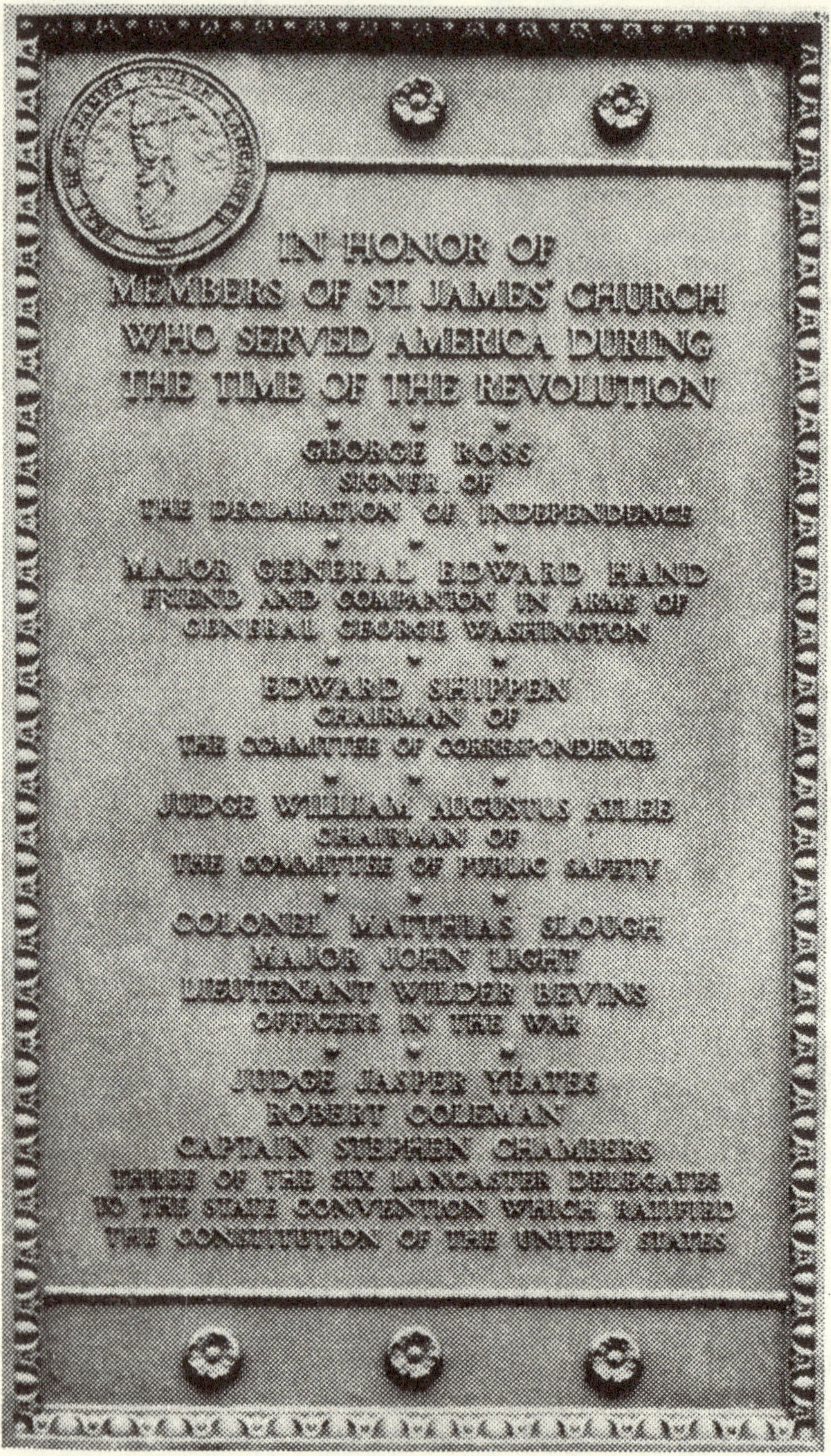

FIGURE 2.3 Tablet on the church building of St. James's, Lancaster, commemorating members of that parish who served in the American Revolutionary War

revolutionary society. That they all retained their posts unmolested until independence was either declared or became imminent is proof that they were not behaving obnoxiously to the patriots. Odell, through his writings, and Batwell, by participating in a conspiracy, were far more militant. But whether passive or active loyalists, they joined their Philadelphia counterparts in opposing the Revolution. William White stood alone from 1778 to 1781.[32]

Creating the Pennsylvania Diocese and the American Episcopal Church

When William White became the assistant rector of Christ Church in 1772, he could not have imagined that within a few years he would be presiding over the only Anglican congregation still functioning in Pennsylvania—indeed, one of a handful remaining in the colonies north of Virginia. The extinction of a church so closely identified with the mother country was a fate he was determined to prevent and that was much on his mind. He knew that during the war several rural parishes were negotiating with the state's leading Lutheran minister, Henry Melchior Muhlenberg, to ordain and provide them with clergy, and that in the absence of either a bishop or British recognition of American independence, the church as it had existed was in serious peril. In August 1782 White published *The Case of the Episcopal Churches in the United States Considered*, the critical document that began the process that resulted in the creation, first, of the Diocese of Pennsylvania and then of the greater American Episcopal Church over the next several years. As he stated in the preface, "a prejudice has prevailed with many, that the Episcopal churches cannot otherwise exist than under the domination of Great Britain. A church government that should contain the constituent principles of the Church of England, and yet be independent of foreign jurisdiction or influence, would remove that anxiety which at present hangs heavy on the minds of many sincere persons."[33]

White argued that "it may reasonably be presumed, that, in general, the members of the Episcopal churches" who lived in America by 1782 "were friendly to the principles by which the government was formed," and thus that any connection with the "spiritual authority in England"—the colonies were part of the bishop of London's diocese—had been "dissolved by the revolution." White, like the former colonists in the political sphere, could also cite English (in this case, church) law, as well as John Locke's notion that people had a right to dissolve their social compact, to support his point. But this was not an Anglican equivalent of the militant Declaration of Independence. White still revered the mother church, if not the mother country, and wished to retain its practices and preserve connections with it to the extent possible. In fact, the Anglican Church itself opened the way for a separate American church in its Thirty-fourth Article, which provided that "every particular or national church hath authority to ordain, change, and abolish ceremonies or rites of the church, ordained only by Man's authority, so that all things be done to edifying." Clearly, prayers for the king as sovereign and an oath of allegiance to the Crown were made obsolete by American independence.[34]

White went on to propose an appropriate government for the American church. "It must have the sanction of all orders of men," both within and outside the church, for it could now exist only as a "voluntary association" rather than a privileged order supported by the state, as in England. White envisioned a "bottom-up" system of representation, given the vast size of the United States, where individual churches would elect representatives to state conventions that would in turn elect delegates to a national convention. These ecclesiastical state and national bodies, much like the state legislatures and Congress, were to meet annually.

But how would America's church, which had no bishops, ordain priests and acquire bishops of its own, who could only be consecrated by three standing bishops? White urged that the church delegates assemble and "include in the proposed frame of government a general approbation of episcopacy, and a declaration of an intention to procure the succession as soon as conveniently may be; but in the mean time to carry the plan into effect without waiting for the succession." White believed that given the absence of bishops, the American people could consecrate their own, and even suggested that if the word "bishop" proved exceptionable, "a president, a superintendent . . . or an overseer" would do just as well. It is significant that White used the word "president" here. The state of Pennsylvania had a president rather than a governor: the word at the time meant a person of very limited powers who usually just kept order at a meeting, and none of White's other suggestions carried a sense of greater power than the person in charge of a specific institution. White cited as precedents several Anglican authorities, including churchmen Richard Hooker and Thomas Cranmer, who held that "a Christian King may on an emergency constitute a bishop." Therefore, White maintained, "much more may the whole body of the church."[35]

In short, White's proposal for a radically reorganized church governed by the laity was the ecclesiastical equivalent of the Pennsylvania constitution

FIGURE 2.4 A middle-aged Bishop William White. Portrait by Charles Willson Peale, 1788

of 1776, a democratic instrument that disregarded the principle of checks and balances in favor of popular control. While White's proposals reflected an immediate and desperate situation, in fact they opened the way to a stronger church. No longer saddled with subservience to an Anglican bishop or British missionaries whose experiences were shaped in England, a church free of overseas connections could flourish in the new Republic.

Nor was a revised polity White's only radical innovation. With the significant help of William Smith, who traveled from Maryland, where he had become president of Washington College, White modified the Book of Common Prayer, discarding the Nicene and Athanasian creeds, along with the doctrine that Christ descended into hell. Historian Robert Prichard has noted that "from 1782 until 1787, White explored the limits of his own church in a theological process of trial and error. At first he perceived the denomination's theology to be pliable. He believed that he was able to reshape the doctrines of the body in whatever way he felt appropriate."[36]

In early 1784, after first talking with the cooperative Samuel Magaw of St. Paul's, and with the approval of his vestry, White called a meeting for May 24 at Christ Church, to which priests and vestries from throughout Pennsylvania were invited. William Currie of the Chester County churches and Joseph Hutchins of St. James's, Lancaster, joined the Philadelphia clergy along with laymen from thirteen congregations throughout the state, ensuring that "the first duly authorized ecclesiastical assembly of Episcopalians in America at which laymen were officially a part" indeed constituted "a full representation of the Episcopal Clergy of the state."[37] This was the founding meeting of the Diocese of Pennsylvania.

Just as state governments preceded and called for a federal union, the first Pennsylvania convention adopted a six-point program that would lead to the creation of a national church. The first two items recognized the disestablishment of the Anglican Church throughout the colonies, constituting it as a church that "is and ought to be independent of all foreign authority"—that is, of the "British church"—and placing it on a level "in common with all other religious societies . . . to regulate the concerns of its own communion." Item three at first glance appeared to backpedal from points one and two: "that the doctrines of the gospel be maintained, as now professed by the Church of England; and uniformity of worship continued . . . to the liturgy of said church." However, the ellipsis contained the words "as near as may be," which in effect opened the door to items four through six. These all made the same point, that "bishops, priests, and deacons" were jointly responsible for choosing the ministry and making "canons or laws," responsibilities exercised in England solely by the bishops. Furthermore, local control was encouraged: "No powers [may] be delegated to a general ecclesiastical government, except such as cannot conveniently be exercised by the clergy and laity, in their respective congregations."[38]

The next step was to bring other states into the sort of episcopal union begun in Pennsylvania. The Philadelphia convention called for a more general meeting in New York on October 6, 1784. Almost immediately after the May 24 convocation, White was writing to clergymen in other states. Many responded positively, among them William West of Maryland. But

West also realized that not only "the most vigorous exertions" but also "the most harmonizing affections" were necessary, given the condition of a church where New England favored clerical rule and the South preferred lay governance. West then drew an analogy between the church and the national government that serves as an excellent way of understanding the process by which the Episcopal Church was formed, at the same time, in much the same manner, and—with respect to the laity—involving many of the same people, as the national government:

> I think the Protestant Episcopal Church in each particular state fully entitled to all the rights and authority that are essentially necessary to form and complete an entire church, and that, as the several states in Confederation have essential rights and powers independent of each other so the church in a state has essential rights and powers independent of those other states. But still as each state harmonizes with its sister states for the common good of the Confederation, in like manner a particular church should harmonize with its sister churches in the different states for the common good.[39]

Fortunately, William White was blessed with a tolerant and accommodating temperament, as were his Pennsylvania supporters. As opposition mounted from Anglicans in both America and England to his revised prayer book and his proposal that bishops be popularly elected, Prichard writes, "he would exercise a more moderate hand in dealing with the church's liturgy and theology. Tradition could not be wholeheartedly rejected, nor could standards easily be set aside."[40] Just as the democratic yet intolerant Pennsylvania constitution of 1776 yielded to the more republican, tolerant, and balanced federal Constitution of 1787, William White led the Episcopal Church down a path in which government balanced between executive and legislative, national and state, clerical and lay authority was incorporated into the new American order.

Historian Deborah Gough has pointed out that it was logical that White and Pennsylvania should take the lead in shaping the new American church, for the colony's diverse churches, like its government, had survived because they had learned to compromise. The Episcopal Church that emerged in the United States was a compromise between the low-church South, which wanted no bishops and total lay control, and the Anglican Church in New England—primarily an elite church, with many ex-loyalist members—which wanted strong bishops and complete clerical rule. Gough writes:

> For Philadelphia churches, independence from England brought fewer changes than it did to any other Episcopal church in the United States. Having always been financially independent, the churches were not forced to look for new sources of income. Never having had any formal relationship with the colonial government, either as an established [supported] church [in the South, New York, and New Jersey], or as an official dissenter [in New England] . . . they had no adjustment to make in this area either. And having had to survive in an atmosphere where religious toleration was stressed and confrontation was frowned upon, they were not startled by the competitive but not combative brand of interdenominational relations which was emerging in the new republic.

After his initial radical proposals were rejected, Gough writes, "White was elevating the unique ecclesiastical structure which had developed in Philadelphia from an unfortunate expedient to a positive good."[41]

White and the Pennsylvanians began their compromising when Episcopal delegates from several states met on October, 24, 1784. The meeting assembled delegates from Massachusetts, Rhode Island, Connecticut, New York, New Jersey, Delaware, and Maryland as well as Pennsylvania. Delaware, Pennsylvania, New Jersey, and New York sent both lay and clerical delegates, whereas the other four states sent only clergy. Virginia sent a clergyman to observe, as the Virginia laity did not permit clergy to vote. Nevertheless, the delegates "recommend[ed] to the clergy and congregations of their communion," in both the represented states and those that did not send delegates, that they elect representatives to form "a general constitution," on the following fundamental principles. Clergy and laity were to deliberate in one body, to meet in September 1785 in Philadelphia, at what was to be the first convention of the American Episcopal Church, although they were to vote separately. Both orders had to agree to all proposals. The seemingly innocuous proposition Pennsylvania had approved in May—that the forms of worship of the Church of England be adhered to "as near as may be"—was replaced with a stronger, more positive assertion of American independence: the new church would "maintain the doctrines of the gospel, as now held by the church of England; and . . . adhere to the liturgy of the said church, as far as shall be consistent with the American Revolution, and the constitutions of the respective states." Immediately following this proposal came the suggestion that every bishop "duly consecrated and settled" could attend the convention, but only ex officio. Proposals that a bishop (if available) was to preside over the convention and vote were deleted at the request of Virginia's David Griffith, who spoke for the southern colonies that were not well disposed toward bishops. The convention also stipulated that each state select a candidate for a bishop.[42]

On June 20, 1785, however, in the interval between the two conventions, America's only bishop, Samuel Seabury, had arrived in Connecticut. Consecrated by three nonjuring Scottish bishops who retained their loyalty to the Roman Catholic House of Stuart and refused to swear allegiance to the Hanoverian succession, Seabury was not even recognized by the British establishment. But he was in New England, and on arriving in America he nevertheless began to throw around his considerable weight. He ordained a dozen priests and numerous deacons, and spoke everywhere criticizing the plan of union that had emanated from the Pennsylvania and New York conventions. Even Hatch Dent, whom Seabury ordained in Maryland, commented to another newly ordained priest, Francis Walker, that "in vulgar language, you and I may hang up our fiddles; the gig is up. The tongue of slander, that fell monster of horrid aspect and hideous stripe, is already issued forth and from her breast disgorging a pestilential steam, diffused her baleful poison over half the land. 'Seabury is no Bishop.'"[43]

Writing to William Smith, Seabury criticized the delegates to the 1784 general convention for "having done wrong in establishing so many, and so precise, fundamental rules," and for "too much circumscribing the power of the bishops." By allowing laymen equal power with the clergy, the American Episcopal Church—as it called itself for the first time at the 1784 New York meeting—had done nothing less than violate "the rights of the Christian Church [which] arise not from nature or compact, but from the institution of Christ."[44]

Seabury did not attend the general convention in September 1785, to which seven states (Pennsylvania, New York, New Jersey, Delaware, Maryland, South Carolina, and Virginia) sent delegates. Nor did the convention have any use for Seabury. It ruled that a bishop could have no authority outside his own state and stipulated that both clerical and lay delegates from each state could meet in convention and recommend the choice of a bishop to the regular British clergy. Yet apart from rejecting Seabury and his proposals, the convention proved compromising, acting toward him as it had toward the South in 1784 to mollify its antagonism toward bishops. Responding to South Carolina's insistence that it would not select a bishop, the convention ruled that each state could decide for itself whether to have a bishop or not and, if so, how to choose him. Nor would a bishop have any authority outside his own state unless another state convention gave it to him. In an effort to conciliate the British hierarchy, to which the convention sent its proceedings, along with its candidates for American bishops, it tabled the controversial article four about permissible changes in the church due to the American Revolution as unnecessarily provocative.[45]

Yet the British bishops had problems with even this conciliatory proposal. They objected to an American convention, including the laity, selecting bishops and pronouncing them fit or unfit to perform their duty; they also insisted that candidates for ordination prove their "moral conduct" for a period of three years. They criticized the elimination of the Nicene and Athanasian creeds from the service, and the removal of the clause "he descended into hell" from the Apostles' Creed. Nor were they happy that the number of hymns (which White would have eliminated altogether) and psalms were reduced. Despite the beautiful morocco bindings prepared by Caleb Burgess of Philadelphia for the use of the English bishops (some five thousand copies were printed altogether but sold very badly), the bishops disliked the simplified American version of the Book of Common Prayer.[46]

Fortunately, both the British and the Americans were willing to compromise. John Moore, the archbishop of Canterbury, who was theologically and personally if not politically tolerant (he became a fierce foe of the French Revolution four years later), shepherded through Parliament an act permitting bishops to be consecrated in America without taking an oath of allegiance to the Crown, even before the Americans had learned of the British objections and taken action on them. The British bishops were also pleased that, despite their objections, the "essential doctrines of our common faith were retained." It was now the Americans' turn to meet the bishops halfway. The next national convention, which met in July 1786, restored the Nicene (although not the Athanasian) Creed as a possible replacement for the Apostles' Creed, and reincorporated the phrase "he descended into hell" in the latter. But on the question of ecclesiastical governance that so troubled Moore, permitting a bishop to be disciplined and if necessary removed by laymen as well as bishops' votes at a convention, the Americans stood firm.[47]

The 1786 convention reached another compromise on the selection of bishops. American states would choose their own but would then send them to Britain for consecration. Once the requisite three American bishops were in place, they could then consecrate more. In consequence, three states chose bishops. Pennsylvania selected William White; New York, Samuel Provoost; and Virginia, David Griffith; all three men had been instrumental in organizing the church conventions and ensuring their success. Maryland chose William Smith, but because he was obnoxiously drunk at the 1784 New York convention, and because he otherwise offended leading churchmen in his state with his "gross acts of immorality," he lost all hope of becoming a bishop when William White convinced the Maryland clergy that the choice would set a bad example. In fact, not until 1790 did Pennsylvania permit Smith to attend its state convention, denying him until then on the grounds that he represented no parish.[48]

* * * * *

Benjamin Rush on William Smith, on the Occasion of Smith's Death

"Why Smith never became a bishop despite his learning, energy, and convivial personality.

"May 14—(1803)—Died this day at 4 o'clock the Rev. Dr. William Smith, formerly Provost of the College of Philadelphia, in the 77th year of his age, being 77 on the 20th of the preceding April. This man's life and character would fill a volume. He was a native of Scotland and arrived in Philadelphia above 50 years ago, and for many years made a distinguished figure in the politicks of Pennsylvania. He possessed genius, taste, and learning. As a teacher he was perspicacious and agreeable, and as a preacher solemn, eloquent, and expressive in a high degree. Unhappily his conduct in all his relations and situations was opposed to his talents and profession. His person was slovenly and his manners awkward and often offensive in company. In the duties he owed to his college he was deficient, insomuch that a person who knew him well, upon being asked where he should find Dr. Smith answered, 'Anywhere but at the College.' His time and talent were principally devoted to acquiring property by taking up new lands. For these he exposed himself to cold, heat and dangers of various kinds, and for these he often made sacrifices it is said of conscience and reputation. . . . From his spending time in the woods and in that kind of a company to which his sad pursuits led him, he early contracted a love for strong drink, and became towards the close of his life an habitual drunkard. He was often seen to reel, and once to fall, in the streets of Philadelphia. His temper was irritable in the highest degree, and when angry he swore in the most extravagant manner. He seldom paid a debt without being sued or without a quarrel. He was extremely avaricious, and lived, after acquiring an estate of £50,000, in penury and filth at a country house he built when a young man at the falls of Schuylkill. In this retired situation he passed the last ten years of his life under the direction and influence of a German who it was

> said not only robbed him, but often treated him with insult and neglect. He had three sons and one daughter, to whom he acted generously in donations or property, but whom he treated so rudely that they avoided his society as much as possible. . . . On his death bed he never spoke upon any subject connected with religion nor his future state, nor was there a Bible or prayer book ever seen in his room. . . . On reviewing the character of the man we are struck with the great contrariety of his morals to his religious principles. . . . He descended to his grave (which he had formed for himself in a mausoleum on a county seat which he left to the church) without being lamented by a human creature."
>
> SOURCE: Rush's Commonplace Book, in *The Autobiography of Benjamin Rush: His Travels Through Life Together with His Commonplace Book*, ed. George Corner (Princeton: Princeton University Press for the American Philosophical Society, 1948), 262–64.

* * * * *

White and Provoost went to England. Armed with letters from Episcopalian laymen John Jay of New York and Richard Henry Lee of Virginia, and assisted by unofficial talks between John Adams, then the minister to England, and the sympathetic archbishop of Canterbury, they were guaranteed advance approval that they would be consecrated. The main concern of the archbishop, whom Adams described as "desirous of doing every thing in his power to promote harmony and good humor," was that in ordaining the first American bishops he not appear to be interfering in American affairs. White and Provoost were treated "with the utmost goodwill," introduced to the king, and brought into the House of Lords, and they assured the British hierarchy that "there is not the least doubt remaining of [the] church retaining the essential doctrine of Christianity established by the Church of England." The British bishops, in fact, refused to consecrate more than three American bishops, insisting that these bishops, in turn, consecrate any others needed in the United States. Ultimately, White participated in the consecration of twenty-five bishops. Only Pennsylvania, New York, and Virginia had candidates for bishop, although Seabury offered to recommend Abraham Jarvis of Massachusetts to the nonjuring bishops. Even the nonjurors' leader, Bishop John Skinner, however, discouraged this move lest it create tension within the American church.[49]

Yet even after Provoost and White were consecrated, the problem remained that there were not yet three American bishops who would act together. Although Virginia Episcopalians endorsed Griffith's candidacy, their failure over the next three years to raise more than £29 to send him overseas for his consecration (Griffith died in August 1789) made their real opinion of bishops abundantly clear. With Provoost implacably opposed to Seabury's legitimacy, and Seabury questioning the validity of a church constructed upward from the laity, the inability to find three American bishops willing to consecrate a fourth threatened to split the church in two, or perhaps three: a northern high church governed by Seabury and the clergy, a Southern low church without bishops, and the middle colonies, capable of going either way or striking out on their own.[50]

However, Bishop White's conciliatory nature, and the realization that the church needed Seabury as much as he needed the church, led to a rapprochement. White always expressed the highest personal regard for Seabury—his portrait still hangs on the wall of White's study. At the moment the United States Constitution was being ratified, William Johnson, president of Columbia College and a delegate to the Convention, along with Connecticut clergyman Jeremiah Leaming, suggested that Bishops White, Seabury, and Provoost meet. While Provoost remained adamant that the New Englanders "have adopted a form of church government which renders them inadmissible as members of the convention or union," White and William Smith did what they could to entice Seabury to join them. White wrote to Seabury on December 9, 1788, that "if any thing should be desired, for the accommodation of the church in any state where the clergy will not admit and the laity do not desire" lay representation, he would be "among the first to advocate some conciliatory expedient."[51]

In 1789 everything fell into line, thanks to the willingness of all parties to practice the traditional Anglican virtue of "adiaphora"—the willingness to remain indifferent, allow diversity, and compromise on matters not deemed essential to salvation and the preservation of the church.[52] First, the national convention had to attract Seabury and the New Englanders. At its July–August meeting, it recognized him as a bishop, a motion that passed thanks in part to Provoost's absence owing to illness. The convention also admitted three priests ordained by Seabury, including Joseph Pilmore, assistant rector of St. Paul's Church in Philadelphia, indicating that his powers were legitimate. With representation left up to the states and his legitimacy confirmed, Seabury was quite willing to work toward "a strong and efficacious union between churches where the usages are different." The convention also established a House of Bishops (with three as a quorum) to placate Seabury. White, too, now preferred a stronger role for bishops than the earlier conventions had proposed. Although a three-fifths vote of the clerical and lay delegates (later changed to four-fifths), who now voted jointly, could override the House of Bishops' decisions, the bishops now served as a council of revision that could not only suggest changes to the other house's rules but could also propose its own rules and changes. A bishop had to be present when another bishop went on trial, although each state could set its own code of conduct for bishops and other clergy. The only failure in 1789 was that Provoost refused to join Seabury and White in consecrating Edward Bass as bishop of Massachusetts; shortly thereafter, Bass married another woman immediately following his wife's death, which called his moral fitness into question. The fourth American bishop, who then joined Seabury and White in consecrating others, was James Madison (not the statesman) of Virginia, who traveled to England at his own expense and was ordained in 1790.[53]

Compromise also marked the final version of the prayer book and liturgy. A priest who believed that Jesus "went into the place of the departed spirits" could substitute that phrase for "He descended into hell" in the Apostles' Creed, or the phrase could be omitted altogether. Priests and congregations were left with considerable latitude as to which prayers, psalms, and rituals they would use, such as standing, sitting, kneeling, or making the sign of the cross at particular points in the service. Other alterations in the prayer book of 1785 were also made, largely, explained the Reverend Joseph Bend (Bend served as curate of the United Churches from 1787 to 1791 and attended the convention), in order to shorten the liturgy. "Men are not angels," Bend wrote, and "become fatigued with too long attention to the same thing; and the most fervent piety flags, in the vain repetition of prayers."[54]

After seven years of uncertainty, the final compromise that established the American Episcopal Church was achieved with remarkable ease, justifying the place of both White and Seabury in the American calendar of Episcopal saints. The Episcopal Church, like the Presbyterians (1785), Reformed (1792 and 1793), and Lutheran (1784) churches, thus established its autonomy from European governance. Even Rome granted America its own hierarchy—John Carroll of Maryland being the first to hold the position of bishop—rather than subordinate American Roman Catholics to the French, as church authorities in Rome had proposed.[55]

* * * * *

Saints of the Episcopal Church

William White and Absalom Jones, the first African American priest ordained by Bishop White, are honored with prayers in the Episcopal calendar of saints on Sundays in mid-July and mid-February.

Episcopalians do not pray to saints, but they remember their deeds and invoke their examples. Among saints in the calendar who were not Episcopalians, Anglicans, or pre-Reformation Catholics are the martyred Catholic archbishop of El Salvador, Oscar Romero, the Reverend Martin Luther King Jr., and Richard Allen, friend of Absalom Jones and founder of "Mother Bethel," the first African Methodist Episcopal church in Philadelphia (indeed, the first anywhere) at about the same time Jones began St. Thomas's Episcopal Church.

Other Episcopalians linked with the Pennsylvania diocese who are commemorated are John Henry Hobart, bishop of New York, who was born in Philadelphia and studied with Bishop White; William Augustus Muhlenberg, also born in Philadelphia and assistant rector to Bishop White before he moved to New York and founded the Episcopal Church school movement; Jackson Kemper, the first missionary bishop of the Episcopal Church, who preached to Native Americans in the West after serving in Pennsylvania from 1814 to 1835; and Phillips Brooks, rector of Trinity Church in Philadelphia from 1862 to 1869, a staunch antislavery advocate, supporter of the Union cause, and the author of "O Little Town of Bethlehem." Samuel Seabury is remembered in mid-November.

The Prayer for Bishop White
O Lord, who in a time of turmoil and confusion didst raise up thy servant William White, and didst endow him with wisdom, patience, and a reconciling temper, that he might lead thy Church into ways of stability and peace: Hear our prayer, we beseech thee, and give us wise and faithful leaders, that through their ministry thy people may be blessed and thy will be done; through Jesus Christ our Lord, who liveth and reigneth with thee and the Holy Spirit, one God, for ever and ever.

The Prayer Honoring Absalom Jones and Richard Allen
Set us free, O heavenly Father, from every bond of prejudice and fear: that, honoring the steadfast courage of thy servants Absalom Jones and Richard Allen, we may show forth in our lives the reconciling love and true freedom of the children of God, which thou hast given us in our Savior Jesus Christ, who liveth and reigneth with thee and the Holy Spirit, one God, now and for ever.

* * * * *

A Revitalized Pennsylvania Church

Just like the national church, the postrevolutionary Episcopal Church in Pennsylvania did a good job of setting its house in order. By 1785 nine Episcopal clergymen were officiating in Pennsylvania. Samuel Magaw of St. Paul's and White in Philadelphia were joined by Robert Blackwell, White's new assistant. Although educated as a Presbyterian at the College of New Jersey, he became dissatisfied with that denomination and took a second AB at Anglican King's College in New York. He supported the Revolution wholeheartedly and became a chaplain and surgeon at Valley Forge. In 1781 the vestry elected him assistant minister of the joint churches, which he served for thirty years. William Currie, age seventy-five, resumed his chores before resigning in 1785. Joseph Hutchins and John Campbell assumed the pulpits in Lancaster and York. The Lutheran T. F. Illing became rector at Pequa, and George Mitchell gathered a congregation in Pittsburgh—a fair number of Virginia Episcopalians had moved to what became western Pennsylvania while Virginia still claimed the area. John Andrews, who had served in York from 1768 to 1771, returned from Maryland as principal of the Episcopal Academy, newly opened in 1785.[56]

The idea of forming the academy first occurred at a meeting of the vestry of the United Churches on October 27, 1784. Episcopalians in general were dissatisfied with what White termed the "political complexion" of the new trustees of the College of Pennsylvania, who had replaced the predominantly Anglican board in 1779. While the trustees still included Benjamin Franklin, he was in France for the next several years, and the board was dominated by Presbyterians and by Constitutionalist leaders Timothy Matlack and David Rittenhouse.[57] But Episcopalians were not the only critics of the newly constituted college. Four days earlier, on October 23, the nation's foremost Lutheran cleric, Henry Melchior Muhlenberg, whose son, the revolutionary general John Peter, was on the board of trustees and had just secured a doctorate of theology for his father, complained of the inflated degrees awarded by the "politico-Christians" who had "brought about a revolution with the help of the assembly of the tribuni plebes." Muhlenberg had nothing but contempt for his own degree: "I have as little fitness for this as an ass has for playing the organ."[58]

Dr. Benjamin Rush was appalled that the college was now headed by Presbyterian John Ewing, who did everything he could to stop Rush, John Dickinson, and others from founding a Presbyterian college in the town of Carlisle (the future Dickinson College), as it would draw students away from the metropolitan institution. Ranting to Scot Charles Nesbit, who later became the first president of Dickinson, Rush complained that "in the vices of the heart" Ewing had "few equals. Revenge, envy, malice, and falsehood rankle forever in his heart." He and his "nefarious" crew had taken over an institution supported by Episcopalians, "without the least aid from the government for 22 years." The college's former faculty Rush considered "ancient inhabitants of the state . . . distinguished for their wealth, virtue, learning, and liberality of manners." It is no wonder that within three years Rush himself had joined the Episcopal Church, precisely when the Constitutional Convention was meeting in Philadelphia. (William White lived next door to him.)[59]

White and his fellow trustees at the Episcopal Academy, including Revs. Blackwell and Magaw and United Churches communicants Francis Hopkinson, Robert Morris, Thomas Willing (president of the Bank of North America), and Richard Peters (nephew of the former rector), moved rapidly. The academy's more than two hundred subscribers included Rush, Dickinson, and Anthony Wayne. The list was headed by Robert Morris, who contributed £100; William White himself offered £37.10. On January 1, 1785, the academy's fundamental rules were established, limiting governance to Episcopal clergymen and vestrymen of the Philadelphia area; by April 7 the faculty and principal John Andrews were in place. Among the most distinguished early faculty members were Noah Webster—who met his wife, Rebecca Greenleaf, during his six months in Philadelphia—and Andrew Ellicott, the geographer who laid out the boundaries of Washington, D.C., and taught mathematics.[60]

Instruction began in April 1785. To satisfy the different constituencies for education at the time, one "school" taught Latin and Greek, another mathematics, another English, and another French, although all students had to study English and mathematics. This curriculum strongly reflected a similar one developed by the Quakers under the Penn charter of 1690 that is still the foundation for the region's numerous charter schools. Morning and evening prayers were led by the Anglican priest, who also instructed the pupils in religion on Sunday; all denominations, however, were welcome.[61]

The rules of conduct at the academy suggest that Episcopalian boys were boys first and Episcopalians second. They were enjoined to refrain "from prophane swearing," "lying and all other mean and dishonest practice," "keep[ing] company with persons of disreputable character," "fighting, quarreling or arguing one to another," "defacing" the building or books, "be[ing] noisy within the building or yard," burning "any dangerous or offensive substance," and "defac[ing] or taking down the copy of these laws"; these prohibitions strongly imply that they were liable to such offenses.[62]

The academy flourished at first. By 1787, encouraged by the decision of the state—now firmly in control of sympathetic Federalists—to grant the academy ten thousand acres of frontier land to sell or rent for its benefit, the trustees decided to abandon the rented quarters and construct a new building, ninety by forty-five feet. But the frontier land was unoccupied and unprofitable, and funds had to be raised to survey and pay taxes on it. Further, in 1789 Pennsylvania restored the college to the surviving trustees of 1779 who had not left the country. In consequence, Andrews, other faculty, and present and prospective students deserted the academy for the more prestigious college. The academy closed its doors from April 1793 until 1816, when it reopened.[63]

In the meantime, however, the trustees had opened a free school, pursuant to the fourth article of the academy's charter, which specified that "a convenient number of youth shall be taught gratis." This institution began in 1788, supported by annual charity sermons at the Philadelphia churches and a bequest of £500 by academy trustee Andrew Doz. Although the trustees proposed to educate boys only, the vestry of the United Churches, noting that the Philadelphia Female Academy—which Episcopal priests and several prominent laymen (including Rush) had enthusiastically supported—had opened the previous year, insisted on a school for girls as well. Moreover, Bishop White also headed the Bray Associates, which educated black children and was named after the British cleric who originally endowed the fund early in the eighteenth century. Although America was independent, the Bray Associates continued to send money. Such schools were crucial for educating the children of Philadelphia, as only in 1818 did the city itself begin to sponsor free public education.[64]

William White's civic interests began with education. In fact, along with Benjamin Rush, he was Benjamin Franklin's successor as the city's foremost creator and supporter of voluntary associations designed to shape the civic life and moral welfare of the city. He was a member of the American Philosophical Society for sixty-eight years, from 1768 until his death in 1836; served as its secretary (1780–82), vice president (1782–1836), and councilor for several years. He was also a trustee of the University of Pennsylvania for sixty-two years, from 1774 until his death (he even survived the 1779 bloodbath, and came within a vote of being elected the new provost, despite the Presbyterian-Constitutionalist majority). White took a special interest in prisoners, to whom he preached frequently, and in 1787 he was a founder and the first president of the Philadelphia Society for Alleviating the Miseries of Public Prisons. Its first action was to petition successfully to free a black man who had been pardoned yet remained in irons for three days thereafter. White headed the list of managers of the Philadelphia Dispensary (his assistant Robert Blackwell and parishioner Samuel Powel were among the others), which provided free medical assistance to the poor. When the intercolonial Corporation for the Relief of Widows and Children of the Clergymen of the Protestant Episcopal Church was revived in 1784 after a ten-year hiatus, White succeeded William Smith as president in 1789. White presided over construction of a new building in 1785 for Christ Church Hospital, established in 1772 by the terms of the will of the church's architect, John Kearsley, "for the support of ten or more poor or distressed women of the Communion of the Church of England." Another bequest in 1789, of land in Philadelphia owned by Joseph Dobbins of South Carolina (who exchanged it for an income of $160 a year for the rest of his life), brought in about $15,000. A relocated and expanded hospital on 49th Street now serves as a nursing home for members of both sexes.[65]

* * * * *

Old-Time Philadelphia Doggerel

Found in William Montgomery White's copy of Bird Wilson's *Memoir of Bishop White*, the following doggerel suggests that White was even more benevolent than Penn and the Quakers, in that he accepted the rat whom the Quakers and city artisans rejected and passed around.

Jack Sprat caught a rat
Behind the miller's door;
The miller ran with all his men
And sent the rat to William Penn.

Mr. Penn got a dish
And sent the rat to Mr. Fish;
Mr. Fish, the biscuit baker
Sent the rat to Moll the Quaker.

Moll the Quaker, full of spite,
Sent the rat to Bishop White;
Bishop White, free from sin,
Opened the door and took it in.

SOURCE: Note transcribed in "Historic Buildings: Report on the Bishop White House," part D, sec. 1, p. 5, notes. Data compiled by M. O. Anderson and David Wallace, staff of Independence Hall National Park, April 1958, copy at Independence Hall National Park Library, Park Headquarters, Philadelphia.

* * * * *

The list went on and on. In 1790 White founded the First Day Society (so called because many Quakers supported it), which taught workingmen how to read and write, and gave them a good dose of morality besides, on their day off. In 1800 he was instrumental in creating the Magdalen Society to care for wayward girls; it is now the White-Williams Foundation and aids poor Philadelphia high school girls who wish to attend college. In 1808 he accepted another first presidency—of the interdenominational Bible Society of Philadelphia, which gave Bibles to poor families—and also participated in the American Bible Society, into which it was later incorporated. The year 1820 added two new charities to his list: the Pennsylvania Institution for the Deaf and Dumb, of which he was the first president, and the House of Refuge for Young Criminal Offenders. The Provident Society for the Employment of the Poor (1824) and the Pennsylvania Institution for the Blind (1833) completed the list of his principal civic involvements.[66]

* * * * *

William White on Slavery

Although he ordained Absalom Jones, the first black priest in Philadelphia, and was friendly toward free blacks, Bishop White did not oppose slavery or join the Pennsylvania Abolition Society. On July 24, 1817, he wrote to Rev. Samuel Turner of Maryland of his sympathy for emancipation but his unwillingness to do anything about it, and expressed his concern about the consequences it might have.

. . . Permission was given to the Jews to have heathen slaves, there can be no doubt. Probably, it was on the humane principle of moderating the cruelties incident to war. . . .

The bearing of the Christian religion on them, I take as follows. The Apostles found the condition of slavery prevalent over the Roman Empire, the mass of those of whom we read under the name of servants, being slaves. There are precepts enjoining on them the respecting and the obeying of their masters. There are also precepts to the latter, of mercy and gentle treatment to their slaves. Bu there is no injunction to set them free. The case of Onesimus is pertinently quoted. The Apostles aimed at the greatest practicable good and not at problematical improvement, to be accomplished if at all, at the expense of the intermediate misery; as we have seen done, in our times by speculative philosophers in their government of St. Domingo. And yet, that the genius of the Christian dispensation is inimical to slavery, appears in the fact that this gradually died away under the attendancy of the other. If the traffic in human flesh became renewed when the scriptures were locked up in languages not generally understood, it is evident that under a renewed manifestation of their contents, there have been the renewed efforts of good men in favor of suffering humanity. On this ground, is it not probable that the efforts now put forth for the Christianizing of the world will gradually have the effect of ameliorating the condition of slaves and even of banishing slavery itself, whenever it can be done without giving occasion to some greater evil? . . .

Considering the conduct of the Apostles in the premises, I cannot countenance any design which tends to make slaves discontented with their condition. Secondly having in view the peculiar circumstance of the southern states and the dreadful consequences of an immediate and general emancipation, I cannot hold it up as the duty of a slaver-holder to give his example and influence toward such as issue. In writing as above, I am not insensible of the magnitude of the evil of slavery. Young people, educated within its sphere, are in great danger of becoming tyrannical and cruel in their dispositions. It is unfavorable to agriculture and to every species of industry. And in the event of war, it exposes it to an invading army. Whether

> public wisdom may hereafter provide a remedy consistent with justice and humanity and whether the colonization scheme on foot may have so happy a tendency, is more than I can foresee. [White was a vice-president of the American Colonization Society.] In the meantime, I abide by the maxim—"Salus Populi suprema Lex." Under which term of people include the black as well as the white, both of whom would be the worse by a change which should arm them against one another.

SOURCE: White to Rev. Samuel Turner, July 24, 1817, Archives, Episcopal Diocese of Maryland, Baltimore.

* * * * *

White's religious and civic charitable activities may be considered the equivalent of what the Philadelphia and national Federalist elite, many of whom were his parishioners and friends, projected for the state and the nation. They included Tench Coxe (Hamilton's assistant secretary of the treasury and the source of many of his financial ideas), Robert Morris (White's brother-in-law, Washington's original choice for secretary of the treasury and the founder of the first American banks), Thomas Willing (president of the first Pennsylvania and national banks), Benjamin Rush (antislavery and temperance advocate and prison reformer), Benjamin Franklin (also a supporter of economic development and opponent of slavery), and George Washington and Alexander Hamilton themselves, who frequently attended Christ Church during the Constitutional Convention and when the national government was headquartered in Philadelphia during the 1790s. White's reforms, like theirs, hoped to give direction to the new nation through the creation of elite-dominated associations that would address social and economic problems.

The checks and balances and separation of powers between state and federal authority brought forth in both the Episcopal and the American constitutions sought to give weight to wisdom and hierarchy as well as to popular consent. Pennsylvanians and northern Federalists launched a series of associations—antislavery, banks, turnpikes, the nation's first stock exchange and insurance companies, encouragement for education, temperance, prison reform, and manufactures, overseas enterprises to the Orient, learned societies and academies—to ensure national prosperity and the general good. White's support of education, prisoners, the sick, the poor, the handicapped, and African Americans (discussed in the next chapter) jibed well with these plans, and represented an equivalent effort to involve the Episcopal Church in shaping a virtuous republic.[67]

White's personal ideas and temperament helped the church in some ways but hindered it in others. Stylistically, he was a democrat. He signed his letters "William White," unlike others—Seabury, for instance, who signed himself "Samuel Bishop Connecticut" in the manner of the British clerics. He bowed to poor as well as rich acquaintances as he took his many walks around the city, and he welcomed all comers to seek him out at home. Simplicity also prevailed when he officiated in church. He thought elaborate ceremonies more likely to create self-satisfaction than the reasoned conversion that he believed was the only true path to benevolence and true, practical Christianity. "I have often been disgusted by seeing light-minded people turn around and stare at the organ loft, when their attention ought to be fixed on their devotions," he wrote later in life to his friend James Kemp, who became bishop of Maryland. "One of the greatest nuisances I have been struggling against during my whole ministry," White continued, "is a disposition manifested in a great proportion of those employed in the musical department to behave as though they were not part of a Christian Congregation and merely called in to relieve the solemnity of the occasion by intermittent diversion." Francis Hopkinson, the American composer who set White's favorite psalms to music, agreed when he advised the bishop on the role of music in the service: "the excellence of an organist consists in his making the instrument subservient and conducive to the purposes of devotion. . . . It is as offensive to hear lilts and jigs from a church organ, as it would be to see a venerable matron frisking through the public streets with all the fantastic airs of a *columbine*."[68]

White also disliked hymns and rarely used them, and he wrote an anonymous magazine article explaining that "no church can want more than from a dozen to twenty tunes," invariably associated with certain psalms. "There is so little of good poetry except the Scriptural, on sacred subjects, and there was so great danger of having selection accommodated to the degree of animal sensibility, affected by those who were the most zealous in the measure, that the discretion of adopting [hymns] seemed questionable." The final version of the American prayer book, however, admitted twenty-seven hymns, a compromise between the fifty-one desired by William Smith and approved in the 1785 prayer book, and the preference of White and Seabury, both of whom wanted to omit them altogether. As Bishop William Bacon Stevens remarked in a speech commemorating the centennial of White's ordination, "Bishop White never bowed at the name of Jesus in the creed, and even wrote two articles in defense of his not doing so. . . . He never turned to the east to say the creed or the Gloria Patri. He never preached in a surplice, but always when not engaged in his Episcopal duties was in the black gown. He never required the people to rise up as he entered the church and at the close of the service to remain standing in their pews until he left the chancel."[69]

For White, religion was largely a matter of reason, which meant that those who preferred more emotional sermons and elaborate ceremonies were not likely to attend. In his autobiography of 1819, White went out of his way to stress at great length that he was not influenced by the great evangelist George Whitefield, whose appeals to the "animal feelings" produced excitement more often than true conversion. Upon White's return from London in 1772, Joseph Pilmore complained of his sermons that "such lifeless discourse will do but little. . . . 'Tis not the sayings of Plato, but the love of Jesus Christ shed abroad in the heart that will promote true benevolence." Even an admirer of White, John Casten, who considered his sermons "well written . . . almost incomparable works of genius and ability, containing the most glowing sentiments and happy figures," doubted whether they "would ever perform half the execution of one of the smooth stories of David," an unclear reference but one pointing to White's rational, elegant, yet hardly uplifting prose. White read his sermons word for word.[70]

During the revolutionary era, the Protestant Episcopal Church decided to adopt, as Benjamin Rush phrased it, "a form of ecclesiastical government purely republican." Rush stressed that its republicanism consisted in establishing a balance of power among bishops, clergy, and laity, between state and national conventions. But the church did not thereby fulfill his wish of becoming "the most popular church in America."[71] Whereas the Episcopal Church embodied the balanced government cherished by the founding fathers, society was becoming more democratic and less republican. But if Episcopalians did not become as numerous as Baptists, Unitarians, Universalists, Presbyterians, and Methodists, by the late eighteenth century their church had come to provide a middle way, a viable alternative for those who felt uncomfortable with the evangelicals' emphasis on emotional expression and enthusiastic exhortation, on the one hand, and the Deists and Unitarians who rejected traditional Christianity and appealed to reasoned argument unleavened by liturgy and aesthetic surroundings, on the other. In so doing, the Episcopal Church became, for better or worse, a church that appealed largely to an educated, cultured elite, but one with a strong tradition of social mission and service that has leavened the natural conservatism of that elite ever since. William White and the Pennsylvania

Episcopal Church he founded thus set the tone that still survives for the national church.

* * * * *

The Bishop White House

Visitors to Independence National Historic Park in Philadelphia are liable to miss the house of Bishop William White at 309 Walnut Street, though it is part of the park. Built in 1787, as soon as White returned from London, where he was ordained a bishop, it remained his residence until his death in 1836. After his wife, Mary, died in 1797, White lived there with his children and (at different times) some of his eighteen grandchildren, and also fostered there the step-granddaughter of George Washington, Nelly Custis.

The White house was an attractive place, located between White's two parish churches, Christ and St. Peter's. Bishop White won universal respect from the inhabitants of Philadelphia for remaining in the city—as did black ministers Richard Allen and Absalom Jones—to comfort the sick and bury the dead during the seven yellow fever epidemics the town experienced from 1793 to 1805. Most wealthy people escaped to the countryside. White stayed at his post, at the age of 84, during the cholera epidemic of 1832. Some scholars guess that White's fondness for cigars (he smoked four a day), Madeira wine, and keeping mosquito netting around his bed spared him from the disease.

One curiosity of the White house is that it contains one of the first indoor privies in Philadelphia, with one seat for an adult and two (side by side) for children. Also, we know what White's library looked like, for one of his daughters had it painted by John Sartain shortly after the bishop's death: 150 volumes from the library, initially donated to the Episcopal Academy, now reside in the house. On the wall hang pictures of Moses leading the Israelites into the promised land, a most appropriate allegory for White's role in founding the Episcopal Church, along with a portrait of Samuel Seabury. Impressive portraits of White's grandparents by Sir Godfrey Knoeller, one of England's finest painters, greet the visitor upon entering the living room. The house has a total of eight levels, including a wine cellar, root cellar, and ice pit. Tours are available from Independence Hall National Park Service, whose headquarters are located across the street in the Merchants' Exchange Building.

* * * * *

NOTES

1. François-Jean, Marquis de Chastellux, *Travels in North America in the Years 1780, 1781, and 1782*, trans. Howard C. Rice, 2 vols. (Chapel Hill: University of North Carolina Press, 1963), 1:167–68.

2. I discuss the clergy's response to the Revolution in more detail in the essay "Out of Many, One: The Anglican Loyalist Clergy of Revolutionary Pennsylvania," in my edited *Pennsylvania's Revolution* (University Park: Pennsylvania State University Press, 2010), 97–119, and in a forthcoming biography of Bishop William White.

3. For enumerations of the Anglican clergy and congregations, all of which differ slightly from one another, see Nancy L. Rhoden, *Revolutionary Anglicanism: The Colonial Church of England During the American Revolution* (New York: New York University Press, 1999), 149; Edgar Legaré Pennington, "The Anglican Clergy of Pennsylvania in the American Revolution," *PMHB* 63 (1939): 430–31. Pennington excludes Richard Peters (who died in 1776) of the United Churches in Philadelphia and includes three Delaware clergymen, while omitting John Andrews, who served in both provinces. Also see J. Wesley Twelves, *A History of the Diocese of Pennsylvania of the Protestant Episcopal Church in the U.S.A., 1784–1968* (Philadelphia: Diocese of Pennsylvania, 1969), 100–123; Episcopal Church, Diocese of Pennsylvania, *Spanning Four Centuries: Pages of Parish History of the Episcopal Diocese of Pennsylvania* (Philadelphia: Diocese of Pennsylvania, 1997); and William Stevens Perry, ed., *Historical Collections Relating to the American Colonial Church*, vol. 2, *Pennsylvania* (Hartford, Conn.: Church Press Co., 1871; reprint, New York: AMS Press, 1969), 458–91. I have tried to include every congregation and clergyman for whose presence there is evidence. White's statement appears in a letter to Bishop John Hobart, September 1, 1819, in appendix to William White, *The Case of the Episcopal Churches in the United States Considered*, ed. Richard G. Salomon (N.p.: Church Historical Society Publications, 1954), 73. On the wealth and nature of early Anglicans, see Deborah Mathias Gough, "Pluralism, Politics, and Power Struggles: The Church of England in Colonial Pennsylvania, 1695–1789" (PhD diss., University of Pennsylvania, 1978), 3, 26–29. For Illing, see Edith L. Baldwin, "Old St. John's Pequa," *Papers of the Lancaster County Historical Society* 6 (1904): 143; R. Chester Ross, *Two Hundred Years of Church History: The History of St. John's Pequa, Protestant Episcopal Church Located at Compass, Chester County* (West Chester: Intelligencer Printing Co., 1929), 6; and *Register of Marriages and Baptisms Kept by the Rev. Traugott Frederick Illing in Connection with the Churches of St. Peter's (Lutheran) Middletown, and Caernarvon (Episcopal) Lancaster County, Penn'a* (Harrisburg: Harrisburg Publishing Co., 1891). On Smith, see "Journals of the Meetings that Led to the Formation of the Diocese of Pennsylvania," Manuscript Minutes of the Standing Committee of the Episcopal Convention, May 23, 1785, Diopa Archives, Lutheran Theological Seminary, Mount Airy (Philadelphia).

4. "Journals of the Meetings that Led to the Formation of the Diocese of Pennsylvania," meeting of April 6, 1784, Diopa Archives; Thomas Claggett to William White, May 8, 1810, and William White to James Kemp, January 29, 1822, Archives of the Episcopal Diocese of Maryland, Baltimore, arranged in chronological order; George Craig to SPG, August 22, 1755, Craig Papers, HSP. In a letter to the SPG dated January 3, 1764, he put the number at one in fifty.

5. Robert James Gough, "Toward a Theory of Class and Social Conflict: A Social History of Wealthy Philadelphians, 1775 and 1800" (PhD diss., University of Pennsylvania, 1977), 137–38, 140; Gough, "Pluralism, Politics, and Power Struggles," 3.

6. Gough, "Toward a Theory of Class and Social Conflict," 193–94.

7. Gough, "Pluralism, Politics, and Power Struggles," 8, 238–39, 243–44, 251–53.

8. E. Digby Baltzell, *An American Business Aristocracy* (New York: Macmillan, 1958), 272, 275. For lists of pewholders, see "Pew Renters of Christ Church, St. Peter's and St. James," microfilm, church reels, 121, HSP; and C. P. B. Jefferys, "The Provincial and Revolutionary History of St. Peter's Church, Philadelphia, 1753–83," *PMHB* 47 (1923): 47, 328–56; *PMHB* 48 (1924): 39–65; 181–192; 251–68; 354–65—pewholders listed on 362–67 for St. Peter's. For a recent history of St. Peter's, see Cordelia Frances Biddle, Elizabeth S. Brown, Alan J. Heavens, and Charles P. Peitz, *St. Peter's Church: Faith in Action for 250 Years* (Philadelphia: Temple University Press, 2012), which came out after this book went to press.

9. Deborah Mathias Gough, *Christ Church, Philadelphia: The Nation's Church in a Changing City* (Philadelphia: University of Pennsylvania Press, 1995), 190–92; for salary complaints from rural missionaries, see Harold Donaldson Eberlein and Cortlandt van Dyke Hubbard, *The Church of St. Peter in the Great Valley, 1700–1940* (Richmond: August Dietz and Son, 1944), 26, 64, 76–77, 87; George Craig to SPG, June 20, 1754, August 5, 1757, September 30, 1759, June 26, 1766, and October 14, 1772, Craig Papers, HSP.

10. William Allen to Benjamin Chew, April 13, 1764, quoted in Margaret B. Tinckom, "Cliveden: The Building of a Philadelphia Country Seat, 1763–1767," *PMHB* 88 (1964): 3–5; and Rev. Henry van Dyke to Rev. James Abercrombie, February 23, 1796, quoted in Rufus Griswold, *The Republican Court* (New York, 1855), 272–73, both cited in Gough, "Toward a Theory of Class and Social Conflict," 434–35.

11. Gough, *Christ Church, Philadelphia*, 128–33, 136–38; Gough, "Pluralism, Politics, and Power Struggles," 516; Gough, "Toward a Theory of Class and Social Conflict," 493.

12. Kevin J. Dellape, "Jacob Duché: Whig-Loyalist?" *Pennsylvania History* 62 (1995): 296 (Dellape is also completing a biography of Duché); Jefferys, "Provincial and Revolutionary History of St. Peter's," *PMHB* 48: 188–89.

13. Bird Wilson, *Memoir of the Life of the Right Reverend William White, D.D., Bishop of the Protestant Episcopal Church in the State of Pennsylvania* (Philadelphia: James Kay Jr. and Brother, 1839), 50–51 (hereafter *Life of White*).

14. William Smith to SPG, July 10, 1775, in Perry, *Historical Collections*, 2:475–80; Philadelphia Clergy to Bishop of London, June 30, 1775, ibid., 2:470–42.

15. See the Pennsylvania SPG missionaries' letters to the SPG, ibid., 2:458–91, for their repeated insistence that they were adhering to the oath taken at the time of their ordination in Britain. The oath appears in William E. Hannum, *The Story of St. John's: Being an Historical Sketch of St. John's Episcopal Church, Concord, Delaware County, Pennsylvania* (Concord: St. John's Episcopal Church, 1959), 17.

16. Jefferys, "Provincial and Revolutionary History of St. Peter's"; Gough, *Christ Church, Philadelphia*, 138.

17. Perry, *Historical Collections*, 2:471; Norris S. Barratt, *Outline of the History of Old St. Paul's Church, Philadelphia, Pennsylvania* (Philadelphia: Colonial Society of Pennsylvania, 1917), 29–34; Gough, *Christ Church, Philadelphia*, 81; H. W. Smith, ed., *Life and Correspondence of the Rev. William Smith*, 2 vols. (N.p., 1879), 2:9–10, 17–82; Albert F. Gegenheimer, *William Smith: Educator and Churchman, 1727–1803* (Philadelphia: University of Pennsylvania Press, 1943), 178–82; J. Walter High, "Thomas Coombe, Loyalist," *Pennsylvania History* 62 (1995): 284–86; Jefferys, "Provincial and Revolutionary History of St. Peter's," 260–61; Dellape, "Jacob Duché," 299–301; Gough, "Pluralism, Politics, and Power Struggles," 558–60; Vestry minutes of the United Churches, September 6–10, 1777, microfilm reel 1, HSP.

18. Vestry minutes of the United Churches, microfilm reel 1, HSP. Annual vestry elections were held in late March or April, 1775–1790. Barratt, *Outline of the History of Old St. Paul's*, 94, 117.

19. Smith, *Life and Correspondence of Smith*, 2:17–29; Gegenheimer, *William Smith*, 178–80; Gough, "Pluralism, Politics, and Power Struggles," 558–60.

20. Eberlein and Hubbard, *Church of St. Peter*, 26, 64, 69–93; Henry Pleasants, *The History of Old St. David's Church, Radnor, in Delaware County, Pennsylvania* (Philadelphia: John Winston and Co., 1907), 92–96, 151, 153; H. M. J. Klein and William F. Diller, *The History of St. James' Church (Protestant Episcopal), 1744–1944* (Lancaster: Vestry of St. James' Church, 1944), 41–57; William

DuHamel, *Historical Annals of Christ Church, Formerly Called St. Mary's, Reading, Pa.* (Douglassville, Pa.: Church Press, 1927), 13–14, 16–18.

21. Barton quoted in Ross, *Two Hundred Years of Church History*, 27.

22. Eberlein and Hubbard, *Church of St. Peter*, 86–93; Pleasants, *History of Old St. David's*, 92–96; *Journal of the Meetings Which Led to the Institution of a Convention of the Protestant Episcopal Church in the State of Pennsylvania* . . . (Philadelphia: Hall and Sellers, 1790), 5; George Craig to SPG, July 17, 1760, June 25, 1762, July 11, 1763, and November 10, 1769, Craig Papers, HSP; William Shaler Johnson, *The Story of Old St. Paul's "On Delaware," 1703–1803* (N.p., n.d.), 4–6; Arthur Chilton Powell, *Historic St. John's: Centennial Sermon Preached in St. John's Episcopal Church, York, Pennsylvania* (York: Gazette Printing Co., 1887), 7–9; Hannum, *Story of St. John's*, 17–19.

23. Eberlein and Hubbard, *Church of St. Peter*, 90–93; Pleasants, *History of Old St. David's*, 92–96.

24. Twelves, *History of the Diocese of Pennsylvania*, 117–23; for Odell, see the biography by Cynthia Dublin Edelberg, *Jonathan Odell: Loyalist Poet of the American Revolution* (Durham: Duke University Press, 1987); for St. James's, see John T. Faris, *Old Churches and Meeting Houses in and Around Philadelphia* (Philadelphia: J. B. Lippincott, 1926), 220–21.

25. See John Frantz and William Pencak, eds., *Beyond Philadelphia: The American Revolution in the Pennsylvania Hinterland* (University Park: Pennsylvania State University Press, 1998), chapters on Berks (Karen Guenther), York (Paul Doutrich), and Cumberland (Robert Crist) counties; for Lancaster, see Jerome Wood, *Conestoga Crossroads: Lancaster, Pennsylvania, 1730–1790* (Harrisburg: Pennsylvania Historical and Museum Commission, 1979).

26. W. Walter van Banaam, *A Brief History of St. John's* (N.p., n.d. [1955?]), unpaginated (9–12 pages into the text; this is a history of St. John the Baptist in York, Pennsylvania, from 1755 to 1955); Powell, *Historic St. John's*, 6–7, 11–15; Samuel Johnson to SPG, November 25, 1776—see also Thomas Barton to SPG, November 25, 1776, both in Perry, *Historical Collections*, 2:487–90; James P. Myers Jr., "The Bermudian Creek Tories," *Adams County History* 3 (1997): 4–40. Myers's use of British military documents proves the existence of the conspiracy and the identity of its leaders.

27. Powell, *Historic St. John's*, 8–10.

28. For Barton's career, see ibid., 5–6; James P. Myers Jr., *The Ordeal of Thomas Barton: Anglican Missionary in the Pennsylvania Backcountry* (Bethlehem: Lehigh University Press, 2010); Marvin F. Russell, "Thomas Barton and the Pennsylvania Colonial Frontier," *Pennsylvania History* 46 (1979): 313–34; Theodore W. Jeffries, "Thomas Barton (1730–1780): Victim of the American Revolution," *Journal of the Lancaster County Historical Society* 81 (1977): 39–74; Klein and Diller, *History of St. James' Church*, 41–57; James P. Myers, Jr., "Homeland Security in the Pennsylvania Backcountry, 1777–1778: The Example of the Rev. Mr. David Batwelle SPG," *Pennsylvania History* 78 (2011): 247–81.

29. Jeffries, "Thomas Barton (1730–1780)," 61; Pennington, "Anglican Clergy of Pennsylvania," 406.

30. Jeffries, "Thomas Barton (1730–1780)," 67–72.

31. Karen Guenther, "'A Faithful Soldier of Christ': The Career of the Reverend Dr. Alexander Murray, Missionary to Berks County, Pa., 1762–1778," *HMPEC* 55 (1986): 5–20; DuHamel, *Historical Annals of Christ Church*, 13–14, 16–18.

32. Rodney Miller, "The Political Ideology of the Anglican Clergy," *HMPEC* 45 (1976): 227–36.

33. The most useful edition of White's *Case of the Episcopal Churches in the United States Considered* is the one cited in note 3 above, edited by Richard G. Salomon. The reference here is to the preface, p. 18.

34. Ibid., 20–21.

35. Ibid., 30, 32, 44–45.

36. Robert W. Prichard, *The Nature of Salvation: Theological Consensus in the Episcopal Church, 1801–73* (Urbana: University of Illinois Press, 1997), chapter 1, esp. 20. See also William Wilson Manross, "Bishop White's Theology," *HMPEC* 15 (1946): 285–97.

37. *Journal of the Meetings*, 1–2.

38. Ibid., 5–6.

39. William West to William White, July 5, 1784, Archives of the Episcopal Diocese of Maryland, Baltimore.

40. Prichard, *Nature of Salvation*, 20.

41. Gough, "Pluralism, Politics, and Power Struggles," 568, 573.

42. *Journal of the Meetings*, 8–9; Frederick V. Mills, *Bishops by Ballot: An Eighteenth-Century Ecclesiastical Revolution* (New York: Oxford University Press, 1978), 233.

43. Hatch Dent to Francis Walker, June 26, 1784; see also Walker to Dent, June 28, 1784, Archives of the Episcopal Diocese of Maryland, Baltimore.

44. Seabury to Smith, August 15, 1785, in *Life and Correspondence of the Right Reverend Samuel Seabury, D.D.*, ed. Eben Edwards Beardsley (Boston: Houghton Mifflin, 1881), 231; Mills, *Bishops by Ballots*, 206–25, 233–37, 247.

45. William Stevens Perry, ed., *Journals of the General Convention of the Protestant Episcopal Church in the United States, 1785–1835* (Claremont: Claremont Manufacturing Co., 1874), 5–9; Gough, "Pluralism, Politics, and Power Struggles," 579; Clara O. Loveland, *The Critical Years: The Restoration of the Anglican Church in the United States, 1780–1789* (Greenwich, Conn.: Seabury Press, 1956), 153–55; Mason Weems to John Adams, n.d., Adams to Weems, March 3, 1784, Adams to President of Congress, April 22, 1784, and William White to John Adams, November 26, 1785, all in John Adams, *The Works of John Adams, Second President of the United States*, ed. Charles Francis Adams, 10 vols. (Boston: Little, Brown, 1950–56), 8:197–99, 184–86, 349–50.

46. Perry, *Journals of the General Convention*, 20–21; Herbert Boyce Satcher, "Music of the Episcopal Church in Pennsylvania in the Eighteenth Century," *HMPEC* 18 (1949): 372–413, esp. 393–400; Hannah D. French, "Caleb Buglass, Binder of the Proposed Book of Common Prayer, Philadelphia, 1786," *Winterthur Portfolio* 6 (1970): 15–32, esp. 32. White had tremendous difficulty selling the books; see his letters of 1786 to William West, in the Archives of the Episcopal Diocese of Maryland, Baltimore.

47. Mills, *Bishops by Ballot*, 250–52; Perry, *Journals of the General Convention*, 32–35.

48. Mills, *Bishops by Ballot*, 257–58; for Smith's misbehavior, see Thomas Craddock to Dr. [John] Andrews, October 27, 1786, Samuel Johnson to Andrews, October 31, 1786, and William West to William White, October, 31, 1786, all in the Archives of the Episcopal Diocese of Maryland, Baltimore. See also "Journals of State [Pennsylvania] Convention," May 22, 1786, June 1, 1790, Diopa Archives.

49. Mills, *Bishops by Ballot*, 258–59; John Adams to John Jay, January 4, 1786, in Adams, *Works*, 8:361–62; Wilson, *Life of White*, 110–11; and letters of William White to the Pennsylvania State Convention, December 6, 1786, January 1, January 22, and February 4, 1787, Diopa Archives.

50. Mills, *Bishops by Ballot*, 249.

51. Bruce Steiner, *Samuel Seabury, 1729–1796: A Study in the High Church Tradition* (Athens: Ohio University Press, 1972), 273; Gough, "Pluralism, Politics, and Power Struggles," 585–86; Mills, *Bishops by Ballots*, 286–87; William West to William White, July 14, 1788, and White to Seabury, December 9, 1788, Archives of the Episcopal Diocese of Maryland, Baltimore.

52. See my "Christian Symbolism and Political Unity in the English Reformation: A Historical Interpretation of the Semiotics of Anglican Doctrines," in my *History, Signing In: Essays in History and Semiotics* (New York: Peter Lang, 1993), 268–87.

53. Mills, *Bishops by Ballot*, 284–86.

54. Bend quoted in Arthur Pierce Middleton, "Prayer Book Revision Explained: Sermons on the Liturgy by Joseph Bend, Rector of St. Paul's, Baltimore, 1791–1812," *Anglican and Episcopal History* 60 (1991): 63; for his opinions, see also 68, 71. Bend served as curate of the United Churches in Philadelphia from 1787 to 1791 and attended the convention of 1789, where the prayer book was hammered out. More generally, see Steiner, *Samuel Seabury, 1729–1796*, 275–80; Mills, *Bishops by Ballot*, 265, 266, 271, 281; Perry, *Journals of the General Convention*, 47–65; Gough, "Pluralism, Politics, and Power Struggles," 585–87; Winfred Douglas, "Early Hymnody of the American Episcopal Church," *HMPEC* 10 (1941): 202–18; Satcher, "Music of the Episcopal Church," 393–400; William Wilson Manross, "The Interstate Meetings and General Conventions of 1784, 1785, 1786, and 1789," *HMPEC* 8 (1939): 257–80; and Martin Dewey Gable Jr., "The Hymnody of the Church—1789–1832," *HMPEC* 36 (1967): 249–74, esp. 253–67.

55. Russell Blaine Nye, *The Cultural Life of the New Nation, 1776–1830* (New York: Harper and Row, 1960), 199–200.

56. Walter Herbert Stowe, Nelson W. Rightmyer, G. McLaren Brydon, Lawrence F. London, and Albert Sidney Thomas, "The Clergy of the Episcopal Church in 1785," *HMPEC* 20 (1951): 243–77, esp. 259–60.

57. Edward Potts Cheyney, *History of the University of Pennsylvania, 1740–1940* (Philadelphia: University of Pennsylvania Press, 1940), 124–25.

58. Henry Melchior Muhlenberg, *The Journals of Henry Melchior Muhlenberg*, ed. Theodore G. Tappert and John W. Doberstein, 3 vols. (Philadelphia: Evangelical Lutheran Ministerium of Pennsylvania, 1942–58), entry for October, 23, 1784, 3:625–26.

59. Rush to Charles Nisbet, August 27, 1784, and Rush to Ashbel Greene, August 11, 1787, both in Benjamin Rush, *Letters of Benjamin Rush*, ed. Lyman H. Butterfield, 2 vols. (Princeton: Princeton University Press, 1951), 1:334–37 and 1:433, respectively.

60. Charles Latham, *The Episcopal Academy, 1785–1984* (Devon, Pa.: W. T. Cooke, 1984), 15–21.

61. Ibid., 218–20.

62. Ibid., 222–23.

63. Ibid., 27–29, 233–35; William White, "Autobiography," ed. Walter Herbert Stowe, *HMPEC* 22 (1953): 379–432, esp. 412–14.

64. Latham, *Episcopal Academy*, 31–33; William C. Kashatus, *A Virtuous Education: Penn's Vision for Philadelphia Schools* (Wallingford, Pa.: Pendle Hill Publications, 1997).

65. George B. Roberts, "Christ Church Hospital," *HMPEC* 45 (1976): 89–102.

66. For more on White's charitable activities, see Wilson, *Life of White;* Walter Herbert Stone, ed., *The Life and Memoirs of Bishop White* (New York: Morehouse, 1937), 107–8, 135–41; Walter Herbert Stowe, "The Corporation for the Relief of Widows and Children of Clergymen," *HMPEC* 3 (1934): 19–33; Myers, Jr., "Homeland Security in the Pennsylvania Backcountry."

67. See William Pencak, "The Promise of Revolution: 1750–1800," in *Pennsylvania: A History of the Commonwealth*, ed. Randall M. Miller and William Pencak (University Park: Pennsylvania State University Press, 2002), 133–37; Gough, "Pluralism, Politics, and Power Struggles," 201.

68. William White to James Kemp, January 4, 1815, Archives of the Episcopal Diocese of Maryland, Baltimore; Francis Hopkinson to William White, printed in the *Columbian Magazine*, September 1792, reprinted in Oscar G. T. Sonneck, *Francis Hopkinson, The First American Poet-Composer (1737–1791) and James Lyon, Patriot, Preacher, Psalmodist (1735–1794)* (originally published in 1905) (New York: Da Capo Press, 1967), 59–62.

69. William White, *Memoirs of the Protestant Episcopal Church in the United States* (Philadelphia: Swords, Stanford, 1835), 236; Satcher, "Music of the Episcopal Church," 396–98; William Bacon Stevens, "Then and Now" (sermon preached on the hundredth anniversary of White's ordination), *The Churchman*, new ser., 6 (1872): 1046, quoted in Barratt, *Outline of the History of Old St. Paul's*, 74.

70. White, "Autobiography," 388–89; Joseph Pilmore, *The Journal of Joseph Pilmore*, ed. Frederick E. Maser and Howard T. Maag (Philadelphia: Historical Society of the Philadelphia Annual Conference of the Methodist Church, 1969), 63 (entry for October 28, 1777); John Casten to William Duke, March 31, 1795, Archives of the Episcopal Diocese of Maryland, Baltimore.

71. Benjamin Rush to Richard Price, October 15, 1785, in Rush, *Letters*, 1:371; see also Muhlenberg, *Journals*, entry for May 17, 1786, 3:707.

3

Identity, Spirituality, and Organization

The Episcopal Church in Early Pennsylvania, 1790–1820

EMMA JONES LAPSANSKY-WERNER

On Wednesday, May 27, 1807, Bishop William White addressed his small audience at the annual convention of the Protestant Episcopal Church. "Twenty years have passed since I became your bishop," he reminded them. Yet, he explained, he was only now delivering his first sermon before this body, "in the form of a pastoral charge."[1]

With his "charge"—the sermon must have been hours long, since in print it ran to more than fifty pages—the bishop apparently aimed to both educate and unify the clergy who reported to him, and to energize them for the challenges ahead. Over the previous two decades, White reported, the Anglican Church had been struggling to redefine itself as the new American Protestant Episcopal Church, adjusting to the dislocation resulting from the Revolution, liturgical and community conflicts, economic difficulties, a precipitous decline in membership, and discord within the leadership. Thus Bishop White had had some busy and stressful years. However, by 1807 the Episcopal Church had reached a level of organization that allowed it the luxury of including a formal sermon as part of its annual gathering.

The American Revolution had focused and actualized the ideas of the Western world's "Enlightenment," thus precipitating new models of participatory government, new notions of individual entitlement, and new challenges for traditional religions. Changing definitions of personal and national identity, realigned allegiances, and shifting economic and demographic boundaries called for fresh approaches to concepts of community, leadership, and loyalty. The Episcopal Church was not immune to these forces. Indeed, its challenges were amplified by its roots in the Anglican Church, with its ties to the now unpopular British Crown.

While upbeat and hopeful, White's message also carried the seriousness of the local implications of the international situation: in the generation following the Revolution, Pennsylvania Episcopalians, centered in Philadelphia, had descended from being the most prestigious church (though not numerically the largest) in the nation's premier city to being just another contender for Christian souls in a region that was rapidly being eclipsed by New York. Christ Church, the seat of power in Pennsylvania's Episcopal world, had an imposing building, a new organ, a renowned musical program,[2] and a widely known and respected leadership. But none of this was holding off the economic wolf at the door, or forestalling the shrinkage in membership.

In 1790 Philadelphia was a city of three vigorous Presbyterian congregations, a handful of Quaker meetings, one Baptist and one Methodist church, two Catholic parishes, and two Lutheran churches. Over the next several decades, the major expansion was among the Presbyterians, who grew to twelve congregations, the Baptists, who gained four churches, and the Methodists, whose evangelical energy increased their number of churches to six. Over the next half century, the Methodists, an impassioned group with historic ties to the Anglican denomination, would outstrip most other Protestants in the competition to "church" America. For a number of understandable but disappointing reasons, the Episcopal Church was clearly losing ground. In Philadelphia, where the enterprising Presbyterians reeled in the upwardly mobile, and the high-profile Methodists scooped up the artisans and skilled workers,[3] there were all too few converts left for Episcopalianism. As one historian described it, "most [postrevolutionary] Philadelphians remained shamelessly unchurched . . . [and] . . . some were openly hostile to mainstream religion," because Protestantism's traditional emphasis on human depravity and an arbitrary God did not sit well with enlightened citizens intent upon human agency and democracy.[4] As he prepared his 1807 sermon, White could hardly have been unaware of these realities surrounding organized religion in the early Republic.

For his part, White had been dreaming up programs and strategies to keep Episcopalians competitive in the race for Americans' souls. Following his own power struggles with colleagues in New England and the South,[5] he had tried to quell the controversies over liturgy and church organization that threatened to rend Episcopal communities, and he had struggled to develop unity among Pennsylvania's Episcopal churches. Under his leadership, the Pennsylvania diocese would sponsor adult schools to "spread the blessings of illumination among the mass of the people,"[6] and establish an academy to train young people for leadership in Episcopal communities. Through the early decades of the nineteenth century, his leadership in joining Presbyterians, Methodists, and other Protestants in philanthropic enterprises, especially those that drew women into active roles, contributed to the visibility of his church.

White encouraged his colleague Jackson Kemper in setting up the Society for the Advancement of Christianity, which aimed to take "our church in[to] the whole western part of the United States."[7] He mentored young idealists like John Henry Hobart, who set out to revive what he believed was the church's "evangelical truth" and "apostolic order."[8]

But the dedicated Episcopalian leader was fighting an uphill battle. Only recently—and then incompletely—has White been examined against the backdrop of the political, economic, and social context of his era.[9] In White's lifetime, the whole Atlantic world went into a tailspin, as revolutions in America, France, and the West Indies realigned political, economic, and indeed religious affiliations, loyalties, and expectations. A figure larger than life both in his own time and in the narratives historians have crafted since, White justifiably holds the position of being the sine qua non for understanding the early development of the Episcopal Church in America. Highly regarded for his levelheadedness and his ability to meld equilibrium out of contesting perspectives, White has come down through history as an intellectually and politically astute strategist whose personal biography often eclipses the development of the organization he led. Yet his story is intimately connected not only to Pennsylvania Episcopalianism; it is also intertwined with broad developments in the wider Atlantic world.

All along the Atlantic rim, in dozens of ways, revolutionized societies and individuals were presented with new questions: Who and what will have authority in the decades and centuries ahead? What aspects of old worlds will endure? In what form? What will be the compelling realities of the future, and how will old communities avoid being marginalized or eradicated by the forces of the new worlds to come?

In the fledgling United States these questions of identity had an extra edge. Having wrenched themselves free from the protection of the most powerful country in the Atlantic world, how would Americans survive? When the contours of the new political experiment jelled, what aspects of colonial culture would be cast aside as too reminiscent of the old order? The American Episcopal Church, born out of an anglicized imperialism to which neither Britain nor America could return, presents a unique lens through which to view some critical aspects of the new Republic: the establishment of identity, values, authority, and community. For with the birth of a new nation came new opportunities for "churching." But, like the postrevolutionary American government, religious organizations would have to adopt an aggressive posture if they were to contend for citizens' loyalty and conformity. Who would have authority and power over whom? How would that power and authority be demonstrated? Who would be responsible for setting behavioral boundaries, and for adjudicating transgressions and conflicts? Could clear definitions of identity and firm guidelines for conduct stave off anarchy?

Shaping Identity in the New Republic

Loyalties could not be taken for granted. Some Americans were hard at work designing a legal and political system that they hoped would inspire the new ideals of liberty and republicanism, and Benjamin Franklin's post–Constitutional Convention quip, "a Republic, ma'am, if you can keep it," encapsulated the political power struggles Franklin knew lay before the new nation. The challenges centered around the balance between "liberty" and the contradictory desires of Americans to develop and maintain a unified political system cemented by mutual duty and trust among citizens. Where should a citizen place first allegiances? To self? To family? To town or region, or to the nation? To political affiliation? To religious community?

In 1775 three denominations dominated the American religious landscape: Congregationalism (mostly in New England), Episcopalianism (predominant in the mid-Atlantic and upper South), and Presbyterianism (all along the Atlantic seaboard). These three denominations accounted for more than half of all Americans' church affiliations. But by 1790, when the first federal census was taken, only about ten thousand of the nation's four million citizens were Episcopalian.[10] Presbyterians were holding their own, but the Methodist and Catholic organizations, with aggressive recruitment and energetic missionaries, were rapidly eclipsing the old established churches, with their ties to the old British traditions. By 1850 conversion and immigration would swell the rolls of the Methodist, Catholic, and Baptist churches, while Congregational membership, which had been vigorous in the revolutionary era, would decline to a state that one historian described as "approach[ing] total collapse."[11]

If the once numerous Congregationalists were "collapsing" after the Revolution, the Episcopal Church was not in much better shape. White reminded his audience that in the years after the Revolution "there were but three clergymen, and for a time, there had been but one, the author of this statement. In the states immediately south of us, most of the clergy had ceased to officiate. . . . To the northward, the clergy were almost universally restrained from officiating."[12] By 1807 White could report some growth in the Pennsylvania diocese, but the numbers—a dozen clergy and a few dozen lay leaders—were still small.

Small in numbers and marked with the stigma of its historical association with England, the Episcopal Church was also constrained by two other limitations—geography and social class. In a country that was largely rural and poor, the Episcopal Church's constituency had traditionally been urban and economically well off. Yet even this description doesn't get at the nuance of the situation, for even though individual members of Episcopal parishes were often among the country's wealthiest men, "wealth" often did not translate into liquid capital, as the United States underwent its bumpy transition to merchant capitalism. Hence, most parishes in the mid-Atlantic region (where Episcopalianism was strongest) had too few members (with too little ready cash) to support a minister, even if an appropriate pastor could be found.[13]

Economic instability, frequent personal dislocations, and community tensions added to the problem of maintaining the churches. At Philadelphia's Christ Church, where White presided, a majority of annual pew rents (an important segment of the church budget) were in arrears for most of the two decades following the Revolution.[14] In addition, postrevolutionary Americans were a highly mobile people. To be sure, the poor moved more frequently than those who were more economically secure,[15] but Pennsylvania's more affluent residents moved often, too, seeking land or other economic opportunities, or escaping from lives that had become somehow unmanageable. What had, a generation before, been a stable and predictable adjunct to a powerful English society was now a constellation of communities within which itinerant new Americans sought to carve out a new identity.

Geography, mobility, and postwar economic volatility destabilized all churches, as newcomers often switched loyalties to whatever denomination offered the warmest welcome. Indeed, argues one historian, early denominational boundaries were surprisingly permeable, with tensions *within* denominations often adding to the itinerant quality of church membership.[16] In particular, the exclusive membership patterns and English holdovers worked against the stability and growth of the Episcopal Church. In addition, the Episcopalians' emphasis on intellectualism, literacy, and relatively expensive architectural and artifactual requirements limited its appeal. A circuit-riding Methodist or Baptist minister, leading hymns outdoors in a call-and-response format that didn't require the congregation to read, could deliver God's message to communicants of lean resources. In the postwar maelstrom of social and economic repositioning, the Episcopal Church was at a disadvantage.

Meanwhile, those who hoped that national attachments would supersede all others were dreaming up symbols around which that new American phenomenon—a citizen—might rally and unify. (Franklin wanted the turkey to be adopted as the emblem of the new nation, because it is a uniquely native bird. He feared that the eagle, which he felt had poor moral character because it feeds on dead things, would not inspire Americans to lofty ideals.)[17] Redesigning dictionaries and spelling books was Noah Webster's contribution to a uniquely American character. And across America, throughout the 1780s and 1790s, parades and public celebrations abounded, as did political debates and rebellions. Local communities, finally freed from British tyranny, sought to knit together a unified polity, while avoiding the imposition of too much government authority. As playwrights satirized Federalist debates and the 1794 Whiskey Rebellion, and immortalized Pocahantas as "the Indian princess," there arose competing ideas and ideals of what it meant to be "American."[18] At every turn, American leaders were acutely aware that although they were fashioning new lives and symbols, persuading the public to commit themselves to those symbols would be no easy task.

Religion, too, was caught up in America's struggle to craft an identity. Predictably, as political and cultural adherents sought to encapsulate their message in symbols, so too did religious advocates. Aided by the increasing availability of paper and the ease of printing, Bible societies sprang up across America—the first of these established, in 1808, by a Protestant alliance in Philadelphia, which White heartily encouraged. By 1812 the Bible Society of Philadelphia, using plates brought in from London, had produced America's first mass-produced—and therefore inexpensive—Bibles. Within three years Philadelphia printers had created their own plates, and the price of Bibles dropped still more. Between 1800 and 1829 more than six hundred different editions of the Bible were published.[19] As religious emissaries rushed to get these sacred symbols into American homes and psyches, Episcopal representatives joined in the effort.[20]

But what should be the place and form of religion in a republic? Some founding philosophers worried about the constrictions of too much mixing of religion and government. Others, including Bishop White, were concerned that "civil governments can't be well-supported without the assistance of religion," and that public servants who lacked respect for God's authority "will have less regard to the laws of men, or to the most solemn oaths or affirmations."[21] Meanwhile, the champions of religion faced a different dilemma. Was it better, these faithful asked themselves, to endeavor to bring the Bible, and some religion, to the unchurched, or was it more important to maintain the purity of denominational tradition, even if that meant excluding those who could not or would not submit to religious discipline? How would the church decide where to set its community boundaries?

One early challenge to the question of how to set membership boundaries arrived in the cloak of one of the new Republic's most vexing, recurring, and pervasive demons: race. Philadelphia's Anglican/Episcopal church had had a long—albeit ambivalent and patronizing—relationship with the black community. Early in the eighteenth century, the Society for the Propagation of the Gospel (SPG) had reached out to slaves, encouraging them to embrace Christianity, with its emphasis on obedience, hierarchy, and acceptance of one's lot in life. By the 1740s, Anglican communicants—who were often among those Philadelphians most able to afford slaves—frequently brought their black servants to be baptized and married at Christ Church or St. Peter's. From this period also, the SPG had opened itself to black recruits through a school set up under an offshoot known as the Associates of Dr. Bray. Thereafter, schools for African American and poor children remained an important aspect of the Anglican Church's outreach, and by the 1770s several hundred black Philadelphians had been baptized into the Anglican fold.[22] After 1780, when the Pennsylvania constitution mandated gradual emancipation, many of Philadelphia's newly freed African Americans found continued comfort in Episcopalian belief systems and forms of worship.

In the postrevolutionary period, however, African Americans increasingly developed community networks of their own design. Historian Gary Nash has documented the story of the origins of both the African Methodist Episcopal denomination and the black parish of the white Protestant Episcopal Church.[23] Like other denominations, Bishop White and the Episcopalians were ambivalent about African American worshippers. Yet religious training was seen as a way to temper what many white Americans considered the undisciplined tendencies of some African Americans, and, at the same time, to encourage the community leadership of exemplary individuals such as Absalom Jones.

Jones had been married in St. Peter's Church, where his master worshipped, in 1770, and within a decade he had borrowed—and repaid—money

FIGURE 3.1 Absalom Jones. Portrait by Raphaelle Peale

to purchase his wife's freedom. Over succeeding years he bought a house and then his own freedom. By 1785 he was a thirty-eight-year-old free property owner.[24] Teaming up with the black Methodist Richard Allen, he helped to spearhead Philadelphia's Free African Society—a black self-help group composed of upwardly mobile black families like his own.

Philadelphia's Free African Society had a sizeable population upon which to draw: more than two hundred independent black households, and perhaps another thousand free people who lived in and served white households but were free to make their own social and religious decisions.

Employment in the bustling city was relatively plentiful, facilitating a vigorous increase in marriages and new households. One estimate suggests that as many as half of Philadelphia's African American marriages during the 1780s and early 1790s took place in Christ Church, St. Peter's, or St. Paul's. Joseph Pilmore, the assistant rector at St. Paul's, was married to a relative of renowned abolitionist Anthony Benezet, and Pilmore himself had a long record of preaching before black parishioners. Between 1789 and 1794 Pilmore performed marriage ceremonies for more than two dozen African American couples. And Pilmore's friend Benjamin Rush, a staunch abolitionist, who was also a member of Christ Church, helped make the Episcopal fold a welcoming place for African Americans.[25]

But not all black Philadelphians felt comfortable in the Episcopal churches. Some—including Jones's good friend Richard Allen—found the humble atmosphere of the Methodists more to their liking. Lay preachers, the simple outdoor meetings, the willingness to simplify the liturgy to accommodate nonreaders, and the Methodists' powerful antislavery posture drew in less affluent black people, leaving the stately Episcopal services to black residents who frequently shared many characteristics with white Episcopalians: they were literate, entrepreneurial, formal, and liturgically conservative.[26] This group included, for example, James Derham, trained by Benjamin Rush and baptized at Christ Church before relocating to New Orleans, where he pursued a successful career as a physician.[27]

By 1794, when White installed Jones as the leader of the segregated St. Thomas's Protestant Episcopal church, Jones had already distinguished himself as one of the city's upstanding residents. To accommodate Jones, the diocese waived its requirement that church officials be proficient in Greek and Latin, and Jones went on to become one of the church's most charismatic leaders, presiding over a congregation that flourished and grew even as some of the region's white parishes languished. St. Thomas's, a congregation of about 250 at its founding in 1794, nearly doubled its membership within a year, and over the next ten years an average of a hundred marriages per year were performed there.[28] Nevertheless, White designated Jones a deacon[29] in 1794 and waited ten more years before promoting him to priest. Jones is never listed among the clergy attending the annual conventions.

Black Episcopalianism flourished in other cities as well: New York had St. Philip's by 1818; St. James's was founded in Baltimore a few years later; and Providence, Rhode Island, opened its Christ Church a few years after that. By 1862, when the Reverend William Douglass—Philadelphia's first black chronicler of Absalom Jones's work—published his *Annals of the First African Church*, many cities, including New Haven, Buffalo, Detroit, and Newark, had thriving black Episcopal congregations. What Douglass described as "a moral earthquake" of Jones's time had produced aftershocks across the nation.[30]

Though it would be many decades before black Episcopalians became equal members of their religious community, the establishment of Philadelphia's African Episcopal Church of St. Thomas—along with its compatriot congregations in other cities—firmly seated an African American presence in the Episcopal community of believers. Thus by the time White delivered his 1807 sermon, the "typical" Episcopalian could be recognized by a common profile that crossed racial boundaries: economically well off, frequently of the landholding class, relatively well educated, and committed to a sober and formal worship service. Rural white and black Americans might be drawn in by the Baptist or Methodist camp meeting, and upwardly mobile urban white workers might find a home among the Presbyterians, but the Episcopalian communities had shaped their pathway to the divine around the urbane dignity of a standardized liturgy.

Spirituality: Approaching "Otherworldliness"

If the role of the church was to provide a sturdy and reliable conduit between the temporal and spiritual worlds, then it was imperative that the church clearly outline the essentials for constructing and maintaining that conduit. Even as White was delivering his stirring sermon in May 1807, his protégé, John Henry Hobart, was developing his own guidelines for supporting such a conduit. Hobart—whom White had baptized, confirmed, tutored, and then, in 1801, ordained—served briefly in Philadelphia before moving on to New York. While in Philadelphia, Hobart had begun to articulate what he felt was the spiritual individuality of the Episcopal Church. Then, from New York, he corresponded with White as he continued to develop the liturgical implications of his conviction that the modern Episcopal Church was the designated descendant of the true Catholic Church as it had emerged in the first several centuries following Christ's death. Hobart argued that since those early centuries saw the foundation of the *true* church, before it was corrupted by the introduction of politics, the primary goal of the modern Episcopal Church should be to restore the Catholic Church to that early level of untarnished purity.

The essence of the church's spiritual health, Hobart was convinced, lay in guarding its claim on religious purity. Therefore, he argued, the Episcopal Church should maintain and protect its ancient traditions. These

FIGURE 3.2 The African Episcopal Church of St. Thomas, Philadelphia, dedicated 1796

traditions included vesting church leadership in a literate and formally trained succession of bishops, ordained within the lineage traceable to those first pure centuries. The church also needed to maintain a focus on the Bible as the word of God and on baptism and Holy Communion as the bedrock of Christian faith.[31] Hobart further advocated a prescribed order to worship services, which centered around a formal sermon founded upon scripture, history, literature, and philosophy, and delivered by a properly ordained minister. The church should also remain loyal to concrete sacred symbols such as an ornate pulpit from which to read from scripture and the Book of Common Prayer, the standard by which to maintain consistency in worship services.[32] Other indicators of proper respect for the divinity included formal vestments, chalice, baptismal font, and a fully appointed Communion table. Many altars also included Hobart's own publication, *Companion for the Altar* (1804), America's first compendium of meditations aimed at preparing communicants to receive the Eucharist.

For Hobart, the true church also included an expectation that communicants would hold an unwavering commitment to the Nicene and Apostles' creeds. Bishops should regularly visit and correspond with parishes in order to remind members of the elements of true faith. It was only within these predictable and time-honored ceremonies and disciplines that worshippers could be assured of attaining the transcendent state necessary to achieve divine grace and repentance. This cluster of orientations and beliefs marked Hobart as the champion of the "high church"—the keepers of a tradition very close to Catholicism itself. For Hobart, the specialness of Episcopalian history signified that the church should remain aloof from other Protestants, because the sacraments of such churches were not grounded in the time-honored traditions of Episcopalianism. Likewise, the church should distance itself from contemporary political, social, and economic affairs. Anything that is not discussed in the scriptures, he insisted, did not belong in the scope of religion, and only the prayers of clergy ordained in apostolic succession were truly effective. Yet for all his focus on religious constrictions and orthodoxy, Hobart apparently was not insensitive to the public mood: his sermons are reputed to have been spirited and passionate—reminiscent of a rousing Methodist address.

* * * * *

The Nicene Creed was developed by religious scholars over several decades during the fourth century to codify beliefs among Christians. Though amended several times in succeeding centuries, it remains a central tenet of Episcopal liturgy. The text reproduced here is from one of two versions printed in the 1790 American Book of Common Prayer.

> I believe in God the Father Almighty, Maker of heaven and earth.
>
> And in Jesus Christ, his only son our Lord who was conceived by the Holy Ghost; Born of the Virgin Mary; suffered under Pontius Pilate, was crucified, dead, and buried. The third day he rose from the dead; He ascended into heaven, and sittith on the right hand of the God the Father Almighty; From thence he shall come to judge the quick and the dead.
>
> I believe in the Holy Ghost, the holy Catholic Church; the communion of saints; the forgiveness of sins; the resurrection of the body, and the Life everlasting. Amen.

SOURCE: *Book of Common Prayer, and Administration of the Sacraments according to the Use of the Protestant Episcopal Church in the United States of America* (Philadelphia: Hall and Sellers, 1790).

* * * * *

But while White could take pride in the accomplishments of his protégé Hobart, he must have known that Presbyterian minister James Patterson was preaching from soapboxes in vacant lots, homes, and factories in the Northern Liberties, just a few blocks north of Christ Church, gathering up souls and developing teams of women to spread far afield and recruit even more.[33] The intellectualism advocated by Hobart was eschewed by Patterson, whose sermons were also likened to those of Methodist preachers. Patterson may not have been upholding the tenets of a true and pure church, but he *was* expanding the Presbyterian fold.

All around him White could see the fruits of evangelicalism, born in the Great Awakening a half century before. Methodists, freeing themselves from formal and hidebound traditions, took to the road with the energy to draw in the lower classes and the dispossessed. Breaking from the constraints of lengthy training and the long wait for a seasoned authority to pronounce one worthy of being a pastor, Methodist preachers could be legitimized simply by hearing the divine calling to "go into all the world and preach the gospel to every creature."[34] Any person who received such a divine summons could be deputized by three other ministers and quickly sent into the field to gather in the Methodists' ever-growing flock. With this kind of pyramid system, the Methodists (and also the Baptists, who had similar emotional appeal and minimal bureaucracy) were outrunning all other denominations in every region of the United States except New England.[35]

In his 1807 call to action, however, White reflected his commitment to the episcopate and to the disciplines in which he had been steeped. He remained faithful to the centrality of the scriptures, to the creeds, to the sacred artifacts, and to the Book of Common Prayer, as these were embedded in his spiritual identity. However, consistent with the Deist philosophy of the era (Benjamin Franklin, a consummate Deist, was Christ Church's most illustrious member), he also embraced the idea that religion should not hold just an emotional or ceremonial place in one's life. Religion should also make sense—and should appeal—to the mind.[36] He thus took a rational approach to questions of identity. What, he pondered, were the best ways to bring the citizenry to religion, and religion to the citizenry?

New members, talented and dedicated leadership, a strong financial base, and a disciplined unity of purpose would, he reasoned, form the foundation from which to address these questions.

White agreed with Hobart that a sermon should be framed around the scriptures—not just the undisciplined ideas that allowed "humans to range without control." Quoting from Genesis and Deuteronomy, he reiterated his concern that the church should unify around a body of the "same leading truths." Noting that clergy must be models of "piety" and the "exercise of human virtue," he reminded his flock that one should serve without regard for "personal interest or glory."[37] But he parted ways with Hobart over questions of outreach strategies, favoring alliances with other Christians and taking a leadership role in founding the ecumenical Bible Society of Philadelphia in 1808, asserting that "making known the contents of the Bible" was a worthy enough cause that it did not matter who participated in it.[38] Likewise, White joined interdenominational efforts to aid prisoners, the poor, and the disabled. By 1817 he was involved in a united effort to promote Sunday schools for adults as well as children.[39]

In shaping its identity, White felt that the Episcopal Church, in seeking to emerge from the lingering shadow of its English past, should not jettison the familiar and beloved forms of liturgical truth that had served its members so well. The familiar and predictable formal service, periodic observances of Holy Communion, a formal sanctuary with predictable appointments, and a clergy with properly legitimized training and vestments remained, for White, the foundation of Episcopal faith. But how would all this be accomplished in such a way as to garner the loyalties of both the old faithful and new recruits? How could traditional standards be upheld in the context of the emotional immediacy of the "democratic" spiritual experience of the evangelical churches?

Here White's answers diverged from those of his protégé Hobart. Over the protest of some of his critics, he led his church to engage with other Protestants and with the concerns of the secular world, and he tried to strike a balance between the traditional formality of his church and the evangelical atmosphere of his day.[40] While affirming his confidence in the importance of appropriately trained and properly ordained clergy, he also insisted that some level of authority be vested in individual congregations, rather than only in a centralized and hierarchical governing body.

Many observers have likened the Protestant Episcopal Church to a "bridge" between the Catholic and Protestant churches—grounded in Catholic liturgy and ceremony, which includes a faith in the apostolic succession, yet steeped in the modern Book of Common Prayer, which reflects a Protestant deemphasizing of the necessity of intermediaries between the individual and the divine.[41] In England, these aspects of worship were protected by the authority of the established church. However, as it developed in the United States, this bridge had two distinct poles, with a continuum of variation in between. "High-church" Episcopalians (like Hobart) clung closely to the liturgy modeled by the Catholic Church—including strict interpretations of the timing and meaning of baptism, divine grace and repentance, and the importance of remaining aloof from other Protestant denominations. "Latitudinarian" adherents, including Bishop White, who held a more "democratic" and flexible position on these subjects, often found themselves at odds with their more conservative brethren.[42] During the American Revolution, the Anglican Church had had a substantial loyalist voice. White, at pains to shed that image and to position the church favorably in the new society, lobbied for a tone of greater democracy in the church's governance.[43]

Some estimates suggest that during the first decades of the nineteenth century, as much as one-third of the total American population was swept up in the camp-meeting movement.[44] With Presbyterians and Methodists throwing themselves headlong into congregation building, how would the Episcopal diocese position itself? Bishop White suggested one strategy: systematizing the organization *within* the diocese while building alliances with other Protestants *outside* the Episcopal communities.

Organization: Committed Churches

Traditional Episcopalians, preferring formality in the preparation of leaders, the worship site, and the liturgical structure, were obliged to proceed more slowly than their more informal compatriots. As one historian has described it, the challenges of the Protestant Episcopal Church, as it emerged from its Anglican origins, were to "create a governing structure" and to develop "authority structures uniquely suited to the American environment."[45] A first step, then, was to strengthen the local authority and the creedal unity of the denomination. Beginning with the establishment of the General Convention in 1785, at which White presided, the Episcopal Church had developed a system of internal governance that included a written statement of the rights and responsibilities of clergy and laity, which was published as part of the proceedings of the 1790 conference.[46] This report signaled a developing bureaucracy, which included standing committees and a regular secretary charged to "keep regular minutes, subject to the inspection of the convention."[47] Such systems served not only to maintain and standardize a consultable history but also to hold those who served to a community uniformity.

White understood that he could not meet all the challenges alone. His vision was to develop, inspire, and nurture new leadership, while attracting, orienting, and retaining new members and new congregations. To this end he took initiatives on many fronts, some of which floundered. The Episcopal Academy, established in 1785, grew in three years to 137 students, but by 1790 the educational facility had closed, not to be revived for more than a decade.[48] Still, White was undaunted. The annual conventions continued, the reports showing evidence of increasing hierarchy, structure, and monitoring of community behavior. By 1794, for example, the convention had started to send out notices weeks ahead of time announcing the time and place of the annual meeting.[49] The following year, rules and guidelines specified that before agreeing to officiate at a wedding, a clergyman had to investigate whether the bride and groom were both old enough to marry and free of other commitments (e.g., other spouses, or indenture contracts).[50] With each passing year, new community-building and community-monitoring strategies were added. By 1801 local congregations were required to send annual reports to one another in preparation for the annual conventions,[51] and by 1808 the convention was printing 250 copies of its proceedings for distribution among local parishes.[52]

The annual conventions were for the leadership, but the new Protestant Episcopal organization did not ignore its loyal supporters. Under the guidance of Bishop White, Robert Blackwell and Matthew Clarkson of Christ Church, and John Chaloner and Gerardus Clarkson of St. Peter's, frequent gatherings were held with a broader membership group. It was agreed that authority should be shared and that local congregations would make their own rules, though they might appeal to the diocese for guidance. Canons and church regulations, however, had to be agreed upon by both clergy and laity. This new partnership between clergy and laity was a bow to life in the new democratic republic. In theory, as outlined by White in his controversial *Case of the Episcopal Churches in the United States Considered*, the new governance structure would simply streamline operations by giving voice to the laity. In reality, it was both revolutionary and troublesome. It was revolutionary in providing increased power to the laity, which brought the Episcopal Church more closely in line with other Protestant denominations and with the political tenor of the day. But it was troublesome because it introduced multiple layers of bureaucracy that could muddy questions of authority and thereby tangle decision making.[53] This commitment to democracy, which underpinned the latitudinarian movement, distressed Episcopal leaders who sought closer adherence to the old English traditions.

At one level, the development of a central organization paid off. Energized by vigorous leadership and improved communication, new congregations committed themselves to the unified effort to restore the Episcopal Diocese of Pennsylvania to its pre-Revolution stature. New parishes arose in and around Philadelphia. In Philadelphia, other parishes evolved as neighborhoods grew: in addition to Christ Church at Second and Market, St. Peter's at Third and Pine, and St. Paul's at Third and Walnut, there appeared St. James's, at Seventh and Market, in 1809, and the special case of St. Thomas's—the African American congregation—established at Fifth and Walnut in 1794.[54] Though the groups often were small and fragile, throughout the 1790s Radnor, Chester, and Marcus Hook began to send representatives to the general conventions. In 1806 White was pleased to report nearly five hundred new baptisms across the region (of which 10 percent were in Philadelphia's African American church).[55]

As early Americans were a highly mobile people, though, the diocese frequently faced the difficulty of evaluating the credentials and character of newcomers who arrived in Pennsylvania from far-flung places.[56] A Methodist minister from Tortola, an Episcopal deacon from South Carolina, a Presbyterian from St. Kitts and several from New Orleans and Ohio were among the newcomers who presented themselves for leadership positions in Pennsylvania's Episcopal community in the early years of the nineteenth century.[57] How to discern the true religious leader from the imposter?

Such questions presented the General Convention with an ever-lengthening list of loopholes to be plugged. By 1795 it had developed local canons clearly stipulating that ministers transferring in from other states must have a letter attesting to "good moral conduct."[58] By 1817 the Standing Committee closed the gate to leadership to everyone except those whom its members could personally vouch for, insisting that "no person shall be the rector or minister of this church, unless he shall have had Episcopal ordination, and unless he be in full standing with the Protestant Episcopal Church of the State of Pennsylvania . . . and recognized as such by the Bishop of this diocese . . . or by the standing committee of the same."[59] These strictures helped maintain high standards, but there soon followed lengthy discussions about how to handle the companion problem of too few credentialed clergy to staff existing or new congregations. The flip side of that concern, in such a volatile environment, was that a minister might find himself with too few communicants to maintain a viable congregation.

Nevertheless, since too much top-down authority could be problematic in a country newly committed to "liberty," the diocese aimed both to maintain some measurable standards of behavior and to allow local parishes to respond to unique local concerns. For example, the convention decided, as of 1793, that it could choose, at its discretion, to waive the requirement that clergy master both Latin and Greek. As noted above, this waiver allowed White to install Absalom Jones as leader of St. Thomas's. In the coming years this waiver would become commonplace.

Having shaped some guidelines, the Pennsylvania Episcopalians proceeded to their next task: boosting membership. A vibrant membership provides energy and attendance for worship services and other events, personnel for church committees, reassurance that one has received and shared God's beneficence, and, critically, economic support to maintain the everyday needs of church life: buildings, supplies, and clergy salaries.

One possible place to garner converts was from among disgruntled members of nearby denominations. Local Quakers, fleeing the constrictions (e.g., prohibitions against slaveholding and bearing arms), helped swell Episcopal membership rolls. So, too, did the region's newly affluent industrialists and developers. Philadelphia's small Jewish population sometimes yielded up converts, especially if geographic proximity or similar class interests brought a member of a Christian merchant family to marry into a Jewish family.[60]

Another effective outreach mechanism was Sunday schools. By the late eighteenth century a number of Protestant denominations in England were experimenting with Sunday schools to occupy and rein in the children of the poor. In 1791 Bishop White encouraged a combined Episcopal/Catholic Sunday school alliance—the first such in the United States. It grew quickly, boasting as many as three hundred students within the first year.[61] Mostly run by women—Sunday schools offered women a new opportunity for leadership roles—the schools taught children to memorize scripture, but many children also learned to read. By 1813 White reported the "constantly accumulating evidence of the utility of Sunday schools." That year, the number of baptisms was up as well.[62]

Sunday schools reached local recruits, and outlying areas of the Philadelphia region spawned some new congregations: St. John's, Norristown (1812), and Christ Church, Pottstown (1825) were joined by congregations at West Chester, Yardley, Honey Brook, West Whiteland, and others in an ever-widening sphere in Lancaster and Berks counties. Sometimes these worship groups had as many as 150 communicants.

Sometimes missionaries were a way to reach those at a greater distance. As early as 1793, Bishop White had had his eye on the frontier, and it took him a few years to persuade his Episcopalian comrades to look westward. But by 1801 the Presbyterians had linked up with the Congregationalists in a joint sweep of new western territories.[63] Then, by 1806, Lewis and Clark's much-heralded forays into the trans-Appalachian west reminded easterners that there was a new world to conquer, with new souls to be gathered in. But it was not until 1808, when White joined with Maryland bishops to write pastoral letters encouraging Episcopal evangelists to go west, that Episcopal missionaries did so in significant numbers. Then they aimed to make up for lost time. By 1812 White had helped found the Society for the Advancement of Christianity, which dispatched clergy to western Pennsylvania, Ohio, West Virginia, and Kentucky to "take our church in[to] the whole western part of the United States." Within a few years, more than three dozen new congregations were reported.[64]

By that time, however, the upstart Methodists were leaving the more conservative easterners behind in the western dust. Needing neither buildings, chalices, surplices, nor formal training, Methodist ministers could hold camp meetings alongside rivers or under the trees, could clone leadership from lay preachers, and could thereby almost instantly create the personnel to blanket the frontier with God's word.[65]

However, it isn't easy to maintain unity in a far-flung community. Historian Neva Specht has dramatically recounted the difficulties that confronted Quaker congregations in maintaining discipline on the Pennsylvania frontier,[66] and other denominations faced similar challenges in trying to stabilize new parishes, even as they attempted to discern whether newcomers were saints or sinners. People often relocated to a frontier to escape a morally checkered past, but in doing so they often took their morally suspect personalities with them. Episcopalian growth faced similar challenges in moving into what Specht terms "a remote place."

Missionary efforts were not inexpensive, and, stationed far from central authorities, missionaries often made questionable decisions. For example, nineteenth-century Methodists became known for their antiliquor crusades, but in the 1790s Methodist circuit riders, crisscrossing the backcountry, reportedly peddled alcohol to attract audiences and to supplement their meager incomes.[67] In general, the remoteness of the frontier seemed to loosen restraint. Typical were the charges of "alleged misconduct" brought before the Episcopal convention in 1802. A Berks County priest was called to task on charges that he "was reported to have been guilty of adultery, with a certain woman, in whose house he was a lodger, [and] had not only neglected to take any measures to disprove the matter . . . but had continued to be a lodger in the house kept by the woman." His behavior, it was felt, had "brought reproach on the clerical character, and on religion in general."[68]

It took many meetings to sort out the issues of alleged misconduct. Finally, in 1804, the accused clergyman was defrocked. However, the process of his deposing is as significant as the outcome. In those meetings, the scattered Episcopal communities confirmed and reinforced the authority of their central leadership. Over succeeding years, congregations and conventions would return to these disciplines defined by White and his colleagues, evaluating themselves in terms of standards and guidelines developed in these deliberations. Was a minister properly ordained? Was his personal conduct above reproach? Were services based upon the Book of Common Prayer? Was the minister working to preserve unity both within his own parish and between his parish and the wider Episcopal communities? Could the congregation provide proper housing for clergy?

The answers to some of these questions were partly economic. If the diocese could both draw sustenance from the local parishes and provide financial support to churches that were less well off, perhaps pastors could be provided with viable incomes, and with parish houses instead of lodgings in boarding houses. Here, too, the diocese made some progress under White's leadership. By charging fees for sermons, by focusing on actually collecting pew rents, and by installing a diocesan treasurer, the conventions were increasingly able to amass a surplus, which was invested in stocks or mortgages and contributed to a growing endowment.[69]

The "Churching" of America

Modern historians still debate the degree to which the United States was "churched" in its early decades. Some argue that most people were loyal to some religious affiliation. Others insist that apathy reigned. Still others insist that Americans resisted formal religion, because it reminded them of the tyranny from which they had just escaped. There is even one school of thought that holds that hostility to religion was an offshoot of economic class tensions.[70] There is still much work to be done in explaining the multiple levels of religious energy in the early Republic. Some things, however, are clear. First, the energy that would soon erupt in the Second Great Awakening was already gathering in the years following the Revolution and the War of 1812. Second, the missionary zeal that began in the mid-eighteenth-century First Great Awakening was carried forward in the rise of Sunday schools, the distribution of Bibles, and Americans' zest for moral and philanthropic efforts. On these rising tides, Episcopal arks were lifted.

Eventually, the Methodists' spectacular conversion sprint would end. Their early ability to be everywhere and everyone at once would sputter out. By the late nineteenth century, Baptists had begun to catch up in Protestant conversions, even while the Catholic Church—firmly established in Florida, Louisiana, Texas, and California, as well as in Pennsylvania, and experiencing phenomenal growth as immigrants from Europe flooded the eastern cities—had become the nation's largest denomination by 1890.[71] In the ensuing return to balance and equilibrium, the Episcopal Diocese of Pennsylvania would recover some of the strength it enjoyed before the Revolution.

It has been argued that the early Republic was a period of decline for the Episcopal Church. But the early national period was hardly a total loss for Episcopalian Pennsylvania. Certainly, it was not a time of rapid expansion in membership. Nevertheless, by the end of the 1820s, diocesan organizational systems had followed Pennsylvania's settlements to the north and west, peppering the northern and western counties with several dozen new parishes, to create more than five dozen new congregations by 1828.[72] The diocese could look with hope at parishes as far away as Berks County. It could take satisfaction in the period of steady consolidation and structuring of systematic record keeping, economic stability, and internal discipline, as well as in the development of a middle road that might be called a democratization of the liturgy—or "low church."

In these first years of the Republic there was some expansion in membership rolls. There was also an expansion of what had traditionally been an upper-class Episcopalian constituency. The growth of African American membership and missionary work in the west resulted in some broadening of the characteristics of the "typical" Episcopalian. Reduced power for bishops (but not the abolition of bishops' power), and a commensurate rise in the congregations' authority to shape their own community life,[73] meant that the Pennsylvania diocese entered the modern era with a streamlined definition of propriety, one less focused on theological minutiae and orthodox doctrine and more aimed at unity. Pennsylvania's Episcopal Church hadn't won the numbers game, but it had established an enduring system of authority, order, participation, and record keeping and economy, a clarity about community, and a sturdy and a reasonably stable liturgical uniformity. Occupying a specialized niche near the top of the American class hierarchy, its membership would never approach that of the Catholic,

Methodist, or Baptist denominations.[74] But as it entered the nineteenth century, the church leadership had grown more flexible, democratic, and responsive to changing realities.

By 1820 most denominations had recovered from the dislocation of the revolutionary years and, having found their moorings and their identity, were proceeding with the "aggressive churching" of America. In that context, the Episcopal diocese had laid claim to its own unique strategy: a successful Episcopal church in Pennsylvania was one where the minister had been ordained in the full episcopate tradition, where worship service was based on the American Book of Common Prayer, and where liturgical and community conflicts were muted.[75] No sooner had Episcopalians stabilized elements of their identity, however, than the challenges of industrialization and international markets, territorial and ethnic expansion, political unrest, and the Second Great Awakening would set their equilibrium rocking again.

NOTES

1. William White, D.D., *A Charge to the Clergy of the Protestant Episcopal Church in the Commonwealth of Pennsylvania, Delivered in Christ Church in the City of Philadelphia, on Wednesday, May 27, 1807* (Philadelphia: Printed at the office of the United States Gazette, n.d.), 5.

2. White apparently preferred chants or psalms to hymns. See Deborah Mathias Gough, *Christ Church, Philadelphia: The Nation's Church in a Changing City* (Philadelphia: University of Pennsylvania Press, 1995), 189.

3. Bruce Laurie, *Working People of Philadelphia, 1800–1850* (Philadelphia: Temple University Press, 1980), 38–40.

4. Ibid., 34–38 (quotation on 36).

5. See David Hein and Gardiner H. Shattuck Jr., *The Episcopalians* (Westport, Conn.: Praeger, 2004), 51–56.

6. Gough, *Christ Church, Philadelphia*, 196–97.

7. Quoted in ibid., 198.

8. Hein and Shattuck, *Episcopalians*, 219.

9. Two recent works that begin this deeper exploration are Gough, *Christ Church, Philadelphia*, and Gary B. Nash, *Forging Freedom: The Formation of Philadelphia's Black Community, 1720–1840* (Cambridge: Harvard University Press, 1988). See also William Pencak, *Jews and Gentiles in Early America, 1654–1800* (Ann Arbor: University of Michigan Press, 2005); Colleen McDannell, *Material Christianity: Religion and Popular Culture in America* (New Haven: Yale University Press, 1995); and Ronald Hoffman and Peter J. Albert, eds., *Religion in a Revolutionary Age* (Charlottesville: University Press of Virginia, 1994).

10. Hein and Shattuck, *Episcopalians*, 60; Roger Finke and Rodney Stark, *The Churching of America, 1776–1990: Winners and Losers in Our Religious Economy* (New Brunswick: Rutgers University Press, 1992), 54–55.

11. Finke and Stark, *Churching of America*, 55.

12. Manuscript Minutes of the Standing Committee of the Episcopal Convention, Diopa Archives, Lutheran Theological Seminary, Mount Airy (Philadelphia) (hereafter Manuscript Minutes of the Standing Committee), vol. 3, 1807 Appendix.

13. Hein and Shattuck, *Episcopalians*, 59–60.

14. Gough, *Christ Church, Philadelphia*, 192.

15. Billy G. Smith, *The "Lower Sort": Philadelphia's Laboring People, 1750–1800* (Ithaca: Cornell University Press, 1990), 151–52. Smith notes that as of 1790, more than 80 percent of Philadelphia's workers had already migrated from Europe, and were likely to move several more times in their lifetimes.

16. Pencak, *Jews and Gentiles*, 201–2.

17. See http://www.loc.gov/exhibits/treasures/franklin-newrepublic.html.

18. Samuel Low's *The Politician Outwitted*, published in 1789, featured the Federalist debates, and Susanna Haswell Rowson's *The Volunteers* (1795) dealt with the power struggles inherent in the Whiskey Rebellion. James Nelson Barker's *The Indian Princess* was performed in Philadelphia in 1808, then revived for London audiences in 1820.

19. McDannell, *Material Christianity*, 69–71.

20. Hein and Shattuck, *Episcopalians*, 68.

21. White quoted in Edwin S. Gaustad, "Religious Tests, Constitutions, and "Christian Nation," in Hoffman and Albert, *Religion in a Revolutionary Age*, 226.

22. Lee Richardson, "The Diocese of Pennsylvania: The Founding Period," manuscript, n.d. (ca. 1970–2004), 6–7.

23. See Nash, *Forging Freedom*, chapters 3 and 4.

24. Ibid., 67–70.

25. Ibid., 76, 126.

26. Ibid., 111; Gough, *Christ Church, Philadelphia*, 87.

27. Nash, *Forging Freedom*, 107.

28. Ibid., 132–33; George F. Bragg, *History of the Afro-American Group of the Episcopal Church* (Baltimore: Church of the Advocate Group, 1922), 59–80.

29. Richardson, "Diocese of Pennsylvania," 7.

30. William Douglass, *Annals of the First African Church in the United States of America, Now Styled the African Episcopal Church of St. Thomas* (Philadelphia, 1862), 119–20, quoted in Nash, *Forging Freedom*, 114. See also Harold T. Lewis, *Yet with a Steady Beat: The African American Struggle for Recognition in the Episcopal Church* (Valley Forge: Trinity Press International, 1996), 29–38.

31. Hein and Shattuck, *Episcopalians*, 6. Belief in transubstantiation—the literal transformation of the symbolic bread and wine of Communion into Christ's body and blood—was also, for many revolutionary-era Episcopalians, an important marker of the true faith.

32. John Paul Williams, *What Americans Believe and How They Worship* (New York: Harper and Brothers, 1952), 169.

33. Laurie, *Working People of Philadelphia*, 42–43.

34. Leigh Schmidt, *Hearing Things: Religion, Illusion, and the American Enlightenment* (Cambridge: Harvard University Press, 2000), 45.

35. Edwin S. Gaustad and Leigh Schmidt, *The Religious History of America* (San Francisco: HarperCollins, 2002), 166–67; Gough, *Christ Church, Philadelphia*, 106; Dee E. Andrews, *The Methodists and Revolutionary America, 1760–1800: The Shaping of an Evangelical Culture* (Princeton: Princeton University Press, 2004), 65–67.

36. Gough, *Christ Church, Philadelphia*, 115, 173.

37. White, *Charge to the Clergy*, 8, 9, 19–20.

38. Vestry minutes, 1823, quoted in Gough, *Christ Church, Philadelphia*, 196.

39. Ibid., 196–97, 199–200.

40. Hein and Shattuck, *Episcopalians*, 66–67.

41. See Williams, *What Americans Believe*, 167–78.

42. Hein and Shattuck, *Episcopalians*, 65.

43. Gough, *Christ Church, Philadelphia*, 142.

44. Gaustad and Schmidt, *Religious History of America*, 146.

45. Gough, *Christ Church, Philadelphia*, 2.

46. *Journal of the Meetings, Which Led to the Institution of a Convention of the Protestant Episcopal Church in the State of Pennsylvania, Together with the Journals of the First Six Conventions of the Said Church* (Philadelphia: Hall and Sellers, 1821), journal of the sixth convention, June 1, 1790, 23–26.

47. Ibid., 6.
48. Gough, *Christ Church, Philadelphia*, 194–95.
49. Protestant Episcopal Church in the State of Pennsylvania, Annual Report, 1794, Diopa Archives.
50. Annual Report, 1795, 27, ibid.
51. Annual Report, 1801, ibid.
52. Annual Report, 1808, ibid.
53. Gough, *Christ Church, Philadelphia*, 153.
54. Richardson, "Diocese of Pennsylvania," 10.
55. Manuscript Minutes of the Standing Committee, June 1818, vol. 4, pp. 24–27.
56. Laurie, *Working People of Philadelphia*, 50.
57. Manuscript Minutes of the Standing Committee, September 1818, vol. 4, p. 34.
58. Ibid., May 30, 1795, 27–28.
59. Ibid., May 31, 1817, vol. 4, p. 159.
60. Pencak, *Jews and Gentiles*, 234.
61. Gough, *Christ Church, Philadelphia*, 196.
62. Manuscript Minutes of the Standing Committee, June 1813, vol. 4, p. 10.
63. Finke and Stark, *Churching of America*, 63.
64. Richardson, "Diocese of Pennsylvania," 8; Gough, *Christ Church, Philadelphia*, 198.
65. Andrews, *Methodists and Revolutionary America*, 62.
66. Neva Specht, "Removing to a Remote Place: Quaker Certificates of Removal and Their Significance in Trans-Appalachian Migration," *Quaker History* 91 (Spring 2002): 45–69.
67. Laurie, *Working People of Philadelphia*, 37.
68. *Journal of the Meetings*, nineteenth annual meeting, May 1802, unpaginated.
69. Manuscript Minutes of the Standing Committee, June 20, 1818, vol. 4, p. 30
70. For this view, see Hoffman and Albert, *Religion in a Revolutionary Age;* Finke and Stark, *Churching of America;* and Smith, *The "Lower Sort."*
71. Finke and Stark, *Churching of America*, 55, 145, 149, 153.
72. Richardson, "Diocese of Pennsylvania," 8.
73. Gough, *Christ Church, Philadelphia*, 103, 153–54.
74. Gaustad and Schmidt, *Religious History of America*, 170.
75. Gough, *Christ Church, Philadelphia*, 103.

4

New Growth and New Challenges, 1820–1840

CHARLES D. CASHDOLLAR

In October 1824 Bishop William White set out on his first visit to the western reaches of the diocese beyond the Allegheny Mountains. It would have been an arduous journey even for a young man, but White was now in his seventy-seventh year, and for him the trip threatened danger as well as difficulty. As he left Lewistown to follow the Juniata River toward Huntingdon, the carriage horse bolted and hurled the bishop to the ground. White suffered a fractured right wrist, as well as minor lacerations and bruises. In one sense he was fortunate—the bishop of Delaware was killed two years later when he was catapulted from a coach. Nonetheless, White was obliged to postpone his westward circuit. The next summer, White set out again, this time successfully reaching congregations as far west as Pittsburgh and Beaver. By the time he returned five weeks later, he had traveled 830 miles.[1]

That 1825 journey—and one into northeastern Pennsylvania in 1826—acknowledged a new reality. The diocese was no longer confined to a small area of southeastern Pennsylvania. As the population scattered westward, so did the church's responsibilities. White had the state's hinterland in mind at the diocese's fortieth anniversary in 1824. "We should be occupied in planting and watering," he said on that event, "looking with humble confidence to the heavenly Husbandman for the increase."[2]

Population growth presented opportunities in eastern Pennsylvania, too. Philadelphia County was expanding more rapidly than the state as a whole. The development of coalfields in the Schuylkill Valley and early mill towns such as Rockdale and Manayunk changed not only the physical landscape but the state's social and religious contours as well.[3] It seemed that new congregations were needed virtually everywhere, and often more quickly than they could be built or supplied with clergy. Inevitably, much of the diocese's energy went into "planting and watering" new churches.

Despite frustrations and disappointments, the number of parishes doubled between 1820 and 1840, and the largest urban congregations burgeoned. This growth was the result, said a clergyman in Carlisle, of "the *good seed* there sown" by numberless Sunday schools, sermons, liturgies, and prayer meetings.[4]

Growth in Philadelphia and Its Environs

Between 1820 and 1840, Philadelphia County added slightly more than 120,000 new residents, and the western edge of the city proper (the area between Vine and South streets) continued to move farther from the Delaware River. In 1820 no Episcopal church sat west of Seventh Street; by 1840 seven did. During the same two decades, the number of congregations in Philadelphia County jumped from five to thirteen. In the surrounding four counties, eleven new congregations joined the twelve from before 1820.

The formation of new parishes throughout the diocese had been, since 1812, under the supervision of the Society for the Advancement of Christianity in Pennsylvania. With contributions given primarily by larger Philadelphia congregations, the society sent missionaries into recently populated areas and provided financial support until churches were self-sustaining. While much of the society's effort was directed to the remote parts of the state, it was also active in the rural areas around Philadelphia and just beyond the city limits across the Schuylkill and to the south in Moyamensing.

Inside the city of Philadelphia proper, however, the diocese allowed a free, entrepreneurial spirit to rule. New congregations sprang up as nearby congregations or the residents of newly developed streets saw the need. In some instances, the bishop was involved in the planning; in others, the work was well along before he was informed. This freelance approach generated a certain spontaneous energy, but the lack of coordination could also lead to unfortunate duplication, as in the early 1830s, when different organizers started All Souls and Ascension within two blocks of each other on Lombard Street; both struggled until they merged efforts.[5]

Real estate agents understood that attractive churches made lots easier to sell. In Hamilton Village, one of the first areas promoted west of the Schuylkill, developer William Hamilton reserved land for an Episcopal church, and St. Mary's was established with support from the Advancement Society. Later, in the 1850s, St. Clement's Church, on Twentieth between Arch and Cherry, was erected on land offered by the developer.[6]

Erecting churches for the newly developed middle-class sections of Philadelphia was the most successful expansion work undertaken in the diocese; resources were plentiful, and the denomination's social status matched the aspirations of the residents. Joining an Episcopal congregation, with its elegant liturgy, splendid music, and fine architecture, was a mark of respectability—that measure of social appropriateness so valued by the rising business and professional families. In rural areas, new congregations might struggle with small numbers and inadequate resources, but in the city there were organs, choirs, and full schedules of Bible classes and worship at the start. A new congregation might meet temporarily in a school or nearby church, but it typically had its own large, often richly appointed, building within a year. The final component of a successful urban parish was a virtuoso preacher, and all of Philadelphia's largest new congregations boasted a rector known for his oratory—Gregory T. Bedell at St. Andrew's, Stephen H. Tyng at Epiphany, and George Suddards at Grace. Once started, the congregation's financial stability was easily secured by pew rents; in popular congregations where crowds exceeded the available space, affluent parishioners were eager to pay quarterly rent for a reserved sitting or family pew.

When all the pieces were available, as they usually were in the city, a new congregation could be launched with astounding speed. Two case studies—St. Andrew's and Epiphany—illustrate the point. In the spring of 1822, Benjamin Allen, rector of St. Paul's, set out to attract fellow evangelical preacher Gregory T. Bedell to Philadelphia. A severe bout of fever and ague had forced Bedell, a New Yorker by birth, to resign his post in rural North Carolina; Allen was determined that Bedell would relocate in Philadelphia. When no ready vacancy presented itself, Allen engineered a plan to launch a new congregation.[7]

When Bedell arrived in Philadelphia in May on his way home to New York, Allen invited him to preach at St. Paul's. The result was exactly what Allen expected and wanted: wealthy pewholders were so enthralled by Bedell's preaching that by midweek they had pledged to finance a new church. Bedell was guaranteed salary for a year while the church was going up, and within a short time $10,000 was raised toward construction. There was controversy; some warned Allen that he would damage his own congregation by setting up a competitor only a few blocks west, and Bishop White was unhappy to have been ignored until after the plans were already in motion. But Allen was confident that there was room for another church, and the planners mollified the bishop by acceding to his preference for a name, St. Andrew's, rather than Grace, which Bedell had initially preferred

FIGURE 4.1 The Reverend Benjamin Allen, rector of St. Paul's, Philadelphia

With plans launched in May 1822, a cornerstone was laid four months later, in September, and by the following May an elegant Greek Revival building was consecrated. In just short of a year, St. Andrew's had gone from nothing to a fully operating congregation. Pews were rented, a Sunday school and Bible classes were formed, and a full schedule of worship, Friday evening lectures, and prayer meetings were offered. The number of worshippers and communicants mushroomed. Bedell began with

FIGURE 4.2 St. Andrew's, Philadelphia, completed 1823

thirty-four communicants, all transfers from other congregations nearby; within five years he counted four times as many. By 1840 the list of communicants reached 540, making St. Andrew's the largest congregation in the diocese.

The Church of the Epiphany, established at Fifteenth and Chestnut amid the westernmost developed blocks of the city in 1834, enjoyed similarly quick success. When a group of laypeople in the area decided that they no longer wanted to travel eastward to worship, they approached Tyng, St. Paul's popular rector, and enticed him to join them in a new venture. By his own telling, Tyng had no reason for leaving St. Paul's, but he considered planting a church as far west as Fifteenth Street so important that he could not turn down the request.[8]

With Tyng's participation secured, the project moved forward. The cornerstone was laid in March 1834, and seven months later, in October, the building was consecrated. By Easter 1835 there were 87 communicants, 66 of them from other congregations in the city. Here, as elsewhere, those who became communicants were but a small part of the congregation.

In all, Epiphany served 92 families comprising 350 souls, about 200 adults and 150 children, in its first year. By the mid-1840s, Epiphany had supplanted St. Andrew's as the largest congregation in the diocese.

* * * * *

Nurturing Episcopal Children in the 1820s and 1830s

Catechesis by the clergy was gradually replaced by lay-led Sunday schools, although in many places the two systems existed side by side for years. The earliest Sunday schools were mission programs that taught literacy as well as religion to poor children outside the congregation. The rise of public education in Pennsylvania (a movement to which rectors such as Benjamin Allen and William Muhlenberg contributed) allowed Sunday schools to narrow their focus to religious instruction, and to imagine such classes as useful to the congregation's own children. By the 1830s virtually every parish had its Sunday school, typically described as "flourishing." Students were divided into boys' and girls' divisions, with the girls always outnumbering the boys. At St. James's in Lancaster there were 200 girls and 60 boys; the gender ratio at Trinity, Southwark, favored girls by 260 to 140, and at St. Stephen's, Philadelphia, by 90 to 20. (This gender gap was mirrored by the predominance of women on the adult communicants' lists.)

Episcopalians recognized that Sunday schools built denominational loyalty. In Bishop Onderdonk's forthright words, the goal was "the thorough indoctrination of children" and "the early intertwining of their habits and affections about the pure principles, and the beautiful services, and the holy institution, of our apostolic communion." Teachers received help from a weekly preparation meeting with the pastor and an abundance of curriculum materials, children's hymnals, children's magazines, and brief liturgies issued by Episcopal Sunday school societies.

At St. Paul's in Philadelphia, Allen noticed that children stopped coming to Sunday school at about age fourteen. His solution, a Bible class for youth, was soon copied elsewhere and, as Allen expected, proved a recruiting ground for future Sunday school teachers. A few years later at St. Andrew's, Gregory Bedell extended the age range in the other direction by starting an "infant school" for children below normal school age; he claimed that this was the first infant school in the United States and, to his knowledge, in the world. Shortly after Stephen Tyng arrived at St. Paul's in 1829, he began conducting monthly children's worship in the afternoon, including sermons geared to young minds; his idea was soon adopted by others in Philadelphia and, by the 1840s, elsewhere in the diocese. The diocese's most famous preacher to children was Richard Newton, rector of St. Paul's (1840–62) and of Church of the Epiphany (1862–81), whose published collections of children's sermons gained him an international following.

SOURCES: Clifton Hartwell Brewer, *A History of Religious Education in the Episcopal Church to 1835* (New Haven: Yale University Press, 1924; reprint, New York: Arno Press, 1969), 164, 171–78, 186, 195–96, 207–10; *JDC 1827*, 42; *JDC 1828*, 50; *JDC 1830*, 35; *JDC 1833*, 15; Benjamin Allen, *Some Account of the Bible Classes of St. Paul's Church, Philadelphia* (London: L. B. Seeley, 1829); Thomas G. Allen, *Memoir of the Rev. Benjamin Allen, Late Rector of St. Paul's Church, Philadelphia* (Philadelphia: Latimer, 1832), 317, 472–73; Anne Ayres, *The Life and Work of William Augustus Muhlenberg* (New York: T. Whittaker, 1889), 60–61; Stephen H. Tyng, "Memoir of Gregory T. Bedell," in Gregory T. Bedell, *Sermons*, 2 vols. (Philadelphia: William Stavely–John Pechin, 1835), 1:clxii; Stephen H. Tyng, *Forty Years Experience in Sunday-Schools* (New York: Sheldon, 1860), 23; and Norris S. Barratt, *Outline of the History of Old St. Paul's Church, Philadelphia, Pennsylvania* (Philadelphia: Colonial Society of Pennsylvania, 1917), 145–46.

* * * * *

Not all churches in Philadelphia could match the phenomenal success of St. Andrew's and Epiphany. If location in a fast-growing section suggested a happy outcome, older congregations now found themselves in less fashionable neighborhoods. The city's shifting demographics raised questions for Christ Church, as congregations representing other denominations—Presbyterian, Baptist, and Lutheran—left for sites farther west. Christ Church stayed but saw its number of pews rented drop by nearly 40 percent in the fifteen years prior to 1828; by 1833 its communicants' list held only 120 names. When Jackson Kemper, having suffered two salary reductions, left in frustration in 1831, he described it as "sinking."[9]

The Christ Church vestry complained that too many new churches were drawing away its parishioners. In actuality, Christ Church's plight was more complicated. An aging Bishop White's pulpit style belonged to an earlier time, and the weight of diocesan theological battles no doubt bore most heavily on his own congregation. But Christ Church's peculiar union with St. Peter's and St. James's was more significant than people at the time realized. The United Churches was a relic of an earlier era that preceded the creation of the diocese. The design once conveyed a better sense of the larger church than separate congregations could, but now the diocese played that role. Rather than a rector and his assistants sharing responsibility for three congregations, nineteenth-century urban churchgoers expected each church to have its own rector—preferably a star preacher—who shaped the congregation's identity and gave voice to its faith. A proposal for separation failed in 1826, but successful votes in 1828 and 1831 led to the separation of first St. James's and then St. Peter's, with the last ties disappearing at White's death in 1836. With a separate identity and fresh pastoral leadership by the Reverend Benjamin Dorr, Christ Church's membership began to grow once again, with a more than 50 percent increase by 1840.

Churches started in poorer districts struggled with less advantageous conditions. All Saints Church began in 1826, when the Female Sunday School Society of St. Peter's opened a school in Moyamensing; by the 1830s a worship service was added and a church organized. The congregation, filled with highly transient, poverty-ridden recent immigrants, did not thrive. "The greatest difficulty we labour under," the congregation decided, "is we are poor altogether."[10]

All Saints, like the Church of the Evangelists, established in Southwark in 1837, was a "free church"—that is, it was funded by offerings rather than pew rents.[11] This was a common adjustment to the financial circumstances of less affluent areas. In the city proper, the Church of the Ascension, started as a Sunday school on Lombard above Thirteenth Street, was also a free church. "Like our common salvation," the congregation said proudly, "it will be free to all, rich and poor."[12]

St. Matthew's Church, Francisville, north of the city proper in Spring Garden, found its work hampered by the same challenges: scarce resources and a highly mobile population. St. Paul's Female Protestant Episcopal Association had initiated church work there in 1822, and a modest building had been constructed. But progress was halting. Large public institutions, such as Eastern Penitentiary (1823) and the House of Refuge (1827), went up nearby but did little to increase the supply of parishioners. The owners of the nearby country estates belonged to congregations in the city, and most of the year-round residents—a mix of dairy farmers and workers—were not Episcopalians.[13]

By the first half of the 1830s, the work at St. Matthew's was in disarray: there was neither rector nor organized vestry. When the Reverend Jacob Douglass arrived in 1835, he found that the district's "fluctuating population, owing to the frequent removals," threatened to undermine his best efforts. A further difficulty was the church's immediate location. By now, the diocese had enough experience with new church development to know that location—a busy street corner or the highest elevation in the village—improved the chances of success. But Douglass found that St. Matthew's was "too far removed from the main street." The church was "unfortunately not well located," he concluded regretfully, "or a greater interest might be excited."[14]

Proximity to wealthy urban congregations could help to alleviate whatever difficulties these congregations on the outskirts of the city faced. St. Matthew's survived because St. Paul's gave it enough human and financial resources to stay afloat. Other congregations helped as well. On one occasion, the ladies of Grace Church donated a fine piece of "drapery for the pulpit," and when Douglass found himself short of Sunday school teachers, "several pious young ladies, and a gentleman, from the larger churches in the city" volunteered.[15] The Church of the Ascension, although the least secure of the new churches in the city, could still boast from its opening day that the "singing has been conducted by an efficient choir."[16] Such advantages could only be envied by congregations farther west.

Growth in Pennsylvania's New Industrial Towns and Villages

There were gristmills along the creeks below Philadelphia, and iron forges and anthracite mines to the northwest of the city by the time of the Revolution, but the decades after 1820 marked a new industrial phase. Water-powered mills sprang up along the fast-running streams, and small manufactories reshaped small villages into towns. A network of turnpikes, canals, and railroads allowed the exploitation of coal and other natural resources from the interior. Forges and rolling mills produced iron plate; power looms turned out lengths of woolen and cotton cloth. Industrial growth demanded more laborers, especially immigrants from England, Wales, and Germany.[17] Each new or expanded district presented the diocese with an opportunity for mission and church development.

In at least two instances, mill owners took the lead in organizing and funding Episcopal churches. In Manayunk, the site of cotton and woolen mills along the Schuylkill north of the city, leading citizens gathered in 1831 to consider starting a church. Reassured by a retired pastor, the Reverend Robert Davis, who had already surveyed the entire town and counted some three hundred individuals who considered themselves Episcopalians, work went forward.[18] The new parish was named St. David's, and with a large gift from one of the vestrymen, a substantial Gothic building was erected in 1835 and equipped with "an organ of fine tone and sufficient power" to ensure "well-conducted worship."[19] How far the industrialists' benevolent spirit extended beyond the erection of churches varied. Joseph Ripka, who donated the land on which St. David's stood, had such a reputation for treating his workers harshly and exploiting child labor that he was the target of an 1837 state legislative investigation; however, the leading vestryman at St. David's, the textile and drug manufacturer Charles Hagner, provided the legislators with a "most thoughtful and extensive review of the factory system," given in a manner that was, according to historian Philip Scranton, "clearly sympathetic to factory workers."[20]

Calvary Church in Rockdale, one of the cotton mill towns along the Chester Creek in Delaware County, owed its existence to the "zeal and energy" of mill owner Richard Somers Smith, his wife, Elizabeth, and their daughters, Clementina and Harriet. Smith's primary business interests were in Philadelphia, where the family kept a fashionable residence and worshipped at St. James's. But the family came to Rockdale in the summers to escape the city heat—and in 1832 also the threat of cholera. Regretting the distance to the nearest Episcopal church, the women first started a Sunday school in 1833 and then urged the creation of a parish, which Smith agreed to underwrite. Unfortunately, Smith's timing was not good; in 1834 cotton textiles entered an unsettled period that became even more turbulent following the Panic of 1837. After a delay, a stylish Gothic church, "substantially built of stone, handsomely finished, and beautifully furnished," was completed in 1839. Smith and his family continued their financial support and participation as Sunday school teachers and, in the case of one daughter, parish organist.[21]

More commonly, the first Episcopal inroads into a new industrial district came from a nearby congregation or pastor. The usual first step was opening a Sunday school, as members of Christ Church, Pottstown, did near the iron ore mines of Phoenixville in 1838. That same year the church in Reading established a school "in the immediate vicinity of a large iron manufactory" nearby. Parishioners from Bristol walked six miles to teach mill workers' children in Hulmeville for five years before Grace Church was established.[22]

FIGURE 4.3 St. David's, Manayunk, Philadelphia, built 1832–1835

Local clergy took responsibility for leading worship among the unchurched populations near them. They found whatever shelter they could—coach shops, schoolhouses, private homes—or, weather permitting, preached outside factories or in open fields. In the late 1820s Jacob Douglass went out from St. John's, Concord, to preach "at the factories on Chester Creek." Dr. Levi Bull planted St. Mark's, Honey Brook, among the area's Welsh iron ore miners. Another Chester County rector, the Reverend George Kirke, reported to the diocese in 1834 that he had "preached ten times at a school house near Doe Run factories."[23]

Providing churches for the English and Welsh coal miners who settled in Schuylkill County proved a more difficult challenge, and one that the diocese met only imperfectly. In 1825 the Schuylkill Canal connected Pottsville to the Schuylkill River and opened a wider market for the region's anthracite. By the mid-1830s towns such as Schuylkill Haven and Minersville were overflowing with potential Episcopalians. In 1837 the Reverend R. A. Hamilton reported to the diocesan convention that all the pews in Pottsville were filled, which left no room for "about three thousand persons, English and Welsh miners and families, who have been connected with the Church of England" and who had recently come to work in the collieries. Hamilton argued vigorously that these workers of Anglican background had "claims upon the Church for pastoral care, and religious instruction." He was doing what he could by preaching in schoolhouses and homes, but he was frustrated, and within a year he had gone.[24]

Four years later, the Reverend Samuel Buel, from St. James's, Schuylkill Haven, was still pleading for more attention to the mining families. Farther away from the resources of Philadelphia and yet lacking the romantic appeal of the mountains and forests to the west, the miners could easily be overlooked. Buel told the convention that the loyalty of the miners could still be retained, but only "if the church is not blind and recreant to her duty." At Buel's urging, a cornerstone was laid for St. Paul's Church in Minersville in 1841, but by the spring of 1843 there was yet no church erected atop, and the congregation was still meeting every other Sunday afternoon in the Methodist church.[25] Compared with the routine ability to put up a substantial church within a year or less in Philadelphia, it was slow progress indeed.

Ministering in industrial towns and districts presented other challenges and frustrations beyond the mere speed of construction. Economic depressions, such as the one following the Panic of 1837, bore down hard on single-industry towns. In 1838 the Rockdale congregation lamented the hardships it faced because "all the mills have either suspended, or very much diminished their operations." That same year, St. David's, Manayunk, reported, "The fiscal derangements of the country . . . have caused the population of this place to be more than usually fluctuating." This population mobility and "the discouragements arising therefrom" were impediments, the rector, the Reverend Frederick Freeman, had more than once noted, to which towns such as his were "always more or less liable."[26]

Rectors also believed that the mill towns were particularly given to immorality. Douglass, examining the Chester Creek factories with an evangelical eye, concluded that they were "seats of vice" and "moral wastes." Manayunk's Freeman, reflecting on the habitual absence of young men at weekly worship, wondered if their being in factories six days a week encouraged them to "make Sunday a day of recreation."[27]

In the minds of many middle-class Episcopalians, the threat of infidelity within the working class was tied to political and labor radicalism. Smith reacted sharply to Rockdale workers who went on strike in 1842: "some of those to whom their beloved pastor dispensed the visible signs and tokens in the Holy Sacrament have violated the covenant of which they were the pledges."[28] It was not so much that wealthy Episcopalians such as Smith consciously thought of churches as ways of controlling their workers, but they did assume that truly converted laborers would recognize God's hand in the ordering of the world and never organize against fellow members of the body of Christ. Sunday schools were thus indispensable means of cultivating faith in working-class youth, and clergy who could preach effectively to workers were admired and promoted, as was Rockdale's rector, Alfred Lee, who became bishop of Delaware in 1841.[29]

The immigrant workers were not always passive recipients. When there was a responsive rector or missionary, they reshaped worship to fit their needs or to match expectations brought from Britain. In Minersville, Welsh and English parishioners asked for churching of women services. The Reverend George Drake admitted that he'd never seen or heard of this being done in America, but he complied with the request and reported proudly to the diocese that three mothers had come forward with their infants.[30]

Growth in Northern and Western Pennsylvania

The diocese's effort to establish an Episcopal presence in the western and northern parts of the state began in August 1812 when the Advancement Society sent young Jackson Kemper to survey the field. By the time he returned in October, he had seen a great deal—"a little flock without a pastor, still faithful to the church and attached to her worship" in Huntingdon; a cluster of churches, all closed, along the Monongahela River near Brownsville; and a band of would-be Episcopalians "utterly ignorant of the liturgy" in Beaver. Kemper recommended that six to eight missionaries could make a good start on the work, and the Advancement Society began to collect funds.[31] Kemper himself stayed in Philadelphia, serving for almost two decades as White's assistant at the United Churches, but by the time of his 1812 mission trip he had already displayed the interest in westward expansion that eventually led to his election in 1835 as bishop of the Northwest.

Unfortunately, by 1812 the diocese was well behind both competing denominations in Pennsylvania and Episcopal dioceses to the north and south. Within the state, Episcopalians frequently were at a disadvantage when they arrived to find Presbyterian, Lutheran, or Methodist congregations already rooted for a decade or more. In Williamsport, a Presbyterian elder bluntly told an arriving Episcopal missionary that he "had no business there, as . . . the ground was occupied."[32]

The Pennsylvania diocese was moving more slowly not only than other denominations but also than neighboring dioceses. To get more missionaries rapidly into the field, Virginia broke with tradition and allowed candidates for the ministry to preach. New York set up a missionary society ten years before Pennsylvania and funded between two and three times as many missionaries. Pennsylvania's urban congregations gave to missions at a lower rate, and the Advancement Society frequently lamented "the scantiness of its funds." As the society approached its twentieth anniversary, there were still seventeen counties with no Episcopal church, and seventeen more with only one. In 1830, with only a dozen missionaries scattered from Chester County to the Ohio border, White noted with considerable understatement, "There are several places where [missionaries] could now be advantageously stationed; and some of our present missionaries ought to have their fields of duty divided."[33]

The reasons for Pennsylvania's inertia are not easily identified. The state's mountain ridges certainly were formidable obstacles, but so were Virginia's and North Carolina's. Philadelphians were kept busy erecting new churches in the city, but so were New Yorkers. It might be suggested that the diocese's contentious high church/evangelical divisions—which *were* sharper than in other states—made it difficult to unite on a common venture, but since those battles did not erupt until the mid-1820s, they can hardly explain the earlier lethargy. Kemper certainly tried—repeatedly—to convey the importance of speed in getting established. But money and a sense of urgency remained in short supply.

The role of the bishop was critical. White (who turned seventy in 1818) was increasingly "set in his ways" and inflexible when confronted with new situations—at least that was Kemper's judgment.[34] Certainly, bishops John Henry Hobart in New York and Richard Moore in Virginia moved more aggressively. In 1825–26 alone, North Carolina's Bishop Ravenscroft logged 2,128 miles, making the rounds of his diocese on horseback and coach.[35] In contrast, White, his energy hampered by age and his time divided between parish and diocese, rarely got outside Philadelphia. Because Episcopalians required the presence of a bishop to confirm new members and consecrate buildings (rites that other denominations handled congregationally), Episcopalians had more difficulty in planting congregations. On this point, the 1827 appointment of Henry Ustick Onderdonk as assistant bishop helped immensely. Onderdonk was both younger and free of parish responsibilities, and he brought firsthand experience as a western pastor in Canandaigua, New York. Within the first year he had visited fifty of the diocese's sixty-seven organized congregations, plus a dozen not yet fully formed. But by 1827, the greatest opportunity in some villages had passed.[36]

One step that might have helped was an earlier splitting of Pennsylvania into more than one diocese. New York created the Diocese of Western New York in 1838 (ironically with Philadelphian William H. DeLancey as its first bishop), but Pennsylvania did not subdivide the area west of the mountains until 1865, or the central counties until 1871.[37] By then, clergy who served beyond the mountains had long been impatient. As early as 1801 the Reverend Joseph Doddridge and the handful of other clergy serving west of the mountains petitioned for separation; eighteen months later came the answer that "nothing could be done." Doddridge lamented, "I lost all hope of ever witnessing any prosperity in our beloved Church in this part of America. Everything connected with it fell into a state of languor."[38]

John Henry Hopkins, the talented rector of Trinity Church, Pittsburgh, pushed a plan to create a seminary in his city in 1829. He pointed out that General Theological Seminary in New York City had only twenty-four students, which even with the addition of the seminarians being trained in Virginia and Ohio could not come close to meeting the needs of the growing nation; in Pennsylvania alone, Hopkins asserted, there were a hundred towns large enough to support an Episcopal church that were "totally untouched." "If Western Pennsylvania [is] to be won," he argued, "it must

FIGURE 4.4 Bishop Henry Ustick Onderdonk

be by clergymen trained on the ground." Hopkins's proposal was referred to a committee dominated by easterners, which he considered a scheme to "smother the Western project as unobtrusively and as inoffensively as possible." Two years later the decision was rendered: Hopkins's plan was "inexpedient." Bitterly disappointed, Hopkins accepted a position in Boston and a year later became bishop of Vermont; the Pennsylvania diocese had lost one of its most innovative priests.[39]

The clergy who did serve in the west faced considerable obstacles. Unlike the English miners of Schuylkill County, who often arrived with a preference for Anglican worship, the Scots and Scots-Irish settlers in western Pennsylvania brought opposite sentiments—a profound aversion to prayer books and bishops. Clergymen spoke of "professed prejudice against our liturgy"; one working near Brownsville reported that episcopacy was "but a scarecrow to the most of my parishioners."[40]

Breaking down these prejudices was difficult because clergy were unable to present what the denomination considered one of its greatest attractions—worship—at its respectable best. With not even an adequate supply of prayer books at hand, let alone organs and choirs, the singing and responses were halting at best, and often inaudible. Rather than the rich interior of a Philadelphia church, these congregations worshipped in dark, drafty log churches. Onderdonk recalled that as he consecrated one church in 1828, "the melting snow dropped freely through holes in the roof upon the slab seats within."[41]

With the exception of Trinity, Pittsburgh, the congregations across the western and northern counties of the diocese were small and fragile. The greatest threat to their survival was the shortage of clergy. Large Philadelphia churches provided upward of two hundred worship services a year—two on Sunday and one midweek, plus festivals and daily worship during Lent. But in the hinterland, worship and sacraments were infrequent. Most churches had clerical leadership only every third, fourth, or even sixth week. In some places there was lay reading during the intervening weeks, but elsewhere churches were not opened at all. William Hilton, a missionary serving in Butler and Armstrong counties, warned of the need to do better "if we wished to hold our own among the other denominations, all of which had their services more frequently than we."[42]

The combination of scarce supply, arduous conditions, and low pay also meant high turnover and long intervals between pastors. In the interim periods, momentum was usually lost. By the time a replacement finally arrived in Brownsville in 1823, he found "these congregations, through want of clergymen to settle in this part of the country, are nearly all gone to other denominations."[43]

The diocese was not unaware of the problems in the interior of the state, and it did take limited action. A Prayer Book Society was organized to give free copies, but it never had enough money for more than small discounts.[44] An 1822 "Committee on the Supply of Vacant Pulpits" proposed that every minister should devote two or three Sundays a year to filling vacant pulpits, but in less than a year travel expenses had exhausted the diocesan treasury, and the work was suspended. White and Onderdonk tried repeatedly to boost salaries as a way of attracting and retaining

FIGURE 4.5 The Reverend John Henry Hopkins, rector of Trinity Church, Pittsburgh, and later bishop of Vermont

clergy—or at the very least of allowing clergy to minister full time rather than having to supplement their incomes by farming or teaching school. In 1842 Onderdonk proposed a diocesan subsidy for any salary under $400, but the motion failed.[45]

Congregations tried, of course, to minimize the time that their pulpits were empty. When clergy left, vestries wrote to influential pastors, sent requests to the bishop, and advertised in denominational newspapers in hopes of getting a quick replacement. But western congregations had few bargaining chips; even Christ Church, Meadville, one of the stronger churches west of the mountains, reported being "unsuccessful in two or three efforts to obtain a minister."[46] Desperate congregations seemed willing to accept even clergy with questionable records. When a rector ousted from a congregation in Huntingdon for frequent public inebriation was about to be suspended by Bishop White, congregations in Bloomsburg and Wilkes-Barre, where the man had relocated, entered a plea for clemency, lest "they may be deprived of his Ministerial Services."[47]

Planting churches in the hinterland was a story of lost opportunities, of occasional spurts of enthusiasm but more persistent inertia and frustration. Yet in spite of everything—the paucity of clergy and myriad other handicaps—congregations were somehow founded, sacraments administered, Sunday schools and Bible classes organized, and "neat, commodious" buildings acquired. Laity proved capable of surviving discouragement and displaying tenacious devotion to the church's government and liturgical forms. Certainly, more foresight, funding, and energy would have brought greater rewards. Bishop Onderdonk, in 1840, looked back with some satisfaction, but perhaps also a certain degree of rationalization, at what had been accomplished: "A quiet and persevering effort is, though slow, the only method from which a good result may be hoped for."[48]

Greater Institutional Strength and Identity for the Diocese

More churches over a wider geographical area made administering the diocese more complicated and time-consuming. Seeking to put the work on a firm footing, leaders transformed existing practices for greater efficiency and developed new procedures for new demands. Henceforth, activity would be based less on personality and more on institutional structure, operations less ad hoc and more regularized. The signs of change were several, from scheduled rather than intermittent meetings of the Standing Committee, to longer meetings of convention, to the decline and eventual death, in 1836, of Bishop White, whose personal character had from the beginning given the diocese its identity.

As it expanded, the diocese sought better-regulated operations. Parochial reports, once highly individualized assessments of congregations' spiritual strength, became more statistical and less narrative. Beginning in 1832, rectors were expected to write their information on a blank form for the sake of consistency. Gone were the days when White would lament his inability even to construct a list that matched clergy to parishes. Consistent language was created and enforced for the charters of new congregations.[49] As a help to clergy and new congregations, Benjamin Dorr's *Churchman's Manual*, the first of several editions of which appeared in 1835, provided a straightforward guide to Episcopal beliefs and practices.[50]

Other developments indicate a similar desire for procedural efficiency. In 1821 the process of incorporating under the laws of Pennsylvania was begun. A new, updated edition of the diocesan constitution, canons, and regulations was published in 1829. And by the early 1840s, the diocese had taken steps for the preservation of its own records. With many of the early papers lost or scattered in private hands, those who proposed an archival collection regretted their late start: "The derangement of the records and papers of the Convention, is such at present as to be almost irremediable."[51]

Modernizing diocesan finances was an important initiative. The need for a full-time bishop, not weighed down by parish responsibilities, was clear to all, and to that end an Episcopal Fund had been established in 1812 in the hope that endowment income would cover a bishop's salary. The fund was still too small when Onderdonk was elected in 1827, but a large, interest-free loan by wealthy laity made it sufficient.[52] The diocese also had a Widows and Orphans Fund, which insured the families of clergy if vestries or the minister himself paid the required premiums. In 1833 the diocese sought the advice of insurance experts and reorganized the fund to put it on a firmer actuarial basis. In 1841 the diocese started a new fund for "clergy unable to continue due to age or disability." Supported by an annual Christmas offering, the fund aimed to supply a modest stipend, up to $250, as needed.[53]

* * * * *

Church Fairs Become Popular, Entertaining Fund-Raisers

During the 1830s, congregations found that they could raise large sums of money by holding church fairs, a fund-raising technique that had become popular in England a decade earlier. Soon after the opening of commercial marketplaces such as London's Soho Bazaar (1815), the idea spread to hospital charities and then to churches. American churches found fund-raising bazaars a triple blessing—women enjoyed one another's company while fashioning "useful and fancy items," the fair itself was a further source of entertainment, and the profits could wipe out debts and ensure a congregation's solvency. Fairs proved especially effective when raising money for a special project, such as an organ or church renovation. More than one all-male vestry acknowledged that the church's debt had been eliminated or a cost covered "almost entirely from the exertions of female members of the church."

SOURCES: F. K. Prochaska, *Women and Philanthropy in Nineteenth-Century England* (Oxford: Clarendon Press, 1980); *JDC 1834*, 33; *JDC 1834*, 44, 52–53; *JDC 1835*, 41, 62–63; *JDC 1839*, 35, 37, 52, 54, 56; *Episcopal Recorder*, September 14, 1839, December 21, 1839, May 2, 1840.

* * * * *

The education of clergy was also modernized. The old apprentice system, based on White's 1801 reading list, was replaced by seminary training after the opening of General Theological Seminary in New York in 1819. White had favored multiple diocesan seminaries, but when the General Convention decided for a *general* denominational seminary, White supported it wholeheartedly. Most Pennsylvania candidates and most of Pennsylvania's money went to the New York school. Diocesan seminaries were not forbidden, although Pennsylvania did not yet create one; Virginia did in 1823, and the school in Alexandria became a favorite of Pennsylvania evangelicals.[54]

In addition to creating seminaries, Episcopalians were also marking out a distinctive denominational identity by founding schools and colleges. Pennsylvanians had a long history of operating schools, such as the Episcopal Academy, which dated from the 1780s. In the first half of the nineteenth century, numerous rural clergy started small schools to supplement their salaries. Although Pennsylvanians did not found any Episcopal colleges that survived more than a few years, the Episcopal Education Society (1825) opened a college in Delaware that in 1833 moved to Bucks County and operated as Bristol College. One of its distinctive features was a manual labor component, which required three hours each day from its students. The college was constructing a larger building and looking forward to growth before the national economic turbulence of the mid-1830s led to its closing in 1837.[55]

Separate voluntary societies were another way of emphasizing denominational identity. America offered numerous nondenominational societies, organized to distribute tracts, promote Sunday schools, champion social reform, or carry out benevolent work. White, however, was skeptical about submerging Episcopal distinctiveness in such societies. The Episcopal Sunday School Society, founded in 1826 by the General Convention, provided a curriculum consistent with Episcopal tenets; for White, it was a matter of "ministerial fidelity" to teach the full truth, not a bland substitute.[56] Likewise, if Sunday schools used Episcopal liturgies, children would learn to say responses and gain an appreciation for the prayer book. White was willing to cooperate with other denominations to distribute Bibles, so long as no partisan commentary was passed out with them. Religious tracts, however, necessarily advocated a particular theological view, and were best produced and distributed by denominational societies. Thus White valued the Episcopal Female Tract Society of Philadelphia (1816), which printed more than ten thousand copies per year, because it could "guard against the erroneous views of other tracts, industriously propagated among the members of our church, by persons extraneous to its pale."[57]

The availability of cheaper printing methods encouraged other ventures, too. Pennsylvania Episcopalians launched several religious newspapers in which readers could find diocesan and congregational news as well as didactic articles, intelligence from around the country and overseas, features for children, and advertisements for schools and colleges, books, church organs, and liturgical supplies and furnishings.[58] The publication of an authorized Episcopal hymnal in 1827 was another marker of denominational identity, one that would serve the church for the next four decades.[59]

Ironically, each of these signs of self-confident denominationalism—seminaries and colleges, voluntary societies, the religious press, and hymnals—also revealed a new and deepening rift within the Episcopal Church between the high-church party and a new, more aggressive breed of evangelicals. High-church seminarians went to New York, evangelicals to Virginia. One Philadelphia evangelical bluntly told a student, "I would go down with Jonah and study theology in the whale's belly, before I should go to the New York Seminary."[60] Evangelical Episcopalians were more ready to unite with evangelicals of other denominations in common voluntary societies, while the high-church group, concerned for Episcopal distinctiveness, wanted to keep its distance. High-church worshippers shared little of the evangelicals' craving to express piety with hymn singing. High-church clergy rallied behind Hobart, the Pennsylvania native who had started his career as curate in Oxford and Perkiomen and was now bishop of New York; evangelicals feared and despised him.[61] The high-church party read the *Banner of the Cross;* evangelicals read the *Episcopal Recorder.* The division appeared everywhere in America, and in England as well. Unlike New York or Virginia, the one dominated by the high-church party and the other overwhelmingly evangelical, Pennsylvania was evenly divided, and thus especially contentious.

* * * * *

Make a Joyful Noise: Early Nineteenth-Century Episcopal Music in Pennsylvania

Episcopalians knew that their church music distinguished them from other Protestant denominations and attracted people to their services. A few congregations, such as St. Stephen's in Philadelphia, gained a reputation for outstanding music. As soon as new congregations were able, they formed choirs and purchased organs. Church weeklies carried frequent advertisements for modestly priced organs of three or four ranks. Large city congregations, of course, could afford more. But whether of good size or merely "small but handsome," the new instrument was "the means of greatly improving the music," the typical congregation reported.

Worshippers were expected to stand and "unite with heart and voice" in the psalms, hymns, and canticles. Although metrical versions of the psalms were still much employed, chanted psalms had been used since the 1780s, when White introduced them at Christ Church, and hymns were gaining in popularity. William Muhlenberg, who served churches in Philadelphia and Lancaster, joined with Pennsylvania's future bishop, hymn writer Henry Ustick Onderdonk, to edit *Hymns of the Protestant Episcopal Church*, which was authorized by the denomination in 1826. When the new hymnal came off the presses the following year, congregations had a selection of 212 hymns. The hymnal's full music edition, *Music of the Church* (1828), also included chanted responses and multiple settings for a dozen canticles.

Two Philadelphia organists provided tunes for *Music of the Church*. William Henry Westray Darley (1810–1872), the organist at St. Stephen's, provided "Darley," and Benjamin Carr (1768–1831) supplied "Philadelphia," "Pennsylvania," "Carr," and "St. Augustine." Carr, a prominent music publisher, organizer of the Music Fund Society, and organist at St. James's as well as St. Augustine's Roman Catholic Church, also wrote service music for Episcopal use, much of it appearing together with Darley's compositions in *Chants of the Episcopal Church* (1840), edited by Darley and Philadelphia organ builder J. C. B. Standbridge.

SOURCES: Kenneth Walter Cameron, ed., *Early Anglican Church Music in America*, 2 vols. (Hartford: Transcendental Books, 1983); W. H. W. Darley and J. C. B. Standbridge, *Chants of the Episcopal Church, Original and Selected: Harmonized for Four Voices and Provided with an Organ Pianoforte Accompaniment* (Philadelphia: L. J. Williams, 1840); Leonard Ellinwood, *The History of American Church Music* (1953; rev. ed., New York: Da Capo, 1970); Henry Wilder Foote, *Three Centuries of American Hymnody* (1940; reprint, Hamden, Conn.: Shoestring Press, 1961); Ann Ayres, *The Life and Work of William Augustus Muhlenberg* (New York: T. Whittaker, 1889), 46–47, 62–67; Byrd Wilson, *Memoir of the Life of the Right Reverend William White, D.D., Bishop of the Protestant Episcopal Church in the State of Pennsylvania* (Philadelphia: James Kay Jr. and Brother, 1839), 348–49; *JDC 1829*, 80; *JDC 1837*, 34; *JDC 1834*, 31.

* * * * *

The Arrival of the New Evangelicals

Those, such as Bishop White, who lived into a new era found familiar categories and parties shifting all around, and words losing their old meanings. The new evangelical party bore little resemblance to what White had known as "low church" in his formative years. The older low-church (or latitudinarian) party, with which White was identified, traced its origins to the Puritan movement of the sixteenth century. By the time of the American Revolution, it had shed much of its Calvinism for a calm Enlightenment rationalism.

The new evangelicals were rooted in the Great Awakening revivalism of George Whitefield and John Wesley.[62] Their warm emotionalism, prayer meetings, revivals, hymn singing, and extemporaneous preaching differentiated them as much from the earlier low church as from the high-church faction of their own era. Evangelicals' theology and methods created controversy and drew heated rebuttals from high-church leaders such as Hobart. Their emphasis on a personal conversion experience contrasted with the high-church focus on baptismal regeneration. Indeed, for evangelicals, powerful preaching was a more effective means of grace than the liturgy and sacraments. Consequently, they often preferred to shorten the prayer book service to gain more time for preaching. It was a strategy that evangelicals argued was more practical, especially in frontier churches, but that their opponents considered a profane disregard for Episcopal verity.

In Pennsylvania, evangelicals favored revivals—called "associations"—such as the ones Dr. Levi Bull organized in Delaware and Chester counties.[63] Several clergy joined to preach on consecutive days, usually with a harvest of new communicants at the end. At Trinity, Southwark, in 1822, it was reported, "Tears of penitence flowed, and sighs of contrition ascended; multitudes pressed eagerly to the public worship, [and] . . . there was here manifested an evident revival of religion."[64] Such protracted meetings strongly resembled the methods of non-Episcopal revivalists such as Charles Finney, but among Episcopalians the services tended to be more restrained and were often tied to the liturgical year; Lent, especially Holy Week, was known to be a season when minds turned easily toward repentance.

Prayer meetings were controversial because they involved extemporaneous prayers rather than the authorized words of the Book of Common Prayer. Bishop White considered it dangerous especially for laity "to exercise themselves in public instruction and in prayer of their own suggestion or devising." But the evangelicals were adamant. When White confronted a member of St. Paul's about his participation, the bishop was told bluntly that prayer meetings were "most helpful to the laymen" and would continue.[65]

In spite of such differences, these two factions had long managed to coexist within the diocese without open warfare. St. Paul's, the leading evangelical center in Pennsylvania, had been founded in the 1760s. For every committed evangelical in Pennsylvania, there was someone who stood on the high-church side, and several more spaced along a continuum in between. Bishop White's moderate, irenic spirit (and perhaps also Pennsylvania's tradition of welcoming religious diversity) opened the diocese to differing perspectives and, for a long while, kept peace among them.

The arrival of the Reverend Benjamin Allen changed all of this.[66] Allen, who became rector of St. Paul's in October 1821, was a different sort of evangelical. He was aggressive, zealous, and deliberately divisive. He thought in party terms, and he employed tactics, such as the caucus and the single-party slate, that were unknown before his arrival. In his mind, evangelicalism was the only true Christianity, and a heart-wrenching conversion the only path to salvation. Allen's sermons were filled with vivid imagery portraying the "anger of God against sin" and the "filthiness of the flesh and spirit." "Unless you believe in the Lord Jesus Christ," he preached, "you must be *damned*."[67]

Allen was not willing to settle for a diocese where evangelicals were merely accepted; he wanted them to dominate. He launched a no-holds-barred crusade to polarize debate, isolate the opposition, and remake the diocese in the mold of Virginia, where he had served before his move to Philadelphia. He campaigned to bring in like-minded clergy from Virginia to fill vacancies in the diocese, and in the hotly contested election of 1826 he hoped to have a Virginian elected as assistant bishop.

The four years leading up to the 1826 election were filled with skirmishes, as the two sides tested their strategies and measured their strengths. Allen had been in the city less than six months before he launched a brash plan to create a second large evangelical church, St. Andrew's, and ignored Bishop White in doing so. The suspicions and recriminations lingered, and the episode was thrown up periodically as an example of evangelical disregard for authority—to which one evangelical pamphleteer tersely replied that the bishop was not "clothed with papal authority."[68]

In May 1822, when the diocesan convention chose its delegates to the General Convention, the evangelicals successfully replaced the Reverend James Abercrombie, one of White's assistants in the United Churches, with an evangelical, the Reverend George Boyd. The following year, with Boyd absent, the vote went the other way, much to the irritation of the evangelicals, who determined not to let an election slip away again. When the convention met in Norristown in 1824, the evangelicals caucused separately, after a prayer meeting, and prepared a written slate of candidates to direct their votes. The high-church party suspected nothing until it was too late; not only had Boyd defeated Abercrombie, but Allen was elected in place of Kemper. When it was over, the Reverend James Montgomery remarked, "We were told they were praying for us; but we soon found that they were preying upon us."[69] That same year, evangelicals captured control of the *Episcopal Recorder*, a paper that had been started by close associates of White as a nonpartisan "record" of church news. They quickly transformed it into a one-party organ and used it to rally their forces.[70]

The more eagerly the evangelicals pushed their cause, the more they drove White to the high-church camp. Hopkins, from his vantage point across the diocese in Pittsburgh, believed that "no one was more alarmed than the venerable Bishop White."[71] In the aftermath of the 1824 convention, White, determined to squelch what he deemed overblown claims about revivals, pared down several parish reports before they were printed in the journal; predictably, the evangelicals were furious. The following year, evangelicals once again arrived at the diocesan convention with an exclusive slate and, claiming that the bishop's supporters could "not represent their views in the General Convention," successfully elected their people.[72]

By the time of the May 1826 convention in Reading, the high-church party had caught up with the evangelicals' tactics. They, too, caucused beforehand and came prepared to vote a straight party slate. To their glee, every one of their candidates was victorious. The Reverend L. S. Ives bragged to Hobart of their victory: "Judging from appearances, Bedell, Allen, etc., were completely humbled. . . . We evinced no signs of extraordinary joy till we found ourselves alone; and then, you may suppose, we indulged our feelings." Ives, with no little amusement, added that Montgomery had been so elated that he "returned *thanks* in a most animated *extemporaneous* prayer!"[73]

The Election of an Assistant Bishop

The victory in May 1826 convinced White and the high-church party that they could confidently call an election for an assistant bishop with right of succession when White died.[74] White and his friends expected to elect the Reverend Bird Wilson, a professor at New York's General Theological Seminary who, as a native Pennsylvanian and protégé of White, kept his canonical residence in the diocese. Allen and the evangelicals had a different plan; they chose William Meade, a thoroughgoing evangelical from Virginia. The moment a special convention was announced for October 1826, both parties sprang into action. Watching from across the border in Delaware, Bishop Kemp correctly predicted "a fierce storm in Pennsylvania."[75]

The evangelicals, the better organized and more active of the two factions, worked diligently to improve their chance of victory. They hurried to organize new churches and bring additional evangelical clergy into the diocese.[76] Two anonymous pamphlets stirred evangelical passions against high-church doctrine that, according to one, "had its origin in hell." Funds were raised to pay travel expenses for those willing to vote for Meade. Boyd was dispatched across the state to plant doubts about the soundness of Wilson's faith; Wilson's friends called it an underhanded attempt at "poisoning minds." White, who at the previous two diocesan conventions had become more outspokenly critical of prayer meetings, felt the sting of the evangelical assault; indeed, the tone of the *Episcopal Recorder* became so unpleasant that White refused to allow the paper into his house.[77]

The high-church party was not inactive, but (perhaps overconfident after their May victories) they were slower and less aggressive in rallying their supporters. By the time the special convention assembled, neither side was certain of victory. The atmosphere was tense and hostile; one lay evangelical, Samuel J. Robbins, openly suggested that White would try to rig the vote by appointing dishonest tellers (to which White's only reply was, "I thank you for the good opinion you entertain of me").[78] Procedures called for the clergy to vote first, and for their choice to be submitted to the laity for approval or disapproval. When the clerical votes were tallied, there were twenty-seven votes for Meade and twenty-six for Wilson. The crestfallen bishop announced the result, but before he could direct the tellers to poll the laity, Philadelphia attorney Joseph Ingersoll interrupted with a reminder that one person—it was Wilson[79]—had abstained. This meant that there were actually fifty-four, not fifty-three, votes. "Mr. President," he asked, "will you be kind enough to tell me by what kind of arithmetic *twenty-seven* is a majority of *fifty-four?*"[80] White quickly saw the point and declared that there was no winner. With matters hopelessly deadlocked, the convention was forced to adjourn.

In the weeks after the failed convention, the diocese was astir with charges and countercharges, schemes and counterschemes. A great number of evangelicals thought Meade should have been declared the winner, and they fumed at the injustice they thought had been done. Meade himself, however, was having second thoughts about coming into a badly divided diocese, and he suggested that both sides agree not to try another election so long as White was living. The idea of postponing another showdown was acceptable to White and the high-church faction, but not to the evangelicals. Undercut by his own supporters, Meade withdrew. Since Wilson, declaring that the episode gave him "more distress and anxiety than all the delays and difficulties connected with obtaining the Episcopate from England," also refused to stand again, both sides were left without an obvious candidate.[81]

A shortage of candidates did nothing to curtail the accusations and recriminations that were flung about in newspapers and strident pamphlets.[82] By the time the two sides arrived in Harrisburg for the annual diocesan convention in May 1827, each believed it faced an opponent set upon its extinction; no room remained for compromise or even reasoned discussion. When one evangelical tried to narrow the distance by suggesting that White was himself really a low churchman and part of the evangelical party, the bishop snapped back that perhaps as the word had been used in England a hundred years earlier, he might have been. "But," he added, "as the word is understood in this country, and among us now, you might as well call me a Turk or a Jew!"[83]

With Wilson now out of the picture, the high-church party looked to Hopkins of Pittsburgh as a nominee. The evangelicals, uncharacteristically, came to Harrisburg without a candidate chosen in advance; most continued to hold out hope for Meade. A quick head count indicated that the high-church party had a one-vote majority among the clergy present, twenty-six to twenty-five. This meant that the high-church party could elect Hopkins, but only if Hopkins would vote for himself—which he adamantly refused to do. With this road blocked, the high-church party was forced to look outside the diocese for a candidate; thus, all twenty-six votes could be employed without anyone voting for himself.

The choice was Henry Ustick Onderdonk, rector of St. Ann's Church, Brooklyn. He was a solid high churchman, but he was also well known as a hymn writer and editor of the denomination's new hymnal—traits that might have made him less objectionable to evangelicals. In addition, he brought experience in frontier congregations. To the high-church party, he seemed a strong candidate. To the evangelicals, however, any New Yorker was unthinkable. In desperation, the evangelicals suggested that if the high-church party would put Hopkins's name forward, they could, if given time to caucus, add enough votes to elect him. Better Hopkins from Pennsylvania than Onderdonk from New York. But such was the level of distrust by this time that the high-church party believed the offer to be another of Allen's devious tricks. The high-church party pressed forward, and Onderdonk carried the clerical vote by 26 to 25, and the lay vote by 72 to 58.[84]

Some evangelicals tried to put the best face on their defeat; Allen wrote to his wife, "We know not what is best so well as God does. I try to praise for every thing."[85] But they did not give up easily. Evangelical clergy refused to sign the paper attesting to Onderdonk's election, and promptly sent a remonstrance to the House of Bishops listing ten reasons why Onderdonk should not be consecrated—among them that Meade had really won in October and that they had no "hope that [Onderdonk] will exercise the office of a Bishop . . . as a wholesome example to the flock of Christ."[86] A majority of bishops denied the protest and consecrated Onderdonk on October 25, 1827, in Christ Church, Philadelphia.[87] But, in an ill omen for the future, none of the evangelical clergy or bishops took part.

White chose Hobart, the evangelicals' archenemy, to preach the consecration sermon, and the New York bishop's exultant words merely confirmed evangelical suspicions.[88] When Bishop Kemp was killed in a stagecoach accident on his way home to Delaware, some evangelicals spoke of it as an act of divine punishment for his role in the consecration.[89]

The weeks following the consecration showed no improvement. In Philadelphia feelings were so acrimonious that Hopkins reported that there was "no communication except bowing in the street, and not always that." Allen vented his fury in a sharp-tongued open letter to Hobart. "In my inmost soul," Allen raged, "I do honestly believe you to be the worst enemy of the Liturgy, the greatest opponent of the spread of Episcopacy, and the certain author of the entire ruin to our Church." For good measure, Allen provided a sixty-four-page appendix detailing the injustices heaped upon his friends by the high-church party; in contrast, the evangelicals "had acted only on the defensive," and pure motives justified all that Allen had done: "No sin against Christian charity is committed by contending earnestly for the faith." The high-church party had a different assessment of Allen's behavior. Kemper bitterly blamed Allen for the sorry state of the diocese: "He, I greatly fear, is a deep intriguer, and is considered by us all as the author of all our troubles, and as somewhat deficient in the organ of conscientiousness."[90]

Bishop Onderdonk's Early Years in the Diocese

For some months after the election, White was despondent. "Considering my advanced years," he lamented, "I have little prospect of witnessing the end of the evil." But he was pleasantly surprised. Two years later, after the 1829 convention, White wrote to Hobart to tell him of a decrease in hostility. When, the following year, he saw "stronger marks of the same decline," he could begin to relax. "For this I lift my heart in gratitude to God, and with prayer for the increase of it," he wrote.[91]

It appears that more than a few people were badly shaken by the events of 1826–27, and, realizing how close they had come to inflicting permanent damage on the diocese, they curbed their words and behavior. This was easier to do after Hobart's death from fever in 1830 deprived the evangelicals of their most detested foe. Allen, Pennsylvania's most divisive evangelical, was also removed from the scene, first by illness and then by death. Severe symptoms—pain in his side, coughing up blood—forced Allen to Britain in the spring of 1828 for what his doctors hoped would be a curative rest. Instead, Allen's condition worsened, and he died at sea during the return voyage.[92] Tyng, Allen's successor at St. Paul's, was as much an evangelical as Allen, but he was by nature a peacemaker, not a polarizer. From the pulpit he called for reconciliation: "We hope the period of controversies and disputes in the Episcopal Church has past [*sic*] for ever. . . . When I came among you I found no just cause for dissension, nor have I since discovered any."[93]

An equally important source of the diocese's newfound harmony was Onderdonk himself. Ironically, he had never been the imperious high churchman that the Evangelicals feared. His devotion to hymn singing was well enough known, but few seemed to realize that Hobart and he had quarreled. When Onderdonk was in Canandaigua, he shortened the liturgy to accommodate the realities of a frontier congregation; Hobart never trusted him again. Onderdonk was not in Pennsylvania long before White, with a smile, was reporting to the convention the "manifest evidences exhibited of the increasing acceptableness of his services."[94] Some of this approval resulted from the energy and commitment he brought to missionary work in the Pennsylvania interior, a cause dear to evangelicals.

Onderdonk's first two Episcopal charges effectively minimized differences and emphasized common elements of faith. In 1829 he called for "Christianity Entire." Neither formalism nor enthusiasm, neither institutions nor doctrines, encompassed the whole of Christianity. His final words would have resonated with evangelicals: "Above all, we must recollect for ourselves, and earnestly impress upon our flocks, that religion of the HEART, steadfastly manifested in a religious LIFE, is essential to give value to our profession of sound Christian doctrine, and to our adherence to the pure Christian institutions. The design of all these doctrines and institutions is to change the hearts of men, and their character, and reclaim them from the dominion of nature and depravity to the dominion of grace."[95] Onderdonk's second charge, delivered five years later, focused on the differences between Protestant and Roman Catholic, between scripture and church tradition. Onderdonk left no doubt that he belonged to a *Protestant* Episcopal Church, not a Catholic one.[96]

By the time of White's death in 1836 and Onderdonk's succession, most of the initial animosity had fallen away. Bird Wilson, assessing Onderdonk's career in 1839, believed that he had acted "with much prudence, conciliation and ability. In the course of a few years, the general harmony of the diocese was happily restored."[97] Following a revival that grew out of Lenten prayer meetings at Epiphany Church in 1837, Onderdonk came to confirm the converts. Tyng, the rector, described the bishop's visit as "a peculiar mercy from the Most High" and noted that Onderdonk preached "a most awakening sermon." While Onderdonk was speaking, Tyng said, "I blessed God . . . that my hands were so upheld, and my labours were so encouraged."[98] Ten years earlier it would have been hard to imagine such an accolade ever coming from a prominent evangelical.

The Oxford Movement Reignites Partisan Warfare

Across the ocean in England, a group of Oxford clergy—most prominently John Keble, Edward Pusey, and John Henry Newman—started in the 1830s to redefine Anglicanism in ways that eventually reignited the evangelical–high church conflict in Pennsylvania and cost Onderdonk his bishopric. The Oxford Movement began in 1833 to issue a series of publications called Tracts for the Times, of which by 1841 there were ninety in all. The writers of the early pamphlets were responding to the changed situation of the Church of England after the end of dissenting and Roman Catholic disabilities and the Reform Act of 1832. With establishment less secure, the Oxford scholars looked to apostolic succession for legitimacy. As Newman and his colleagues developed their arguments, they delved into patristic and medieval sources, which they read in a manner befitting the age's romantic spirit. But the early tracts drew only limited attention in the United States, where disestablishment was an earlier generation's worry.[99]

Indeed, one high-church Pennsylvanian had anticipated the tractarians' interest in early church writers by nearly a full decade. Hopkins, in the mid-1820s, launched an extensive self-study of patristics, which occupied him for some eighteen years. He began by borrowing books from the local Roman Catholic priest, and then, as he progressed, buying his own copies. Frustrated by biased Roman translations, he tackled the original languages to assure himself that Episcopalians were on solid ground. The more he studied, the more he was enthralled by practices that had been cast aside during the Reformation. In his Pittsburgh congregation, he began adding water to the eucharistic wine, baking his own thin, unleavened Communion bread, and employing "rich colored and embroidered vestments, and lights, and incense." Before he left Pittsburgh in 1831, he founded "a band of *Christian Sisters*" to work among the poor and sick. All of this in the Diocese of Pennsylvania before any of the Oxford tracts or Keble's *Christian Year* was published in England. From this beginning, there was a direct line to the American Anglo-Catholic ritualists of the late 1860s.[100]

The appearance in 1839 of an American edition of the tracts for the first time focused widespread attention on the Oxford writers. Evangelical reviewers were uniformly critical. In Philadelphia, the *Episcopal Recorder* kept up a steady drumbeat against the "exceedingly false and dangerous doctrines of the Oxford Tracts." The "poison contained in them" was "a revival of the worst evils of the Romish system."[101] When the last of the Oxford series, tract no. 90, appeared in February 1841, it brought back all the worst of the old party animosity in Pennsylvania. Newman's thesis was that the Thirty-Nine Articles were compatible with Roman Catholic theology. Whatever Newman's intention, many read it as a call for Romanizing the Episcopal Church—or for defection to Rome.[102] In Pennsylvania, matters were made worse in July 1841 by an open letter from Philadelphia's Roman Catholic bishop, Francis Patrick Kenrick, inviting Episcopal conversions.[103]

Tempers ran high, and reports of General Theological Seminary students using the Roman breviary or hearing private confessions focused attention there, especially on Arthur Carey, a young graduate seeking ordination in the Diocese of New York. Evangelicals tried to block the ordination, but without success. The unfortunate Carey died shortly after being ordained by Bishop Benjamin Onderdonk (the younger brother of Pennsylvania's bishop), but evangelical outrage lived on.[104]

Frustrated, evangelicals attacked on new fronts in 1844. They came to the1844 General Convention in Philadelphia with a motion condemning the "errors and abuses of Tractarianism as inconsistent with the Gospel and with the principles of our Protestant Episcopal Church."[105] The city was hardly an ideal place for a calm discussion of the nuances of Catholic and Episcopal theology; only five months earlier, Philadelphia had been rocked by violent anti-Catholic riots.[106] In spite of the atmosphere, the motion lost decisively. Evangelicals were, however, able to persuade the House of Bishops to launch an investigation of General Theological Seminary; the inquiry caused much grief, and two students were eventually forced out, but the seminary survived.[107]

Concurrently, the evangelicals also moved against leading high-church bishops—the two Onderdonks and George Washington Doane of New Jersey.[108] A recent procedural change had made bishops accountable to their peers, not to their dioceses. Ironically, this had been a high-church idea to enhance the status of bishops, but it now meant that a high-church bishop, even one in a reliably high-church diocese, could be removed by the majority of evangelical bishops across the denomination.[109] Pennsylvania's bishop was especially vulnerable.

The Resignation of Bishop Onderdonk

Onderdonk's controversial election had left wounds that could be easily reopened. In fact, Bishop Meade of Virginia, whom evangelicals had fought to make assistant bishop of Pennsylvania in 1826–27, was about to play a decisive role in the remainder of Onderdonk's story. Beyond his vulnerability to old grudges, Onderdonk's use of alcohol left him especially exposed. Less than a year after he arrived in Pennsylvania, he developed a chronic intestinal disorder for which his physician prescribed daily use of brandy. By the early 1840s, the disease had become more severe, and Onderdonk suffered from "enduring fatigue," "faintishness," and "excruciating" pain in the bowels. "All this terrible exacerbation of my suffering," he explained, "demanded a large use of brandy and water, as the only means of alleviating them; for, taking frequent opiates would be incompatible with my almost constant official engagements."[110] Witnesses differed as to the public damage caused by the generous dosages Onderdonk ingested. But to evangelicals who preached abstinence from their pulpits, neither the amount nor the purpose mattered. What evangelicals saw was a tractarian supporter who matched their anti-Catholic image of the inebriated Roman priest.[111]

In May 1844, in a series of private meetings concurrent with the diocesan convention, evangelicals drafted formal charges against Onderdonk, and they called upon him late in the evening of May 25 to deliver their specifications. The bishop, caught by surprise, complained that his accusers had failed to follow the biblical injunction to seek a private amendment of the fault before taking the matter to the entire church. Quite the opposite, he had been met by "daily smiles"—"not a frown, not a hint of the gathering storm, not one alarm-note of my impending annihilation"—from the very people plotting his downfall.[112]

Onderdonk undertook, beginning that day, "the absolute relinquishment of every kind of spirituous drink, except the wine at the Holy Communion," a resolution to which he was reportedly faithful. But within two weeks, on June 5, his medical symptoms unabated and accusations swirling around him, Onderdonk submitted his resignation "on account of the state of my health." At a special convention in September, the resignation was quickly accepted, and Onderdonk's tenure as bishop of Pennsylvania was over.[113]

But the story did not end there. Onderdonk's carefully worded letter of resignation had specified as his reason failing health—not the moral lapse of intemperance. But in the ensuing weeks, newspaper coverage and public comment implied that he had been forced out because of drunkenness.

Onderdonk, in a move he must have regretted later, and that his friend Horace Binney, the Philadelphia attorney and Episcopal lay leader, advised against, wrote to the House of Bishops asking for an investigation to clear his name.[114]

The response of the House of Bishops was swift and harsh; they indefinitely suspended Onderdonk from all public ministry, as both bishop and priest.[115] The suspension, which was not lifted until 1856, was a continual source of friction in both the diocese and the House of Bishops. Appeals for his restoration came forward in 1847, 1850, and 1853, only to be blocked by Meade of Virginia. Meade never relented, insisting that Onderdonk was guilty "in other respects" beyond intemperance, that he was inadequately penitent, and that even "if he were to appear before his brethren and in the posture and with the language of a penitent pray for restoration—though all had confidence in his professions, and freely mingled their tears of joy with his tears of godly sorrow—*this alone* would not be sufficient to justify the termination of the sentence." The penalty, Meade had come to believe, was the church's declaration of "abhorrence of the offense" and could not be lifted.[116] When the restoration did come, largely through the persistence of Binney and the mediation of Onderdonk's successor, Bishop Potter, it was over Meade's continued objection.[117]

If the most zealous of Pennsylvania evangelicals believed that the removal of Onderdonk would guarantee their long-term dominance, they were disappointed. Although few Pennsylvanians followed Newman's example and joined the Roman Catholic Church,[118] the subtle influence of Oxford theology, worship, and arts continued to grow in the following two decades, as illustrated most specifically by the founding of such Philadelphia parishes as St. James the Less (1846) and St. Mark's (1848). Further ahead, in 1873, lay a more serious confrontation.

* * * * *

The Classical and Gothic Revivals in Architecture

Architects of the new nation built according to Greco-Roman classical forms. Was not America a democracy, like ancient Greece, and a republic, like Rome? In Philadelphia, St. Andrew's Church (1822–23) displayed a portico supported by Ionic columns. The church (now the Greek Orthodox Cathedral of St. George) was the work of a member of the congregation, the prominent English-born architect John Haviland. Another fine Philadelphia example was the Doric-porticoed Church of the Epiphany (1833), designed by Thomas U. Walter. Although by the end of the 1830s classical styles were less favored, Thomas Somerville Stewart included eight Corinthian columns in his design for St. Luke's Church (1839–40).

During the mid-nineteenth century, a Gothic Revival gained an enthusiastic following. The earliest Philadelphia example was St. Stephen's Church (1822–23), by William Strickland. The diocese's most energetic promoter of the Gothic Revival was on the other side of the state, in Pittsburgh. John Henry Hopkins, rector of Trinity Church, had passed through a number of occupations—art teacher, iron mill manager, attorney, and church organist—before entering the priesthood. Liking none of the plans submitted for a larger Pittsburgh church, he created one himself in the Gothic style, which he found appropriately reminiscent of English cathedrals. Trinity's new edifice in 1823 gave Hopkins a reputation as an amateur architect, and he soon was receiving more requests than he had time to fulfill. In 1836, after he left Pennsylvania for New England, he published his *Essay on Gothic Architecture* (1836), including plans that could be adapted to local use. The Gothic style became obligatory not only for large urban churches but also for more modest churches in western Pennsylvania's villages, such as St. Peter's (1830) in the canal town of Blairsville or Christ Church in Meadville, and in eastern Pennsylvania's industrial towns, such as St. David's (1835) in Manayunk or the Hopkins-designed Calvary (1836) in Rockdale.

Congregations that inherited buildings could at least redecorate their interiors in more romantic Gothic hues. In the 1830s, St. Peter's, Philadelphia, repainted its colonial white walls a deep ochre shade and applied dark brown graining to its woodwork. Affluent urban parishioners found that the rich colors, ornate silver, pew cushions, and carpet matched the respectability they had already achieved by furnishing their private houses for style and comfort.

In time, Episcopalians regarded Gothic style as particularly suited to their Anglican heritage and current liturgical needs. In the 1840s, Philadelphia congregations associated with the Anglo-Catholic movement built historically accurate Gothic structures with assistance from England's Ecclesiological Society—St. James the Less (1846–48), on specifications of a thirteenth-century chapel in Cambridgeshire, England, and St. Mark's (1848–49), on a fourteenth-century English plan adapted by noted Philadelphia architect John Notman.

SOURCES: Roger W. Moss, *Historic Sacred Places of Philadelphia* (Philadelphia: University of Pennsylvania Press, 2005); John Henry Hopkins, *Essay on Gothic Architecture, with Various Plans and Drawings for Churches: Designed Chiefly for the Use of the Clergy* (Burlington, Vt.: Smith and Harrington, 1836); John Henry Hopkins Jr., *The Life of the Late Right Reverend John Henry Hopkins*, 2d ed. (New York: Huntington, 1875); *JDC 1831*, 24; *Episcopal Recorder*, November 30, 1839; J. Wesley Twelves, *A History of the Diocese of Pennsylvania of the Protestant Episcopal Church in the U.S.A., 1784–1968* (Philadelphia: Diocese of Pennsylvania, 1969), 150; Clarence Stephenson, *Indiana County: A 175th Anniversary History*, 5 vols. (Indiana, Pa.: Halldin, 1978–95), 1:293; Episcopal Church, Diopa, *Spanning Four Centuries: Pages of Parish Histories of the Episcopal Diocese of Pennsylvania* (Philadelphia: Episcopal Diocese of Pennsylvania, 1997), sec. 1, p. 22.

* * * * *

Changing Diocese, Changing Congregations

By the mid-1840s, when it sought a successor to Onderdonk, the diocese was no longer the simple, geographically limited entity that White had led a quarter-century earlier. It had more churches, more widely scattered across the state. Consequently, it had become more complex and more difficult to administer, although the task was not yet so overwhelming as to demand partition. The diocese now had a full-time bishop unburdened by parish responsibilities, and it had new institutional structures and habits to manage its work. Unfortunately, its peace had been repeatedly disrupted by acrimony between the high-church and evangelical factions, personality clashes, and disagreements about the best ways to stimulate, and absorb, the new growth.

How much this diocesan friction was noticed inside congregations is debatable. Local congregations were more homogeneous than the diocese, and even the most engaged diocesan warriors tried to shield their parishioners from the wider conflicts; Allen, after the angry 1826 election, wrote to his wife, "The friends in the Church must not think any thing has gone wrong."[119] Life within the congregation—that is, life for the laity, whose primary identification was almost always local, not diocesan—was still comparatively simple, in two senses. Worship remained plain and unadorned, even though one could see stirrings of new sensibilities that in due course would lead to greater ritualism—a romantic aesthetic, a commitment to patristic and biblical integrity, and a middle-class demand for the social graces that conveyed respectability. Congregations were also simpler in the sense that historian E. Brooks Holifield means when he refers to them as "devotional," in contrast to the "social" congregations of the late nineteenth and early twentieth centuries.[120] They concentrated on worship, pastoral care, children's education, and above all the cultivation of piety. But they were a far cry from the institutions of the late industrial era that, in addition, launched ambitious urban mission projects, provided a full menu of fellowship and recreational enticements, and incorporated more businesslike methods of budgeting and administration.

NOTES

1. *JDC 1825*, 11–12; *JDC 1826*, 14, 17; Bird Wilson, *Memoir of the Life of the Right Reverend William White, D.D., Bishop of the Protestant Episcopal Church in the State of Pennsylvania* (Philadelphia: James Kay Jr. and Brother, 1839), 215–16 (hereafter *Life of White*).

2. *JDC 1824*, 14.

3. Roger D. Simon, *Philadelphia: A Brief History* (University Park: Pennsylvania Historical Association, 2003), 27–34; Emma Lapsansky, "Building Democratic Communities: 1800–1850," in *Pennsylvania: A History of the Commonwealth*, ed. Randall M. Miller and William Pencak (University Park: Pennsylvania State University Press, 2002), 155–57.

4. *JDC 1835*, 55.

5. J. Wesley Twelves, *A History of the Diocese of Pennsylvania of the Protestant Episcopal Church in the U.S.A., 1784–1968* (Philadelphia: Diocese of Pennsylvania, 1969), 145–47. Philadelphians also had the advantage of a free-ranging city missionary during the 1830s. Operating out of his house, the Reverend Timothy Allen preached and visited where he saw the need. He conducted worship regularly at the Widow's Asylum (monthly), the Magdalen Asylum (weekly), and the Wills Hospital (monthly). On Sundays he could be found on street corners or in halls, "as the Lord in His providence directs." *JDC 1836*, 70; *JDC 1839*, 70.

6. Episcopal Church, Diocese of Pennsylvania, *Spanning Four Centuries: Pages of Parish Histories of the Episcopal Diocese of Pennsylvania* (Philadelphia: Diocese of Pennsylvania, 1997), sec. 2, p. 8; sec. 3, p. 16.

7. On the founding of St. Andrew's, see Thomas G. Allen, *Memoir of the Rev. Benjamin Allen, Late Rector of St. Paul's Church, Philadelphia* (Philadelphia: Latimer, 1832), 289–99; Stephen H. Tyng, "Memoir of Gregory T. Bedell," in Gregory T. Bedell, *Sermons*, 2 vols. (Philadelphia: William Stavely-John Pechin, 1835), 1:lxii–lxxi; William Bacon Stevens, *Past and Present of St. Andrew's* (Philadelphia: Sherman, 1858), 10–18; and annual parish reports in the *JDC*.

8. On Epiphany's organization, see C. R. Tyng, *Record of the Life and Work of the Rev. Stephen Higginson Tyng* (New York: Dutton, 1890), 108–12; Francis Wells, *Fifty Years: A Historic Sketch of the Church of the Epiphany from 1834–1884* (Philadelphia: Patterson and White, 1884), 3–7; Church of the Epiphany, Philadelphia, Pastoral Reports of the Church of the Epiphany, 1835–1845, HSP.

9. The information on Christ Church is based on Deborah Mathias Gough, *Christ Church, Philadelphia: The Nation's Church in a Changing City* (Philadelphia: University of Pennsylvania Press, 1995), 209–28, 233 (Kemper quoted on 210).

10. Diopa, *Spanning Four Centuries*, sec. 2, p. 10; Twelves, *History of the Diocese of Pennsylvania*, 140; *JDC 1836*, 36; *JDC 1837*, 39.

11. *Episcopal Recorder,* May 18, 1839; *JDC 1839,* 16.

12. *JDC 1836,* 39.

13. Franklin S. Edmonds, *History of St. Matthew's Church, Francisville, Philadelphia, 1822–1925* (Philadelphia: St. Matthew's Church, 1925), 41–76.

14. *JDC 1835,* 67; *JDC 1838,* 50; *JDC 1839,* 45.

15. *Episcopal Recorder,* September 21, 1839; *JDC 1835,* 45.

16. *JDC 1836,* 39.

17. Lapsansky, "Building Democratic Communities," 178–89; Walter Licht, "Civil Wars: 1850–1900," in *Pennsylvania,* 178–89, ed. Miller and Pencak, 219–23; Thomas Cochran, *Pennsylvania: A History* (New York: W. W. Norton, 1978), 86–101; Nicholas B. Wainwright, "The Age of Nicholas Biddle, 1825–1841," in *Philadelphia: A 300-Year History,* ed. Russell F. Weigley (New York: W. W. Norton, 1982), 266–80; Walter Licht, *Industrializing America* (Baltimore: Johns Hopkins University Press, 1995), 30–34; Philip Scranton, *Proprietary Capitalism: The Textile Manufacture at Philadelphia, 1800–1885* (Cambridge: Cambridge University Press, 1983); and Bruce Laurie, *Working People of Philadelphia, 1800–1850* (Philadelphia: Temple University Press, 1980).

18. *JDC 1834,* 30; Charles V. Hagner, *Early History of the Falls of Schuylkill, Manayunk, Schuylkill, and Lehigh Navigation Companies, Fairmount Waterworks, Etc.* (Philadelphia: Claxton, Remson and Haffelfinger, 1869), 91–92; Cynthia Shelton, *The Mills of Manayunk: Industrialization and Social Conflict in the Philadelphia Region, 1787–1837* (Baltimore: Johns Hopkins University Press, 1986), 109; Scranton, *Proprietary Capitalism,* 135–61.

19. *JDC 1836,* 45.

20. Scranton, *Proprietary Capitalism,* 153–56. Ripka claimed that his use of children under the age of twelve was a charitable act designed to provide money to impoverished mothers.

21. *JDC 1835,* 35; *JDC 1837,* 56; *JDC 1840,* 15; see also Anthony F. C. Wallace, *Rockdale: The Growth of an American Village in the Early Industrial Revolution* (New York: Knopf, 1978), 17–18, 296–302; Scranton, *Proprietary Capitalism,* 36–39.

22. *JDC 1839,* 61; Diopa, *Spanning Four Centuries,* sec. 2, pp. 11, 23.

23. *JDC 1829,* 68; *JDC 1834,* 39; Diopa, *Spanning Four Centuries,* sec. 2, pp. 20–21; Samuel F. Hotchkin, *Country Clergy of Pennsylvania* (Philadelphia: P. W. Ziegler, 1890), 30–40.

24. *JDC 1837,* 54; see also *JDC 1838, 66–67.*

25. *JDC 1842,* 57; *JDC 1843,* 55.

26. *JDC 1836,* 45; *JDC 1837,* 51; *JDC 1838,* 54, 59.

27. *JDC 1829,* 68; *JDC 1837,* 51.

28. Quoted in Wallace, *Rockdale,* 348.

29. Ibid., 308.

30. *JDC 1843,* 55.

31. Greenough White, *An Apostle of the Western Church: Memoir of the Rt. Rev. Jackson Kemper* (New York: Thomas Whittaker, 1900), 24–25; Hotchkin, *Country Clergy of Pennsylvania,* 25–27; *JDC 1883,* 18. The Reverend Joseph Pilmore, rector of St. Paul's, Philadelphia, was sent on a similar expedition to ascertain the Advancement Society's needs in the eastern part of the state.

32. *JDC 1843,* 64.

33. William Wilson Manross, *The Episcopal Church in the United States, 1800–1840* (1938; reprint, New York: AMS Press, 1967), 114–16; James Thayer Addison, *The Episcopal Church in the United States, 1789–1931* (1951; reprint, Hamden, Conn.: Archon Books, 1969), 127; *JDC 1820,* 11; *JDC 1830,* 17 (quotation from White); *JDC 1831,* 18.

34. White, *Apostle of the Western Church,* 62.

35. Walter H. Conser Jr., *Church and Confession: Conservative Theologians in Germany, England, and America, 1815–1866* (Macon: Mercer University Press, 1984), 301; Manross, *Episcopal Church in the United States,* 56.

36. *JDC 1828,* 20; Manross, *Episcopal Church in the United States,* 62; Hotchkin, *Country Clergy of Pennsylvania,* 15.

37. William Wilson Manross, *A History of the American Episcopal Church,* 3rd ed. (New York: Morehouse-Gorham, 1959), 228.

38. Quoted in John Henry Hopkins Jr., *The Life of the Late Right Reverend John Henry Hopkins,* 2d ed. (New York: Huntington, 1875), 69 (hereafter *Life of Hopkins*). Fifteen years later, Doddridge

complained to Hobart, "Had we initiated at an early period the example of other Christian communities, employed the same means for collecting our people into societies and building Churches with the same zeal, . . . we should have occupied the first and highest station among the Christian societies of the West." Ibid.

39. Ibid., 122–26; *JDC 1830*, 43–45.

40. *JDC 1837*, 48; *JDC 1834*, 33; see also *JDC 1827*, 44.

41. *JDC 1843*, 16–17.

42. *JDC 1833*, 33–34.

43. Hopkins, *Life of Hopkins*, 70.

44. *JDC 1822*, 11. The following year, the Prayer Book Society was merged into the Society for the Advancement of Christianity. *JDC 1823*, 11.

45. *JDC 1823*, 23–24; *JDC 1824*, 18; *JDC 1842*, 36; St. Paul's, Philadelphia, Vestry Minutes, June 7, 1825, Closed Parish Records, box 2, Diopa Archives, Lutheran Theological Seminary, Mount Airy (Philadelphia).

46. *JDC 1834*, 25.

47. Standing Committee Minutes, March 28, April 23, May 29, and July 12, 1822, December 24, 1824, Diopa Archives. The man, the Reverend Charles Snowden, was soon in trouble in Wilkes-Barre for "repeated acts of inebriation, profane cursing and swearing, profanation of the Lord's day, quarreling, striking, and threatening to stab and to kill, wanton nude and indecent behavior towards females, and vain trifling and irreligious conduct and conversation." He was deposed, but a year and a half later, still another tiny congregation, this time in Mifflin County, was petitioning White for Snowden's reinstatement so that they might have a minister.

48. *JDC 1840*, 19.

49. *JDC 1832*, 43; *JDC 1828*, 18 (White blamed his inability on "the neglect of sending to him official information of the periods for the commencements and of the dissolutions of pastoral connexions"); *JDC 1825*, Appendix, 53–57. An 1821 canon required that congregations say explicitly that they "accede[d] to the constitution, canons, doctrines, discipline, and worship" of the Protestant Episcopal Church. See Standing Committee Minutes, October 17, 1826, Diopa Archives.

50. Benjamin Dorr, *Churchman's Manual: An Exposition of the Doctrines, Ministry, and Worship of the Protestant Episcopal Church in the United States* (Burlington, N.J.: J. H. Powell Missionary Press, 1835).

51. *JDC 1842*, 27–29.

52. *JDC 1812*, 6–7. The fund, begun with a small bequest from the estate of attorney Benjamin Doz, had grown to about $20,000 by 1827; the interest-free loan of $30,000 was promised for the duration of Onderdonk's tenure and brought the principal to approximately $50,000, which, invested in 5 percent state stock, yielded a salary of $2,500 per year for the bishop. *JDC 1828*, 28.

53. Standing Committee Minutes, May 22, 1833, Diopa Archives; *JDC 1841*, 24–25.

54. Manross, *Episcopal Church in the United States*, 78–97; Wilson, *Life of White*, 206.

55. Clifton Hartwell Brewer, *A History of Religious Education in the Episcopal Church to 1835* (New Haven: Yale University Press, 1924; reprint, New York: Arno Press, 1969), 145, 252–54; E. Clowes Chorley, *Men and Movements in the American Episcopal Church* (1946; reprint, Hamden, Conn.: Archon Books, 1961), 115–16; Tyng, *Life and Work of the Rev. Stephen Higginson Tyng*, 115.

56. *JDC 1827*, 17–18; *JDC 1828*, 12. White spoke of the need for schools to teach "exclusively according to our religious system." *JDC 1825*, 14–15.

57. *JDC 1825*, 14; *JDC 1830*, 12.

58. Manross, *Episcopal Church in the United States*, 192–93n; Brewer, *History of Religious Education*, chapter 16. Beginning with the short-lived *Episcopal Magazine* (1820–21), Philadelphians edited the *Christian Warrior* (1828), soon renamed *Christian Magazine* (1828–29); the *Philadelphia Recorder* (1823–31), which continued as the *Episcopal Recorder* (from 1831); the *Church Register* (1826–29), which was succeeded by the *Protestant Episcopalian and Church Register* (1830–38); and the *Banner of the Cross* (1839–52).

59. *Hymns of the Protestant Episcopal Church in the United States of America* (Philadelphia: Bradford, 1827). See also Kenneth Walter Cameron, *Early Anglican Church Music in America*, 2 vols. (Hartford: Transcendental Books, 1983).

60. Quoted in Norris S. Barratt, *Outline of the History of Old St. Paul's Church, Philadelphia, Pennsylvania* (Philadelphia: Colonial Society of Pennsylvania, 1917), 145.

61. David Hein and Gardiner H. Shattuck Jr., *The Episcopalians* (Westport, Conn.: Praeger, 2004), 218.

62. Manross, *Episcopal Church in the United States*, 48–51; Chorley, *Men and Movements*, 59–110; Diana Hochstedt Butler, *Standing Against the Whirlwind: Evangelical Episcopalians in Nineteenth-Century America* (New York: Oxford University Press, 1995), passim. On the changing meaning of party labels in England, see Peter Benedict Nockles, *The Oxford Movement in Context: Anglican High Churchmanship, 1760–1857* (Cambridge: Cambridge University Press, 1994).

63. *JDC 1833*, 27; Hotchkin, *Country Clergy of Pennsylvania*, 33.

64. *JDC 1822*, 22.

65. *JDC 1825*, 16–17; Barratt, *Outline of the History of Old St. Paul's*, 147.

66. See Gough, *Christ Church, Philadelphia*, 211–12.

67. Allen, *Memoir of the Rev. Benjamin Allen*, 272–74.

68. Plain Fact, *An Answer to a Pamphlet Recently Addressed to the Episcopalians Under the Signature of Plain Truth* (Philadelphia, 1827), 7; Allen, *Memoir of the Rev. Benjamin Allen*, 289–95.

69. Quoted in Hopkins, *Life of Hopkins*, 85 and n3.

70. *JDC 1822*, 27–28; *JDC 1823*, 16; *JDC 1824*, 29; Hopkins, *Life of Hopkins*, 86.

71. Hopkins, *Life of Hopkins*, 84.

72. Plain Truth [William H. DeLancey], *Candid Address to the Episcopalians of Pennsylvania, in Relation to the Present Situation of the Affairs of the Diocese* (Philadelphia, April 1827), 3.

73. Ives to Hobart, May 13, 1826, quoted in Hopkins, *Life of Hopkins*, 87n1.

74. On this election, see *JDC (Special), October 1826;* see also David L. Holmes, "The Making of the Bishop of Pennsylvania, 1826–1827," *HMPEC* 41 (1972): 225–62, and 42 (1973): 171–97.

75. Kemp to Hobart, August 30, 1826, quoted in Hopkins, *Life of Hopkins*, 88n1; John Johns, *A Memoir of the Life of the Rt. Rev. William Meade* (Baltimore: Innes, 1867), 134.

76. Holmes, "Making of the Bishop," 252, notes that the evangelical scheme to "pack" the convention was certainly successful: "Of the twenty-seven clerical members of the Diocese who voted for Meade at the 1826 Special Convention, almost half—thirteen—were not rectors in the Diocese. Five held missionary posts, seven were simply listed as 'residing' in a diocesan city (most often Philadelphia), and one—Norman Nash, Meade's former associate in Virginia—served as a missionary in Wisconsin but returned temporarily to Pennsylvania in order to cast a vote for Meade."

77. Hopkins, *Life of Hopkins*, 88–89; see Plain Fact, *Answer to a Pamphlet*, 19.

78. Quoted in Holmes, "Making of the Bishop," 254. The tellers were evangelical Levi Bull and high churchman John Henry Hopkins (ibid., 258); see also Plain Truth [DeLancey], *Candid Address to the Episcopalians*, 5.

79. William W. Bronson, *A Memorial of the Rev. Bird Wilson* (Philadelphia: J. B. Lippincott, 1864), 82.

80. *JDC (Special), October 1826*, 27; Holmes, "Making of the Bishop," 259–60. Apparently, it was convention secretary DeLancey who prodded Ingersoll to ask the question.

81. Bronson, *Memorial of the Rev. Bird Wilson*, 84. Meade was elected assistant bishop of Virginia in 1829 and bishop in 1841. Hein and Shattuck, *Episcopalians*, 249–50.

82. In January 1827 a committee of correspondence composed of leading evangelicals (Boyd, Bedell, Rev. Charles Dupuy, and lay leaders Samuel Robbins and Joseph Riley) circulated a confidential flyer urging their followers to hold fast. The circular was made public and challenged by An Episcopalian, *An Appeal to the Lay Members of the Protestant Episcopal Church in Pennsylvania* (Philadelphia, April 1827), which charged that an evangelical victory would have led to "oppression and persecution in their worst forms." In April 1827 William H. DeLancey, writing under the pseudonym Plain Truth, laid out in *A Candid Address to the Episcopalians of Pennsylvania* the high-church version of recent events—that evangelicals were waging a vicious "war of extermination." DeLancey's pamphlet drew return fire. Plain Truth, Junior, in *Another Candid Address to the Episcopalians of Pennsylvania* (Philadelphia, 1827), found DeLancey's description "so gross, so insulting, so unmeasured, so unkind, so exquisitely cruel, that I know not how to give it an answer." A second pamphlet by Plain Fact—*An Answer to a Pamphlet Recently Addressed to the Episcopalians Under the*

Signature of Plain Truth—claimed that the evangelicals' tactics were purely defensive and innocent of guile. In May, DeLancey replied in *Three Letters: One to the Committee of Correspondence; One to 'Plain Truth, Junior'; and One to 'Plain Fact'* (Philadelphia, 1827); he asserted that the evangelicals were really Methodists, not Episcopalians, and that the "fierce recriminations" heaped on him simply demonstrated that the evangelicals had no reasonable counterarguments.

83. Quoted in Hopkins, *Life of Hopkins*, 101.

84. *JDC 1827*, 26–27. The vote among the clergy was Onderdonk 26, Hopkins 18, Wilson 1, James Milnor 2, and Meade 2. One vote was cast simply for "assistant bishop," and one voter abstained. An unsuspecting person looking at the tally might have assumed that Hopkins was the leading evangelical candidate against Onderdonk. An ironic side effect of the episode is that when Hopkins moved to New England, the events in Pennsylvania gave him credibility with both high-church and evangelical factions. Hopkins, *Life of Hopkins*, 105, 135–36. Onderdonk, unaware that he was even being considered, was informed of his election by his fellow hymnbook editor Muhlenberg, who called on him at his home in Brooklyn. After prodding Onderdonk to guess who had been elected and replying to each wrong name that it was "a man more after your own heart," Muhlenberg finally said, "Let me now take leave of you as a fellow presbyter and fellow hymn-monger, and salute you as Henry, Bishop of Pennsylvania." Muhlenberg recalled, "He seemed considerably affected, and received the intelligence, I thought, like a Christian man." Anne Ayres, *The Life and Work of William Augustus Muhlenberg* (New York: T. Whittaker, 1889), 95–96.

85. Allen, *Memoir of the Rev. Benjamin Allen*, 330.

86. Standing Committee Minutes, October 24, 1827, Diopa Archives.

87. *Decision of the Bishops Who United in the Consecration of the Rev. Henry U. Onderdonk, D.D., on the Reasons Presented to Them Against the Said Act* (Philadelphia: Jesper Harding, 1827); Standing Committee of the Diocese of Pennsylvania, *Narrative of the Consecration of the Rev. Henry U. Onderdonk, D.D., with the Address of the Presiding Bishop* (Philadelphia: Jesper Harding, 1827). The bishops supporting the consecration were White, Hobart of New York, James Kemp of Delaware, John Croes of New Jersey, and Nathaniel Bowen of South Carolina. Some evangelicals apparently held out hope that Bishop Philander Chase of Ohio would consecrate one of them as an "anti-bishop" in Pennsylvania. Holmes, "Making of the Bishop," 191.

88. John Henry Hobart, *The Christian Bishop Approving Himself unto God* (Philadelphia: Jesper Harding, 1827). In "Making of the Bishop," 191, Holmes rightly characterized Hobart's sermon as "triumphant."

89. Hopkins, *Life of Hopkins*, 108n1.

90. Ibid., 108; Benjamin Allen, *Letter to the Right Reverend John Henry Hobart* (Philadelphia: Russell and Martien, 1827), 30, 32, i–lxiv; Kemper to Hobart, November 3, 1826, quoted in Hopkins, *Life of Hopkins*, 92n1.

91. Wilson, *Life of White*, 217–19.

92. Allen, *Memoir of the Rev. Benjamin Allen*, 479–507.

93. Stephen H. Tyng, *Sermon Preached at the Consecration of St. Paul's Church, Philadelphia, January 1, 1831* (Philadelphia: William Stavely, 1831), 20–22.

94. *JDC 1829*, 17.

95. Henry U. Onderdonk, *Sermons and Episcopal Charges*, 2 vols. (Philadelphia: C. Sherman, 1851), 2:255.

96. Ibid., 2:256–309.

97. Wilson, *Life of White*, 228.

98. Church of the Epiphany, Philadelphia, Pastoral Report, 1837, 61–62, HSP.

99. Robert Bruce Mullin, in his *Episcopal Vision/American Reality: Theological and Social Thought in Evangelical America* (New Haven: Yale University Press, 1986), demonstrates that the rise of the Hobartian high-church theology was the American Episcopal answer to the end of establishment.

100. Hopkins, *Life of Hopkins*, 114–15; Charles F. Sweet, *A Champion of the Cross, Being the Life of John Henry Hopkins, S.T.D.* (New York: James Pott, 1894), 8. Later, after he moved to New England, Hopkins published *The Primitive Church Compared with the Protestant Episcopal Church of the Present Day* (Burlington, Vt.: Smith and Harrington, 1835). See John Henry Hopkins, *The Law of Ritualism* (New York: Hurd and Houghton, 1866). Hopkins visited Newman and Pusey in Oxford in

1839 and commented, "Certainly I was very pleased with them." Hopkins's enthusiasm for Oxford waned in the early 1840s after the publication of tract no. 90, but the sharpness of his criticism later mellowed. Hopkins, *Life of Hopkins*, 375–76. Hopkins's son, John Henry Hopkins Jr., followed in his father's footsteps as a pioneer in ecclesiastical arts and music, and is known today for his carol "We Three Kings of Orient Are." Born in Pittsburgh and raised in New England, Hopkins Jr. returned to Pennsylvania in 1876 as rector of Christ Church, Williamsport, a congregation that was by then separated in the new Diocese of Central Pennsylvania. Sweet, *Champion of the Cross*, 193.

101. *Episcopal Recorder*, March 30 and April 6, 1839.

102. John Henry Newman, *Remarks on Certain Passages in the Thirty-Nine Articles*, Tracts for the Times no. 90 (New York: Sparks, 1841); Conser, *Church and Confession*, 197–209.

103. Butler, *Standing Against the Whirlwind*, 108; George E. DeMille, *The Catholic Movement in the American Episcopal Church*, 2d ed. (Philadelphia: Church Historical Society, 1950), 55.

104. Butler, *Standing Against the Whirlwind*, 109; Mullin, *Episcopal Vision/American Reality*, 161; DeMille, *Catholic Movement*, 55–58; Stephen H. Tyng, *A Letter Sustaining the Recent Ordination of Mr. Arthur Carey* (Philadelphia: Appleton, 1843). Tyng, though an evangelical, refused to criticize the ordination; Carey had passed all his examinations, and Tyng was astute enough to see that if a bishop could at the last moment refuse ordination for someone with tractarian sympathies, he could do so for evangelical ones; it was a precedent Tyng did not wish to have set.

105. Quoted in DeMille, *Catholic Movement*, 59.

106. An exchange of pamphlets between Hopkins, now bishop of Vermont, and Kenrick only added to the polarization. Hein and Shattuck, *Episcopalians*, 71; Robert W. Prichard, *A History of the Episcopal Church* (Harrisburg: Morehouse, 1991), 139.

107. Bronson, *Memorial of the Rev. Bird Wilson*, 109–16.

108. Benjamin Onderdonk was tried for sexual harassment and intoxication and suspended in January 1845. Hein and Shattuck, *Episcopalians*, 266–67. Doane had written the introduction to an American edition of Keble's *The Christian Year* (Philadelphia: Carey, Lea & Blanchard, 1834). In 1852–53, Doane was tried for financial mismanagement but acquitted. Conser, *Church and Confession*, 307. Conser suggests that the evangelicals were encouraged in their attacks by the suspension of Pusey from preaching in May 1843.

109. Butler, *Standing Against the Whirlwind*, 115; *JDC 1839*, 13–14.

110. *JDC (Special), September 1844*, 28–29.

111. Benjamin Onderdonk's conviction, of course, mirrored both of the era's stereotypical priestly sins, intoxication and sexual abuse of women. See Hein and Shattuck, *Episcopalians*, 266–67; DeMille, *Catholic Movement*, 63–65.

112. *JDC (Special), September 1844*, 32–33.

113. Ibid., 16–47; Charles C. Binney, *The Life of Horace Binney* (Philadelphia: J. B. Lippincott, 1903), 242.

114. Binney, *Life of Horace Binney*, 242–43; Onderdonk to House of Bishops, October 8, 1844, in Member of the Church [Horace Binney], *The Case of the Right Rev. Henry U. Onderdonk, D.D.: Stated and Considered with Reference to His Continued Suspension* (Philadelphia: T. K. and P. G. Collins, 1853), 17–18.

115. The text of the bishops' suspension can be found in "A Member of the Church" [Binney], *Case of the Right Rev. Henry U. Onderdonk*, 22–23.

116. Quoted in Johns, *Memoir of the Life of the Rt. Rev. William Meade*, 388–99.

117. Binney, writing under the pseudonym A Member of the Church, engaged in a pamphlet duel with Meade, beginning with Binney's *Case of the Right Rev. Henry U. Onderdonk* and followed by William Meade, *A Counter Statement of the Case of Bishop H. U. Onderdonk* (Philadelphia: T. K. and P. G. Collins, 1854). The exchange continued with Binney's *Review of Bishop Meade's Counterstatement of the Case of Bishop H. U. Onderdonk* (Philadelphia: C. Sherman, 1854); Meade's *Bishop Meade's Second Pamphlet on the Case of Bishop H. U. Onderdonk* (Winchester, Va.: Senseney and Coffroth, 1854); and Binney's *Reply to Bishop Meade's Second Pamphlet and to Bishop Hopkins's Letter to the Clergy and Laity* (Philadelphia: C. Sherman, 1854). In building his argument, Binney sought precedent in early church practice in *The Law of Suspension of the Clergy in the Primitive Church* (Philadelphia: C. Sherman, 1855). During the suspension, a group of Philadelphia clergy and laity prevailed upon

Onderdonk to publish, at their expense, a collection of his writings to "alleviate this loss to themselves, to their families, and to the public . . . of your personal ministrations." The two-volume set, *Sermons and Episcopal Charges*, appeared in 1851, with a dedication "To Horace Binney, an Offering of Profound Gratitude from the Author."

118. The author of "Romish Perverts," which appeared in the *American Quarterly Church Review* in July 1860, listed four Pennsylvania clerical defections: Henry Major (1846), George Allen (1847), Dwight Edwards Lyman (1853), and George Foote (1857). None of the four was raised in the Episcopal Church; the first two were originally Methodists and the last two were Presbyterians. The most prominent Episcopal convert was Bishop Levi Silliman Ives of South Carolina; during Pennsylvania's diocesan conflicts of the 1820s, he served Trinity Church, Southwark (1823–26), and St. James's Church, Lancaster (1827–28).

119. Allen, *Memoir of the Rev. Benjamin Allen*, 330.

120. E. Brooks Holifield, "Toward a History of American Congregations," in *American Congregations*, ed. James P. Wind and James W. Lewis, 2 vols. (Chicago: University of Chicago Press, 1994), 2:23–53.

5

The Church and the City, 1840–1865

MARIE CONN

For Bishop Alonzo Potter and the Episcopal Church in Philadelphia, as for all residents of the city, the years leading up to the Civil War were a period of great growth, change, and almost overwhelming challenge.

* * * * *

A Historian's Description of Mid-Nineteenth-Century Philadelphia

Cities . . . change over time. The Colonial city of Philadelphia, with a population of about 24,000 on the eve of the Revolution, has little in common with the booming industrial city of 1860 which contained more than half a million people. . . . Colonial Philadelphia was a walking city extending from the Delaware River to Seventh Street, from South to Vine. All parts of the city, and the rich farm lands on the outskirts, were within easy walking distance. Artisan, businessman, and day laborer all lived close together and worked in or near their residences. They met each other on the street and frequented the same taverns. By 1860 over half a million people (about 30 percent foreign-born) lived crowded together in a city which covered more than six square miles. . . . No longer was it possible to walk across the city. . . . No longer could most people live and work in the same neighborhood. . . . The process of residential segregation and the desertion of the center city by the wealthy had begun.

SOURCE: Allan F. Davis, "Introduction," in *The Peoples of Philadelphia: A History of Ethnic Groups and Lower-Class Life, 1790–1940*, ed. Allan F. Davis and Mark H. Haller (Philadelphia: Temple University Press, 1973), 6.

* * * * *

The three decades between the death of Bishop White and the end of the Civil War saw a huge increase in both the number of immigrants and their countries of origin, a fractious divide between abolitionists and those who supported slavery, the remaking of the boundaries of the city itself, the rise of nativist parties and the resulting Know-Nothing riots, growing demands by blacks to be treated as equals in the church and in society, and the emergence of Philadelphia as a major industrial center.

Echoes of the Oxford Movement

In the nineteenth century, many Christian denominations were looking for ways to clarify their teachings on salvation. Episcopalians taught that salvation was assured by baptism, which established a covenant relationship with God, and by good works, which were the true sign of individual renewal. They therefore had no need for the predestination of Calvinists or the conversion experience of evangelicals.[1]

After Bishop White's death in 1836, the future of the Episcopal Church lay somewhere between evangelicals and high churchmen. According to the historian S. D. McConnell, "The line of cleavage did not run sharply through the mass. The two contrasted principles mingled in varying proportions in individuals. The same man might, and often did, embrace them both. He held to the conscious religious life with the Evangelical, and dreamed of ecclesiastical empire with the High Churchmen."[2] When action seemed necessary, however, party lines were drawn. The General Convention of 1844 witnessed an especially heated debate, spurred by the tractarian movement.

The Oxford Movement, which took its name from the Tracts for the Times, ninety tracts written at Oxford, mainly by John Henry Newman, John Keble, and Edward Pusey, and published between 1833 and 1841, emphasized the points that the Church of England had in common with Roman Catholicism, with the goal of reclaiming the Catholic theological and devotional heritage of the church.[3] Tractarians wished to reconcile Roman Catholic dogma with the Thirty-Nine Articles of the Church of England. This caused an uproar among the evangelicals, but it also conflicted with the traditional high-church emphasis on apostolic order and authority in the Church of England.[4]

By rejecting the Episcopal understanding of the renewed life and the baptismal covenant, the Oxford Movement also disrupted the essential agreement about the assurance of salvation that had marked the previous decades of the nineteenth century. Many first-generation adherents of the movement converted to Roman Catholicism when they felt that their beliefs were being met with hostility. After the war, however, most second-generation adherents of the Oxford Movement stayed within the Episcopal Church. Their views, and the reaction of the evangelicals to those views, ended the theological consensus of the first three quarters of the century and eventually opened the door to the broader theological pluralism that would mark later Episcopalianism.

These differences in emphasis took on added significance because this was the period of Protestant revivalism. The high-church emphasis on baptism put more value on that sacrament than did other Protestants, thus stressing the distinctiveness of Episcopalian doctrine, while the evangelical emphasis on renewal was more in keeping with the broader Protestant preoccupation with the faith of the individual believer. In addition, the Oxford Movement's emphasis on feeling resonated with the romantic movement of the day and with evangelical Protestantism.[5]

At the General Convention of 1844, the evangelicals wanted what they saw as the errors of tractarianism condemned, but "they failed to convince the House of Deputies that Anglican theological standards were actually threatened by the movement," in the words of Hein and Shattuck. The House of Bishops did, however, issue a pastoral letter affirming the Episcopalian belief in the Protestant doctrine of justification by faith and condemning the Roman Catholic doctrine of transubstantiation.[6]

* * * * *

Bishop Alonzo Potter

The child of a Quaker upbringing, Bishop Potter had a strong sense of social concern. After college, he moved to Philadelphia, where he was baptized by Bishop White; he eventually studied for the ministry under Dr. Samuel H. Turner and was ordained at the age of twenty-four. In 1826 he became rector of St. Paul's Church in Boston; the church had been founded a few years before at the end of the Unitarian controversy. It was meant to embody a "vital type of orthodoxy" and to be a "refuge for those who desired the security offered by a fixed creed and uniform Liturgy, and yet would hear the truths which they embodied proclaimed from the pulpit with pungency and power." The year after his consecration, Bishop Potter established the western and northeastern convocations of his diocese. The bishop worked for the establishment of the Hospital of the Protestant Episcopal Church and the Philadelphia Divinity School. An advocate of temperance, Bishop Potter was also an opponent of slavery. The editor and author of several collections of sermons and lectures, he traveled to Europe for his health in 1858; while sailing from New York to California, he died onboard a ship in San Francisco harbor on July 4, 1865.

SOURCE: M. A. DeWolfe Howe, *Memoirs of the Life and Services of the Rt. Rev. Alonzo Potter, DD, LL.D* (Philadelphia: J. B. Lippincott, 1871), 18–20, 24.

* * * * *

Bishop White had been succeeded by a high churchman, Henry Ustick Onderdonk of New York, but the divisions remained deep. At the General Convention of 1844, changes were made in the trial procedures so that a bishop who confessed his guilt could avoid such proceedings. It was also decided that the resignation of a bishop required the consent of the House of Bishops. Bishop Onderdonk of Philadelphia was one of the first bishops to resign under this system, rather than face a trial on charges of drunkenness.[7] After Onderdonk's resignation in 1844, the choice of Alonzo Potter, a moderate, as his successor created an atmosphere in which improvement seemed possible.[8]

Bishop Potter was considered one who could reconcile various factions in the church. The bishop was elected largely by supporters of Onderdonk, but also by others who found him, in the words of his biographer, "large-minded and large-hearted, holding his own opinions frankly, kindly, tolerantly—a man from whom others could differ without incurring his utter distrust and condemnation; a Low Churchman indeed, but no partisan; an earnest, Evangelical Christian, but no self-righteous and proscriptive zealot."[9]

At the General Convention of 1847, Bishop Potter, lamenting a clergyman who went over to Rome, warned against an "overfond pursuit of what calls itself Catholic," thereby rejecting the "very first principles of true Catholicism." Potter called for an immersion in the "broad and comprehensive principles" on which the Reformation and the Anglican Church were based and called all to "be tolerant of diversities in doctrine and practice." Potter felt that Rome remained superstitious, still falling into the very errors that the first generation of reformers had rejected. He urged that externals avoid both "pomp and pageantry" and "slovenly negligence."

FIGURE 5.1 Bishop Alonzo Potter

Sacraments should be balanced by preaching, and personal zeal was more important than "doubtful theories of priestly authority." People should be empowered to think and to read the scriptures while maintaining respect for authority.[10]

The Muhlenberg Memorial

At the General Convention of 1853, a group led by the Reverend William Augustus Muhlenberg, a Philadelphia native then living in New York, introduced what became known as the Muhlenberg Memorial. It urged relaxation of obligatory rubrics and greater flexibility and variety in the liturgy. Muhlenberg has been described as the most influential Episcopal priest of the mid-nineteenth century.[11] Greatly influenced by the Oxford Movement, Muhlenberg dubbed his approach evangelical Catholicism, a sort of overlay of Anglo-Catholic usages onto a moderate evangelical theology. The Muhlenberg group also raised questions about the relationship of the Episcopal Church to the pressing social issues of the time. "Muhlenberg and his colleagues feared that internal dissension caused by the ongoing conflict between the high church and evangelical Episcopalians was starting to hinder the mission" of the church.[12] In a pamphlet titled *What the Memorialists Want*, written in 1856, Muhlenberg claimed that "all they asked for was a greater degree of liturgical freedom within the Church."[13]

In addition to more flexibility in worship and prayer book services, the Muhlenberg group recommended the recruitment of clergy in other denominations who were open to being ordained by Episcopal bishops but who would not be required to follow all the customs and rules of the Episcopal Church. "An ecumenical gesture like that would not only extend the reach of the Episcopal Church but also represent a major step toward effecting the union of all Protestants in the United States," writes historian Robert Bruce Mullin.[14]

According to McConnell, the main objective of the Muhlenberg Memorial was "the emancipation of the Episcopate." Rome was subject to the Pope; England was subject to the state; America was bound by the Protestant Episcopal sect. It needed to be more open, more "catholic." Muhlenberg supporters also felt that the liturgy (which they themselves loved) was bound by too much required uniformity and needed to be adaptable to parish needs. They also wished to revive the order of permanent deacons, which would allow a place in church ministry for less educated men. "The ultimate object toward which all their aims pointed was the Unity of

Protestant Christendom."[15] The goals espoused by Muhlenberg and his followers give evidence of a yearning for a new broad-church movement, a movement that could heal divisions between high-church supporters and evangelicals and, ultimately, unite all Christians into one church that honored both Catholic and Protestant traditions and roots.

Bishop Potter championed the memorial and formed a committee to study it. The committee recommended the practice of extemporaneous preaching; the use of traveling evangelists; the ministry of women in some sort of sisterhood; greater attention to the education of the young; the rigorous training of candidates for the ministry; more congregational participation in services; an increase in ecumenism; the separation of the litany and morning prayer from the Communion service; and the adoption of some special prayers. The bishop advised that each diocese be allowed to decide the terms of admitting Protestant ministers into the ministry and to explore the idea of a permanent diaconate. He urged that congregations have the freedom to use the established liturgy or not.[16] Because the document represented the evangelical viewpoint, however, it was resisted by high-church clergy. Despite several years of discussion, the Muhlenberg Memorial was dropped after the General Convention of 1858. Although the movement had no immediate effect, it did set the stage for later changes.[17]

Architecture and New Churches

The Oxford Movement was also echoed in the architectural plans for churches designed and built in Philadelphia during this period. The churches were part of the broader growth of architecture in the city. An article in New York's *United States Gazette* on April 18, 1836, had this to say about Philadelphia's buildings: "The best architectural taste in the country is found at Philadelphia, as her public buildings make manifest."[18]

As the nineteenth century progressed, wealthy Philadelphians gradually moved westward, settling west of Broad Street and south of Market Street. Walnut Street was especially desirable. New churches, like John Notman's Gothic Revival St. Mark's, in the 1600 block of Locust Street, and St. Clement's on Twentieth Street north of Market, which Russell Weigley describes as "the second of [Notman's] temples to High Church Anglicanism," began to appear.[19]

The original Gothic style had been a product of medieval culture, and since Christianity was, in the words of George B. Tatum, "the one

FIGURE 5.2 St. James the Less, Philadelphia, completed in 1850 and said to be modeled after St. Michael's Church, Long Staunton, Cambridgeshire, England

factor which, more than any other, separated the Middle Ages from the Ancient World . . . it was inevitable that nineteenth-century architecture would find in the Gothic style one of the most fruitful sources for the designs of churches."[20] So the design of some of the period's most architecturally outstanding churches, reflecting a return to the Gothic style in England, resulted from a resurgence of interest in medieval liturgy and construction.[21]

This Gothic Revival encouraged the belief that the past was superior to the present. The preference for an earlier style, seen as closer to the original doctrines, was embraced especially by Roman Catholics and Anglo-Catholics. According to Donald Egbert, although Episcopal churches with Gothic details had been built prior to 1836, it was the publication in that year of John Henry Hopkins's *Essay on Gothic Architecture*, the first publication devoted wholly to the style, that influenced the architecture of many new Episcopal churches. Egbert sees here the influence of the Oxford Movement.[22]

The Church of St. James the Less (1846–50), at Clearfield Street and Hunting Park Avenue, was commissioned for the growing community of mill families and summer residents in the Falls of Schuylkill section of

FIGURE 5.3 St. James the Less, interior

Philadelphia. The English Cambridge Camden Society, founded in 1836, advocated proper Gothic design and construction, and architects Robert Ralston and John Carver consulted drawings of a thirteenth-century English parish church. St. James's became a model for many other Gothic Revival churches in America. According to architectural historian John Gallery, "it remains unsurpassed for the authenticity and completeness with which it interpreted the English model."[23]

St. Mark's Church (1848–51), a brownstone building at 1625 Locust Street designed by John Notman, is, in Theodore B. White's opinion, "one of the most successful examples of the archaeological phase of the Gothic Revival in this country, and the best of the period in Philadelphia."[24] St. Mark's, according to Gallery, was "founded with the express purpose of 'restoring Catholic worship' in the Episcopal Church. St. Mark's is rightly regarded as one of the first American churches to show the influence of the religious revival identified in England with the Camden Society and the Oxford Movement." Notman's plans were in fact sent to the Cambridge Camden Society in England for approval. Notman left some of the capitals on the piers uncarved as a symbolic reminder that the church's work is never done.[25]

Philadelphia's Floating Church of the Redeemer, set up by the Destitute Sailors' Asylum on Dock Street on the Delaware River, and modeled

FIGURE 5.4 Holy Trinity, Rittenhouse Square, Philadelphia, designed by John Notman and completed in 1859

after London's "floating church," provided Anglican services for seamen. Built in 1849, the wooden church was designed by Clement L. Dennington. Usually moored at the foot of Dock Street, the church served the seamen in the port of Philadelphia. The church, ninety feet long, thirty feet wide, and seating about five hundred people, rested on the hulls of two boats placed ten feet apart. The Floating Church was an example of the "rural Gothic" or "carpenter's Gothic" style, which used more modest wooden structures for parishes without funds. "So famous was Philadelphia's floating church," Tatum writes, "that a model of it was exhibited in the American Section at the Great Exhibition at London in 1851."[26]

At the same time that the Gothic Revival style became popular, a Romanesque Revival was also evident in the United States. The Romanesque style retained Roman features like the rounded arch and a considerable massiveness. Egbert points to Trinity Episcopal Church in Boston, built between 1873 and 1877, as an influential example of this style, but Philadelphia's Church of the Holy Trinity represents an earlier Romanesque plan.[27]

The Church of the Holy Trinity (1857–59), on Rittenhouse Square at Nineteenth and Walnut streets and designed by John Notman, has a Romanesque façade.[28] The church is one of the first accurate renditions of the Romanesque style in the country. The interior is relatively simple, in keeping with the simple service of the low church. St. Timothy's Protestant Episcopal Church (1862–66), designed by Emlen T. Littell and Charles Burns and located at 5720 Ridge Avenue, was meant to be a handsome country parish church set within a walled churchyard. The church is built in the high Victorian Gothic style.[29]

Blacks and Their Churches

The role of the church in the lives of black people in the nineteenth century cannot be overstated. In the words of W. E. B. Du Bois, "The church really represented all that was left of African tribal life, and was the sole expression of the organized efforts of the slaves."[30] The black church thus became a key institution for Philadelphia's Negro population. Religion offered spiritual sustenance and the promise of a better life in the next world for oppressed people. The churches also offered an avenue to organization in other areas, such as politics and economic issues, and some life in a society that virtually shut them out. Black Protestantism grew rapidly; about 7 percent of churchgoing blacks were Episcopalian.[31]

In 1796 the African Episcopal Church of St. Thomas, with Absalom Jones as its first minister, had become the first legally incorporated Negro church in the United States. St. Thomas's had offered itself to the Episcopal Church at its founding and had been accepted on the condition that the members take no part in the government of the general church. In 1849, attempts to gain full recognition in the church began with a demand for delegates to the General Convention. It took fifteen years; the Negro congregation was not received into full fellowship until 1864. Du Bois remarked that the membership of St. Thomas's consisted of the most cultured and wealthy blacks in the city. Noting that black churches acted as centers of social interaction to a greater degree than white churches, Du Bois described the members of St. Thomas's as affluent, well educated, and well bred, but "rather cold and reserved to strangers or newcomers."[32]

By the 1850s there were two independent black Episcopal churches, St. Thomas's and the Church of the Crucifixion at Eighth and Bainbridge streets. Crucifixion was especially active in outreach work, including the Fresh Air Fund, a vacation school, parish visitors, university extension courses, an insurance society, a Home for the Homeless on Lombard Street, and special care for the neglected poor.[33]

In 1862 the black Episcopalian minister William Douglass gathered membership lists, records of births and baptisms, the minutes of church committees, and the recollections of older parishioners, and wrote a documentary history of Absalom Jones and St. Thomas's called *Annals of the First African Church in the United States of America, Now Styled the African Church of St. Thomas.*[34]

During this period, Richard Allen and his followers founded Bethel African Methodist Episcopal Church at Sixth and Lombard streets. In this way, the city's free black community founded the first independent black denomination in the country.[35]

Slavery and Abolition

Historians of nineteenth-century Philadelphia nearly always observe that Philadelphia was, in general, opposed to abolition. It was in fact seen as the most anti-Negro, anti-abolition city in the North, if not in the entire country. Allan F. Davis, for example, observes that "of all northern cities, none treated abolitionists and blacks worse than did Philadelphia."[36] Philadelphia had segregated schools, churches, libraries, and voluntary associations. It supported the Fugitive Slave Act of 1850. It disenfranchised black men.[37]

After the 1830s, few clergymen preached against slavery. The Reverend Benjamin Dorr's Christ Church congregation, for example, stayed out of the abolition debate for the most part, focusing instead on more tradition methods of outreach.[38] Pierce Butler, a vestryman of the Episcopal Church of the Epiphany, owned more than nine hundred slaves on St. Simon's and

Butler islands in Georgia. When his minister, Rev. Dudley Tyng, did speak out against slavery in 1856, Butler led the parishioners in driving Tyng from the pulpit.[39]

Another fearless advocate of abolition was Rev. Phillips Brooks, the rector at the Episcopal Church of the Holy Trinity on Rittenhouse Square from 1862 to 1869 and perhaps the greatest preacher in the history of the Episcopal Church. A theological liberal, Brooks believed in each person's goodness and potential for spiritual growth, preferring this approach to an emphasis on sinfulness. He also considered ethical behavior more important than orthodoxy and insisted that faith play a part in one's daily life. Brooks became known as a steadfast voice in the fight for emancipation, and later for the right of the former slaves to vote.[40]

Philadelphians did not generally believe that the controversy over slavery would lead to a civil war. The city also retained a deep attachment to the South. Politically, the Republicans were the antislavery party. The Democrats were officially neutral but tended to support slavery. In the presidential election of 1856, the Democratic candidate, James Buchanan, from Lancaster, Pennsylvania, won 53 percent of the Philadelphia vote. His election was seen as a rejection of the antislavery movement. Philadelphians were not willing to agitate the South, and they had little time for blacks.[41]

White Episcopalians in Philadelphia regarded the outbreak of the war with great ambivalence, hoping they could keep the disaster at a distance. According to Episcopal Church historians David Hein and Gardiner H. Shattuck, "the Civil War challenged the institutional fabric of Anglicanism in America. Like the American Revolution, it revealed how estranged many of the church's clerical leaders were from the mainstream."[42] Phillips Brooks accused his fellow Episcopalians of dragging their feet, as if they were unsure "whether there was a war going on or not, and whether if there was it would be safe for them to say so."[43]

It took time, but by 1861 Philadelphians seemed to come to the realization that their historic heritage demanded support of the Union, even if that meant acknowledging the equality of blacks.[44] So Philadelphians in general came to support the war, but they did so primarily to preserve the unity of the nation born in their own city, and not primarily to free the slaves. William Meredith, a member of Christ Church, helped found the Union League as a "refuge of loyalty," to show that some of Philadelphia's first families supported the war. Like Philadelphia as a whole, however, the membership of Christ Church was divided on slavery and the war.[45]

* * * * *

The Union League

Many other public buildings of architectural interest went up in this period. The Union League Club, an ornate structure in red brick and brownstone designed by John Fraser and located at Broad and Sansom (built in 1865, with additions in 1910–11), is mentioned here because of its connection to the ambivalent attitude of many Philadelphians as the South moved toward secession and the nation moved toward civil war. The Union League was one of many political clubs organized during the Civil War; it was an outgrowth of the Union Club, organized by a group of aristocrats to raise funds and recruit troops for the Union. The building, in the French Renaissance style then popular, with a curving exterior stairway, tower, and mansard roof, was one of the few erected in Philadelphia during the war; it is an early example of the Second Empire style.

* * * * *

In 1861, in the aftermath of the South's secession, southern Episcopalians established the Protestant Episcopal Church in the Confederate States of America. Its constitution, canons, prayer book, and organization "almost exactly mirrored" those of the church in the North. As Hein and Shattuck point out, however, when its members held their first General Council in November of the following year, they made clear their conviction that slavery played a "crucial role in the moral and religious elevation of the people of Africa."[46] The southern churches supplied chaplains for Confederate troops, but they also continued their ministry to the slaves. Their commitment to their work among the slaves was explicit: "Slaves of the South are not merely so much property," read the journals of the southern church, "but are a sacred trust committed to us, as a people, to be prepared for the work which God may have for them to do, in the future."[47]

The General Convention of the now truncated national church met in 1862, shortly after the Union victory at Antietam and Abraham Lincoln's Emancipation Proclamation, but "neither the House of Bishops nor the House of Deputies believed it wise to comment on those events," according to Hein and Shattuck. The bishops supported the Union as private citizens but remained neutral as church officials. The general trend among evangelicals was to favor abolition and oppose slavery, while the high-church tendency was to view abolitionists with suspicion.[48]

The slavery controversy caused no lasting division in the Episcopal Church. Northern evangelicals who opposed slavery were far outnumbered by high churchmen and southern evangelicals who either remained neutral or supported slavery. No resolution condemning slavery could possibly have succeeded at a General Convention.

The General Convention of 1862 also took a diplomatic approach to the war. While it did not want to alienate the South, members did want to express loyalty to the Union. Not wishing to condemn the secessionists, but fearing the evil that could result from permanent secession, the convention adopted a resolution setting apart a day of "fasting, humiliation, and prayer for the ills of the nation." The members observed that "to hate rebellion, so uncaused, is duty; but to hate those engaged therein, is the opposite of Christian duty."[49]

The southern denomination had dissolved soon after the Union victory, and the presiding bishop, John Henry Hopkins, invited bishops Henry C. Lay of Arkansas and Thomas Atkinson of North Carolina to attend the General Convention of 1865, held in Philadelphia. No resolution offering thanks for the Union victory was offered; "the assembly followed Hopkins's irenic approach and adopted a statement simply thanking God for the return of peace and the prospective restoration of unity within the church."

Racial and Religious Riots

Historian Michael Feldberg has characterized the period from 1835 to 1850 as the most violent in Philadelphia history. In addition to anti-Negro, anti-abolitionist, and anti-Catholic riots, tradesmen like the weavers turned labor strikes into pitched battles. But Feldberg also points out that violence already had a long history as a political tool in Philadelphia, as it did in other cities. Skilled workmen considered it their right to defend their territory, and the threat of physical harm was often used as a political bargaining chip.[50] And as Philadelphia came to terms with the Industrial Revolution, there were multiple causes for the increased violence, among them the explosive growth in population, an uneasy mixture of people with differing racial, ethnic, and religious backgrounds, a lack of adequate housing, and an uneven distribution of wealth, as well as political mischief.[51]

The first serious racial attack occurred in November 1829. It was reportedly caused by a "loud and emotional" church service, but, as Nash points out, whites had rioted two months earlier to protest lectures by feminist abolitionist Fanny Wright on racial equality. A dozen years later, on August 1, 1842, the Negro Young Men's Vigilant Association paraded to commemorate the emancipation of slaves in the British West Indies in 1834. The parade was attacked, and a riot broke out that went on for two days. The Second African Presbyterian Church and Smith Beneficial Hall, used for educational, moral, literary, and religious programs, were razed. The marchers were eventually blamed and charged with inciting the whites by presuming to use public space. Later, Moyamensing Township ordered the New Temperance Hall torn down, purportedly out of fear that it could not be protected from arsonists.[52]

Catholics were the targets of the American Republican Party, a nativist organization founded in Philadelphia in 1837 in response to economic instability and the arrival of thousands of Irish Catholics. An even larger influx of Irish followed the potato famine of 1846–47. Most Irish immigrants had lived in rural areas back home, and now they found themselves thrust into an urban setting. The Irish arrived during Philadelphia's period of great industrial and population growth, just before consolidation and not long before the Civil War. These immigrants took advantage of the new economic opportunities, founding building-and-loan associations and even acquiring property. To serve their religious needs, some twenty-four Catholic churches were built between 1840 and 1870, in the city and its outlying districts.[53]

In response to this inrush of southern Irish "popery," Philadelphia became home to one of the largest anti-Catholic movements in the country. Philadelphia's Protestant revivalism made it a "major operating base" for the so-called Protestant crusade. In 1842 the American Protestant Association, a coalition of fifty Philadelphia clergymen, entered into ideological warfare on "popery," hoping to combat Catholicism's growing presence. As Jay P. Dolan observes, "students at the University of Pennsylvania believed that nativists were justified in burning the homes of their Catholic neighbors during the Bible riots of 1844."[54] Among the influential congregations represented in the association was St. Paul's Protestant Episcopal Church and its preacher, Stephen Tyng.[55]

In 1850 the American Party was founded by men who deemed Catholicism incompatible with America's democratic government. Because members were advised by party leaders to say "I know nothing" when asked about their organization, their opponents dubbed the group the Know-Nothing Party, and the name stuck.

After the Act of Consolidation of 1854 was passed, Know-Nothing support helped the nativist Robert L. Conrad to become the first mayor of

FIGURE 5.5 Anti-Catholic rioting in Philadelphia, July 1844

the newly configured city of Philadelphia. Conrad vowed to recruit nine hundred men, all of American birth, as policemen. Conrad also influenced the Sunday "blue laws," which banned a host of economic and social activities on the Christian Sabbath. In fact, many of the police later called in to quiet scuffles were themselves former gang members. "The early police specialized in legalized violence as their weapon against the unlegalized kind," Weigley observes.[56]

The Role of Women

The women of Christ Church ran successful Sunday schools and sponsored a parochial day school both to instill church discipline and to see to it that poor children learned to read. These women carried on many fund-raising activities and engaged in projects like the Ladies' Missionary Associations. As a monument to Bishop White, a *free* church, considered revolutionary and unorthodox at the time, was established in the Northern Liberties section of Philadelphia. The cornerstone of Calvary Monumental Church was laid in 1851 and the building was completed the following year; a school was built next to the church.[57]

By the 1830s, women had taken over the Magdalen Society of Philadelphia as well. The Magdalen Society Asylum had been founded in Philadelphia early in the nineteenth century, and Bishop White was one of the leaders involved with the asylum. The goal was to help women who had "been seduced from the paths of virtue, and [were] desirous of returning to a life of rectitude."[58] The Magdalen system had its roots in Victorian England but flourished in eighteenth- and nineteenth-century Ireland, where countless women were forced to do laundry in convents overseen by religious women like the Good Shepherd Sisters. While the system is now rightly seen as a form of "cruel and unjust punishment," it is also true that there were few options open to women at the time.[59]

The original Philadelphia asylum was on North Twentieth Street, now the site of the Franklin Institute Science Museum's Futures Center. Lu Ann DeCunzo observes that this put it on the outskirts of the city, effectively separating the women from their former lives and identities. Eventually, a thirteen-foot wall was built around the property, and a new building was built in the 1840s. DeCunzo contrasts the living conditions in the Magdalen building with those of Bishop's White's home. Ultimately, the Philadelphia Magdalen Society became the White-Williams Foundation, which encourages high school students to complete their education.[60]

Both the Quaker Lucretia Mott and the Episcopalian Sarah Josepha Hall came to Philadelphia in the early nineteenth century. Hall arrived in 1841, but her interest in women's suffrage was not linked to the cause of abolition, as it was with Mott. Hall became the editor of *Godey's Lady's Book*, a popular women's magazine of the period. Although the magazine dealt only with traditional "women's issues," such as child care, furniture, and fashion, Hall did advocate education and intellectual respect for women. She promoted the Female Medical College of Pennsylvania, founded in 1850 as the first medical school for women in the country.[61]

The women of Christ Church founded the Dorcas Society in 1859. The society took its name from the story of Dorcas, or Tabitha, found in the ninth chapter of the book of Acts. Dorcas was a widow in Jappa who was completely occupied with good deeds and almsgiving. Among other things, she made tunics and cloaks. When she died, the people were so distraught that they begged for help from Peter, who raised her from the dead. The women of the Dorcas Society provided clothing for the poor and worked hard to provide for the soldiers. They made clothing but also sent other necessities, like tobacco, that the men could not afford.[62]

An Era of Reform

In the mid-1800s America saw a wave of spiritual commitment, which often expressed itself through social reform. Philadelphia, despite its reputation for racial and religious prejudice and accompanying mob violence, was one of the major centers of this movement, which stressed the perfection of society and the individual.[63]

This impetus to reform reflected the broader social and religious movements sweeping the nation in the mid-nineteenth century. After the Second Great Awakening, revivalists linked social reform with the need to hasten the coming of the new Kingdom of God. Utopian societies, like New Harmony in Illinois and Brook Farm in Massachusetts, emerged, as did religious groups like the Shakers and the Mormons. Reform issues included religious and secular education, temperance, crime and the penal system, care for the sick and needy, attention to orphans and the deaf, and many more.[64]

In 1847 a group of Philadelphia women founded the Rosine Association. It rejected the reform program of the Magdalen Society, blaming its ineffectiveness on the men in charge. The founders of the Rosine Association believed that only women could truly care for other women. The association determined that women needed marketable skills and training in household management, so their approach included education and even some free time, with no emphasis on moral regeneration.[65] Eventually, the Magdalen Society followed the lead of the Rosine Association and changed its approach in turn.

The years between 1846 and 1850 saw the revitalization of the Episcopal Academy at Juniper and Locust streets. The academy had been founded in 1785 by Bishop White at the old Christ Church as an all-boys school; it was originally located on the east side of Fourth Street. In 1798 the academy was reconstituted as a free school. After other changes, the school was reconstituted again in 1846 as the Third Classical Academy, moving to the building at Juniper and Locust in 1850. The academy moved again, to Merion, in 1921.[66]

Concerned about the gangs in Moyamensing, Bishop Alonzo Potter attempted to get their members into night schools. This led to the establishment of the Young Men's Institute and Spring Garden Institute in 1850.[67]

Founded in 1858, the Philadelphia Divinity School was respected for its pioneering efforts in the study of pastoral theology. The school was among the first Episcopal seminaries to admit black students, even allowing them to live on campus. It was also a pioneer in training women for ministry. In 1974 the school merged with the Episcopal Theological School in Cambridge, Massachusetts, to form the Episcopal Divinity School in that city. The Philadelphia Divinity School's campus, bounded by Forty-second and Forty-third streets and Locust and Spruce streets, is now part of the University of Pennsylvania.

The Episcopal Church also established three hospitals during this period. Episcopal Hospital at Lehigh Avenue and Front Street, which opened in 1852, was designed by Samuel Sloan. Those who describe the hospital's architecture as in the "Norman style" overlook the plan's Renaissance balance and regularity. Sloan modeled his parallel pavilions on the Hôpital Lariboisière in Paris.

Christ Church Hospital was established near Bala Cynwyd in 1861. The matron was charged by the board with running the hospital like a Christian family, caring for all patients with equal patience and dignity. And the Hospital of the Protestant Episcopal Church was established in 1852 on property bequeathed to the church by the Leamy family. Originally housed in the Leamy mansion, the hospital soon outgrew its space, and a new building was completed in 1862, just in time to admit the many soldiers wounded in the Civil War. A total of 705 Union soldiers were treated at the hospital, of whom only thirty-three died.

Conclusions

Like the rest of the nation, Philadelphia's Episcopal Church found itself in a period of ferment at the end of the war. It had weathered debates over war and peace, slavery and abolition, high and low church, the place of black congregations, and the relationship between the Episcopal Church and other denominations. During the period covered in this chapter, some sixty-four churches were added to the diocese, and institutions such as the Episcopal Academy were revived.[68] The connection between high and low forms of worship and architectural styles became clear: medieval churches instilled medieval sentiments.[69]

Before leaving on what would be his final voyage, Bishop Potter prepared his address for the General Convention of 1865. The address was delivered after his death and closed with the bishop's "strong confidence" about the future of the diocese and the church:

> Whatsoever may be the appointments of the Most High in regard to any human life, I feel an abiding, yea, a strong confidence, brethren, that if you look to God, your Parishes and this Diocese will be visited with larger and yet larger manifestations of his favor. Institutions which are now in their infancy will gather might from year to year. Their foundations will be deepened and consolidated, their structures shall widen and mount upward. Kindred institutions of

> different names shall rise to attest your thoughtful zeal and your unstinted and unresting liberality. The benediction of the sanctifying spirit and of a gracious Providence shall rest upon your persons and your families, and you shall own that God, even our God, is your refuge and strength.[70]

One of the effects of the Civil War was the breakdown of the sectarian isolation of the Episcopal Church. Wounded soldiers were nursed by Roman Catholic sisters. Soldiers prayed with ministers of other denominations. The world became "bigger" for many people. The restlessness of the broader society had an impact on the churches. A new interest in evolution and historical criticism was taking hold. The westward movement was in full swing. "The 'Church Idea,'" as McConnell writes, "was to be infused with American Protestantism. The task of the memorialists was to be taken up again, and the Liturgy revised to fit the exigencies of common life. The idea of a mechanical uniformity was to be unconsciously forsaken. The Episcopate was to break from its trammels, and proclaim to the divided Christian world the Church's hope and plan for Unity."[71] Like the nation, the Episcopal Church was poised on the edge of a challenging and unknown future.

NOTES

1. Robert W. Prichard, *The Nature of Salvation: Theological Consensus in the Episcopal Church, 1801–73* (Urbana: University of Illinois Press, 1997), 1. Chapter 6 of Prichard's book, "The End of an Era," gives a comprehensive summary of the Oxford Movement as it began in England and then was received in the United States.

2. S. D. McConnell, *History of the American Episcopal Church, from the Planting of the Colonies to the End of the Civil War* (New York: Thomas Whittaker, 1890), 320.

3. David Hein and Gardiner H. Shattuck Jr., *The Episcopalians* (Westport, Conn.: Praeger, 2004), 70.

4. Ibid.; Deborah Mathias Gough, *Christ Church, Philadelphia: The Nation's Church in a Changing City* (Philadelphia: University of Pennsylvania Press, 1995), 226.

5. Hein and Shattuck, *Episcopalians*, 71; Prichard, *Nature of Salvation*, 4, 19.

6. Hein and Shattuck, *Episcopalians*, 71.

7. Raymond W. Albright, *A History of the Protestant Episcopal Church* (New York: Macmillan, 1964), 241.

8. Gough, *Christ Church, Philadelphia*, 213.

9. M. A. DeWolfe Howe, *Memoirs of the Life and Services of the Rt. Rev. Alonzo Potter, DD, LL.D* (Philadelphia: J. B. Lippincott, 1871), 104.

10. *JDC 1845*, 63, 46.

11. Hein and Shattuck, *Episcopalians*, 255.

12. "Muhlenberg Memorial, 1853," in *Documents of Witnesses: A History of the Episcopal Church, 1782–1985*, ed. Don S. Armentrout and Robert Boak Slocum (New York: Church Hymnal Corporation, 1994), 209–10, quoted in Hein and Shattuck, *Episcopalians*, 74.

13. Quoted in William Wilson Manross, *A History of the American Episcopal Church* (New York: Morehouse, 1935), 285–86.

14. Robert Bruce Mullin, *Episcopal Vision/American Reality: Theological and Social Thought in Evangelical America* (New Haven: Yale University Press, 1986), 181–82, quoted in Hein and Shattuck, *Episcopalians*, 74.

15. McConnell, *History of the American Episcopal Church*, 348–50.

16. Ibid., 350–51.

17. Hein and Shattuck, *Episcopalians*, 75; William Sydnor, *The Story of the Real Prayer Book, 1549–1979* (Wilton, Conn.: Morehouse, 1989), 61.

18. Quoted in Nicholas B. Wainwright, "The Age of Nicholas Biddle, 1825–1841," in *Philadelphia: A 300-Year History*, ed. Russell F. Weigley (New York: W. W. Norton, 1982), 284.

19. Russell F. Weigley, "The Border City in Civil War, 1854–1865," *Philadelphia*, ed. Weigley, 382. See also Elizabeth M. Geffen, "Industrial Development and Social Crisis, 1841–1854," in the same volume, 310–11.

20. George B. Tatum, *Penn's Great Town: 250 Years of Philadelphia Architecture Illustrated in Prints and Drawings* (Philadelphia: University of Pennsylvania Press, 1961), 81; see also Theodore B. White, *Philadelphia Architecture in the Nineteenth Century* (Philadelphia: University of Pennsylvania Press, 1953), 26.

21. John Andrew Gallery, *Philadelphia Architecture: A Guide to the City* (Cambridge: MIT Press, 1984), 4.

22. Donald Drew Egbert, "Religious Expression in American Architecture," in *Religious Perspectives in American Culture*, ed. James Ward Smith and A. Leland Jamison (Princeton: Princeton University Press, 1961), 387–89.

23. Gallery, *Philadelphia Architecture*, 51.

24. White, *Philadelphia Architecture in the Nineteenth Century*, 28.

25. Gallery, *Philadelphia Architecture*, 52; see also Tatum, *Penn's Great Town*, 83.

26. Tatum, *Penn's Great Town*, 83; see also White, *Philadelphia Architecture in the Nineteenth Century*, 28. In New York, the Seamen's Church Institute was founded in 1834 to minister to merchant seamen. In 1844 floating chapels were launched on the East River for the benefit of sailors who were less comfortable on dry land. Although the floating chapels have disappeared, the institute continues its work to this day.

27. Egbert, "Religious Expression in American Architecture," 390–91.

28. White, *Philadelphia Architecture in the Nineteenth Century*, 29.

29. Gallery, *Philadelphia Architecture*, 58, 60.

30. W. E. B. Du Bois, *The Philadelphia Negro: A Social Study* (Philadelphia: University of Pennsylvania Press, 1899), 197.

31. Theodore Hershberg, "Free Blacks in Antebellum Philadelphia," in *The Peoples of Philadelphia: A History of Ethnic Groups and Lower-Class Life, 1790–1940*, ed. Allan F. Davis and Mark H. Haller (Philadelphia: Temple University Press, 1973), 120–21.

32. DuBois, *Philadelphia Negro*, 198, 203.

33. Ibid., 217.

34. See Gary B. Nash, *First City: Philadelphia and the Forging of Historical Memory* (Philadelphia: University of Pennsylvania Press, 2002), 149–50.

35. Steven Conn, *Metropolitan Philadelphia: Living with the Presence of the Past* (Philadelphia: University of Pennsylvania Press, 2006), 35. See also Du Bois, *Philadelphia Negro*, 199.

36. Allan F. Davis, "Introduction," in Davis and Haller, *Peoples of Philadelphia*, 10–11.

37. This information is widely available. See, for example, Gough, *Christ Church, Philadelphia*, 232–33.

38. Ibid., 233.

39. Nash, *First City*, 189, 195. Butler sold about half his slaves in the late 1850s to cover gambling debts and financial losses. See also Malcolm Bell Jr., *Major Butler's Legacy: Five Generations of a Slaveholding Family* (Athens: University of Georgia Press, 1987).

40. See http://htrit.org/phillipsbrooks.html (accessed August 12, 2006). Brooks, of course, is also remembered for writing the words to the Christmas hymn "O Little Town of Bethlehem" in 1867, following a trip to the Holy Land. See also Hein and Shattuck, *Episcopalians*, 177.

41. Weigley, "Border City in Civil War," 383–85.

42. Hein and Shattuck, *Episcopalians*, 77.

43. Quoted in Alexander V. G. Allen, *Life and Letters of Phillips Brooks*, vol. 1 (New York: E. P. Dutton, 1901), 428, cited in Hein and Shattuck, *Episcopalians*, 76–77.

44. Weigley, "Border City in Civil War," 394.

45. Gough, *Christ Church, Philadelphia*, 241–42.

46. Hein and Shattuck, *Episcopalians*, 78.

47. William A. Clesback, ed., *Journals of the Protestant Episcopal Church in the Confederate States of America* (Austin, Tex.: Church Historical Society, 1962), part 3, 266, quoted in Albright, *History of the Protestant Episcopal Church*, 252.

48. Hein and Shattuck, *Episcopalians*, 79.

49. "Muhlenberg Memorial, 1853," quoted in Hein and Shattuck, *Episcopalians*, 79. See also Robert Bruce Mullin, "Trends in the Study of the History of the Episcopal Church," *Anglican and Episcopal History* 72, no. 2 (2003): 201–5; and S. D. McConnell, *History of the American Episcopal Church, 1600–1915*, 11th ed. (New York: Morehouse, 1934), 261–69. See also Manross, *History of the American Episcopal Church*, 290–91.

50. Michael Feldberg, "Urbanization as a Cause of Violence: Philadelphia as a Test Case," in Davis and Haller, *Peoples of Philadelphia*, 55–56.

51. Geffen, "Industrial Development and Social Crisis," 307–8.

52. Nash, *First City*, 167–69.

53. Dennis J. Clark, "The Philadelphia Irish: Persistent Presence," in *Peoples of Philadelphia*, ed. Davis and Haller, 135–37.

54. Jay P. Dolan, *In Search of an American Catholicism: A History of Religion and Culture in Tension* (New York: Oxford University Press, 2002), 57.

55. Geffen, "Industrial Development and Social Crisis," 356. See also Gough, *Christ Church, Philadelphia*, 231–32. Gough notes that, at the same time, Presbyterians, Methodists, and Baptists were all growing. Revivals were becoming common: the majority of the more than 250 places of worship in Philadelphia were evangelical (231).

56. Weigley, "Border City in Civil War," 369–70.

57. Gough, *Christ Church, Philadelphia*, 236–38.

58. Magdalen Society of Philadelphia's Pact of Incorporation, sec. A1, 1802, quoted in Lu Ann DeCunzo, "Reform, Respite, Ritual: An Archaeology of Institutions; The Magdalen Society of Philadelphia, 1800–1850," *Historical Archaeology* 29, no. 2 (1995): 1.

59. The existence of the laundries in Ireland became generally known in the 1990s. The most comprehensive scholarly treatment to date is Frances Finnegan, *Do Penance or Perish: A Study of Magdalen Asylums in Ireland* (Piltdown, County Kilkenny: Congrave Press, 2001).

60. See DeCunzo, "Reform, Respite, Ritual," 50.

61. Nash, *First City*, 185.

62. Gough, *Christ Church, Philadelphia*, 242.

63. See, for example, Nash, *First City*, 176ff.

64. Greg D. Feldmeth, "U.S. History Resources," http://home.earthlink.net/~gfeldmeth/USHistory.html, March 31, 1998 (accessed April 13, 2007).

65. DeCunzo, "Reform, Respite, Ritual," 30.

66. See http://www.ea.pvt.k12.pa.us.

67. Geffen, "Industrial Development and Social Crisis," 340–41.

68. For information on these churches, see J. Wesley Twelves, *A History of the Diocese of Pennsylvania of the Protestant Episcopal Church in the U.S.A., 1784–1968* (Philadelphia: Diocese of Pennsylvania, 1969), 148–87.

69. Howe, *Memoirs of the Life and Services*, 251.

70. Quoted in ibid., 354.

71. McConnell, *History of the American Episcopal Church*, 380.

6

The Gilded Age and Progressive Era, 1865–1910

ANN NORTON GREENE

Bishop Alonzo Potter died in July 1865, while en route to California from Central America. He had been on a trip through the region, attempting to restore his worsening health. Because it took five weeks to return Potter's body to Philadelphia, it was September before a funeral could be held.[1] William Bacon Stevens, now diocesan bishop, conducted services at Christ Church and the interment at Laurel Hill Cemetery. Many of the attendees had also paid respects at Lincoln's coffin when it lay in state at Independence Hall the previous April. In the space of five months, Philadelphia Episcopalians mourned a president and a bishop. In contrast to what subsequently transpired in the national government, the transition in diocesan leadership, though sad, was smooth. Stevens had been elected assistant bishop to succeed Potter (the term "coadjutor" did not come into use until 1902), had been consecrated in early 1862, and was already handling duties in Potter's absence, including presiding over the diocesan convention in the spring of 1865.

Bishop Stevens presided over a geographically smaller diocese than his predecessors had. After several years of discussion and planning, the portion of the diocese that lay west of the Alleghenies became the Diocese of Pittsburgh in 1865. The enormous physical size of the diocese had always made oversight and visitation difficult, but the growing number of parishes to the west made it increasingly unmanageable. Stevens estimated that he had traveled eight thousand miles between the conventions of 1864 and 1865.[2] Six years after this division, the region on the eastern side of the Alleghenies became the Diocese of Central Pennsylvania, with its bishop based in Harrisburg. This move further reduced the geographical size of the Pennsylvania diocese. Finally, with the creation of the Diocese of Bethlehem in the northeastern corner of the state, the Diocese of Philadelphia acquired its current size, encompassing all of Philadelphia, Chester,

Delaware, and Montgomery counties and part of Bucks County. By 1910, after the creation of the Diocese of Erie in 1910 (now the Diocese of Northwestern Pennsylvania), the state of Pennsylvania would contain five dioceses. Western and urban development caused this process of division to occur across the American East and the upper Midwest. New York first divided in 1839, and again in 1869, to form the dioceses of Albany, central New York, and Long Island; further west, the same process of growth led to the establishment of the Diocese of Fond du Lac in 1875 and the Diocese of Central Illinois in 1877.

The changing physical borders of dioceses reflected shifts in less tangible but no less important boundaries in American society between the Civil War and World War I, a period known as the Gilded Age and the Progressive Era. Every aspect of American society altered because of rapid industrialization, and the outlines of the twentieth-century world took shape. Historian Alan Trachtenberg calls this process "the incorporation of America," because all across society, not just in the business world, there was a trend toward more institutional development, more structure and organization, and new hierarchies of power and influence.[3] In the Diocese of Philadelphia and elsewhere, the Episcopal Church tried to mediate the transition between an earlier society that was largely rural, agricultural, atomistic, homogenous, and decentralized, and an emerging society that was urban, industrial, systems-based, heterogeneous, and centralized. It underwent changes as an institution, but as it defined its role in an increasingly complex, secular, urban industrial world, the Episcopal Church became an agent of change as well.

* * * * *

The Gilded Age, the Progressive Era, and Victorian America

Historians employ these terms to describe stages of late nineteenth- and early twentieth-century American history. The "Gilded Age," a phrase coined by Mark Twain in 1873, refers to the period between the Civil War and the end of the century. With this phrase, Twain contrasted the superficial golden glitter of rapidly accumulating wealth with the dark realities of rampant political corruption and wrenching social and economic problems. The appellation, though not always entirely adequate or accurate, has stuck. Most usefully, the term "Gilded Age" describes a period when Americans experienced the dramatic material and structural transformations brought about by industrial production and business incorporation.

The Progressive Era early acquired a positive reputation in contrast to the negative image of the Gilded Age. It was a period of political reform, a time of active political response to the dislocating impact of industrialization and incorporation on democratic society. Progressivism is best understood as a mindset or attitude rather than a specific set of programs, since its adherents ranged across the political spectrum from right to left. Progressives valued efficiency, science, management, democratic reforms, and executive power. Historians date its start to 1896, with the election of McKinley, or to 1900 or 1905, coinciding with Theodore Roosevelt's presidency. The end of Progressivism varies from 1914, the outbreak of World War I in Europe, 1920, when the Republicans regained the presidency, or 1933, the start of the New Deal.

Whereas "Gilded Age" and "Progressive Era" have political, economic, and social connotations, the term "Victorian" is distinctly cultural. The reign of Queen Victoria in Great Britain, from 1837 to 1901, gives Victorianism approximate boundaries. It was a transatlantic Anglo-American phenomenon coterminous with the rise of industrial capitalism, and many of its characteristic features both celebrate and attempt to modulate the impact of industrialization on society. Victorianism denotes a self-conscious cultural style that was largely British-American, Protestant-evangelical, and middle-class in values. Victorians believed in a rational and objective social order maintained through highly disciplined personal behavior and morality, education, self-improvement, and social responsibility. Aggressively forward-looking and scientific in outlook, Victorians were also sentimental and traditional, and, concerning women, family, and sexuality, downright stuffy, often in contrast to their startlingly progressive views on other matters. Even as they laid the groundwork for modern society, Victorians were nostalgic about the medieval period, which they believed represented a stable, faith-based social order and moral code.

* * * * *

Industrialization and American Society

The term "industrialization" describes a broad process of material transformation spanning two hundred years, from the mid-eighteenth century to the mid-twentieth. At its heart lay changes in manufacturing and agricultural production, which created new combinations of machines, humans, and energy sources (water, wind, animal muscle, and steam) and achieved increases in output and in the diversity and standardization of products. These changes were facilitated and accelerated by advances in metallurgy, transportation, and communication. Changes in economic institutions, work relations, and the amount and distribution of wealth had far-reaching social, political, and cultural consequences, with enormous implications for the Episcopal Church and all churches. Industrialization stimulated urbanization, with all of its opportunities and challenges. Enormous new wealth permitted the expansion and proliferation of all kinds of cultural and social institutions, including churches but also schools, social clubs, charities, professional groups, museums, orchestras, operas, literary societies, and reform organizations. The Diocese of Pennsylvania underwent "incorporation," developing a more centralized and formally organized diocesan structure in a newly established Church House. Industrialization broadened the middle class, adding new occupations in management and the professions. Mental boundaries expanded along with the physical boundaries of time and space as transportation and communication became faster, easier, and more widely available.

However, industrialization also created troubling conditions that challenged and eroded traditional values and assumptions about society and government. No wonder that newspapers and magazines described their times as a "nervous" age! As Bishop Ozi Whitaker said in 1906, "We are living at a rate much faster than that of our forefathers . . . the pressure to go faster and faster is felt in every department and relation of life. In business, to keep up with others in securing results; in pleasure, to satisfy the insatiable craving for new sensations. The continual strain is making multitudes of men and women feverish and restless! The number of insane is increasing faster than the population."[4] The strains and anxieties of industrialization included the concentrated wealth and power of big business, rampant corruption in business and politics, a widening gap between rich and poor, terrible labor conditions, horrendous poverty, racial and gender inequality, and the rise of consumer culture, all of which seemed to exceed the capacity of existing institutions to maintain stability and order. Furthermore, social conflict and outbreaks of violence in the final decades of the nineteenth century left the comfortable classes with a pervasive sense of peril. The politics of reunification and the failure of Reconstruction in the South, nationwide labor strikes, economic downturns of frightening intensity and increasing frequency, warfare in the Philippines, Caribbean,

Pacific, Latin America, and the American West, millions of immigrants from unfamiliar ethnicities, and a tidal wave of lynchings of black Americans strained the social and political structures of the United States. New ideas of germ theory, evolution, biblical scholarship, Freudian psychology, genetics, and modern literature, music, and visual arts presented further challenges to customary beliefs.

The position of the Episcopal Church amid these developments was paradoxical. On the one hand, it was increasingly a bastion of the wealthy and privileged. On the other, the church did more than simply comfort the comfortable, and it was active in the reform impulses known collectively as the Social Gospel Movement. The contradictions that defined the Episcopal Church in the twentieth century took shape in the Gilded Age.

City and Diocese

Philadelphia was one of the nation's largest and most industrialized cities, with many small and midsize companies producing a wide array of products. It was also a transportation center and home to the powerful Pennsylvania Railroad. It boasted one of the nation's largest mass transit systems. In 1876, commemorating its role in the Revolution, it hosted the Centennial Exposition, constructing Memorial Hall and other edifices for the occasion in Fairmont Park. The forty-foot-high Corliss engine, which dominated the central hall and powered the entire exposition, became a national symbol of technological progress.

The city exemplified all the benefits and costs of industrial capitalism. Between 1860 and 1900 Philadelphia's population increased by 138 percent. Compared to other cities, Philadelphia received relatively little of the "new" immigration that began in the 1880s, bringing millions of southern and eastern Europeans to the United States, in contrast to earlier waves of immigration from northern Europe and the British Isles. Philadelphia's foreign-born residents made up only 24 percent of the population in 1880, a figure that had dropped by 1900, making its experience different from that of New York, Boston, or Pittsburgh.[5] Philadelphia's population growth was a result of the vast rural-urban migration that also drove urban growth in the Gilded Age. As in other cities, problems of poverty, housing, sanitation, and disease outstripped both physical infrastructure and government capabilities. Between the scramble to build streets, railways, sewers, and buildings, and the raw competition of a nascent industrial capitalism, both public and private opportunities for illicit gain abounded, and Philadelphia gained a reputation for corruption and a place in the powerful Republican political machine that dominated state politics between the Civil War and the Depression.

Thus the era was a period of both problems and promise for Philadelphia and its environs. It certainly was a time of enormous growth in the Episcopal Church on both the national and diocesan levels. By 1906 one out of every ninety-five Americans was Episcopalian. Between 1880 and 1920, as the American population doubled, the church added half again as many dioceses, doubled the number of parishes, and tripled the number of parishioners. The proliferation of parishes inhibited the growth in parish size; even as parishes increased 102 percent in number, they increased in size only 55 percent on average.[6]

In the Diocese of Pennsylvania, the number of Episcopalians increased 318 percent between 1860 and 1900. Although the geographical area of the diocese shrank during this time, it remained one of largest dioceses in the United States in terms of numbers of parishes and clergy. In 1872 the diocese had 113 parishes and 176 clergy; by 1910 it had 138 parishes and almost 300 clergy.[7] Philadelphia and its environs were urbanizing and suburbanizing. The 352-mile horse-drawn transit system more than doubled the residential commuting area, while steam-powered trains created suburbs both within city lines—Germantown, Mount Airy, and Chestnut Hill—and outside the city along the "Main Line."[8] Most new parishes were in new neighborhoods. Others were founded as missions to serve particular classes or social groups. Still others were established when parishes divided over theological and liturgical differences, or over the personality and style of a particular rector.

* * * * *

Bishop Stevens

William Bacon Stevens (1815–1887) was born in Maine and attended Phillips Academy in Andover, Massachusetts. He began medical studies at the Medical School of Dartmouth College in Hanover, New Hampshire, but poor health took him south, where he completed his degree in 1838 at the Medical College of South Carolina. He began medical practice in Savannah, Georgia, quickly becoming part of that city's society by joining the Georgia Hussars, becoming an Episcopalian, and marrying into a prominent family. In 1841 this New Englander was named the state historian of Georgia and was commissioned to write a state history. At the same time, he began studying for the ordained ministry. In 1844 he was ordained a

FIGURE 6.1 Bishop William Bacon Stevens

priest and also named professor of belles-lettres, oratory, and moral philosophy at the University of Georgia. In 1848 he was called as rector of St. Andrew's in Philadelphia, a large evangelical parish located at Eighth and Spruce. Stevens first turned down the call; he was well established in Georgia and committed to helping establish the university. The parish reiterated its call after a day of fasting, prayer, and discernment, and Stevens accepted, perhaps because Bishop Potter had encouraged him to become an Episcopalian years earlier. Stevens spent thirteen years at St. Andrew's, and the church continued to reserve a pew for Stevens and his family after he became bishop.

SOURCE: Vestry Minutes of St. Andrew's Church, 1845–1887, box 16, Closed Parish Records, Diopa Archives, Lutheran Theological Seminary, Mount Airy, Philadelphia.

* * * * *

The Ritualist Controversy

From the beginning of his episcopacy, Stevens had to handle the ongoing quarrel between the high- and low-church parties. Known as the "ritualism" controversy, it was more than a continuation of the antebellum conflict between high church and evangelical (see chapter 4). The tractarian or Oxford Movement of the 1840s had not only reignited the conflict but also changed the terms of the dispute.

In the antebellum period the high-church position, also known as formalism, emphasized piety and rationalism. Following the "forms"—the rites, liturgies, and sacraments—was considered preparation for salvation. For example, after a baptism, the priest pronounced the child "regenerate," or saved. However, during the bitter conflicts of the 1820s and 1830s, the term "high church" meant "not-evangelical" as well as a "high" or more formalistic understanding of the church. The evangelical or low-church position emphasized a religion of the heart in which scripture was more important than theology or tradition. Baptism was important, but salvation required going through a personal, wrenching conversion experience and demonstrating salvation by living an exemplary life, evangelizing, and performing good works. Evangelicals emphasized the Protestant side of their heritage from the Church of England, and believed that their version of Protestantism was central to American national identity and mission. The low-church or evangelical party grew out of the revivals of the Second Great Awakening and the mass politics of Jacksonian democracy, and distanced itself from the traditional association of the Episcopal Church with monarchy, established religion, and aristocratic privilege and practice.[9]

By the 1840s, the high-low distinction had been altered by the appearance of the Oxford Movement. Originating in Britain, the Oxford Movement was a reform movement aimed at laxity and decline in the Church of England and talk in Parliament of disestablishment. However, it also became an aggressive attempt to "de-Protestantize" Anglicanism and return it to its Roman Catholic roots by holding up a romantic image of medieval Christianity. At Oxford University, John Henry Newman wrote Tract 90, which attacked the fathers of the English church and tried to reconcile the Thirty-Nine Articles with Roman Catholicism. In the United States the Oxford Movement generally involved the use of more elaborate liturgies, emphasized communion over preaching and priesthood over ministry, placed the authority of tradition alongside that of scripture, and founded monastic orders for both men and women. However, American responses to the Oxford Movement were complicated not only by theological and liturgical issues within the Episcopal Church but also by rising anti-Catholicism in the United States, as thousands of Irish immigrants arrived in the 1830s and 1840s and the number of Roman Catholic churches and schools increased. Nor did the 1841 invitation from the Roman Catholic bishop of Philadelphia to Episcopal bishops to "return" to the true church help matters.[10]

The high-church group in the American church, always more formalistic, supported the ritualistic practices of the Oxford Movement, though not its movement toward Roman Catholicism. A new low-church position developed that was composed of moderates, former high-party formalists who opposed the Oxford Movement, and some evangelicals, though the evangelical position persisted. To complicate matters further, another position emerged based on the 1860 publication of *Essays and Reviews.* This collection, written by seven English churchmen, articulated a liberal theology that emphasized reconciling modern thought with Christianity. It argued for the recognition that all truth, even new scientific or historical truths, came from God, that Christian truth was of a different nature from "factual" truth, and that Christian truth did not depend on miracles or supernatural revelation. *Essays and Reviews* became the basis of the emerging "broad-church" position, which was anathema to both high churchmen and evangelicals. The broad-church position in the United States was associated with Phillips Brooks, its most powerful and well-known proponent.[11]

* * * * *

Anti-Catholicism in Nineteenth-Century America

Anti-Catholicism was religious, racial, and political. It was an outgrowth of centuries-old religious differences, perceptions, and conflicts between Catholics and Protestants. It was racial because, in the United States, Catholicism was associated with the Irish, who immigrated in large numbers beginning in the antebellum period. Native-born white Protestants did not consider the Irish "white" but saw them as a different race. Some Americans were anti-Catholic because they didn't like the Irish, and they didn't like the Irish because the Irish were predominantly Catholic. Anti-Catholicism was political because many Americans believed that Catholicism was anti-democratic. For example, in 1864 Pope Pius IX denounced science, rationalism, and liberalism (of the nineteenth-century variety) and opposed nationalistic movements in Europe, and in 1870 he proclaimed the doctrine of papal infallibility in political and social matters. Consequently, for many American Protestants, Catholicism was a force that had to be resisted at home and abroad, and this perception stimulated missionary activity among the Protestant churches designed to counter what were perceived as expanding missionary efforts on the part of the Roman Catholic Church around the globe.

Anti-Catholicism became a factor in the intense partisan politics of late nineteenth-century America because Irish Catholics were an influential faction within the Democratic Party. One divisive issue was public education. Democrats tended to favor local autonomy for schools; in addition, Catholics often wanted public funding for parochial schools. Republicans supported federal and state funding for centralized school systems. Catholics objected to the use of the King James Bible in public schools, while Protestants saw Bible reading as a way of disseminating their values and creating social unity. Another issue was temperance. Anti-Catholicism intersected with the temperance issue because of the association of the Irish with drinking and the opposition of the Democrats in general to any temperance laws. Finally, Anti-Catholicism reared its head in urban reform movements when reformers—often native-born white Republicans and Protestants—fought political machines dominated by Irish Catholics, like the famous Tammany Hall machine in New York City.

SOURCES: Mark W. Summers, *The Gilded Age, or The Hazard of New Functions* (Upper Saddle River, N.J.: Prentice Hall, 1997), 217–18; Rebecca Edwards, *New Spirits: Americans in the Gilded Age, 1865–1905* (New York: Oxford University Press, 2006), 184–85.

* * * * *

The Reformed Episcopal Church

The Episcopal Church experienced a schism in the early 1870s when the evangelicals revolted. Just as John Henry Newman, despairing of reforming Anglicanism along more Catholic lines, had left the church and become a Roman Catholic, a group of evangelicals at the other end of the spectrum, despairing of liberal theology and of what they saw as the church's weakness in responding to ritualism, exited the church as well. Led by Bishop George David Cummins of Kentucky, they established the Reformed Episcopal Church in 1873. Another of their number was the Reverend Charles Cheney of Chicago, who was deposed by his bishop for omitting the word "regenerate" from the baptismal service. The eight clergymen and nineteen laymen who organized the Reformed Episcopal Church saw themselves as more evangelical than episcopal, and believed that they were upholding the Protestant and evangelical heritage of the Episcopal Church. The evangelicals who stayed in the church after 1873 tended to be those who saw themselves as more episcopal than evangelical. As fundamentalism emerged in the late nineteenth century, it was less a factor in the Episcopal Church than in other denominations because of the schism of 1873; the evangelicals who remained affirmed the Anglican tradition of both reason and scripture.[12]

Bishop Stevens opposed the schism and hoped that the General Convention would condemn the practices and doctrines of the "so-called Catholic party," thus depriving the separatist party of its raison d'être. When the Roman Catholic Church adopted the doctrine of papal infallibility in political matters in 1870, he hoped that this would strengthen the opposition to ritualism. Stevens denounced the doctrine of infallibility as an "arrogant claim," a "soul-enslaving dogma," and "an attack made upon freedom of conscience in religious affairs" by declaring the pope to be "the voice of God."[13] He emphasized the Protestant character of the church unambiguously, asserting that the church had never adopted any "Romish errors." He vowed to reject any candidate for holy orders who belonged to any of the "secret orders" that promoted ritual practices and teaching. He rejected the notion that there were "romanizing germs" in the prayer book, and criticized the "polluting influences" of the confessional, purgatory, indulgences, invocation of saints, Mariolatry, making the priest the "dispenser of grace and judgment," and withdrawing of the right of private judgment in spiritual matters and Bible reading. According to Stevens, it was the ritualistic party that was schismatic, disloyal to church authority, libelous to the reformers, and thoroughly anti-Protestant.[14]

In Philadelphia, only one church seems to have been directly affected by the schism. Bishop Stevens reported in 1874 that the Reverend Walter Windeyer, rector of Trinity Church in East Falls, had "abandoned our communion" to cast his lot with the reformed group, and that a portion of the congregation had "followed their pastor." There was little that Stevens could do about it, however. Though Windeyer's group continued to worship in one of Trinity's buildings, it was owned by a parishioner and not by the church, which left the diocese no grounds on which to prevent Windeyer and his followers from meeting there.[15]

In general, Stevens followed the traditional Philadelphia Episcopal path of balancing congregational autonomy, priestly authority, and the authority of the diocese and bishop. For Stevens and his successors, it would be a difficult path to walk when controversies divided parishioners into warring factions and pitted parishioners against rectors, rectors against vestries, and parishes against the diocese.

Christ Church, Germantown, St. Peter's, St. Martin-in-the-Fields, and St. Clement's

The ritualist controversy that divided Christ Church, Germantown, in 1871 was one instance of such battles. The vestry of Christ Church called Dr. Theodore Rumney as rector in 1870. Rumney was nominated by vestrymen Henry H. Houston and E. A. Crenshaw after nine vestry meetings had failed to produce a consensus on a new rector. Houston and Crenshaw, who had interviewed Rumney, assured the vestry that he understood that Christ Church was low church and supported many evangelical societies. However, within a year the parish was split into factions over his "innovations," his invitations to clergy "who were entirely different in their views from [Christ Church's] dearly loved preachers," and his alleged failure to support the evangelical societies.[16] The records do not detail these charges, but they imply that Rumney followed high-church liturgical practices and theology.

In 1871 the vestry asked Rumney to resign, but he refused, maintaining that he had done nothing wrong. Both sides—the vestry majority and their supporters, and Rumney and his supporters—appealed to the diocese, and both published pamphlets defending their positions. A diocesan Board of Presbyters investigated, cleared Rumney of charges, and affirmed him as the rector of Christ Church.[17] At this point Henry H. Houston, who had become a close friend of Rumney's, decided that despite the ruling,

FIGURE 6.2 St. Martin-in-the-Fields, Chestnut Hill, Philadelphia, completed 1889

Rumney's position at Christ Church was untenable. His solution was to build St. Peter's Church, on a lot he owned a mere four blocks away, and install Rumney as rector. Houston was Rumney's warden at St. Peter's for many years, and he supported the church financially for the rest of his life, remaining a member even after moving to Chestnut Hill and founding the Church of St. Martin-in-the-Fields in 1889. When Houston died in 1895, Rumney conducted the private family service that preceded Houston's public funeral at St. Martin's.[18] Houston was one of the wealthiest and most influential men not only in the diocese but in Philadelphia, and there seems to have been little that Stevens and the diocese were willing or able to do to mediate the situation at Christ Church, or to prevent the needless proliferation of churches by persuading Houston not to build St. Peter's around the corner.

Bishop Stevens did rebuke clergy when he thought they were using liturgical practices that were too "high" or were unauthorized. In 1870 he wrote the Reverend J. Pinckney Hammond of Christ Church, Reading, objecting to several features of worship there. The list included Pinckney's use of stoles, mixing water into the wine during Holy Communion, interposing "a sentence" after the offertory was laid on the table, crossing himself at any time during the service, and genuflecting when placing the elements on the table. Stevens informed Pinckney that all of these changes had been made without consulting the bishop, were unauthorized by the rubrics, and should be discontinued.[19]

The most serious conflict over ritualism occurred between Stevens and St. Clement's Church in the 1870s. This parish already had a reputation for high-church practices, but Stevens had supported the rector against some complaints in 1869, writing to the vestry,

> Your communication of the 5th gave me real sorrow. In it however you speak not as a vestry but as individuals being in number a minority of the Vestry. I can therefore take no official action. . . . From the peculiar relations which subsist between the clergy and myself I shall ever stand forth as their defender and shall ever recognize them as in good standing until proved otherwise by due course of law. . . . I think that the time has come when these too long continued altercations should cease. They disturb your community, injure the church and are a scandal to Christian Men.[20]

However, he also warned the rector of St. Clement's that "the multiplication of services outside of those prescribed in the Book is to be deplored; especially in view of the unauthorized proceedings of a certain class of men who are seeking to enjoy new or obsolete services [other than?] the accepted or recognized ritual of our Church. . . . Our Prayer Book in judicious hands is sufficiently flexible for all our needs, and it is better to adapt what we have to varying circumstances of time and place than introduce new forms and thus virtually ignore the old."[21]

St. Clement's underwent more tumult in 1871, when rector H. G. Batteson, accused of improprieties with choirboys, was fired, an action that Stevens supported but that was eventually overturned in civil court. Then, in 1875, St. Clement's called Oliver S. Prescott as rector. Prescott was a member of the Order of the Society of St. John the Evangelist, founded in 1866 at Cowley, near Oxford, as one of a number of monastic orders established in the mid- to late nineteenth century in England and America. Cowley fathers took a vow of obedience to the bishop of Oxford, and Americans trained at Cowley were known for their missionary zeal in restoring Roman Catholic liturgical and spiritual practices to Anglicanism.[22] The relationship between Stevens, with his moderate evangelical background, and Prescott, a Cowley father, got off to a poor start when Prescott invited a bishop other than Stevens, his diocesan bishop, to officiate at Prescott's institution as rector. The vestry invited Stevens to attend as well, but he declined "complying with this request as I could not conscientiously take part in such an institution as Mr. Pres[cott] can not delegate my power to any Presbyter to act as Institutor."[23]

Over the next year, relations between Prescott and Stevens deteriorated further. In October 1876 Prescott preached and conducted retreats in Montreal without getting permission from its bishop, Ashton Oxendon, who promptly forbade him to function again in that diocese. In response, Prescott published their exchange of letters, one of which stated that Prescott believed he was licensed by the bishop of Oxford for all activities anywhere, implying that the bishop of Oxford superseded the authority of any diocesan bishop. Then Stevens learned that Prescott was celebrating daily Communion by himself—a ritualistic practice—in the rectory at St. Clement's. He instructed Prescott to "immediately discontinue such celebrations as contrary both to the order and spirit of the Protestant Episcopal Church in these United States." After stating that the church did not recognize "divided allegiance" between two bishops, Stevens commented caustically, "I respectfully request that you make your selection as to which of the two Dioceses you will solely and canonically attach yourself and inform me of your decision at the earliest moment."[24]

Prescott waited a week and a half before replying—a significant delay considering that urban mail delivery often made same-day responses possible. "Will you please tell me what the omissions and additions to the communion service are to which you allude?" he wrote, adding, "As to the election [of which bishop to serve] for which you ask, I beg leave to say that I consider that such election was made when I accepted a care of souls in the Diocese of Pennsylvania. If you think otherwise will you please embody your idea in such a form as may suit you and transmit it to me?" Stevens shot back, "I regret to find that you evade the main issues and have not complied with either of my requests."[25]

The rector's warden of St. Clement's told Stevens that the parish was not violating the canons or doctrines of the church: "Our people are . . . attached to their rector, and are unanimous in his support. . . . They claim for themselves and they accord to others . . . that liberty of action with regard to forms of worship, which has always been a distinguishing feature of the Anglican Church. . . . We should most deeply regret to be involved in an unseemly conflict with the official authority of this diocese. But it is our right, as it will be our endeavor, under all circumstances, to maintain the ecclesiastical and legal rights of this parish."[26]

The standoff between Stevens and Prescott continued, Stevens demanding that Prescott clarify his status and Prescott insisting that Stevens send him the proper "form" on which he could state his allegiance.

Prescott invited Stevens for a visitation, "that you should know something of the ways and work of this important Parish from personal observations," but Stevens refused to visit St. Clement's until Prescott complied with his previous requests. Prescott retorted that he wouldn't comply because of Stevens's "disobedience" of the canons on visitation.[27] The degeneration of the handwriting of their letters into angry scrawl reflects the escalation of the dispute, as parties to the conflict published pamphlets and the newspapers reported the ongoing story.

The 1878 diocesan convention voted to send a committee to investigate the practices at St. Clement's. It reported at the next convention "that there is truth in many of the rumors referred to," among them "numerous celebrations of the Holy Supper on the same day" and Communion services at which "it is not unusual for the officiating priest to partake of the sacred elements alone . . . it is by *request* of the clergy that none of the congregation commune at these celebrations." The committee concluded that St. Clement's was in violation of "the Prayer Book, Constitution, Canons and Usages of the Protestant Episcopal Church in the *United States*, and those of the Diocese of Pennsylvania."[28] On the basis of this report, Bishop Stevens, in consultation with the Standing Committee, issued Prescott an "official admonition and judgment" requiring that he cease these practices at St. Clement's.[29] Prescott left St. Clement's by 1882.[30] However, despite this exercise of authority by bishop and diocese over Prescott, the parish of St. Clement's would continue to follow ritualistic practices.

Prayer Book and Hymnal

The committee report to the 1879 convention described services at St. Clement's:

> There are processions of boys and men, in surplices, not merely into the Church, but *into* and through it; processions headed by a crucifer, or person carrying aloft a large cross, and attended by a boy at each side of him carrying large sized decorated candles; and other boys or men in the procession carrying banners, with representations on them, of the Virgin and Child, of the vessels used in the Eucharist, and of the Dove; *during* the processions, as afterwards, in parts of the celebrations, hymns or sentences being sung, not authorized by this Church. . . . At other parts of the celebrations, referred to, numerous candles standing on the super-altar, are

> lighted; other candles on *it* and on the altar itself, having been *previously* lighted; that the priest celebrant on such occasions, officiates in vestments entirely unusual in this Church; that he is attended, during his ministrations, by boys, who perform a variety of offices, some of them mysterious, except to the initiated, and who, as well as the clergy, are careful to bow, or bend the knee, as often as they pass in front of the holy table, or even approach it. And, in addition to all that, immediately after consecrations, the elements are lifted up by the celebrant.[31]

That this service was considered shocking, and evidence of transgression at St. Clement's, reveals something about average liturgical practice in the diocese in the 1870s; that little about this service would surprise a twenty-first-century Episcopalian reveals the extent to which the practices of the Oxford Movement eventually permeated the church, resulting in a range of liturgical practices within the Episcopal Church, and often within dioceses, from low-church liturgies, where nary a chasuble or candle was to be seen, to high-church "smells and bells," and a wide range of liturgies that fell somewhere in between.

By the 1890s the ritualism controversy had calmed down substantially. While differences still existed, and churches were proud of their high, low, or broad identity, public animosity subsided significantly, and toleration of a range of practices grew. There was a softening of traditional Protestant ideas about religious art and ritual within the expansion of high culture in the late nineteenth century. The late Victorian fascination with all things medieval led to a Gothic Revival that drew a visual and atmospheric connection between American churches and the great cathedrals of Europe and Britain. The growing wealth generated by industrialization supported music, fine art, and architecture. By the end of this period, Americans were building cathedrals themselves, in particular St. John the Divine in New York City and the National Cathedral in Washington, D.C. In the bustling urban world of the Gilded Age, churches emerged as places of repose and refreshment that was both spiritual and cultural. As Robert Prichard notes, "American Episcopalians increasingly saw their denomination as a tradition in its own right."[32]

Two liturgical changes occurred in the 1890s, neither of which would have been possible in the contentious 1870s. The first was the approval of a revised hymnal at the 1892 General Convention. This project had begun in 1886 and continued the broadening of church music beyond metrical psalms. *The Hymnal, Revised and Enlarged with Music* had 679 hymns,

FIGURE 6.3 St. Mark's, Philadelphia, inspired by the Oxford Movement, designed by John Notman and completed in 1849

including Anglican and Gregorian chants, and romantic and Victorian hymnology.[33]

The other significant change was the approval at the same General Convention of a revised Book of Common Prayer. This concluded a twelve-year process of committee reports and drafts. The 1892 BCP was considered a conservative revision of the 1790 edition, but it nonetheless added more prayers and thanksgivings, permitted a range of additions and omissions at points in the service, and included elements valued by the ritualists. It encompassed a wider range of liturgical choices than previous prayer books had done.[34] That it easily received the required approval of two consecutive triennial conventions showed that liturgical and theological passions were cooling, at least for the time being. However, this does not mean that controversy was entirely gone. In 1903 Bishop Whitaker opposed removing "Protestant" from the church's name, as was discussed at General Convention, because it stood for resistance to "the erroneous teaching and practice of the Church of Rome," with its "tyrannous pretensions."[35]

Anglophilia

The widening acceptance of high liturgical practices and the Gothic Revival in church design was a sign of the growing Anglophilia of the wealthy classes that dominated the Episcopal Church. Anglophilia had a basis in the general rapprochement and growing commonality of interests between the United States and Great Britain that occurred in the second half of the nineteenth century. Middle- and upper-class Americans participated in transatlantic Victorian culture by ethnicity and cultural preference. Even as this group benefited from the growth of industrial capitalism, the social disorder of the times encouraged nostalgia for an imagined aristocratic past. In particular, the middle and upper classes became fascinated with medieval culture, which they saw as a robust source of aesthetic, spiritual, and social inspiration. They were attracted to images of martial knights, ethereal women, chivalric ideals, and spiritual quests, set in Gothic cathedrals and castles. This cultural impulse accounted in part for the attraction of the Oxford Movement and high-church practices.

The new moneyed elite, with their shallow genealogies and deep pockets, adopted the trappings of English gentry culture as part of their quest for upward mobility and social prestige. They built Gothic mansions and castles and created country estates with British names, as Henry H. Houston did in Chestnut Hill, naming his estate "Drum Muir" to highlight his Scottish ancestry. They built English-style churches like St. Martin-in-the-Fields, named after one of the most famous churches in Britain. They founded sporting and country clubs, such as the Merion Cricket Club and Philadelphia Cricket Club, where they played cricket, golf, and lawn tennis. They developed a horse-based social culture, playing polo, introduced to America in the 1870s by Philadelphian Fairman Rogers,

FIGURE 6.4 Henry Howard Houston, a railroad magnate and multimillionaire who built St. Martin-in-the-Fields and developed an upscale planned railroad suburb around the church

and engaging in horseback riding, coaching, and wintertime sleigh rides. Houston hosted the Philadelphia (now Devon) Horse Show in 1892 near his home in Chestnut Hill. During the 1890s coaching as a social activity and display of conspicuous consumption swelled in popularity, and parents made sure their daughters learned to ride sidesaddle. To remove their children from the diverse and dirty cities and make sure they associated with the right people, they established boarding schools and country day schools in bucolic settings with neo-Gothic buildings, where grades were called "forms," the dining hall "the refectory," and the faculty "masters" and "mistresses." These schools prepared their children for admission to suitable colleges and marriage to suitable people. Families traveled to Britain and Europe, decorated their houses in British style, and looked for titled husbands for their daughters. Even as the American population of British descent shrank and lost the demographic battle, it won the cultural war, for the trappings of social status in American society were defined as English for more than a century. As in other cities, in Philadelphia Episcopalians dominated the upper classes and institutions.[36]

The Rise of the Social Gospel

The social dislocations caused by industrialization, urbanization, and immigration raised new questions about the role of the church in society. Social reform always played an important role for Episcopalians and other Protestants in nineteenth-century America, as an expression of true religion on the part of individual believers and a way for churches to regenerate and purify American society. Individual or collective, private or political, social reform was seen as providing the moral basis for American Christian civilization in the absence of an established church.[37] Episcopalians liked to describe the church as an ambulance that rescued individuals in need, and as a school that produced moral citizens who would be the conscience of the community.

Thoughtful church members were appalled by the broad poverty and narrow wealth created by industrial capitalism, and the ways that it eroded the institution of the family and individual moral standards by reducing the lives of many to a struggle for survival. At the same time, the leaders of industry seemed to have unchecked power, restrained by neither morality nor government. The Social Gospel Movement was a broad-based attempt to make industrial society more moral and just. Primarily a phenomenon in the northern Protestant churches, it also resonated in the Roman Catholic Church. It was the descendant of the antebellum evangelical reform movements and long-standing beliefs in persuasion, but the Social Gospel Movement differed in focusing on structures and institutions rather than individuals as a source of sin.

During the Gilded Age, Episcopalians played a leading role in promoting the Social Gospel, founding effective organizations and making the denomination known for social ministry and worship rather than doctrine.[38] Bishop Stevens made a passion for social mission a hallmark of his episcopacy from the start, urging the church to "not only speak with its mouth but work with its hands and walk with its feet."[39] Over the next decades, the diocese was instrumental in founding and supporting more institutions than can be discussed here. Concern for the care and education of children is evident in the founding of the Lincoln Institute for Orphaned Boys (1866), the Sunday School Association (1869), the Sheltering Arms (1872) for abandoned children and unwed mothers, and in the diocese's provision of funds for educating the children of clergy. Bishop Stevens collaborated with philanthropist Asa Packer to found Lehigh University in Bethlehem as an Episcopal school (1865). The Board of Missions (1872) was entrusted with the supervision of all missions in the diocese. In 1877 Stevens ordained John Winter Syle, a deaf mute, who established the Mission to the Deaf, which later became All Souls Church for the Deaf (1888). There was an Italian Mission (for Italian immigrants), several missions "to the Colored People," such as St. Barnabas, and also work in the West with American Indians, in the South with African Americans, and in foreign countries.

One of the most important institutions was the City Mission (1870), the forerunner of today's Episcopal Community Services. It served those in penal institutions and hospitals, with a special ministry to consumptives and the blind. The diocese supported Episcopal Hospital and created the Church Dispensary in Southwark (1872). By 1872 Bishop Stevens could report with satisfaction on the church's good works. "As I move about from Parish to Parish . . . I am penetrated with a feeling of thanksgiving that our beloved church, which has been so long stigmatized as only The Rich Man's Church, as being the Aristocratic Church, is in her sphere, doing more about the lower and degraded classes for their temporal benefit, their mental culture and their spiritual welfare than any other body of Christians."[40]

Severe economic depression throughout the 1870s and growing labor unrest culminating in the Great Strike of 1877 caused growing anxiety among the comfortable classes about the social order. The strike was precipitated by repeated wage cuts by the major railroad companies, which at the same time increased executive salaries and stockholder dividends. It began when workers along the B & O Line refused to run the trains, and spread throughout the system of eastern railroads and then across the country. Because of the importance of railroads in Pennsylvania, the state saw a great deal of strike activity. Violence erupted between workers and police in several cities, among them Pittsburgh; the strike was broken by calling out the National Guard and the U.S. Army.

Bishop Stevens was concerned about the poverty, scared by the violence, and alarmed by the idea of labor unions and by the private armies that had sprung up among the comfortable classes. He noted that it had been "a year of great trial to all classes of persons by reason of the financial stringency which affects all work and income," and he described the "approaching evil" of the nascent labor movement. "The effort now being made, ostensibly, in behalf of the laboring men," he said, "but really by communistic infidels to bring about a conflict between labor and capital, the rich and the poor, the workmen and corporations . . . cannot but result in devastation and ruin." He was alarmed by "associations and gathering and drillings with military manuals and arms, of this dangerous and inflammation element." This evil had to be met by physical force and by the moral force of the gospel of the workingman's divine friend, Jesus of Nazareth.[41]

Stevens's response reflects the growing tension between the traditional belief that poverty was an individual, moral problem, and newer arguments that poverty was a structural problem of political economy. The inequities of wealth and power that were being exacerbated by industrialization did not fit easily into conventional ideas about social amelioration. The national church in 1877 was concerned that the working classes were alienated from the church; as the report of an official committee of the House of Bishops observed, "property and culture, and social and official position, have no rights that do not impose equivalent obligations."[42] The diocesan Committee on the Neglected and the Poor reported that

> the pertinacity of human suffering caused by the weakness and misfortune, the necessities and strifes of society and by the depravity of their victims, through generations of civilized life; the ever increasing complexity of man's social, industrial and political relations; the wide field of benevolent effort littered with the wrecks of useless plans and occupied by still unconcluded experiments; the growing sense of the dependence of each man's powers upon the others for their efficiency, rendering fruitless the schemes which aim at the relief of a single class of wants, present a problem that well may be called "the unsolved riddle of the age."[43]

In the parochial reports of that year, churches in working-class neighborhoods, such as St. Mark's in Frankford, reported, "the troubles of the times have deeply affected the people of the Parish."[44]

How to carry out social ministry as a diocese was unclear. The convocations (now called deaneries) established in 1885 carried out social ministry, called missionary activity. In 1896 the convention changed the diocesan canons to allow an archdeacon to oversee all missionary work in the diocese. Cyrus J. Brady, a mission priest from Kansas, was called to be the first archdeacon. However, he suffered from a poorly defined job description that did not make clear how the archdeacon fit into the convocation missionary system already in place. Furthermore, his relationship with the Board of Missions was poor, and he managed to rub influential Philadelphians the wrong way. Brady left for three months to serve as chaplain to the First Pennsylvania Regiment of the U.S. Volunteer Infantry in the Spanish-American War, and then was sick for an additional three months, all the while still drawing his salary from the diocese. He was asked to resign, and the convention removed the provision for an archdeacon from Canon VIII, placing ministry back in the hands of churches and convocations.[45]

Social Gospel work was supported by all parties in the church, high and low, liberal and conservative. Anglophilia played a role. Many progressive Episcopalians were influenced by the Christian socialist movement in England. But Social Gospel belief was also important in high-church circles, where it was precisely a belief in aristocracy and hierarchy that inspired a sense of social responsibility. The national Episcopal Church took the lead in recognizing the right of labor to organize.[46] The Church Association for the Advancement of the Interests of Labor, founded in 1887, got support from conservatives and high-church types. In 1890 the Church Social Union was established to promote discussion of social questions in the church.[47] In Philadelphia and in the national church, Social Gospel organizations were important forerunners of progressive reforms and the development of liberal government in the twentieth century.

Women and the Diocese

The social ministry of the church would not have been possible without the women of the church. Industrialization created a growing class of educated women eager for work. Participation in evangelical societies, the temperance movement, the abolition movement, and the women's rights movement during the antebellum period, and hospital nursing and U.S. Sanitary Commission work during the war, had created wider roles for women and proved their effectiveness. In 1864 Bishop Potter urged "more organized employment of Christian women," describing them as "a fund of power, which, properly drilled and organized, could move the world." The Reverend D. S. Miller marveled at their effectiveness not only in teaching but also in "real Pastoral work . . . the special province of the minister of the Gospel."[48] Women became the backbone of the Social Gospel Movement and broadened the definition of ministry, even though they were denied formal church leadership and ordained ministry.

In 1865 Bishop Stevens, with the generous support of Mr. and Mrs. William Welsh of St. Mark's Church, established the Bishop Potter Memorial House in a mansion adjacent to Episcopal Hospital to provide training for women to serve in church-related institutions—the first school of its kind. Stevens emphasized that the program would not compete with marriage or take women out of their proper place—it was to be strictly under male supervision—and that the women were not taking vows or leaving the world. The Bishop Potter House was not going to open the door to the establishment of Catholic orders, he vowed![49] By 1872 it had trained thirty-seven women as deaconesses.[50] Graduates worked as teachers, parish assistants, hospital administrators, and in missions to the Indians, the freedmen, and the poor of other cities, and in missions abroad. Unfortunately, after William Welsh died in 1878, the Potter House floundered; Stevens tried to reorganize it, but it was so closely identified with the Welshes that it had few other sources of support. It was formally adopted as a diocesan institution in 1879 in an attempt to broaden its support[51] but eventually closed in 1891 and served only as a residence in its final years. When the 1889 General Convention finally approved a canon establishing an order of deaconesses, the Church Training and Deaconess School opened in Philadelphia in 1891 under the supervision of Miss Mary Coles. However, it was not a continuation of the Bishop Potter House, nor was it a diocesan institution. As one historian writes, "The closing of the Bishop Potter Memorial House demonstrated a problem that was to continue to plague the Church. Though many leaders were eager to enlist the services of women workers, they were not realistically prepared to pay for them."[52]

Episcopal women were also active in the social settlement movement, and many settlements were started by churches. Deaconesses at the school in Philadelphia studied social work at the settlement of St. Martha's (1901), run by Deaconess Jean W. Colesberry, and worked at St. Agnes House, another settlement. With church workers in settlement houses and settlement workers in church programs, a network began to evolve. Another organization that linked parish and settlement work was the 1884 Society of the Companions of the Holy Cross, dedicated to Christian lifestyle, intercessory prayer, and social justice. By 1897 there was a chapter in Philadelphia. There were also thirteen monastic orders for women in the nation by 1880. The Woman's Auxiliary of the Board of Missions was an especially important organization. It was organized into four committees: the Indians Hope Association, the Domestic Committee, the Foreign Committee, and the Freedman's Committee. It had importance beyond Philadelphia as well. Along with the Girls' Friendly Society, the Church Periodical Society, and the Daughters of the King, the Woman's Auxiliary developed extensive, powerful networks that carved out a place for women to exercise leadership in the church and provided them with diocesan and national connections.

Another group of women in the diocese remains largely hidden from history—the women of clergy families, especially clergy wives. These women contributed to building the institutions of parish life, providing unpaid and often unrecognized work. They appear in diocesan records obliquely, the beneficiaries of the Widows and Orphans Corporation, the Christmas Fund, or the Fund for the Education of Clergy Daughters.[53] They lurk in the background of discussions of clergy pay, or appear in the records as victims or causes of conflicts between parish and priest.[54]

* * * * *

Women and Missionary Work

"The women's missionary movement of the late nineteenth century was the largest grass-roots movement of American Protestant women of its day," according to historian Dana L. Robert. Missionaries are sometimes portrayed as militant agents of American imperialism and racism, but the gender politics of missionary work make it a far more complicated story both in the United States and in missions abroad. Within the overall expansion of missionary work that occurred in this period, the role of women changed and expanded dramatically. Missionary work provided opportunities for education and training and a sphere for action and leadership. The money they raised and the programs they directed gave women a role in church matters and social reform movements that they otherwise lacked. Training as a missionary was acceptable in ways that training for work or for ministry was not. In addition, it opened up a world of travel and adventure, but defined in acceptable and often traditional terms. Fund-raising, lecture series, and the establishment of training programs and missions built powerful networks among individual women, among organizations in separate churches, and eventually among denominations. Women missionaries abroad often focused on improving conditions for women, especially by creating educational and vocational opportunities.

The Woman's Auxiliary of the Board of Missions, established in 1872, became "the most influential framework of support for women's vocations in the Episcopal Church," according to historian Fredrica Thompsett, in addition to its role in missionary work. The auxiliary organized a centralized network of women's missionary societies. Beginning in 1880, the auxiliary met every three years alongside the General Convention, and the triennial became "a parallel organization to the church's male hierarchy." In 1889 the triennial inaugurated an annual united offering (which became the United Thank Offering) as a supplemental fund given to the Board of Missions and designated for women's missionary work. As a result, the auxiliary could recruit, train, deploy, and fund women missionaries, and had a national network for fund-raising and communication.

SOURCES: Dana L. Robert, *American Women in Mission: A Social History of Their Thought and Practice* (Macon: Mercer University Press, 1996), 188; Fredrica Harris Thompsett, "Women in the American Episcopal Church," in *Encyclopedia of Women and Religion in North America*, ed. Rosemary Skinner Keller and Rosemary Radford Ruether, 3 vols. (Bloomington: Indiana University Press, 2006), 1:269–79 (quotations on 274).

* * * * *

Race Matters

In the years following the Civil War, most Americans chose reconciliation between the North and the South over racial justice, and the Episcopal Church largely mirrored rather than challenged these conditions. The racial beliefs crystallizing in the late nineteenth century justified the disenfranchisement of black Episcopalians, while the growing Anglo-Saxon identity of the church made the idea of black Episcopalians seem oxymoronic. The church wanted both to evangelize and to marginalize. The "Sewanee canon" of 1883 proposed reducing all blacks to missionary status by placing them in nongeographical districts or dioceses, effectively disenfranchising them within the church. Not officially adopted by the national church, it was the de facto reality in some southern dioceses.

Historically, Philadelphia had had one of the largest populations of free blacks in the country, and could boast strong leaders like Absalom Jones. In 1865 St. Thomas's finally achieved representation at the annual convention, after removing a provision, at the convention's insistence, that only those of African descent could serve on the vestry. Pennsylvania women took the lead in establishing freedom schools in the South after the Civil War. The Freedman's Commission of the Protestant Episcopal Church, a coalition of aid organizations, encouraged the creation of women's auxiliaries to support the aid societies. The Pennsylvania auxiliary, headed by Isabella Batchelder James, was "the only organization in the Episcopal Church that provided support for freedmen's programs," raising funds and supplying teachers.[55] However, the national church did not support the commission, and it gradually collapsed and voted to disband in 1877—the same year that the federal government abandoned Reconstruction policy. But the extensive use of women in missions to southern blacks laid the groundwork for foreign missionary work, as well as providing experience in fund-raising and connecting Episcopal women through diocesan and national networks.[56]

Missionary efforts continued to increase the number of black Episcopalians. In 1910 the League for Work Among Colored People estimated that there were ninety-five thousand blacks in the geographical diocese.[57] Missions established included St. Barnabas's, which later became a school, and St. Augustine's. Deaconesses trained at Bishop Potter House or, later, the Church Training and Deaconess School continued to work among African Americans in the South.

They also worked in missions and schools for American Indians. In this period the nation tried simultaneously to exterminate, segregate, and assimilate Indians. Stevens, in a rare mention of national politics, attacked federal Indian policy in his convention address of 1872, and called for missions and Episcopal oversight of the heathen Indians. The Indian wars ended in the 1890s with the massacre at Wounded Knee; missionary activity and schools for Indian children continued, though in 1899 there was a complaint to the Indian Rights Association that the Educational Home for Indian Children had bad facilities, was poorly managed, and was failing to accomplish its mission.[58] The Indians' Hope of Philadelphia (1868) came under the auspices of the Woman's Auxiliary in 1873 and received support from the women of the diocese throughout this period.[59]

FIGURE 6.5 Bishop Ozi W. Whitaker

The Election of Bishop Whitaker

By 1886 Stevens had been a bishop for nearly a quarter-century. He had suffered poor health his entire life, even before becoming bishop. In the early 1870s he was ill for the better part of two years, and had been severely ill in 1885. On the centenary of Bishop White's consecration, Stevens called for an assistant bishop. The election for an assistant bishop went to ten ballots before electing Phillips Brooks, who had been rector of

Holy Trinity on Rittenhouse Square in the 1860s and was currently rector of Trinity Church in Boston. It was a controversial election because of Brooks's strong broad-church position. However, Brooks declined the call. A second convention elected the Right Reverend Ozi W. Whitaker, missionary bishop of Nevada, shortly before Stevens died on June 11, 1887.

* * * * *

Bishop Whitaker

Ozi William Whitaker (1830–1911) was a native New Englander and a graduate of Middlebury College. He taught school for four years, then attended General Theological Seminary in New York and was ordained in 1863. Before becoming bishop of Pennsylvania, he spent most of his career in Nevada. In 1868 the General Convention elected Whitaker missionary bishop of Nevada. Whitaker also received the degree of DD that year from Kenyon College in Ohio.

Whitaker was a moderate churchman who balanced Protestant concerns with a new appreciation of ritual, asserted the centrality of the prayer book, and tolerated a range of liturgical practices. He stated a few general principles to which he wanted all parishes to adhere: deliver Holy Communion of both kinds into the hands of the people; provide sufficient opportunity for those present to communicate; consume leftover consecrated bread and wine reverently immediately after the blessing. Finally, he held that parishes and parishioners should not contravene any rubric or teaching in the prayer book.

Whitaker presided over a church that was struggling to encompass both tradition and modernity during a time of rapid change. The values of scientific management, practical social reform, and efficiency that were infusing American society also affected the church. Whitaker called for church organizations to organize themselves more effectively in order to carry out their work. "In view of the increasing tendency to organize society for accomplishing all sorts of purposes, it seems evident that it would be well, before making any new organization for the benefit of any class, to consider whether the desired end may not be secured by the adoption and better use of agencies already existing. . . . There are dangers connected with too much organization and too many societies." He lifted up the Woman's Auxiliary as an example. "Its organization is as simple as possible," he wrote. "It goes on quietly. It is conducted without expense. It devotes all its resources to the one end for which it exists: the building up of the Redeemer's Kingdom."

SOURCES: *JDC 1893*, 61–62; *JDC 1888*, 35.

* * * * *

Diocesan Matters

Since the seventeenth century, one of the ongoing tensions in American society has been between central and local authority. The nineteenth-century church did not escape this tension. Within the diocese, the boundaries between the authority of the bishop and the independence of the parishes, and between laity and clergy, were always being tested. Sometimes parishes wanted maximum independence; at other times they wanted the bishop to intervene and fix their problems. The diocese became increasingly "corporate" during the Gilded Age and Progressive Era by creating a more formal diocesan structure and becoming more legalistic in its charters and canons.

In 1869 the diocese purchased a residence for the bishop at 1633 Spruce (sold in 1901 and replaced by a residence at 4027 Walnut). Stevens did not live to see the fulfillment of his dream of a Diocesan House, finally established after disputes over location, the purchase of property, and raising funds.[60] Bishop Whitaker set the cornerstone for the new building at Twelfth and Walnut in 1894 as part of the twenty-fifth anniversary of his consecration as a bishop, and it was completed in 1896. It contained the Diocesan Library and Reading Room, the Church Club (a men's social club), offices and meeting rooms, and a fireproof vault for securing diocesan records. In 1898 a committee on parish histories began contacting parishes and urging them to compile their histories with the goal of accumulating a complete set.[61]

Whitaker urged parishes to become more organized and businesslike. In particular, he emphasized the importance of keeping accurate parish records of baptisms, marriages, confirmations, and numbers of communicants. Citing the canons of the diocese and the national church, he told the clergy that "neglect of a plain duty is not only unbusinesslike; it is wrong." This became a recurrent theme. He also reminded clergy of the importance of financial propriety, especially in the use of their private discretionary funds.[62] Whitaker told vestries that they had to comply with changes in civil law regarding corporations, and keep records of their proceedings in accordance with civil and ecclesiastical law.[63]

Whitaker was particularly worried that there were more parishes than the diocese could support. There had never been a diocesan policy on establishing new parishes, and as a result there were situations, as with St. Peter's and Christ Church in Germantown, where two small parishes existed adjacent to each other. "The policy of concentration, which is fast becoming the rule in all business enterprises," Whitaker wrote, "may to a large extent be profitably followed in the Church. . . . One strong Parish . . . will be more efficient in influencing the lives of men, than if the same amount of energy and money were expended through the instrumentality of two or three weaker organizations." Whitaker knew that it would be difficult to consolidate these "feeble" parishes, acknowledging the

> very natural affection which old and almost deserted parishes feel for the building in which worship has been carried on. . . . Such a parish may consist of only a handful of people gathered into a dingy and inconvenient edifice. Nevertheless, people cling to their old church, and often expect the Convocation to supply funds to support it, forgetting that, however praiseworthy their affection may be, it is still the duty of those responsible for raising funds to carefully husband all resources and to relinquish a sacred dollar from the collection plate only where it can be expended under a most solemn sense of responsibility. Great difficulties have been experienced this past year in concentrating the work of the church, owing to the action of some vestries, based on feelings with which we sympathize, but which cannot be approved. It is to be hoped that a higher conception of duty will gradually increase in strength, and that the people of these smaller parishes will more and more realize that the church is not merely a sentimental but also a scientific association and one consequently and sacredly bound to apply its energies only where they will do the most good.[64]

Another problem was the impulse toward suburbanization already evident in the closing years of the nineteenth century. Parishes had a tendency to relocate when the neighborhood changed, following their parishioners to more prosperous neighborhoods, possibly impinging on existing churches while abandoning the old neighborhood. Whitaker described these moves as "blunders" worthy of "just reproach," and admonished such parishes, "I think we are too often inclined to be needlessly alarmed by changes in population."[65]

The problems of feeble and failing parishes and the concentration of parishes owing to relocations were related to another chronic problem—inadequate clergy salaries. Bishop Stevens discussed this issue in his first address as bishop at the 1866 convention and reiterated it numerous times, as did Bishop Whitaker. Perhaps Bishop Alexander Mackay-Smith put it best: "While our clergymen are not serving for money they require money to live."[66] The Committee on Inadequate Support of Many Clergymen took a systematic look at salaries across the diocese and, having determined what constituted a minimum level of support, proposed a system for augmenting salaries, providing for disabled and infirm clergy, and supporting unemployed clergy who had at least three years of service in the diocese. The diocese had a sustentation fund that augmented clergy salaries in parishes that applied for assistance, without reducing those parishes to mission status. Nine parishes received help in 1900, twelve in 1903, and fifteen in 1909.

In 1901 Whitaker called for a coadjutor. He collapsed at the annual conference of the Woman's Auxiliary in November and had to be removed by ambulance. In February 1902 Dr. Alexander Mackay-Smith, rector of St. John's in Washington, D.C., was elected bishop coadjutor (the first time this term was used in the diocese). Mackay-Smith's election was something of an upset, as Dr. Richard H. Nelson, rector of old St. Peter's Church, was expected to win. Mackay-Smith had a long wait before becoming bishop. Whitaker recovered his health and returned to the diocese after a five-month leave, remaining diocesan bishop until his death on February 9, 1911. At the convention that spring, his own health failing, Bishop Mackay-Smith called for the immediate election of a coadjutor. The diocese elected Dr. Philip M. Rhinelander. In October, Mackay-Smith announced his intention to retire to Washington, D.C., and to donate his house at 251 South Twenty-second Street to the diocese for use as a residence for future bishops. Mackay-Smith resigned immediately after Rhinelander's consecration in October and died nineteen days later. His widow, Virginia Stewart Mackay-Smith, renewed the offer of the house, which the diocese accepted.

* * * * *

Bishop Mackay-Smith

Alexander Mackay-Smith (1850–1911) hailed from New England, like bishops Stevens and Whitaker before him. Mackay-Smith came

FIGURE 6.6 Bishop Alexander Mackay-Smith

from an important Connecticut family—his grandfather, Nathan Smith, was a U.S. senator from Connecticut, and his older half brother was a prominent clergyman in New York City—and at his death was described by the *New York Times* as one of the wealthiest clergymen in America. After graduating from Trinity College, Mackay-Smith attended General Theological Seminary and studied abroad in England and Germany. He was rector of churches in Boston and New York City before becoming archdeacon of New York in 1887. In 1893 he became rector of St. John's, Lafayette Square, in Washington, D.C., where he served until he was elected bishop coadjutor in Pennsylvania in 1902. Mackay-Smith was active in the good government movement and served on the Civil Service Reform Association of Pennsylvania. He was also a published poet. He and his wife had three daughters.

* * * * *

The Diocese, the Nation, and the World

The Episcopal Church had traditionally stayed out of politics, but the changing conditions brought on by the rise of industrial capitalism made it increasingly difficult to separate church concerns from questions of social organization and political economy, or from national and world events. While commentary on current events remained rare in parish and diocesan records, it did become more frequent. In 1893 Bishop Whitaker referred to the impact of the depression of 1893 (the most severe in American history until the Great Depression of the 1930s) on the City Mission. At the 1898 convention he commented at length in support of the Spanish-American War and in subsequent years on the opportunities for the church in "regenerating the morals of the [Cuban] people."[67] In 1901 the Standing Committee recommended an appeal to the diocese for special collections for "the extraordinary emergency of the Diocese of Texas" after the hurricane at Galveston, and in 1906 the diocese collected money and supplies to send to victims of the San Francisco earthquake.[68] The increasing speed with which news reached remote locations and the growing use of photography in newspapers made such distant events more immediate to people than ever before. Furthermore, urban growth made concentrated populations far more vulnerable to natural and man-made disasters than before. Whitaker also commented on the problems arising from increased immigration at the turn of the century, and on the political corruption of the times.

Sometimes moral concerns drew the church into political matters. Stevens attacked divorce and opposed state attempts to liberalize divorce laws. In 1894 Whitaker took part in the efforts of the National Reform Association to secure uniform divorce laws across the nation. In Philadelphia, Whitaker helped mediate the Union Traction Company strike in 1896. Regarding the founding of the Christian Social Union, Whitaker said, "there are those who think that this is going beyond their sphere, but in fact it is going into the very heart of it. It is putting into practice what our Lord preached."[69] It was hard for the church to find a comfortable position on issues involving labor, especially since so many Episcopalians were from the moneyed classes. In 1910 Whitaker reminded the diocese that Christ "showed no disposition to interfere with the existing and political order of his time," but added, "the Church is obliged to resist that which destroys individual worth and to take active measures."[70] The growing power of the state raised the possibility of enshrining moral positions in state and federal legislation, one of the goals of Progressive reformers.

The years of the Gilded Age and Progressive Era also saw the church become more involved in ecumenical and international associations. The presiding bishop had put Stevens in charge of all the American churches in Europe between 1868 and 1874. In 1874 the first Church Congress met to create a forum for presentations on church and world issues. And although Stevens did not attend the first Lambeth Conference in 1867, he did attend in 1878. He emphasized that "the Anglican Communion" provided unity among the various churches but did not constitute a governing body that could dictate to the American church.[71]

The history of the diocese between the Civil War and World War I shows the extent to which the political liberalism of a more active and expanded government associated with the Progressive Era was presaged in the social ministries of the Episcopal Church. The Diocese of Philadelphia played a leading role. In these years, the privatist evangelical impulse central to mainstream antebellum Protestantism gave way to a Social Gospel Movement that emphasized ministries that were public and de facto political, and the church began to shift its emphasis to the material world of pragmatic results rather than the purely spiritual world of regeneration. As Bishop Mackay-Smith said in 1909, "The intensity and complexity of modern life add greatly to the difficulty and the number of problems with which the church has to deal. Especially this is true along social lines. . . . [Conditions] have been freshly created by the forces of modern progress."[72]

NOTES

1. J. Wesley Twelves, *A History of the Diocese of Pennsylvania of the Protestant Episcopal Church in the U.S.A., 1784–1968* (Philadelphia: Diocese of Pennsylvania, 1969), 93.
2. *JDC 1865*, 55.
3. Alan Trachtenberg, *The Incorporation of America: Culture and Society in the Gilded Age* (New York: Hill and Wang, 1982), 3–4.

4. *JDC 1906*, 71.

5. Nathaniel Burt and Wallace E. Davies, "The Iron Age, 1876–1905," in *Philadelphia: A 300-Year History*, ed. Russell F. Weigley (New York: W. W. Norton, 1982), 488.

6. Robert W. Prichard, *A History of the Episcopal Church*, rev. ed. (Harrisburg: Morehouse, 1999), 174, 183.

7. Burt and Davies, "Iron Age," 488; *JDC 1872*; *JDC 1910*.

8. Clay McShane and Joel A. Tarr, "The Centrality of the Horse in the Nineteenth-Century American City," in *The Making of Urban America*, 2d ed., ed. Raymond Mohl (Wilmington, Del.: SR Books, 1997), 111; David R. Contosta, *Suburb in the City: Chestnut Hill, Philadelphia, 1850–1990* (Columbus: Ohio State University Press, 1992), 6–7.

9. George Marsden, *Fundamentalism and American Culture*, 2d ed. (New York: Oxford University Press, 2006), 12.

10. Diana Hochstedt Butler, *Standing Against the Whirlwind: Evangelical Episcopalians in Nineteenth-Century America* (New York: Oxford University Press, 1995), 100, 108.

11. Ibid., 180.

12. Ibid., 211–12.

13. *JDC 1872*, 29.

14. *JDC 1874*, 33–41.

15. Ibid., 38.

16. "Statement of the Vestry of Christ Church, Germantown, Regarding Their Controversy with the Rector, February, 1872," in *Statement and Answer in the Matter of Christ Church, Germantown* (Philadelphia: King and Baird, 1872), 9.

17. "Answer on Behalf of the Rector to the Statement of the Vestry of Christ Church, Germantown, as Read Before the Board of Presbyters, February 29th, 1872," in ibid.

18. David R. Contosta, *A Philadelphia Family: The Houstons and Woodwards of Chestnut Hill* (Philadelphia: University of Pennsylvania Press, 1988), 28–29.

19. Stevens to Pinckney, November 9, 1870, RG 1.5, box 1, file 1, Diopa Archives, Lutheran Theological Seminary, Mount Airy (Philadelphia).

20. Stevens to Vestry of St. Clement's, October 30, 1869, ibid., file 2.

21. Stevens to William Meade, November 2, 1869, ibid.

22. T. Jackson Lears, *No Place of Grace: Antimodernism and the Transformation of American Culture, 1880–1920* (Chicago: University of Chicago Press, 1981), 200.

23. Stevens to Vestry of St. Clement's, January 12, 1876, RG 1, box 8, file 2, Diopa Archives.

24. Stevens to Prescott, October 18, 1876, ibid.

25. Prescott to Stevens, October 29, 1876; Stevens to Prescott, October 30, 1876, ibid.

26. Rector's warden to Stevens, November 1, 1876, ibid.

27. Correspondence between Stevens and Prescott, January 1877, ibid.

28. *JDC 1879*, 46.

29. Ibid., 58; Prescott to Stevens, March 8, 1880, RG 1.5, box 8, file 25, Diopa Archives.

30. *JDC 1882*, 184.

31. *JDC 1879*, 47.

32. Prichard, *History of the Episcopal Church*, 157.

33. William Sydnor, *The Story of the Real Prayer Book, 1549–1979* (Wilton, Conn.: Morehouse, 1989), 67–68.

34. Ibid., 66.

35. *JDC 1903*, 73.

36. Contosta, *Philadelphia Family*, 28; Sam Bass Warner, *The Private City: Philadelphia in Three Periods of Its Growth* (Philadelphia: University of Pennsylvania Press, 1968); E. Digby Baltzell, *An American Business Aristocracy* (New York: Collier Books, 1962), 253.

37. Marsden, *Fundamentalism and American Culture*, 12, 91.

38. M. Moran Weston, *Social Policy of the Episcopal Church in the Twentieth Century* (New York: Seabury Press, 1964), 4–15; Prichard, *History of the Episcopal Church*, 164; Henry F. May, *Protestant Churches and Industrial America* (New York: Octagon Books, 1963), 182, 184.

39. *JDC 1867*, 159.

40. *JDC 1872*, 37.
41. *JDC 1878*, 47, 49–50.
42. Quoted in Charles Howard Hopkins, *The Rise of the Social Gospel in American Protestantism, 1865–1915* (New Haven: Yale University Press, 1967), 39.
43. *JDC 1878*, 214.
44. Ibid., 126.
45. R. Francis Wood to Cyrus Brady, January 30, 1899; John Fulton to Cyrus Brady, January 20, 1899, RG 1.6, box 4, file 19, Diopa Archives.
46. Baltzell, *American Business Aristocracy*, 264.
47. May, *Protestant Churches and Industrial America*, 184–85.
48. *JDC 1864*, 264, 275–76.
49. *JDC 1872*, 38, 39.
50. *JDC 1872*.
51. *JDC 1879*, 68.
52. Mary Sudman Donovan, *A Different Call: Women's Ministries in the Episcopal Church, 1850–1920* (Wilton, Conn.: Morehouse-Barlow, 1986), 64.
53. *JDC 1895*.
54. See, for example, a complaint from the vestry of Trinity Church in Williamsport that the wife of Trinity's rector, the Reverend Henry Spackman, was too intimate with a "Romish priest" and tended toward the "Romish church." Vestry of Trinity Church to Stevens, September 8, 1868, RG 1.5, Stevens General Correspondence, 1861–87, Diopa Archives.
55. Donovan, *Different Call*, 54.
56. Ibid., 57.
57. *JDC 1910*.
58. Report of the Committee of the Board of Council, February 16, 1899, RG 1.6, box 6, file 11, Diopa Archives.
59. *JDC 1872*; Donovan, *Different Call*, 64, 68–69.
60. The story of Diocesan House is practically a chapter in itself, with lots being donated and rejected, purchased and sold; committee decisions being challenged and revisited; arguments over locations north and south of Market; and, of course, problems reaching agreement, securing cooperation, and raising funds.
61. *JDC 1899*; *JDC 1908*.
62. *JDC 1899*, 103, 104.
63. Ozi W. Whitaker to wardens of the Church of St. Simeon, October 18, 1910, RG 1.6, box 7, Diopa Archives; for legal opinion on churches as corporations, see box 2, file 19.
64. *JDC 1892*, 58.
65. *JDC 1906*, 104–5.
66. *JDC 1911*, 64.
67. *JDC 1900*, 101; *JDC 1901*, 88.
68. *JDC 1901*; *JDC 1906*, 62.
69. *JDC 1906*, 64.
70. *JDC 1910*, 122.
71. *JDC 1877*, 45; *JDC 1880*.
72. *JDC 1909*, 120–21.

7

The Church in Prosperity, Depression, and War, 1910–1945

THOMAS F. RZEZNIK

On Thanksgiving Day 1918, Bishop Philip Mercer Rhinelander gave thanks to God for the blessings of peace. The occasion was both solemn and festive, a time to celebrate the homecoming of those who had fought in World War I and to honor those who had died in service to the country. Rhinelander also used the Thanksgiving service as an opportunity to promote plans for the new diocesan cathedral, a monumental project that would be "a temple of God's peace, a house of prayer for all God's people," and "a thank-offering for victory."[1] As he envisioned it, the cathedral would be the city's religious crown jewel and a fitting tribute to the mother diocese of the Episcopal Church.

The cathedral project epitomized the spirit of the Diocese of Pennsylvania in the opening decades of the twentieth century and reflected the theological and social outlook of its members. The period was marked by economic prosperity and a remarkable sense of confidence. Institutional maturity and diocesan centralization were bolstered by an increasingly national and nationalistic vision of the church's role in public life and a fuller theological embrace of the church's Catholic heritage. The cathedral plans embodied all of these developments.

The triumphalism of the age, however, was soon tempered by depression and war. Yet those dark years were also an opportunity for the diocese to shine with a spirit of service and sacrifice. In adapting to the changing fortunes of the period, the diocese and its members responded to the new realities of modern American life.

Prosperity and National Prominence

In the opening decades of the twentieth century, the Philadelphia area prospered as a center of industry, commerce, and finance. Major corporations like the Pennsylvania Railroad, Baldwin Locomotive, and Curtis Publishing shared the stage with a host of smaller firms that manufactured everything from soup (Campbell's) to nuts and bolts (William Sellers & Co.). Between 1900 and 1950 Philadelphia consistently ranked as the third-largest city in the country, and for much of that time was the third-richest, too.[2]

The diocese benefited from the region's good fortune. Between 1910 and 1930 the number of communicants in the diocese rose from 55,561 to 70,288, a 26.5 percent increase.[3] In contrast, membership stagnated during the lean years that followed, so that by the end of World War II there were slightly fewer communicants than in 1932. Nevertheless, the diocese maintained a position of prominence within the national church, behind only New York in size and wealth.[4]

Growth inevitably transformed the physical and social geography of the city and surrounding counties. Rail and streetcar transportation opened up new districts to settlement. The grand estates in Chestnut Hill, the Whitemarsh Valley, and along the Main Line were converted from summer retreats to year-round residences, while middle-class families flocked to blossoming neighborhoods in West and North Philadelphia. The increased use of private automobiles led to the construction of new boulevards connecting far-flung areas—a development that almost cost the diocese one of its churches, St. Clement's. When the city decided to widen Twentieth Street to accommodate downtown traffic, the building, in a feat of engineering, was lifted off its foundation and moved back forty feet to be spared demolition.[5]

With the membership gains and suburbanization of the 1910s and 1920s, the number of parishes and missions in the diocese increased, although the rate of expansion was slower than in the previous three decades.[6] Church growth during these two decades was characterized by alterations, additions, and embellishments. Prosperity enabled many parishes to improve and expand their facilities in response to membership gains, especially once wartime scarcity ended and the government lifted construction restrictions. Temporary chapels were replaced with more permanent (and more impressive) structures.[7] Benefactors lavished memorial windows, altars, statues, and other adornments on both new and existing churches. As in the earlier industrial period, some donors single-handedly financed the construction of new buildings, if not entire parishes.[8]

Parish beautification projects were a boon to local artists, artisans, and architects, and helped Philadelphia develop as a center for ecclesiastical art and architecture. Stained glass from the studios of Nicola D'Ascenzo and William Willett and decorative metalwork produced by Samuel Yellin garnered a national reputation for their beauty and craftsmanship.[9] They and other designers worked closely with local architects, many of whom had trained at the University of Pennsylvania under the careful eye of Theophilus Parsons Chandler Jr., a leading ecclesiastical architect and master of the English Gothic style popular within the diocese. A devout Episcopalian, Chandler capped his career by designing and financing the Chapel of St. Martin, Ithan (now Christ Church, Ithan), which he and his wife donated to the diocese in 1919.[10]

Perhaps more than ever before, Episcopalians became obsessed with the "character" of their churches. Refinement reigned: "Why not have a little more of the beauty of the useful arts in our Church?" asked one author. Editorials in the diocesan newspaper addressed such crucial matters as "shrubbery" and "the latest trends in tombstones."[11] The diocese began to take a more active role in church planning in 1913 with the establishment of the Church Building Commission, to help parishes "avoid making mistakes in location and design." The creation of the commission also reflected diocesan concerns over the nature and direction of parish growth. With parishes too often clustered in wealthy districts, the commission encouraged greater support for diocesan missions and church extension.[12]

As church growth shifted from the city to the suburban periphery, architectural styles underwent a notable change. New parishes favored churches that blended into the natural landscape, with towers kept below the tree line and vast churchyards creating a buffer between buildings and surrounding roads. Suburban churches were often modeled on English parish churches and their earlier counterparts in the diocese, such as St. James the Less and St. Timothy's, Roxborough. Usually constructed of local stone, they featured rich interior woodwork and decorative elements drawn from the English ecclesiastical tradition, including rood screens, choir stalls, and eagle lecterns.[13]

While the "parish church" revival reflected the intense Anglophilia of the Philadelphia upper class, it was both a catalyst for and a product of the changing theological orientation of the Episcopal Church. Enlarged chancels and extended choirs signaled the acceptance of high-church principles by emphasizing ritual over preaching. These ecclesiastical spaces also fostered a new sense of community and mission. Unlike "city churches," which were designed to accommodate and evangelize the urban masses, these smaller parish churches emphasized a more intimate sense of community.[14] And to some extent they served as the perfect ecclesiastical accessories to the country estates of the Philadelphia upper class, helping them to envision themselves as heirs to the English gentry.

On the diocesan level, this same prosperity allowed a number of institutions to acquire new facilities or expand existing ones. Nineteen twenty-one stood out as a remarkable year. That April the diocese relocated Church House from Walnut Street to a residence adjoining the Church of the Holy Trinity on Rittenhouse Square that had been acquired "on favorable terms" from Mrs. Alexander J. Cassatt, the widow of the former president of the Pennsylvania Railroad. In July the Philadelphia Divinity School began construction of its new campus in West Philadelphia. Then, in the fall, the Episcopal Academy transferred from Locust Street to "Yorklynne," an Overbrook estate originally built for a wealthy snuff manufacturer. Its forty-room mansion would house the venerable educational institution for the next fifty years. The Episcopal Hospital, however, waited another decade to replace its eighty-seven-year-old central pavilion, dedicating its new landmark spire-topped tower in 1933.[15]

In addition to sustaining physical expansion, industrial-era wealth allowed many parishes and other diocesan institutions to build endowments. St. Asaph's in Bala Cynwyd had dedicated its annual Easter offering since 1895 for its endowment, which had grown to $50,000 by 1930.[16] At the Church of the Holy Trinity, Rittenhouse Square, rectors William McVickar and Floyd W. Tomkins spoke often of the need to save during years of plenty for eventual lean times ahead. Their efforts resulted in a remarkable $500,000 endowment by the mid-1920s.[17] It became increasingly common for parish leaders and diocesan officials to remind the faithful to remember the church in their wills, with model bequest clauses provided to help donors get the legal language right.[18] Admittedly, rising income and inheritance taxes contributed to this outpouring of generosity, as wealthy individuals preferred that their money go to the church rather than the government. But regardless of donors' motives, their financial legacies provided a vital source of income for many parishes.

Gifts, of course, came from sources both large and small. In 1927 the diocese hosted a national ceremony to mark the fiftieth anniversary of the Lenten Mite Offering, a program that had originated at St. John's Church in Lower Merion as a way to encourage Sunday school students to support the missions. The "Bishop's Bricks Fund," instituted around 1915, relied on ten-cent donations to support diocesan extension. Members of the Episcopal Churchwomen, the diocesan women's auxiliary, were among the most tireless fund-raisers for various diocesan charities, including settlement houses, dispensaries, immigrant aid, child welfare programs, poor relief, and food and fuel assistance.[19]

Prosperity, however, also led to unforeseen pastoral problems. As the diocesan population continued to shift from the city to the suburban periphery, many older parishes experienced severe declines in membership and financial support. Some parochial restructuring was inevitable as the growing central business district consumed residential neighborhoods, but even churches in less commercial districts were adversely affected by residential mobility. After growing steadily in the 1910s and early 1920s, communicant rolls at the Church of the Holy Trinity fell from 1,294 in 1910 to 760 in 1934. Membership at the Church of the Saviour in West Philadelphia fell by half between 1920 and 1935.[20] In an attempt to solve the problem of declining attendance, one center city rector encouraged his parishioners to purchase cars so that they might more easily travel from the suburbs. Another complained that his congregation was "scattered all over the city and suburbs, so that it often takes a half day to make a pastoral visit." As leading families moved away, many churches struggled to recruit lay leaders to fill vestry seats and head parish organizations. When the Reverend Joseph Fort Newton arrived at the Church of St. Luke and the Epiphany in 1938, he described the vestry of the downtown congregation as "a skeleton of its former strength."[21]

Congregations faced with empty pews were left with a difficult choice. If they could not attract new members—a formidable task in districts increasingly inhabited by recent Catholic and Jewish immigrants—they often had no alternative but to relocate or merge. In 1932 the Church of the Holy Trinity was approached by St. James's, which had earlier moved from Seventh and Market to the Rittenhouse Square district in response to neighborhood transition. After merger plans fell through, St. James's, the third-oldest parish in the city, hobbled through the Great Depression before dissolving in 1946.[22] St. Thomas's Church, the oldest African American Episcopalian congregation in the country, transferred to West Philadelphia in 1938.[23] Such incidents, by no means isolated, foreshadowed the more pronounced parochial changes of the second half of the twentieth century.

The demographic changes caused by suburbanization left many downtown parishes struggling to maintain their ministry to the city's poor and immigrant classes. Since each parish functioned as an independent corporation governed by its members, the diocese had no legal or canonical authority to force parishes to remain downtown or to reinvest in the city. In the 1930s the diocesan convention voted against changes in the system of apportionment that would have provided greater financial support for "city churches." Those committed to urban ministry did not hide their sense of moral outrage. They criticized the diocese for abandoning the city, turning its back on its historic parishes, and "deserting the people." In an impassioned plea for greater awareness to the "changes in our churches," one rector could not help but cry out, "Wake up, Philadelphia Episcopalians!"[24]

The general prosperity of the diocese and its parishes made Episcopalians easy targets for criticism. In the eyes of one observer, many were members of "class churches" who built luxurious sanctuaries for use on Sunday mornings but left them "shut up all the rest of the week."[25] Some within the diocese grew concerned about complacency among the faithful. At the 1921 convention, Bishop Rhinelander declared that "the rank and file" must cease "to regard their Parish Church as a 'reluctant Sunday Morning Club.'" There was also a sense that parishes had developed an unhealthy dependence on a handful of wealthy donors, whose financial influence allowed them to dominate parochial affairs. Speaking before the diocesan convention in 1927, Bishop Thomas J. Garland, Rhinelander's successor, suggested that reform of parish vestries was "a matter for serious consideration." He argued that the "self-perpetuating" vestries found at some parishes "surely [do] not represent the democratic principles on which the Church [was] founded." Gradually, in order to broaden representation, many parishes passed provisions that limited the number of consecutive terms a member of the vestry could serve.[26]

Similar concerns were raised at the diocesan level, where some felt that larger parishes should receive greater lay representation at the annual convention. Efforts to institute a system of "proportionate representation," however, consistently failed, as they had when first proposed in the 1880s and 1890s. Diocesan officials and convention delegates held firmly to the principle that the parish was the basic unit of the diocese and that, as such, each should receive an equal voice.[27] This also meant that diocesan and parochial missions remained ineligible for representation. Attempts to extend voting privileges to these communities, which were often located in poorer neighborhoods or made up of racial and ethnic minorities, similarly met with little success.[28]

As the Episcopal Church continued to draw disproportionately from the ranks of the city's comfortable classes, some reformers within the diocese argued that not enough was being done to keep the working classes in the fold. They feared that the church would lose them to labor radicalism or socialism. The Episcopal Church had a mixed record on issues of labor and economic reform. During the late nineteenth century the church had been a leading voice in the Social Gospel Movement and had done much to advocate for improved labor relations through the Church Association for the Advancement of the Interests of Labor. In the early twentieth century the diocese produced progressives like Dr. George Woodward, who worked to end child labor and promote housing reform, but also many who defended the social and economic status quo.[29] The Reverend George Chalmers Richmond, one of the more radical activists in the diocese, landed in trouble with his ecclesiastical superiors when he declared that "the moral vision of the clergy [has] been restricted . . . by the power of special interests, vested rights and rich laymen."[30]

* * * * *

The Richmond Ecclesiastical Trial

Matters of church discipline are usually conducted quietly, but that was not the case when the Reverend George Chalmers Richmond was brought before an ecclesiastical court in 1916. Over the course of eight months, Richmond defended himself against more than 140 charges, ranging from minor lapses, such as failure to maintain proper parish records, to major offenses, including "conduct unbecoming a clergyman" and violations of his ordination vows. The trial made headlines in the local papers and was followed closely by members of the diocese on account of the sensational figure at its center.

Richmond, the rector of St. John's Church in Northern Liberties, had come to Philadelphia in 1909 from the Diocese of Central New York, where he had served as secretary to Bishop Frederic Dan Huntington, one of the leading figures in the Social Gospel Movement within the Episcopal Church. A committed advocate for the poor and working classes, Richmond spoke out against child labor and actively supported local unionization efforts. Among the actions that brought him to the attention of diocesan officials was his involvement with the Central Labor Union, the group responsible for igniting the violent 1909 carmen's strike that crippled the city's streetcar network.

Richmond also railed against the concentration of wealth and power in the hands of the elite, and openly denounced the "money power" within the Episcopal Church. Such pronouncements earned him the loyalty of his working-class congregation but angered many influential members of the diocesan laity who were directly or indirectly implicated by them. Richmond's views also worried his ecclesiastical superiors, especially when he seemed to speak on behalf of the diocese.

The Richmond ecclesiastical trial, which resulted in a two-year suspension for Richmond and contributed to his eventual defrocking, was one of the more colorful episodes in the history of the diocese. Although diocesan historian J. Wesley Twelves suggested that the trial stemmed from a misunderstanding between Richmond and the bishops that had been blown out of proportion, the matter was symptomatic of more complex issues. Most significantly, the trial reflected the class tensions prevalent within the diocese during this period of prosperity and the church's aversion to social radicalism.

SOURCES: For an account of the proceedings, see "George Chalmers Richmond Ecclesiastical Trial," George Chalmers Richmond Papers, Collection 550, HSP. For a brief biographical sketch of Huntington, see David Hein and Gardiner H. Shattuck Jr., *The Episcopalians* (Westport, Conn.: Praeger, 2004), 225. Richmond also wrote a tribute to Huntington, *Frederic Dan Huntington: A Tribute* (Rochester, N.Y., 1908). On the carmen's strike against the Philadelphia Rapid Transit Company, see Lloyd M. Abernathy, "Progressivism, 1905–1919," in *Philadelphia: A 300-Year History*, ed. Russell F. Weigley (New York: W. W. Norton, 1982), 547–49. See also "Richmond Declares Money Power Has Dominated Church" (n.d.), typed transcript of a newspaper report, in Rhinelander Letters, box 6, George Chalmers Richmond Papers, Collection 550, HSP; "Rev. G. C. Richmond, Clergyman, 72, Dies," *New York Times*, January 16, 1938; J. Wesley Twelves, *A History of the Diocese of Pennsylvania of the Protestant Episcopal Church in the U.S.A., 1784–1968* (Philadelphia: Diocese of Pennsylvania, 1969), 35–36.

* * * * *

The Episcopal Church's close ties to the social and economic elite may have made it seem socially exclusive, but they also provided the church with an indisputable air of confidence, particularly in the years following World War I, the so-called Anglo-Saxon decade. During these years, Episcopalians held positions of power in the nation's economic and political life in rates far disproportionate to their overall numbers. They brought their professional expertise to bear on church affairs as members of parish vestries and diocesan commissions, and held firmly to a patrician creed of civic responsibility and public service.[31] Senator George Wharton Pepper, one of the leading laymen of the diocese, believed that through the Christian faith, as professed by the Episcopal Church, one might "develop all the qualities of the good citizen." In Philadelphia this ethos was prevalent at the University of Pennsylvania, the training ground for the city's leading citizens, where members of the diocese dominated the upper echelons of the administration and the board of trustees.[32]

As part of their growing national influence, members of the Episcopal Church increasingly affirmed their "American" identity. Speaking before a gathering of the Episcopal Churchwomen in 1919, Bishop Rhinelander stressed that Episcopalians had a "national responsibility to unify the church of America." Given Philadelphia's history, members of the diocese focused on their forebears' role in the struggle for independence and the spiritual growth of the nation. Their historical consciousness was on prominent display at the 1926 Sesquicentennial Exposition, where volunteers representing various parishes and organizations staffed the diocesan booth. It featured a filmstrip about the diocese and a model of Christ Church that allowed onlookers to peer through the roof "to observe the pew where Washington and other patriots worshipped." Many who attended the exposition also took the opportunity to visit the city's historic churches, advertised in a diocesan pamphlet as the "spiritual sources" from which the signers of the Declaration of Independence "drew their inspiration."[33]

This patriotic sensibility shaped Episcopalians' sense of mission. In 1921 Bishop Garland claimed that the Episcopal Church had a unique obligation to help "mold [immigrants] into American citizens." To advance this work, the diocese supported the creation of a number of missions to serve various ethnic communities, especially Poles and Italians. These efforts, however, met with limited success. Missions that did not close within a few years of their founding rarely lasted more than a generation or two.[34] Linguistic differences and cultural biases hindered outreach efforts. Church workers assumed that Catholic immigrants wanted to free themselves of papal influence and join an "American Church," and they misinterpreted the nature of Catholic devotional practices as an "appalling" "ignorance of Christianity." Church outreach toward Philadelphia's growing Jewish population presented its own set of challenges, including protests from Jewish leaders who objected to Christian proselytizing and Americanization efforts.[35] In addition, those involved in evangelization constantly struggled against the perception that membership in the Episcopal Church was reserved for those of English ancestry.[36]

Episcopalians had more success among African Americans, long a presence in the diocese. Lured in part by wartime jobs, Philadelphia's black population swelled to 134,000 by 1920, more than double their number in

1900. In response, parishes and the diocese increased support for "colored work" and established several new mission chapels for that purpose.[37] To help guide this expansion, the Reverend Henry L. Phillips was appointed archdeacon for work among the colored in 1913. Between 1900 and 1945, twenty-seven black candidates for orders graduated from the Philadelphia Divinity School, many of whom remained to serve the local community.[38] The place of blacks within the diocese was hardly ideal, given the segregated nature of parish life, but their commitment to the church remained strong and their growth robust. While the total number of communicants within the diocese dropped slightly between 1930 and 1945, the number of those in "colored" congregations grew by more than 80 percent, from 3,159 to 5,733. In the same period, several missions matured into independent parishes, and two churches, St. Thomas's and St. Simon the Cyrenian, each reported more than a thousand members.[39]

Diocesan outreach to ethnic and racial minorities may have stemmed first from Episcopalians' concern for those less fortunate, but it also reflected their distinct vision of the church's role in civic and religious affairs. More than ever before, Episcopalians saw themselves not simply as members of a national church (in terms of geographic reach), but as *the* church of the nation, the de facto religious establishment. One manifestation of this sense of religious identity was the Episcopal Church's lead in establishing national houses of worship, such as the National Cathedral in Washington, D.C., and the Washington Memorial Chapel at Valley Forge.[40]

* * * * *

Washington Memorial Chapel

Of the thousands who visit the Washington Memorial Chapel at Valley Forge each year, many do not realize that it is an independent Episcopalian parish. Instead, they believe that the chapel was part of the government's plan for the park, a presumption that speaks to the remarkable success of the Episcopal Church in placing itself within the life of the nation.

Plans for the chapel were first proposed in 1903 by the Reverend W. Herbert Burk, the rector of All Saints' Church in Norristown, who sought to erect a shrine to the memory of George Washington and all the patriots who fought for American independence. He dreamed that it would serve as the "American Westminster," a "House of Prayer . . . great enough to be the Nation's symbol of thankfulness to God for his manifold gifts."

Initial lack of support from the diocese did not deter Burk, but constant financial difficulties put the project in jeopardy. The diocese took charge of the project in 1913, and within four years the main sanctuary was completed. Attention then shifted to the cloister of the colonies, the defender's gate (which currently houses parish offices), and other portions of the chapel complex. The redesigned bell tower, with its noted carillon, was not completed until 1953, after receiving considerable support from the Daughters of the American Revolution.

Although local architect Milton B. Medary Jr. designed the chapel, Burk was unquestionably the project's visionary. He was solely responsible for determining how Washington and the Revolution would be commemorated. Patriotic imagery infuses the space. One of the chapel's most impressive features is the window above the main entrance. Its thirty-six medallions depict scenes from Washington's life, from his baptism and early education through his military career and presidential service. Other patriots are commemorated in the aisle windows, each of which illustrates a particular American theme or value, such as discovery, settlement, mission, patriotism, and democracy. As Burk intended, the chapel's design "use[s] art to glorify religion and to illustrate history."

To this day, the Washington Memorial Chapel serves as a shrine to the American people and marks the site of the revolutionary encampment as hallowed ground. It reflects the lasting influence of the nationalistic vision that guided the Episcopal Church and its members during the opening decades of the twentieth century.

SOURCES: See W. Herbert Burk, *Valley Forge: What It Is, Where It Is, and What to See There* (North Wales, Pa.: Norman B. Nuss, 1928), 91. For the history of the chapel's development, see Lorett Treese, *Valley Forge: Making and Remaking a National Symbol* (University Park: Pennsylvania State University Press, 1995), 81–103. For a description of the chapel's various elements, see Louise Walker, "Memorial at Valley Forge," *Stained Glass* (Spring 1976): 20–23; and "Welcome to Washington Memorial Chapel" (n.d.), pamphlet courtesy of the Washington Memorial Chapel. On the chapel's mission, see W. Herbert Burk, "The American Westminster," *DAR Magazine*, December 1923, 709, cited in Treese, *Valley Forge*, 99.

* * * * *

Ironically, this increased identification with the nation came at a time when the composition of the Episcopal Church was becoming increasingly out of step with the national population. The cultural and religious authority of white, Anglo-Saxon Protestantism exemplified by members of the Episcopal Church would fade by midcentury.[41]

New Episcopal Leadership and Cathedral Dreams

The diocese witnessed a new style of episcopal leadership during this period. In 1911 Philip Mercer Rhinelander was elected bishop following the sudden death of Alexander Mackay-Smith, who had been elevated only eight months earlier. At the time of Rhinelander's election, the convention also selected Thomas J. Garland as the new suffragan bishop. When Rhinelander resigned in 1923, Garland was elected the diocesan ordinary, a position he held until his death in 1931. The two men, who were fewer than three years apart in age, represented a generational shift in diocesan leadership. Despite their distinct personalities and different theological orientations, Garland and Rhinelander shared a common vision for the diocese and a similar understanding of their episcopal office, particularly in their administrative capacity to oversee parochial affairs. Their successor, Francis Marion Taitt, who was elected coadjutor in 1929 and served as diocesan ordinary from Garland's death until his own in 1943, would follow the course they set.

At the time of Rhinelander's election, parochialism and church politics continued to have a powerful influence on diocesan affairs. The contest between high, low, and broad factions made it difficult for the convention to reach consensus on any number of matters, not least of which was the selection of a bishop. (As one rector remarked, the Episcopal Church, with "so many varieties," was "very much like Heinz's Pickles!")[42] Rhinelander, favored by the high-church faction, was elected fairly quickly—on the second ballot—when two other candidates split the low and broad party bloc.[43] Garland's subsequent election was thus an attempt by those parties to place in office someone more in line with their views. They thought that Garland, who had served as Bishop Ozi Whitaker's personal secretary for eight years, would keep Rhinelander in check and preserve his predecessor's low-church and evangelical style.[44]

The contrast between Rhinelander and Whitaker was unmistakable. Elected at the age of forty-two, Rhinelander brought youthful vitality to the bishop's chair. He was born in Newport, Rhode Island, in 1869, the youngest of nine children in a prominent family with strong ties to the Episcopal Church. Educated at St. Paul's School, Harvard College, the General Theological Seminary, and Oxford, he developed an appreciation for the historic traditions of Anglicanism during his studies in England. After his ordination in 1897, he served briefly in parish work in the Diocese of Washington before accepting faculty positions first at the Berkeley Divinity School in Connecticut and then at the Episcopal Theological School in Massachusetts.[45]

To characterize Rhinelander simply as a high churchman is to conflate his theological views with his understanding of his role as bishop. As his biographer explained, Rhinelander "leaned to the English conception of a bishop's duty and privilege." Ritualism was less important to him than the defense of the apostolic heritage of the church and its historic doctrines. He believed that the episcopal office provided the "sacramental security" necessary for the "continuity of the Church's spiritual life." At a time when "higher criticism" and scientific analysis were reshaping theological study, Rhinelander ardently defended the creed and other matters of faith.[46]

To Rhinelander, the spiritual authority of the bishop obligated him to push for greater diocesan centralization. Although Whitaker had done much to turn the diocese into a working unit, he had not altered the system of decentralized parochial authority. Rhinelander, in contrast, wanted to place "the diocese at the center of things."[47] Whereas Whitaker spoke of "church unity," with an emphasis on Christ and ties to other Protestant bodies, Rhinelander stressed "diocesan unity." Speaking before the convention in 1917, he pleaded "for a larger and more generous recognition of the Diocese as such . . . [for] the Diocese, rather than the Parish, is both the working unit of the Church's organization and the cell of its organic life and growth." Garland echoed these sentiments in 1925. "There is no room for pure 'parochialism' in the Episcopal Church," he insisted. Rather, "there must be co-ordination, and a full realization of the duty of every member of the church, not merely to his parish, but also to his Diocese, and to the whole Church."[48] To the dismay of those who had pushed for his election, it was clear that Garland was following in Rhinelander's, not Whitaker's, footsteps.

Rhinelander, believing that the office of bishop could serve as "both symbol and instrument of our unity," found ways to extend his influence. In 1912 he supported the creation of *The Church News* to serve as the official voice of the diocese (and loyal defender of his policies).[49] He restructured the convocation system to streamline diocesan organization and, where possible, he placed more authority in diocesan bodies or appointed

FIGURE 7.1 Bishop Philip Mercer Rhinelander

executives. The oversight of diocesan committees, departments, and offices increased tremendously during Rhinelander's tenure. He also sought to extend the financial reach of the diocese by increasing the number and size of funds under its control.

Many of these changes met with considerable resistance, if not outright hostility. Although Rhinelander's policies did not detract from the authority traditionally reserved for parish vestries, particularly in financial matters, the shift in the balance of power between the diocese and its parishes was evident. In exercising greater spiritual oversight, Rhinelander reined in some of the theological liberties individual parishes had enjoyed. An intellectual conservative, he defended the doctrines of the "Catholic faith" and favored greater uniformity in ritual and worship. Tensions grew to such a point that at the diocesan convention of 1919 Rhinelander was compelled to publicly refute charges that he was a "Romanizer." Frustrated by the opposition, and with his health in question, Rhinelander resigned his office in 1923 and accepted a post as the first dean of the College of Preachers, a "post-graduate school for preaching" housed on the grounds of the National Cathedral in Washington, D.C.[50]

The shift toward greater diocesan centralization mirrored changes taking place within the national church. In 1919 the General Convention approved a comprehensive restructuring of the church's administrative organization. The twenty-four-member National Council was established as the denomination's main governing body, with seats divided equally among the bishops, clergy, and lay deputies. The convention also modified the office of presiding bishop, making it an elected six-year post rather than an appointment based on seniority. Together, he and the council oversaw the operations of five newly consolidated central departments: missions and church extension, religious education, Christian social service, finance, and publicity. The convention also increased the power of the provincial synods that had been established six years earlier.[51] These changes, which flowed from the corporate organizational imperatives of the day, modernized the administrative operation of the Episcopal Church.

National and diocesan restructuring also responded to women's demands for greater inclusion in church administration in an official capacity. In 1919 the Woman's Auxiliary, which previously reported to the Board of Missions, was recognized as an auxiliary to the National Council, with its own executive secretary and board. Then, in 1934, representatives of the Woman's Auxiliary were given seats on the National Council.[52] These changes recognized women's increasing power and importance in the work of the church, particularly in fund-raising and missionary activities.

Responding to the women's suffrage movement and the 1920 Lambeth encyclical, which recommended that women be admitted to church councils "on equal terms as men," the 1921 diocesan convention considered a motion to allow for women delegates, but the measure was voted down the following year.[53]

If Rhinelander contributed the impetus and theological rationale for diocesan centralization, then Garland provided the corporate impulse. Prior to entering the ministry, Garland had been an executive in the steel industry. His financial acumen and administrative experience brought him to the attention of Bishop Whitaker. In addition to serving as the bishop's secretary, Garland was placed in charge of the missionary department of the national church. To put the diocese on firmer financial ground, he instituted and directed the $3.5 million Campaign for Missions and Institutions in 1926. Shortly before his death, members of the National Council described him as "the best financial genius in the Church."[54] The dominant cultural values of order and efficiency enabled Garland to promote diocesan reorganization and administrative consolidation as a practical and prudent business strategy.

Despite his relative youth, Garland was described as always having been a "frail man." On account of his weak health, which was undoubtedly strained by administrative stress, Garland asked the convention in 1928 to name a coadjutor, preferably someone younger than he. The election proved unexpectedly difficult, as each of the first five men called declined the nomination. It has been suggested that owing to Garland's relatively young age some may not have wanted to endure a long term as coadjutor. Ultimately, a special convention had to be held, at which time Francis Marion Taitt, a respected member of the local clergy, accepted the nomination.[55]

Garland and Taitt both benefited from an intimate prior knowledge of the diocese and its people. Both were elevated from within, unlike many of their predecessors. Although Garland, born in Belfast, Ireland, and educated at St. Bees College in England, was not a native Philadelphian, he had become an adopted son. He received his training for the ministry at the Philadelphia Divinity School and spent many of his early years in local parish work. Taitt, likewise a PDS alumnus, dedicated his entire career to the diocese, including a remarkable thirty-six years as rector of St. Paul's Church in Chester. He also served as dean of the Convocation of Chester from 1903 to 1929, during which time he developed a fruitful working relationship with local parishes and their clergy.[56] His devotion to the diocese and his deep personal concern for the welfare of all those who lived in the Philadelphia region were especially apparent as he led the diocesan

FIGURE 7.2 Bishop Thomas J. Garland

response to the Great Depression and World War II, rallying support for the diocese and its institutions during those difficult years.

The careers of bishops Rhinelander, Garland, and Taitt were bound together by their common support for the diocesan cathedral, one of the greatest undertakings in diocesan history. No project was more important or more symbolic to the local church, and none would prove more difficult. Bishop Whitaker had withheld support for a cathedral, citing his belief that "the Rectors and Laymen of the diocese preferred the existing

FIGURE 7.3 Bishop Francis Marion Taitt

distribution of work among the Parishes rather than centralization of it in and around a cathedral."[57] But in an age of American cathedral building, with monumental edifices rising up in Washington, D.C., New York City, San Francisco, and other cities, some found it distressing that the mother diocese of the Episcopal Church was without its own cathedral.

Over the years, several individuals had attempted to remedy this situation on their own. In 1886 the family of George W. South provided money for the construction of the Church of the Advocate, erecting a magnificent high French Gothic "cathedral in miniature" with the intent that it might someday serve as the diocesan church. When Rhinelander selected it as the site of his episcopal consecration, their hopes quickened. The Reverend W. Herbert Burk similarly thought that his "wayside chapel" at Valley Forge would make a suitable cathedral for the diocese. And in 1916 the diocese received a $100,000 bequest from Mrs. Henry W. Watson in support of a diocesan church in South Philadelphia.[58]

The official diocesan stance changed under Rhinelander, who threw his support behind the cathedral. This was not unexpected, since he was a disciple of Bishop Henry Yates Satterlee of Washington, D.C., the driving force behind the National Cathedral.[59] Shortly after his election, Rhinelander selected the Church of the Ascension at Broad and South streets to serve as the pro-cathedral until a proper cathedral could be built. He then established the Cathedral Foundation to hold funds for the project, and set out on the important task of selecting a location. For many years the diocese eyed a site on the Benjamin Franklin Parkway, the city's recently completed beaux arts thoroughfare. Problems securing the land forced officials to reconsider, and in 1927 a hundred-acre site was selected in Upper Roxborough.[60] According to diocesan reports, this location would place the cathedral at the highest point in the city, an obvious source of pride.[61]

As a prestige project for the diocese and the city, the cathedral gained the support of many of Philadelphia's most distinguished and prosperous families. Sallie Drexel van Rensselaer, for instance, held the honorary presidency of the Cathedral League, the project's influential women's auxiliary.[62] William Ellis Scull, a founding member of the Cathedral Chapter, hosted luncheons and dinners at his Overbrook estate to promote interest in the work.[63] After the Roxborough site was selected, members of the Houston and Woodward families cleared the mortgage on the land. Garland actively courted the city's "men and women of great wealth" and encouraged them to take a "vital interest" in the cathedral as "patriotic Pennsylvanians and loyal Churchmen." Then again, some simply wanted to demonstrate that Roman Catholics did not "have a monopoly of Cathedrals in America."[64]

The envisioned cathedral complex was immense. According to the original plan, the campus would include the cathedral, a bishop's house, a deanery, a cloister of canons, and a synod hall. In time, it would also comprise a deaconess house, a home for the aged, a home for children, schools, and other institutions, making it the focal point of diocesan spiritual life

FIGURE 7.4 Architect's model of the unrealized cathedral in Roxborough. The circled area represents St. Mary's Chapel, the only section to be completed. It later became the parish church of St. Mary's, Cathedral Road.

and "the natural seat of all Diocesan agencies and activities." The cathedral itself, as a "house of prayer for all people," was intended to be a theologically inclusive space that united persons of all faiths in worship.[65] Diocesan reports praised the Roxborough location as the geographic center of the metropolitan area and the population center of the diocese. (The plan also included a proposed Chestnut Hill–Bryn Mawr Road that would bridge the Schuylkill River and make the cathedral the link between the two elite suburban regions.) The cathedral was intended to advance the diocese's nationalist enterprise, with supporters believing it destined to "become the Mecca of our people, as it will bear witness to the faith of our fathers and to their contribution in the making of our Nation."[66]

Despite this passion, the cathedral vision was never realized. Ground was not broken until 1932, by which time the Depression had dried up streams of financial support.[67] The project was also a victim of diocesan hubris. Cathedral boosters, thinking that the prosperity of the early twentieth century would continue unabated, had envisioned a structure that would rival the great cathedrals of the world. The proposed dimensions stood at a total length 460 feet, with transepts stretching 160 feet, a nave 45 feet wide, and a main tower rising 279 feet. Even though the plans were scaled down in the 1930s, only the Lady Chapel and two side chapels were completed by the time the project was halted in the 1960s. The structure now serves as a parish church, St. Mary's, Cathedral Road.[68]

Theology and Faith Life

Styles of episcopal leadership and administrative organization helped to shape the character of the diocese, but they did not define the spirit of the church, which grew from the beliefs of the community. In an age characterized by the rise of secular modernism, economic hardship, and the devastation of two world wars, Episcopalians embraced theological perspectives and spiritual practices that enabled them to respond to contemporary moral issues, to enrich worship and parish life, and to promote interreligious cooperation.

The theological landscape of the diocese shifted considerably in the early twentieth century. The old party divisions remained in place, but those allegiances no longer seemed as relevant as they once had. Subscribing to high-, low-, or broad-church principles did not easily determine a person's response to the theological challenges presented by scientific rationalism, evolutionary biology, biblical "high criticism," and other hallmark issues of "modernism." One sign of these emerging influences came in 1913 when the alumni association of the Philadelphia Divinity School issued a "Memorial on the Subject of Higher Theological Learning," which called on the General Convention to support advanced theological study among the clergy. That same year, the Reverend Nathanael Groton, rector of St. Thomas's, Whitemarsh, described one of his confirmation students as "an intellectual doubter . . . [and] champion of science!"[69]

Episcopalians may not have suffered bitter division on account of these debates, but neither did they emerge unscathed. The greatest controversy centered on the creed and the ultimate validity of some of its constitutive elements, such as the virgin birth and bodily resurrection of Christ. Modernists contended that these nonscriptural elements could not be interpreted literally, since they were neither scientifically plausible nor rationally sound. Those holding more "traditional" views—a unique coalition that drew from both Anglo-Catholics and evangelicals—worried that scientific approaches to theological study would eviscerate the faith by stripping it of its historic teachings and essential doctrines, many of which could not be "proved" in any definitive sense.[70]

The debate over creeds raised the question of which beliefs, if any, were essential to the faith. Tensions came to a head in 1923, when the House of Bishops issued a pastoral letter that affirmed a traditional interpretation of the creed. Modernist critics charged that the bishops had overstepped their authority in defining doctrine. In the wake of the controversy, church leaders trod a fine line. They sought to promote theological inquiry without jettisoning established beliefs, distinguishing between articles of faith and statements of fact. One commentator argued that those who did not believe in the creed as the repository of theological truths might nevertheless accept its recitation as a "spiritual exercise" that recalled the "historic origin of our formulary."[71] Bishop Rhinelander, however, remained resolute in his defense of the creed, which he deemed "absolutely crucial" to the life of the church. He argued that any officer of the church who disowned the essential statement of faith was "guilty of the breach of a most sacred trust which they have sworn to keep inviolate."[72]

While such theological debates were somewhat removed from the daily lives of ordinary Episcopalians, the same cannot be said about the church's stance on various social and moral issues, especially those related to marriage and family life. Traditional views on the sacramental nature of marriage and the sanctity of the family had not lost their weight, but the effects of changing cultural assumptions were evident. In 1922 the General Convention struck the words "serve" and "obey" and the phrase "with all my worldly goods I thee endow" from the marriage service as part of a larger revision of the prayer book and church rubrics. This signaled the church's recognition of the changing relation between husband and wife that had emerged as part of the women's suffrage movement. The decline in church weddings and rising rates of interfaith marriage also garnered the attention of church leaders.[73]

Efforts to liberalize the church's position on divorce proved particularly contentious. While some wanted to outlaw divorce entirely, more moderate voices sought the passage of uniform divorce laws that would prevent states with less restrictive statutes from becoming "divorce mills." For religious leaders, however, the problem was not divorce per se but remarriage. The belief in the indissolubility of sacramental marriage meant that the church could not bless the marriage of a divorced person so long as his or her former spouse was still living, nor could it extend Communion to those who remarried.[74] As social pressure for change increased, church leaders recognized the need to reexamine church teachings and clarify directives. Delegates to the 1930 Lambeth Conference discussed the matter intensely, and while they reaffirmed many traditional teachings, they did allow bishops greater discretion, particularly in extending Communion to innocent parties in instances of adultery, should they remarry in a civil ceremony.[75]

The 1930 Lambeth encyclical further fueled discussion on divorce within the Episcopal Church. The issue came before the General Convention each time it met in the 1930s and 1940s. In 1937 the preliminary commission report recommended that local bishops be given discretion to allow for the possibility of remarriage for all divorced persons, not just the innocent party. The proposal was defeated by the House of Deputies and sent back to the commission for further study.[76] Three years later, efforts to liberalize church canons again failed. The House of Bishops had sought to make it possible for all divorced and remarried persons to seek ecclesiastical blessing after waiting one year, but lay deputies voted down the measure by a large margin. Although the bishops' openness to change may have seemed counterintuitive, it made sense for the clergy to seek greater flexibility so that they might respond to couples in a pastorally sensitive way. Even though these debates yielded no satisfactory resolution, they signaled to some a lack of a "sound, basic 'theology of marriage'" among Episcopalians and a need for the church to promote proper instruction about the nature of holy matrimony.[77]

The moral debate over divorce was also colored by the rising incidence of birth control, declining family size, and the specter of "race suicide" among the nation's prosperous "native" population. Low birth rates coupled with family instability, many Episcopalians worried, would result in the passing of their great Anglo-Teutonic race, and possibly their church as well. In addressing the issue of birth control, one editorial in the diocesan newspaper urged "every Churchman . . . [to] adjust his thinking to its economic, social and religious consequences," including "the startling decrease in the white population of Sunday School age."[78] Although the 1930 Lambeth Conference reaffirmed its "abhorrence of the sinful practice of abortion," for the first time it permitted the use of contraception by couples for "morally sound reasons." The General Convention likewise rescinded its opposition to birth control within marriage in 1934. At that time, the convention also supported efforts by doctors and medical clinics to "convey such information as is in accord with the highest principles of eugenics and a more wholesome life, wherein parenthood may be undertaken with due respect for the health of mothers and the welfare of the children."[79] Proponents of eugenics had earlier sought to protect the "integrity of the race and the home" by lobbying for mandatory health examinations to "prevent the securing of licenses of those who are morally and physically unfit" to wed, but church leaders countered that reception of the sacrament should not be restricted on medical grounds.[80]

Another perceived threat to family life was the rise of "youth culture." A more nebulous problem, it was difficult to address comprehensively. The Public Morals Committee of the diocese's Department of Christian Social Service issued lists of approved motion pictures in an effort to guide families to wholesome entertainment.[81] Parishes and other groups sponsored a variety of programs to help improve the physical and spiritual welfare of children, especially those from underprivileged backgrounds. In 1918 the Reverend Charles W. Shreiner founded the Church Farm School to provide for the educational needs of boys "without adequate home environment."[82] Since college students seemed most prone to moral laxity, a number of efforts focused on that population. In 1914 the administration of the University of Pennsylvania, under Episcopalian provost Charles Custis Harrison, brought Billy Sunday and his evangelical crusade to campus in an effort to revive religious interest among students. Penn students also formed their own vestry at the Church of the Transfiguration, which served as the university chapel from 1921 to 1933.[83] With relatively few church-sponsored colleges and universities, there was a national effort to promote Episcopalian chaplaincy programs.[84]

Many programs within the diocese were aimed at cultivating churchgoing, family piety, and greater religious involvement. Parishes held "go-to-church" Sundays to bring people back into the pews, and many organized societies that targeted specific segments of their membership.[85] In an effort to keep men and boys active in the life of the church, a number promoted the "muscular Christianity" of the era. At the Church of the Holy Trinity, Rittenhouse Square, the famous Drexel Biddle Bible classes taught that true manliness required both piety and physical prowess. The Stonemen's Fellowship, which also originated at Holy Trinity under the direction of the Reverend H. Charles Stone, recruited men to serve as agents of evangelization.[86] The Brotherhood of St. Andrew, however, was probably the most influential group. A national organization with strong roots in the diocese, the brotherhood sponsored a variety of programs to support the spiritual needs of men and boys, including Bible study, corporate Communion, and "coaching" programs to help junior members "comprehend the fullness of religion." It also encouraged men to assume leadership in family religious life.[87] Women were encouraged to join the Episcopal Churchwomen, the Girls' Friendly Society, the Daughters of the King, and other groups that promoted parish service, volunteerism, and missionary outreach. Such associations responded to changing gender roles and gender relations in society by preserving traditional spheres of activities for men and women.

When it came to other social issues, Episcopalians avoided overt moralizing. The national church did not take an official stance on Prohibition, but rather asked that citizens respect the rule of law.[88] Senator George Wharton Pepper, speaking unofficially for many within the diocese, insisted that the use of alcohol should be a personal moral choice, favoring temperance but not prohibition. In his autobiography, he recalled being "brought up to believe that the moral significance of conduct depends upon whether it is the result of compulsion or of an exercise of free will." Several prominent members of the diocese joined the Association Against the Prohibition Amendment, which viewed the law as unenforceable and therefore poor public policy.[89] Episcopalians likewise recognized the inherent difficulties of Sabbatarianist legislation and held that respect for the lord's day should spring from the informed conscience, not state mandate.[90]

Amid the theological and moral debates of the first half of the twentieth century, Episcopalians found unity in the bonds of common worship. Although congregations still defined themselves according to high- and low-church orientation, the church as a whole had moved toward a greater acceptance of formalized liturgical practice. Emphasis on ritual increasingly defined the character of the Episcopal Church and distinguished it from other denominations. In speaking of "church unity," Bishop Rhinelander maintained that "without uniformity in worship we may, indeed, secure a certain liberty to worship God according to our taste or conscience, but it is apt to be a freedom of a rather lonely and delusive kind, and the loss would seem far greater than the gain." This trend also reflected the continued strength of the Catholic revival in England and throughout the Anglican Communion. To mark the centenary of the Oxford Movement in 1933, the diocese played host to the "Catholic Congress," whose conferences and special liturgies drew thousands of participants from across the country.[91]

The liturgical revival of the early twentieth century led to a revision of the church's key liturgical text, the Book of Common Prayer. A new edition of the prayer book had been issued in 1892, but many within the church felt the need for a more comprehensive and systematic revision. Demands for a new prayer book first reached the General Convention in 1913, but the outbreak of World War I—coupled with some procedural problems within the committee—delayed sustained consideration of the matter until the 1920s. Members of the evangelical wing of the church questioned the need for revisions, concerned that changes would only provide further capitulation to ritualism and high-church influences. "If there are some who desire ornate ritual and observance of customs long since left behind," the rector of the Church of the Holy Trinity, Rittenhouse Square, announced in 1916, "we need not deny them their freedom; but we must not allow them to force upon us, through changes in our beloved Prayer Book, the things which are contrary to our evangelical inheritance and contradictory to the history and teaching of our Church."[92]

The 1928 edition was not as radical as critics had feared. Many of the changes were more stylistic than substantive. Prayers, collects, and thanksgivings were "mercifully edited" and cleansed of their archaic language and usages. Among other alterations, the burial service was expanded and an office for the visitation of the sick was added, while the three baptismal services that had appeared in earlier editions were condensed into one, with emphasis placed on the Resurrection rather than original sin. The only major point of contention was the proposal to excise the Articles of Religion. Although proponents of the measure argued that the Thirty-Nine Articles had no place in the prayer book, the majority at the General Convention refused to eliminate this "bulwark against a pro-Roman interpretation of the doctrines" and "strong safeguard" against "radical interpretation" of church teachings.[93]

The revised book allowed for greater flexibility in worship without mandating change. New rubrics simply sanctioned the trend toward more formalized worship that had already been taking place. Like church buildings themselves, altar settings became more elaborate and refined, as items once regarded as "too high" gained acceptance. As donors lavished altar wares, liturgical vestments, and other church goods on their parishes, they contributed, whether intentionally or not, to the changing style of worship. It was now common to find full frontals draped across the altar, and the presence of candles and flower arrangements within the sanctuary no longer caused a stir. If anything, the new prayer book unified worship by ending the period of experimentation and "rubrical laxity" that had emerged during the fifteen-year lapse between the first call for revision and its publication in 1928, when church leaders declared it to be the only authorized edition.[94]

Even with this emphasis on ritual, preaching continued to play a vital role in Episcopalian worship. Noted orators like Floyd W. Tomkins at Holy Trinity drew large crowds to their services, and parish committees continued to evaluate candidates for vacant rectorships on their preaching ability. These expectations meant that rectors devoted considerable attention to their sermons. In his first years as rector of St. Thomas's, Whitemarsh, Nathanael Groton frequently spent the greater part of a day crafting his weekly remarks.[95] At the Philadelphia Divinity School, homiletics remained an integral aspect of seminary formation as part of the course of "practical theology." Distinguished speakers from throughout the diocese were invited to participate in the annual Lenten preaching missions first conducted in the city in 1928.[96]

The importance of music as a part of worship prompted two revisions of the hymnal during this period, the first in 1916 and the second in 1940. Both reflected the theological and social conditions of their day. With the outbreak of World War I, several patriotic hymns were added to the 1916 edition, while six hymns for peace followed in 1940. In response to the ecumenical movement, the latter edition also incorporated more works from the "rich heritage of Christian hymnody" of other churches, as well as sacred folk melodies from around the world. In both editions, the arrangement of hymns continued to follow the "prayer book order," with groupings set to correspond with the liturgical season and particular themes. Complaints invariably poured in from those who found their favorite hymns sacrificed to make room for new ones, but parishes were reminded that they were not obligated to employ the new hymnals and could supplement them with old favorites.[97]

In addition to its new content, the 1940 hymnal was significant because it emphasized new musical praxis. "Congregational in character," the hymnal was intended to promote hymn singing and congregational participation. The editors simplified the musical notation by substituting melody lines for the four-part arrangements of previous editions, and made the layout of the text more visually pleasing. While not seeking to supplant the rich choral tradition of the church, the national commission responsible for the revisions wanted music to be seen as part of participatory worship, rather than performance. The commission also issued a companion handbook to the 1940 hymnal that included historical essays on each hymn and a compendium of biographical sketches on composers and arrangers intended to "lead to wider and more intelligent use of its contents."[98]

Within the diocese, the Department of Church Music was instrumental in promoting these and other musical innovations. Under the direction of Harold W. Gilbert, the choirmaster at St. Peter's Church, Philadelphia, and headmaster of its choir school, the department established a music lending library and provided parishes with practical advice on a variety of topics, such as choosing Easter music and the "appropriate speed in hymn singing," in its regular column in the diocesan paper.[99] Bringing its influence to bear in the national church, the department showcased its work at several general conventions to help advance new trends.

The theological developments of the early twentieth century contributed to the transformation of seminary education in the diocese. In 1914 the trustees and managers of the Philadelphia Divinity School unveiled a plan for the future of the divinity school, which established committees to evaluate the course of studies and investigate the possibility of moving the school to a new campus closer to the University of Pennsylvania. Following the example of other seminaries, the report called for the implementation of an electives system that would help the school "keep pace with universities in advancing higher education," and introduced a new curriculum that included instruction in such areas as "social questions," missions, and music. The plan sought to make divinity degrees akin to graduate degrees and transform the divinity school into a place where students pursued "professional" rather than simply "vocational" training.[100]

The plan also addressed the school's chronic financial instability. Dubbed "the forgotten school" in one report, the PDS struggled to secure dedicated support from the local dioceses and parishes, even though it had long enjoyed the second-largest enrollment of the nation's Episcopalian seminaries.[101] Funding became a major issue once ground was broken for the school's new West Philadelphia campus, which occupied the city block between Locust and Spruce and Forty-second and Forty-third streets. While the new space would allow the school to implement its plans to raise academic standards, introduce new programs, and expand the school's national influence, the trustees and overseers also believed that the school's new and more prominent location would increase awareness of the need to support ministerial formation.[102]

In keeping with the appeal of all things English, the new campus evoked the beauty of "an Oxford College." The collegiate Gothic buildings included classrooms, a library, the deanery, faculty houses, and dormitories. The chapel, the showpiece of the entire plan, was strategically planted on the highest spot on the property. Designed by the firm of Zantzinger, Borie and Medary, with windows by the D'Ascenzo Studios and ironwork by the Yellin workshop, the "noble" Gothic chapel defied the "restraint and simplicity" school officials claimed characterized the campus. It was known as St. Andrew's Collegiate Chapel in honor of the generosity of St. Andrew's Church, Philadelphia, which had housed divinity school classes in its vestry rooms in the 1860s. When the parish dissolved in 1921, the congregation voted to dedicate proceeds from the sale of their buildings to the chapel.[103] This gift, in addition to a substantial bequest from the estate of Harry Louis Peak, financed the soaring chapel and its rich program of architectural and decorative detail.[104]

More comprehensive changes to the curriculum and administration came in the 1930s, following the loss of a considerable number of faculty and students on account of economic difficulties and policy disputes. In 1936 the Reverend Allen Evans Jr. accepted a position as dean of the school on the condition that the boards approve his "new plan of theological

FIGURE 7.5 Architect's model for the Philadelphia Divinity School, only part of which was completed

education," which emphasized preparation for pastoral ministry through fieldwork, practicums, and clinical training. Evans also demanded greater autonomy in hiring faculty and admitting students, in an effort to "create an entirely new school upon the foundations of the old." In return, he promised to use his personal and professional connections to raise funds for the school. He instituted a "system of support" that included the solicitation of funds from alumni, direct mail appeals to potential donors, and offerings collected from parishes within those dioceses served by the school. He also planned to start rebuilding the endowment as soon as the economy permitted.[105]

The mission of the school expanded in a new direction in 1938, when the Church Training and Deaconess House moved from Spruce Street to the PDS campus and a department of women was established to train those interested in becoming "church workers."[106] The development of the new department reflected the professionalization of women's roles in religious education and social service ministries. It also signaled women's changing personal expectations. Whereas deaconesses were required to relinquish their position upon marriage, church workers could perform similar work without foregoing family. Diocesan records reveal their preference. Of the ten deaconesses in the diocese in 1945, all but two were retired. In contrast, there were thirteen active "women workers" that year.[107] Their numbers were never large, but their role in church life prefigured laywomen's increased ministerial role in later decades.

The theological developments of the first half of the twentieth century also influenced Episcopalians' relationship with other churches. Evolving belief and worship underscored the denomination's historical connection to the broader Anglican Communion. As it was a center of Anglo-Catholicism in the United States, many within the diocese affirmed the church's Catholic heritage, stressing the legitimacy of its creeds, sacraments, worship, and orders.[108] For others, however, this trend was disturbing. The diocese was still reeling from the "defection" of the Reverend William McGarvey and several other Anglo-Catholic clergy to Roman Catholicism in 1908.[109] Other high-profile conversions among the clergy and laity in the early decades of the twentieth century fueled fears that the Episcopal Church was moving toward a dangerous embrace of Romanism.[110] At their 1927 meeting in Philadelphia, members of the National Church League issued a statement reasserting the denomination's Protestant character.[111]

As the Episcopal Church and the wider Anglican Communion rediscovered their Catholic heritage, they commenced more earnest dialogue with the Orthodox, Eastern, and Old Catholic churches, who were invited to send representatives to the 1930 Lambeth Conference. Full communion with the Old Catholic churches was restored the following year. (Anglican–Roman Catholic discussions had begun in 1921, but they ended in 1928 when Pope Pius XI forbade further Catholic participation.)[112] These developments also led Episcopalians to greater study of Orthodox liturgical practice and sacramental theology. The diocese had taken an early interest in the matter with the creation of the Orthodox-Eastern Commission in 1910, and Bishop Rhinelander issued reminders of the validity of Orthodox sacraments as early as 1914.[113]

The Episcopal Church also participated in various ecumenical movements within the Protestant sphere, both at home and abroad, especially in the wake of World War I, when interest in interreligious cooperation increased tremendously. Although reluctant to join the Federal Council of Churches when it was established in 1908, the Episcopal Church played an instrumental role in organizing the World Conference on Faith and Order, which convened in Lucerne, Switzerland, in 1927. The forum, intended to bring together representatives of all Christian communions to promote peace and goodwill, was the precursor to the World Council of Churches.[114] Conflicting views of the purpose of the body, however, limited its effectiveness. It was uncertain whether members were to form one church body or whether they would participate in a central council as autonomous churches.

Among these ecumenical ventures, the most sustained and fruitful dialogue took place with the Presbyterian Church.[115] Efforts were followed closely in Philadelphia, since both churches had a strong presence in the city and a history of local cooperation. (For many years, Church House and the Witherspoon Building, which housed many national Presbyterian offices, stood only one block apart on Walnut Street.)[116] The two churches had appointed commissions in 1886 to study the possibility of union. Discussions led to accord on scripture, the creed, and the sacraments but ultimately collapsed when they could not overcome differences on the nature of religious authority. Episcopalians demanded recognition of the historic episcopate, while Presbyterians sought to preserve the presbytery, a form of governance in which power was shared equally between the clergy and laity. The matter remained stagnant until the post–World War I ecumenical movement revived interest in the subject on both sides. Talks resumed in 1929, and a tentative concordat was presented in 1939. Unlike the previous effort, this plan respected the two distinct historical traditions of the two churches, allowing freedom of governance until a common form could be developed. A statement on joint ordination followed the next year.[117]

Even with these advances, union was far from certain. The most vocal opposition came from Anglo-Catholics who objected to the proposed spiritual and liturgical equality extended to Presbyterian ministers, something theological liberals in the Episcopal Church were willing to concede. In 1907 the General Convention had approved the "open pulpit," a measure that permitted ministers of other churches to preach at Episcopal services. This move enraged defenders of Catholic orthodoxy, who did not accept as valid the ministry of those with non-Episcopal ordinations. With members of the American Church Union, an Anglo-Catholic body, threatening a break, church officials approached the deliberations with caution. The irony that efforts at union with the Presbyterian Church might split their own church did not go unnoticed. When the matter reached the General Convention in 1946, the nature of ordinations and the authority of the bishops remained major sticking points. With Presbyterian support uncertain, the convention ended its deliberations by issuing a statement that, although allowing for the possibility of continued talks, effectively ended the venture. Ultimately, neither denomination was prepared to shed its distinct identity and established form of governance.[118]

The lack of formal union, however, did not halt interdenominational cooperation, with joint prayer services, coordinated fund drives, and other programs proving that it was possible to find common theological ground. Yet it remained unclear whether the Episcopal Church was a Protestant denomination standing in opposition to Romanism, or whether it was, in the words of one observer, "a branch of the true Church trying to free itself from alien Protestantism."[119] In their attempt to make their church the national religious establishment, Episcopalians struggled to fashion a cohesive yet comprehensive theological identity. They wanted the church to be all things to all people. In describing the character of the planned diocesan cathedral in 1934, George Wharton Pepper praised the space as the embodiment of both "the beauty of Catholic ceremonial" and "the simplicity and quietness which characterizes Friends' Meeting."[120] Unlike the broad-church movement of the nineteenth century, which endeavored to establish a via media between high- and low-church factions, the new program of unity sought to make room for those of every religious persuasion under one all-encompassing theological umbrella.

Service and Mission in Depression and War

The outbreak of two world wars and the economic crisis of the 1930s sustained a sense of collective mission among church members in ways that intentional efforts to promote "diocesan unity" could not. Domestic and international turmoil kindled a spirit of service and sacrifice that revealed the power of faith in action. Overwhelming need, however, also forced the diocese to recognize its own limitations, prompting new financial and organizational strategies to maintain institutions and ministries.

When the United States entered the international fray in 1917 and again in 1941, the call to service received a tremendous response.[121] During both wars, *The Church News* printed letters from soldiers, chaplains, and nurses from the diocese serving overseas. A number spoke of how their faith gave them strength. One nurse serving in World War I wrote, "Sometimes the tasks set before me seemed impossible and then, as I'd look at these men dying, I could almost see our Lord and His presence made all the tasks possible." A soldier also serving in the Great War recalled how the prayer book for soldiers and sailors comforted him during the long nights in camp and "pulled him through" battle.[122] Through a national program during World War II, military personnel from the diocese were presented with specially designed "war crosses." In a letter of appreciation, one army private described his as "a never ceasing consolation . . . [and] a constant reminder that I am serving in a high and noble cause."[123]

Members of the diocesan clergy contributed to the "war work" by accepting chaplaincy commissions. Often serving as the sole Protestant cleric in a battalion, they found themselves caring for men of all churches and creeds. As one ministering in World War I commented, "we had Church-Unity as near as it is possible to have it."[124] In addition to conducting services and offering the sacraments, chaplains provided spiritual counsel, led informal prayer sessions, and consoled the dying. Those in the diocesan "clergy reserve corps" volunteered as part-time chaplains at local bases such as the Philadelphia Navy Yard and accepted short-term appointments at other domestic military sites. Local parishes and the diocesan altar guild aided the chaplains by donating linens, sacred vessels, and other items they needed to hold Communion services.[125]

Many home-front activities were directed by the Diocesan War Commission, a temporary body first established in October 1917 and then reconvened by the bishop in December 1941. The commission subsidized the work of parishes located near local military bases and set up hospitality centers where soldiers and those engaged in wartime industry might be able to "pass their free time comfortably." It also coordinated volunteer efforts within the parishes, working with groups like the Boy Scouts, Girls' Friendly Society, and Woman's Auxiliary.[126] Many parishes sponsored Red Cross chapters, where volunteers rolled bandages and prepared medical kits. Women also nursed troops returning to local hospitals and military bases.

In October 1917, wartime medical volunteers were mobilized to confront a different concern: the sudden outbreak of the global influenza epidemic. Philadelphia was among the hardest-hit cities in the United States, perhaps because of the large number of military personnel stationed at the Navy Yard and nearby Fort Dix and Fort Meade. By the time the epidemic subsided, thousands had died. On October 10 alone, 759 were reported dead. By government order, churches throughout the city canceled services to help prevent the spread of infection.[127] The number of patients at the Episcopal Hospital doubled in a matter of days, forcing the staff to fashion makeshift wards in every available space. Volunteers and emergency aides supplemented the regular staff, many of whom had fallen ill caring for others.[128]

In addition to direct service, members of the diocese supported the war effort through prayer and patriotism. The congregation at Christ Church declared its support for the government and offered the use of its buildings for the "national cause" during World War I. Invoking the "spirit of the Revolutionary fathers who knelt in this sanctuary," parishioners dedicated themselves to "mobilizing the powers of our religion . . . to advance the kingdom of the Prince of Peace." In cooperation with the American Legion, St. Mark's Church in the city's Frankford section held annual services in the 1930s and 1940s for the blessing of flags and military standards.[129] Even traditional Lenten observances of fasting and sacrifice were

FIGURE 7.6 Members of the honor guard of St. Mark's Church, Frankford, join the Reverend Albert Fischer and the Reverend Edmund H. Carhart during the "Churching of the Colors" in 1954

recast as patriotic duties. In 1917, St. James's, St. Mark's, and Holy Trinity, the three parishes near Rittenhouse Square, conducted "union services" to conserve fuel.[130]

Yet there was also a degree of ambivalence toward the triumphant tone of the war effort. Some felt it wrong to glorify the war or to politicize the work of the church. During World War I, Archibald Campbell Knowles, the rector of St. Alban's, Olney, insisted that the parish remain a "place of peace," and forbade discussion of the war in the church or guild house. "I never believed," he wrote, "that the House of God should be made the propaganda of War."[131] Even if such views were in the minority, they resonated in Philadelphia because of the strong pacifist stance of the local Quaker community. At Christ Church, patriotism was set in the context of global citizenship when the parish dedicated a shrine to the United Nations in 1943.[132]

International events also inspired interest in the missions, in terms of both personal service and financial support. The Deaconess House trained many workers for foreign fields, and numerous parishes organized societies to raise funds and collect supplies for the missions. The United Thank

Offering (as the united offering became known in 1919) continued to raise large sums for the missions and the training of mission workers. According to diocesan figures for 1928, fully half of every budget dollar for that year went to support the national church and its missions (32.5 percent) or the foreign missions (17.5 percent).[133] Considerable support went to those areas that had been supported by the Church of England. In 1941 the diocese exceeded its $30,000 pledge to aid the British missions, 10 percent of the total sought by the national church. This matched the amount promised earlier for the church in China, one of the Episcopal Church's main missionary fields, which was devastated by events of the 1930s and '40s.[134]

Demobilization after World War I presented both challenges and opportunities for the diocese. Church leaders hoped that the spirit of service would remain strong. Within days of the armistice, Bishop Garland announced "a campaign for personal service" in parish life, diocesan work, and the missionary fields. Invoking the military spirit of the day, he stated that this was not a financial campaign but a drive for personal commitment and "obedience to the marching orders of the Master."[135] More broadly, the "return to normalcy" offered a chance for the Episcopal Church to reexamine its organizational structures and to recommit itself to its social mission. Church leaders looked for new ways to shore up struggling parishes, support missionary work both domestically and abroad, and sustain the network of denominational institutions that had sprung up in the preceding decades. In 1926 the diocese organized a $3.5 million Campaign for Missions and Institutions. Although the five-year campaign raised only $2 million, it placed more than fifty diocesan mission churches and other institutions on firmer financial footing.[136]

Diocesan funding was also affected by the 1919 implementation of a nationwide campaign by the national church as part of its organizational restructuring. Promoted as a means to increase the "devotion and loyalty of our Church members," the campaign was really an effort to systematize funding for national and diocesan institutions by consolidating collections.[137] The new program attempted to smooth fluctuations in annual giving by asking members to pledge toward "expectations" based on predetermined national and diocesan budgets. Implementation, however, did not go as well as hoped. Dioceses were slow to conduct the required comprehensive surveys, and parishes were unaccustomed to canvassing their members.[138] Some parishes in the diocese protested when they saw a large jump in their expected contributions in the campaign's first year. Even when it was explained that the $650,000 would be split evenly between the national church and the diocese, many still felt that "expectations" had been set too high.[139] Some churchgoers objected to the required pledging, finding it odd to be asked to approximate "voluntary" giving.[140]

The system was put to the real test during the Great Depression, when resources were stretched thin. Many parishes failed to meet their expectations, and the diocese struggled to fulfill its obligations to the national church.[141] Just one year after the bishops' 1932 pastoral letter offered "fullest assurance that the business of the church will be carried on," the diocese faced a $35,000 deficit that threatened cuts in salaries and the elimination of some church departments, and curtailed support for missions and social service agencies.[142] As voluntary giving dried up and investment returns fell flat, diocesan social welfare institutions and charitable agencies were hard pressed to sustain their programs. Parishes, many with heavy mortgages, likewise suffered, and often failed to meet basic obligations, like clergy salaries.[143]

The diocese and its institutions could do little to reverse the nation's economic fortunes, but they were able to assist with relief efforts. In 1936 the superintendent of the City Mission reported that 2,729 families had been aided, five thousand home visits conducted, and seventy-six thousand milk orders filled. Members of Christ Church organized a daily bread line in 1929, expanded the activities of their "neighborhood house" in 1932, and took over operation of St. John's Settlement in 1935 when diocesan support ceased.[144] Some wealthier parishes partnered with poorer ones, as was the case with St. Paul's, Chestnut Hill, which sponsored programs at St. Barnabas's in the mill districts of Kensington. The dispensary of the Episcopal Hospital recorded more than 133,000 visits in 1937. As evidence of the hospital's commitment to its charitable mission, figures for 1940 reported that 21 percent of ward service had been provided for free and an additional 19 percent at partial cost.[145]

Even before the Depression made it clear that parochial and diocesan institutions needed to pool resources and develop cooperative strategies, a number of diocesan institutions had begun to experiment with new financial arrangements. Several were among the first to affiliate with the Philadelphia Welfare Federation, a local community chest that organized united fund drives for member institutions. In 1922 the rector of St. Thomas's, Whitemarsh, reminded his congregation that any gift made to one of the twelve church institutions associated with the federation would "be credited by the diocese to the parish."[146] Episcopalians were more willing to join community chests and other nondenominational initiatives than their Catholic or Jewish contemporaries (who feared the Protestant nature of these organizations), since they were well represented among their leadership. George Wharton Pepper, E. T. Stotesbury, and George Woodward, for instance, were among the trustees of the Welfare Federation in 1924, and Lewis N. Lukens Jr., a communicant of St. Paul's Church, Chestnut Hill, directed the 1940 United Charities Campaign, which supported nine Episcopal institutions.[147]

At the same time, a number of institutions shed their religious affiliation in order to become eligible for government support, as operational expenses stretched beyond parochial abilities. The change was particularly evident in the field of health care, as rising costs, technological demands, and administrative complexity presented a challenge to church-run institutions. In 1920 the vestry of St. Timothy's parish and the board of St. Timothy's Hospital, Roxborough, agreed to sever their legal connection in order for the hospital to become eligible for state funding.[148] The Episcopal Hospital bucked the trend until 1949 because of the commitment of church leaders and broad-based diocesan support, including the annual Thanksgiving Day offering dedicated for its benefit. Although the hospital retained its name and religious identity, it too eventually severed its official connection with the diocese in order to tap into state funds.[149]

There is no question that such decisions were prompted by the changing financial circumstances of diocesan institutions, but they were also a reflection of the new religious landscape that had emerged by midcentury. Even though peacetime conditions brought prosperity, confidence, and full pews, just as they had in the 1920s, the Episcopal Church would no longer command the same prominence and cultural authority that it had in preceding decades. The Anglo-Saxon decade had given way to postwar religious pluralism. Nonetheless, for those in the diocese, the church remained a powerful symbol of stability and certainty in an age of social mobility and cold war conflict. For those who endured depression and war, the years provided a period of renewal and revival, a seemingly calm interlude before the turbulence of the 1960s.

NOTES

I would like to express gratitude to the following parishes for providing information and access to their records: Church of the Holy Trinity, Rittenhouse Square; St. Asaph's, Bala Cynwyd; St. Mark's, Locust Street; St. Mark's, Frankford; St. Mary's, Cathedral Road; St. Thomas's, Whitemarsh; and the Washington Memorial Chapel, Valley Forge. A note of appreciation is also extended to Nathanael Groton Jr., who generously shared the diaries of his father, the Reverend Nathanael Groton, the former rector of St. Thomas's, Whitemarsh.

1. "Victory Gives New Spirit to Thanksgiving," and "Parkway Cathedral Will Be P.E. Memorial," both in *Philadelphia Public Ledger*, November 29, 1918. The text of Rhinelander's speech was also reprinted as a special insert to *TCN* (December 1918).

2. Arthur P. Dudden, "The City Embraces 'Normalcy,' 1919–1929," in *Philadelphia: A 300-Year History*, ed. Russell F. Weigley (New York: W. W. Norton, 1982), 596, 602; and Joseph S. Clark Jr. and Dennis J. Clark, "Rally and Relapse, 1946–1968," in ibid., 668.

3. Communicant numbers stood at 75,031 in 1945. Statistics are derived from the diocesan figures published in the *Living Church Annual and Whittaker's Churchman's Almanac* (Milwaukee: Young Churchman Co., 1911); and *Living Church Annual* (Milwaukee: Morehouse, 1931, 1932, and 1946). For the national church, domestic communicant numbers grew from 928,780 to 1,254,227 during the same period, a 35 percent increase. See "Comparative Statistics for Fifty-Five Years," *Living Church Annual* (1932), unpaginated.

4. Wealth comparisons are based on total contributions to the national church. See figures for 1910 in the "General Table of Statistics," *Living Church Annual and Whittaker's Churchman's Almanac*, 350–53; and, for 1930, "General Table of Statistics," *Living Church Annual* (1931), 504–9.

5. The city later repaid the parish for the project. See May Lilly, *The Story of St. Clement's Church, Philadelphia* ([Philadelphia: St. Clement's Church], 1964), 41–44.

6. According to the *Living Church Annual* (1911, 1931, 1946), the number of parishes and missions increased from 190 to 222 between 1910 and 1930, but then dropped to 204 by 1945. The growth during the first period was impressive, but not as substantial as the institutional expansion that had taken place under Bishop Whitaker between 1887 and 1910, when more than seventy new parishes and missions were established. The decline between 1930 and 1945 reflects the effects of the Great Depression, as well as the retreat from establishing new missions for ethnic groups.

7. According to the parish histories compiled in J. Wesley Twelves, *The History of the Diocese of Pennsylvania of the Protestant Episcopal Church in the U.S.A., 1784–1968* (Philadelphia: Diocese of Pennsylvania, 1969), those parishes with new or expanded sanctuaries included St. Paul's, Chestnut Hill (1911); Church of the Redemption, Philadelphia (1914); Church of the Redeemer, Bryn Mawr (1914); St. Paul's, Overbrook (1922); and Trinity, Swarthmore (1932). Many more built parish houses during these years. To name just a handful: St. Paul's Memorial, Philadelphia (1912); Good Shepherd, Rosemont (1914); St. Nathanael's, Kensington (1915); St. James the Less, Philadelphia (1918); St. James's, Langhorne (1924); and All Hallows, Wyncote (1927). Most of the growth occurred in suburban districts.

8. From its inception in 1912, the diocesan newspaper *The Church News* regularly mentioned memorial gifts and other substantial donations. For an example of a parish's debt to a single benefactor, see the history of St. George's Church in Ardmore, which was established in 1929 through a bequest from the estate of George Washington Nevil, in Twelves, *History of the Diocese of Pennsylvania*, 252–53.

9. Ralph Adams Cram, the nation's leading exponent of Gothic design, praised D'Ascenzo and Yellin for their commitment to religious craft and the principles of organic design. See Cram, *Church Building: A Study of the Principles of Architecture in Their Relation to the Church*, 3rd ed. (Boston: Marshall Jones, 1924), 222–24. See also Rider College, *D'Ascenzo: The Art of Stained Glass from the Collection of Stanley Switlik* (Trenton: Rider College, 1973); Myra Tolmach Davis, *Sketches in Iron: Samuel Yellin, American Master of Wrought Iron, 1885–1940* (Washington, D.C.: George Washington University, 1971); and Sandra L. Tatman, "The Integration of Stained-Glass Windows into the Architectural Church Styles of the Nineteenth and Twentieth Centuries," in *Stained Glass in Catholic Philadelphia*, ed. Jean M. Farnsworth, Carmen R. Croce, and Joseph F. Chorpenning (Philadelphia: Saint Joseph's University Press, 2002). A database of their work has been compiled by the Philadelphia Athenaeum through its Philadelphia Architects and Buildings Project, available online at http://www.philadelphiabuildings.org/.

10. William B. Bassett, "T. P. Chandler, Jr., FAIA—an Introduction" (bachelor's thesis, University of Pennsylvania, 1967); and "Christ Church, Ithan, Villanova, PA: A Short History" (1961), courtesy of Christ Church, Ithan.

11. "Renovation," *TCN* (April 1928), 230–31; "Shrubbery," *TCN* (November 1928), 42; and "The Latest Trends in Tombstones," *TCN* (April 1933), 238–39.

12. On the organization of the commission, see "Report of the Commission of Church Building of the Diocese," *JDC 1914*, Appendix T. See also Rev. Francis C. Hartshorne, "The Parishes and

Missions of the Convocation of Norristown," *TCN* (October 1915), 9. At least one parish agreed to let the commission approve its memorial designs, to "prevent the erection of grave-stones that are not at all in keeping with our churchyard." See Rector's Letter, *St. Thomas' Messenger*, May 15, 1921, St. Thomas's Church (Whitemarsh) Archives (hereafter STCA).

13. Among the churches fitting this architectural style are those located in the suburban communities of the Main Line, Chestnut Hill, and other suburban areas. Representative examples include St. Asaph's, Bala Cynwyd; Church of the Redeemer, Bryn Mawr; Church of the Good Shepherd, Rosemont; St. Martin-in-the-Fields, Chestnut Hill; St. Paul's, Chestnut Hill; St. Timothy's, Roxborough; and St. Thomas's, Whitemarsh. Although many of these parishes had been founded, or had rebuilt their churches, in the years between 1880 and 1910, their membership would increase significantly in the 1910s and 1920s.

14. This analysis is borrowed from ideas suggested in Jeanne Halgren Kilde, *When Church Became Theatre: The Transformation of Evangelical Architecture and Worship in Nineteenth-Century America* (New York: Oxford University Press, 2002); and Alison Lurie, "God's Houses," Part I, *New York Review of Books*, July 3, 2003, 30–32.

15. "The New Church House," *TCN* (April 1921), 209; Stanley R. West, *Centennial History of the Philadelphia Divinity School: The Divinity School of the Protestant Episcopal Church in Philadelphia, 1857–1957* (Philadelphia: S. R. West, 1971), 138; William Morrison, *The Main Line: Country Houses of Philadelphia's Storied Suburb, 1870–1930* (New York: Acanthus Press, 2002), 55–58; Charles Latham, *The Episcopal Academy, 1785–1984* (Devon, Pa.: W. T. Cooke, 1984), 127–39; and "Episcopal Hospital—and What It's Doing," *TCN* (November 1941), 10–11.

16. Spencer Ervin, *History of the Church of St. Asaph, 1888–1838* (typescript, n.d.), 47, Church of St. Asaph Archives; and "S. Asaph, Bala," *JDC 1930*, 160.

17. See, in particular, the rector's letters of 1895–96, 1900, 1910, and 1924, and financial reports for 1922–29 in the annual parish *Yearbook*, Church of the Holy Trinity Archives.

18. "Bishop's Address," *JDC 1925*, 79. For sample bequest clauses, see "Rector's Letter," Church of the Holy Trinity, *Yearbook* (1895–96), Church of the Holy Trinity Archives; and the inside front cover of the Philadelphia Divinity School Bulletin (1920), Philadelphia Divinity School (PDS) Records, Episcopal Divinity School (EDS) Archives. On the practice, see also Richard Byfield and James P. Shaw, *Your Money and Your Church* (Garden City, N.Y.: Doubleday, 1959), 219–20.

19. On the Lenten Mite Offering, see "Episcopal Leaders Meet Here June 5," *Philadelphia Public Ledger*, May 28, 1927, 10. On women's work, see Minutes, 1898–1920, Episcopal Churchwomen Records, Collection 2106, HSP. The Bishop's Bricks Fund is mentioned in the minutes for October 27, 1915.

20. Figures are based on the communicant numbers that appear in the *JDC* for the years mentioned. The decline, however, may have been more gradual than the reports suggest because some parishes kept members on the rolls even after they had moved. The effects of the Depression encouraged parishes to purge their rolls in the 1930s, since diocesan assessments were often based on communicant numbers.

21. "Church Folk Urged to Purchase Autos," *Philadelphia Public Ledger*, March 7, 1927; "Incarnation Parish, Phila., Faces Crisis," *TCN* (February 1926), 179; and Joseph Fort Newton, *River of Years: An Autobiography* (Philadelphia: J. B. Lippincott, 1946), 260.

22. "The Proposed Merger of St. James and Holy Trinity," *TCN* (March 1932), 249.

23. Plans for relocation had been discussed within the parish since the early 1920s. See "St. Thomas' Will Move," *TCN* (March 1923), 180. On the relocation, see "Department of Property Report," *JDC 1938*, 270; "St. Thomas' Church, Founded in 1793, Buys Large Edifice from Methodists," *TCN* (May 1941), 24; and Twelves, *History of the Diocese of Pennsylvania*, 125.

24. See "Report of the Committee on Problem of City Churches," *JDC 1934*, 357–62; "Changing Philadelphia," *TCN* (December 1928), 90; and David M. Steele, "The Problem of the Central City Church," *TCN* (March 1933), 213.

25. Russell H. Conwell, "Shall the Rich Divide the Poor?" *Temple Review*, May 5, 1922. Although Conwell did not direct his comments specifically at members of the Episcopal Church, the implication was evident.

26. Characteristics of self-perpetuating vestries included the allowance of members to serve consecutive terms, authorization for members to fill vacancies that arose between meetings of the

congregation, and the ability to present the vestry as a slate for approval by the congregation. On discussions within the Diocese of Pennsylvania, see "Bishop's Address," *JDC 1921*, 48; "Bishop's Address," *JDC 1927*, 83; and, for an example of a parochial clash between the rector and vestry over the issue of dependence, Nicholas B. Wainwright, *History of the Church of the Messiah, Gwynedd: Its First Hundred Years, 1866–1966* (Gwynedd, Pa.: Church of the Messiah, 1966), 29–30.

27. On the debates over proportionate representation, see "Rector's Letter," *St. Thomas' Messenger*, May 1922, STCA; and "Report of the Chancellor and the Committee on Canons in re S. John, Northern Liberties," *JDC 1930*, 42. For similar debates in an earlier period, see Rev. Dr. McConnell, "Report of the Special Commission of Proportionate Lay Representation of the Parishes," *JDC 1890*, 125–26.

28. For mention of such efforts, see Rev. George Copeland, "The 143rd Annual Convention of the Diocese," *TCN* (May–June 1927), 270; and Rev. Francis C. Hartshorne, "The Coming Diocesan Convention: So What?" *TCN* (April 1937), 239–40.

29. George Woodward, *Memoirs of a Mediocre Man* (Philadelphia: Harris, 1935); Cynthia Ann MacLeod, "Arts and Crafts Architecture in Suburban Philadelphia, Sponsored by Dr. George Woodward" (master's thesis, University of Virginia, 1979); and David R. Contosta, *A Philadelphia Family: The Houstons and Woodwards of Chestnut Hill* (Philadelphia: University of Pennsylvania Press, 1988).

30. "Richmond Declares Money Power Has Dominated Church" (n.d.), in Rhinelander Letters, box 6, George Chalmers Richmond Trial Records, Collection 550, HSP.

31. On Episcopalians broadly, see Kit Konolige and Frederica Konolige, *The Power of Their Glory: America's Ruling Class, the Episcopalians* (New York: Wyden Books, 1978). On members of the local diocese, see John Lukacs, *Philadelphia Patricians and Philistines, 1900–1950* (New York: Farrar, Straus and Giroux, 1981); and E. Digby Baltzell, *The Protestant Establishment: Aristocracy and Caste in America* (New York: Random House, 1964).

32. On Pepper's views on citizenship, see George Wharton Pepper, *Philadelphia Lawyer: An Autobiography* (Philadelphia: J. B. Lippincott, 1944), 290. On the cultivation of "power of service" at the university, see Pepper, "Why the University?" in *Men and Issues: A Selection of Speeches and Articles*, comp. Horace Green (New York: Duffield & Co., 1924), 13–24; and on its Episcopal character, see E. Digby Baltzell, *Philadelphia Gentlemen: The Making of a National Upper Class* (Chicago: Quadrangle Books, 1971), 322–26.

33. For Rhinelander's comment, see Minutes, May 1918, Episcopal Churchwomen Records, Collection 2106, HSP. On the exposition, see "Church Exhibit at the Sesqui-Centennial," and "Spiritual Sources from Which Signers Drew Their Inspiration," both in *TCN* (October 1926), 12 and 18–19, respectively.

34. Among Poles, these missions included Advent Mission (1918, closed 1966); Redeemer, Port Richmond (1918, closed 1966); St. Mary's, Manayunk (1920, closed 1944); and Holy Trinity, Conshohocken (1928, closed 1938). Among Italians, they included St. Mary of the Annunciation, Kensington (1914, closed 1968); and St. Francis of Assisi (1931, closed 1936). See parish histories in Twelves, *History of the Diocese of Pennsylvania*, 237–57.

35. See Minutes, January 31, 1917, and December 18, 1918, Episcopal Churchwomen Records, Collection 2106, HSP; "Deny Jews Need to be Americanized: Indignation Meeting Held to Resent Charges of Bishop Garland and Rev. Dr. Zacker," *New York Times*, November 25, 1919; "Denies Reflection on Jews: Dr. Burgess Explains Scope of Episcopal Church Program," and "Deny Proselytizing: Pennsylvania Episcopalians Reply to Jewish Statement," both in *New York Times*, September 26, 1919.

36. Minutes, May 1918, Episcopal Churchwomen Records, Collection 2106, HSP; and "The State of the Church and the Bishops' Crusade," *TCN* (January 1927), 118–19.

37. For population figures, see Lloyd M. Abernathy, "Progressivism, 1905–1919," in Weigley, *Philadelphia*, 531. On the expansion of missions, which included Phillips Brooks Memorial Chapel of Holy Trinity (1914), St. Cyprian Mission, West Philadelphia (1916), St. John the Divine, West Philadelphia (1920), St. Augustine Chapel, Norristown (1929), St. Christopher Mission, North Philadelphia (1930), Holy Spirit Mission, South Philadelphia (1930), and St. Paul Mission, North Philadelphia (1934), see Twelves, *History of the Diocese of Pennsylvania*, 237–57.

38. Phillips was the first African American graduate of the Philadelphia Divinity School. See Twelves, *History of the Diocese of Pennsylvania*, 161; and "List of Black Philadelphia Divinity School Alumni, 1857–1974," RG 8, box 1; PDS Records, EDS.

39. These figures are derived from the diocesan listings that appear in the *Living Church Annual* of 1931 and 1946. They do not distinguish, however, between the diocese's historically black churches, like St. Thomas's, and chapels for "colored" congregations sponsored by other parishes.

40. The Episcopal Church was the first denomination to recognize the need for a national church in the capital, obtaining a charter from Congress in 1893 for the project. Other denominations followed suit with their own projects, most notably with Catholic plans for a national shrine in 1913 and the creation of the National Presbyterian Church in 1947, but none would achieve the success of the National Cathedral. On the National Cathedral, see Richard T. Feller and Marshall W. Fishwick, *For Thy Great Glory*, 2d ed. (Culpeper, Va.: Community Press, 1979).

41. By the 1940s, the Episcopal Church's hold on the upper class had begun to slip. Even though 42 percent of those listed in Philadelphia's *Social Register* for 1940 were affiliated with the Episcopal Church, its role in shaping the life of "proper Philadelphia" had declined considerably since its peak in the late Victorian era. See Baltzell, *Philadelphia Gentlemen*, 236, 260.

42. Archibald Campbell Knowles, *Reminiscences of a Parish Priest* (New York: Morehouse, 1935), 51.

43. One report described the election politics this way: "It should not be forgotten that this same Doctor Mann was one of the candidates for Bishop Coadjutor of the Diocese of Pennsylvania at the time Bishop Rhinelander was elected. Doctor Mann was a candidate for the low and broad church party, which split its vote between him and the Rev. Dr. William M. Groton, a tactical error which spelled success for the adherents of Doctor Rhinelander." A copy of the unattributed newspaper clipping is located in the 1913 diary of Groton's son, the Reverend Nathanael Groton. (The diary is held privately by Nathanael Groton Jr.)

44. On this claim, see Henry Bradford Washburn, *Philip Mercer Rhinelander: Seventh Bishop of Pennsylvania, First Warden of the College of Preachers* (New York: Morehouse-Gorham, 1950), 122.

45. Ibid., chapters 1–6; and Twelves, *History of the Diocese of Pennsylvania*, 33–35.

46. On Rhinelander's views, see Washburn, *Philip Mercer Rhinelander*, 136; and Rhinelander, *The Things Most Surely Believed Among Us* (Philadelphia: Education Department, Diocese of Pennsylvania, 1920), 77. Within the national church, the challenge to traditional theological belief came to the fore at the heresy trial of the Reverend Algernon Sidney Crapsey, a self-professed evolutionist, rationalist, and "disciple of the Higher Criticism," in the Diocese of Western New York in 1906. See Algernon Sidney Crapsey, *The Last of the Heretics* (New York: Knopf, 1924), vii.

47. Twelves, *History of the Diocese of Pennsylvania*, 34.

48. "Bishop's Address," *JDC 1917*, 110; and "Bishop's Address," *JDC 1925*, 92.

49. "Bishop Rhinelander, Founder of 'The *TCN*,' Sends Anniversary Greetings," *TCN* (October 1936), 8. Although the *Church Standard* had been published in Philadelphia prior to this, it was an independent, national publication, not an organ of the Diocese of Pennsylvania. For a reflection on the creation of *TCN*, see Rev. Francis C. Hartshorne, "Twenty-Five Years of '*The Church News*,'" ibid., 10.

50. See "Bishop's Address," *JDC 1914*, 114–15; "Bishop's Address," *JDC 1919*, 102–3; and Washburn, *Philip Mercer Rhinelander*, 165–75.

51. "A Blackboard—What Convention Did," *Churchman* (November 15, 1919), 15–16; and Robert W. Prichard, *A History of the Episcopal Church* (Harrisburg: Morehouse, 1991), 174–75.

52. "A Blackboard—What the Women Did," *Churchman* (November 15, 1919), 17; and Mary Sudman Donovan, *A Different Call: Women's Ministries in the Episcopal Church, 1850–1920* (Wilton, Conn.: Morehouse-Barlow, 1986), 162–65.

53. The measure would have amended the language of the diocesan constitution so that the convention would have consisted of "clergymen and lay deputies" rather than "laymen." See "Report of the Committee on Canons," *JDC 1921*, 85; and "Report of Diocesan Commission on Membership of Women in the Convention," *JDC 1922*, Appendix T, 347–63.

54. Twelves, *History of the Diocese of Pennsylvania*, 36–37; *Lloyd's Clerical Directory* (Chicago: American Church Publishing Co., 1910), 147; and "Milestones," *Time*, March 9, 1931.

55. See Twelves, *History of the Diocese of Pennsylvania*, 37–39; and, for the account of the special convention, "Journal of the Special Convention of June, 1929," *JDC 1930*, Appendix T, 333–53.

56. "Bishop Taitt: An Appreciation," *TCN* (October 1943), 2–3.

57. Rev. J. DeWolf Perry, DD, *Memorial Sermon Preached at the Convention of the Diocese of Pennsylvania, May 9, 1911 in Memory of The Rt. Rev. O. W. Whitaker, DD, LLD* (Philadelphia, 1911), 7.

Whitaker's reluctance is also hinted at in "The Bishop Announces Selection of Site for Cathedral," *TCN* (January 1927), 114–15.

58. A good history of the Church of the Advocate can be found in the National Historic Landmark nomination form for the church prepared by Susan Glassman and edited by Carolyn Pitts, dated June 23, 1995. A copy of the completed form is located at http://www.cr.nps.gov/nhl/designations/samples/pa/advocate.pdf. See also Twelves, *History of the Diocese of Pennsylvania*, 207–8. On the diocesan decision not to use the Church of the Advocate as a cathedral, see "Bishop Announces Selection of Site," 114. On Burk's cathedral plans, see Lorett Treese, *Valley Forge: Making and Remaking a National Symbol* (University Park: Pennsylvania State University Press, 1995), 119–20. On the Watson bequest, see "Death of Henry W. Watson," *TCN* (October 1933), 26.

59. On Rhinelander's connection to Satterlee, see Washburn, *Philip Mercer Rhinelander*, chapter 4. On Satterlee's support of the National Cathedral, see Feller and Fishwick, *For Thy Great Glory*, 5–17.

60. One report suggests that the parkway site was abandoned because the city had offered to lease the land to the diocese rather than sell it outright. See "Bishop Announces Selection of Site," 114. It is also possible that the parkway site's proximity to the Roman Catholic cathedral on Logan Square may have played a role. This is hinted at in *Cathedral Church of Christ of the Diocese of Pennsylvania* (Philadelphia: Diocese of Pennsylvania, [1934]), HSP. In particular, see the anti-Catholic overtones that appear in the operetta "The Parkway Squad," which appears in Appendix B. On the formation of the Cathedral Foundation and its role in promoting the project, see William Ellis Scull, *William Ellis Scull, Sometime Quaker: An Autobiography* (Philadelphia: John C. Winston, 1939), 176–84.

61. This claim appears in *Cathedral Church of Christ* and "The Bishop's Address at Cathedral League Meeting," *TCN* (April 1920), 179. A newspaper account at the time of the groundbreaking, however, reported that it was only the second-highest. See "Site of Cathedral Unit Is Dedicated," *Philadelphia Public Ledger*, June 26, 1932.

62. "The Cathedral League," *TCN* (April 1925), 253.

63. On Scull, who was also responsible for issuing a pamphlet, *First Ten Years Founding a Cathedral for the Diocese of Pennsylvania*, that chronicled the project's early steps, see Scull, *William Ellis Scull*, 176–78.

64. See "Bishop's Address," *JDC 1925*, 90; and the address of George William Douglas in *Cathedral Church of the Diocese of Pennsylvania* (Philadelphia: Diocese of Pennsylvania, [1922]), HSP.

65. "Bishop Announces Selection of Site," 114–15; and "The Use of a Cathedral," *TCN* (April 1920), 180–81.

66. The plan and map were included in a special insert to *TCN* (January 1936). See also Thomas J. Garland, "Address to the Diocesan Convention," May 5, 1925, reprinted in *Cathedral Church of Christ*.

67. Reports at the time, however, did not hint at any financial problems. See "The Bishop Breaks Ground for St. Mary's Chapel on the Cathedral Site in Upper Roxborough," *TCN* (October 1932), 22–23; and "P.E. Group Begins on Cathedral Site," *Philadelphia Public Ledger*, June 25, 1932.

68. On the original plan, see "Bishop Breaks Ground for St. Mary's"; and Frank R. Watson, "The Cathedral Vision for Philadelphia," *Cathedral Age* (Easter 1933), 19. The scaled-down, though still grand, plans appeared as part of a special insert, "The Cathedral of the Diocese of Pennsylvania," to vol. 24 of *TCN* (1935–36). See also "Chapter Announced Changes in Plans for Cathedral," *TCN* (February 1936), 141. On the eventual fate of the cathedral, see Francis A. Shearer, ed., *Cathedral Village: The First Decade, 1979–1989;* and *St. Mary's Church, Cathedral Road*, pamphlet courtesy of the church.

69. See "Memorial on the Subject of Higher Theological Learning" (Easter Monday, 1913), RG 8, box 1, PDS Records, EDS; and Nathanael Groton's diary entry for September 11, 1913.

70. For a challenge to the creed, see Crapsey, *Last of the Heretics;* and on theological developments more broadly, see Prichard, *History of the Episcopal Church*, 206–14.

71. Prichard, *History of the Episcopal Church*, 206–11; and Cecil Roberts, "The Use of Creeds," *TCN* (April 1924), 240.

72. Rhinelander's comments, as well as the bishops' 1923 pastoral letter, were issued in response to comments made by Bishop William Lawrence of the Diocese of Massachusetts, in which

Lawrence expressed his personal doubts about the virgin birth as an essential belief. See [Rhinelander], "The Creed: Its Place in the Life of the Church and in the Duty of the Church's Offices," *TCN* (May–June 1923), 263; and William Lawrence, *Memories of a Happy Life* (Boston: Houghton Mifflin, 1926).

73. "The General Convention," *TCN* (October 1922), 5–6; and "Flotsam and Jetsam," *Church Standard*, April 14, 1906, 801.

74. For an overview of divorce debates in America, see Glenda Riley, *Divorce: An American Tradition* (New York: Oxford University Press, 1991). Unlike the Roman Catholic Church, the Episcopal Church did not have an established system of annulment to address these problems.

75. The Lambeth encyclical was reprinted as a supplement to the October 1930 issue of *TCN*. It is also available at http://www.lambethconference.org/resolutions/1930.

76. "Commission on Marriage and Divorce Completes Final Report," *TCN* (October 1937), 11; and "A Review of the General Convention Meeting in Cincinnati," *TCN* (November 1937), 42–44.

77. "Episcopalian Divorce Canon Is Retained," *Washington Post*, October 20, 1940; A. O. J., "Marriage Canons," *TCN* (January 1945), 6; and "Committee on Marriage Proposes New Canon," *JDC 1945*, Appendix U.

78. "Good-Bye Mr. Quiverfull!" *TCN* (November 1935), 11. See also "The Children in Our Midst," *TCN* (October 1940), 12; and Leslie Woodcock Tentler, *Catholics and Contraception: An American History* (Ithaca: Cornell University Press, 2004), 5.

79. See resolutions 15 and 16 of the 1930 Lambeth encyclical, and "Summary of the General Convention," *TCN* (November 1934), 46.

80. The proposal originated with the Social Service Commission of the Diocese of Chicago but received attention in dioceses across the country. See "Must Be Normal and Well to Wed," *New York Times*, March 25, 1912; and "Report of the Commission on Social Service," *TCN* (June 1913), 16.

81. See "Approved Motion Pictures," *TCN* (March 1925), 204. For later views on censorship, see "A Diocesan Trans Lux," *TCN* (January 1939), 10.

82. For an example of a parish enterprise, see Timothy D. Hufnagle, *A Brief History of Holy Trinity's Holiday House of Sellersville, Pennsylvania* (2003), pamphlet courtesy of the Church of the Holy Trinity. On Shreiner's work, see "The Church Farm School," *TCN* (April 1920), 182–83; and Twelves, *History of the Diocese of Pennsylvania*, 60.

83. On Billy Sunday's visit to the university, see Ken Fones-Wolf, *Trade Union Gospel: Christianity and Labor in Industrial Philadelphia, 1865–1915* (Philadelphia: Temple University Press, 1989), 187–88; Lightner Witmer, *The Nearing Case: The Limitation of Academic Freedom at the University of Pennsylvania by Act of the Board of Trustees, June 14, 1915* (New York: B. W. Huebsch, 1915), 44–45; and Nathanael Groton's diary entry for March 30, 1914. On the student vestry, see "Dr. Kelly Addresses Church Students," *TCN* (February 1925), 156; and Twelves, *History of the Diocese of Pennsylvania*, 199.

84. The result of this effort can be seen in the comprehensive chaplaincy listings found in the *Living Church Annual*. See, for instance, the list of clergy ministering to college students under the "National Organization for College Work," *Living Church Annual* (1928), 179–84. See also "Consecration of Episcopal Church at State College," *TCN* (June 1928), 75. By the 1920s there were only five schools of theology and the arts affiliated with the Episcopal Church: Hobart, Trinity (Connecticut), Kenyon, University of the South, and St. Stephen's (Annandale, New York). On the secularization of mainline Protestant colleges and universities, see George Marsden, *The Soul of the American University: From Protestant Establishment to Established Nonbelief* (New York: Oxford University Press, 1994).

85. See Nathanael Groton's diary entry for March 1, 1913.

86. On the local organizations, see "Rector's Letter," Church of the Holy Trinity, *Yearbook* (1912), Church of the Holy Trinity Archives; Cordelia Drexel Biddle, *My Philadelphia Father* (Garden City, N.Y.: Doubleday, 1955), 71–72; and Washburn, *Philip Mercer Rhinelander*, 153. For a broader view, see Clifford Putney, *Muscular Christianity: Manhood and Sports in Protestant America, 1880–1920* (Cambridge: Harvard University Press, 2001). For concerns about men in the church, see also George Parkin Atwater, *The Episcopal Church: Its Message for Men of Today* (New York: Morehouse-Barlow, 1962), originally published in 1917.

87. "The Boy Problem," and "Family Prayer and Religion at Home," *St. Andrew's Cross*, January 1922, 99–100.

88. The diocesan convention voiced its approval of the prohibition amendment in 1918, but support was not unanimous, as reflected in editorial stances in the diocesan newspaper and an earlier preference for the "local option" rather than national legislation. See "The Church and Drink," *TCN* (April 1918), 212; "Two Convention Resolutions," *TCN* (May–June 1918), 246–47; and "Dr. Tomkins Is 77, Criticizes Courts: Blames Tribunals Largely for Failure to Enforce Prohibition," *Philadelphia Public Ledger*, February 8, 1927.

89. Pepper, *Philadelphia Lawyer*, 211. For a representative list of AAPA members from Philadelphia, see the letterhead of the organization's Pennsylvania division on the letter of 1925 in box 1, folder 1, William Wallace Atterbury Papers, Acc. 2053, Hagley Museum and Library, Wilmington, Delaware. In response to the "Pinchot Dry Amendment" in Pennsylvania, members of the AAPA argued that an "attempt to make Prohibition enforceable by increasing the police power will be ineffective here as it has been everywhere else where tried, and involves the abandonment and violation of fundamental principles of American Constitutional law designed to protect individual liberty." See William Wallace Atterbury to Charles S. Wood, March 12, 1923, in the same location.

90. Although Sabbatarianism was not a dominant issue within the diocese, George Wharton Pepper did spar publicly over the issue with the Reverend Floyd W. Tomkins of the Church of the Holy Trinity. Wharton, in addition to his defense of individual will, noted the hypocrisy of Sabbatarian policies. Members of the privileged class could play golf or tennis at private clubs, for instance, but members of other classes would be barred from Sunday recreations at public parks. See Pepper, *Philadelphia Lawyer*, 130.

91. See "Bishop's Address," *JDC 1914*, 116; "The Anglo-Catholic Centenary," *TCN* (December 1932), 91; "The Oxford Centenary Celebration," *TCN* (October 1933), 10; and "Centenary Draws Episcopal Throng: Thousands Are Gathering in Philadelphia for the Catholic Congress," *New York Times*, October 22, 1933.

92. William Sydnor, *The Real Prayer Book: 1549 to the Present* (Wilton, Conn.: Morehouse-Barlow, 1978), 69–76; and Floyd W. Tomkins, "Rector's Letter," Church of the Holy Trinity, *Yearbook* (1916), 17–18, Church of the Holy Trinity Archives.

93. Sydnor, *Real Prayer Book*, 77–79; and "Bishop's Address," *JDC 1928*, 101.

94. See Sydnor, *Real Prayer Book*, 81; and for a good description and illustrations of the changing appearance of the altar setting, *Our Common Prayer: A Bicentennial Book Celebrating the History of the Episcopal Diocese of Pennsylvania, 1784–1984* (Philadelphia: Diocese of Pennsylvania, 1984), 22–23.

95. See "Dr. Tomkins, Trinity Rector 33 Years, Dies," *Philadelphia Inquirer*, March 25, 1932; and Nathanael Groton's diary entries for September 26 and March 8, 1913, and September 26, 1914.

96. *Philadelphia Divinity School Catalog* (1910), EDS; and "Program for Ninth Annual Diocesan Lenten Preaching Missions," *TCN* (February 1936), 137. Although the annual series was formally instituted in 1928, the program had grown from Lenten noonday meetings for businessmen sponsored by St. Stephen's Church. See "Philadelphia," *Church Standard*, March 2, 1901, 611–12.

97. *The Hymnal of the Protestant Episcopal Church in the United States of America, 1940* (New York: Church Pension Fund, 1940), v; and John W. Norris, "The New Hymnal—When, How, Why," *TCN* (March 1941), 13, 24–25.

98. *The Hymnal 1940 Companion*, 2d ed. (New York: Church Pension Fund, 1951), quotation on vi.

99. Gilbert was also a member of the Joint Commission on Church Music responsible for the 1940 revisions. See Harold W. Gilbert, "Appropriate Speed in Hymn Singing," and "Choosing the Easter Music," *TCN* (February 1937), 172–73; Gilbert, "Our Campaign for Better Church Music," *TCN* (November 1937), 50–51; and N. Herbert Caley, "Pennsylvania Gives the Beat," *TCN* (October 1940), 11.

100. See West, *Centennial History of the Philadelphia Divinity School;* and Minutes of the Joint Board, January 1915, Board of Overseers Ledger, PDS Records, EDS.

101. "The Forgotten School: An Open Letter in Which the Philadelphia Divinity School Admits You Candidly into Its Confidence," *TCN* (April 1917), 229–31. Primary support for the school came from the five dioceses in Pennsylvania and the Diocese of Delaware.

102. Total construction costs were estimated to be between $500,000 and $900,000. See West, *Centennial History of the Philadelphia Divinity School*, 123–24.

103. For the history of the funding arrangement between the divinity school and the church, see the Resolution of the Standing Committee of the Diocese of Pennsylvania, January 11, 1974, regarding the "Disposition by St. Andrew's Church of Certain Funds Received From the Philadelphia Divinity School Upon Termination of Agreement Between the Church and the School," RG 4, box 2, PDS Records, EDS. See also "General Information: History and Purposes," *Philadelphia Divinity School Catalog* (1925), 25.

104. On the architecture, see Costen Fitz-Gibbon, "The Philadelphia Divinity School," *Architectural Record* 54 (August 1923): 106–20; James D. van Trump, "The Chapel on the Hill," *Charette* 47 (September–October 1967): 13–16; and Dorothy Grafly, "Paen of Color Rises in Chapel" (n.d.), in Clipping File, RG 6, box 1, PDS Records, EDS. On the Peak bequest, see also "Bishop Coadjutor Report," *JDC 1930*, 60.

105. Allen Evans, "Memoranda on the Divinity School in Philadelphia" (May 1938), RG 2, box 1, PDS Records, EDS. Evans's proposed "system of support" appears as point 11 to his "memoranda." For a description of its implications for the course of study, see *Philadelphia Divinity School Catalog* (1938), 17.

106. West, *Centennial History of the Philadelphia Divinity School*, 178–79. A resolution to admit women students at the PDS had passed in 1930, but the destabilizing effects of the Depression hindered advances in this field for much of the decade.

107. Donovan, *Different Call*, chapters 7–8; and *Living Church Annual* (1946), 333.

108. Cecil Roberts, "Was the English Church at Its Foundation Roman Catholic?" *TCN* (November 1922), 46–47. Earlier works written by members of the diocese to promote the Catholic revival include Archibald Campbell Knowles (later rector of St. Alban's, Olney), *The Belief and Worship of the Anglican Church* (Philadelphia: George W. Jacobs, 1896); and Rev. Alfred G. Mortimer (rector, St. Mark's, Philadelphia), *Catholic Faith and Practice: A Manual of Theological Instruction for Confirmation and First Communion* (New York: Longmans, Green, 1897).

109. See Twelves, *History of the Diocese of Pennsylvania*, 36; and "Converts to Be Priests: Six Former Episcopal Clergymen to Join Catholic Secular Priesthood," *New York Times*, July 23, 1908. See also James P. Lafferty, *Religious Unrest: The Way Out; Comments on Lectures of Rev. Alfred G. Mortimer, D.D., Rector of St. Mark's P.E. Church, Philadelphia* (Philadelphia: Catholic Standard and Times, 1908). Mortimer gave the lectures in response to McGarvey's conversion and the "open pulpit" controversy. Lafferty contends that the 1907 decision to open Episcopal pulpits to clergy from other Protestant denominations was in part a response to the flow of Episcopalians toward Rome.

110. In the Diocese of Delaware, Bishop Frederick J. Kinsman resigned his post in 1919 and was later received into the Catholic Church. See Charles A. Silliman, *The Episcopal Church in Delaware, 1785–1954* (Wilmington: Diocese of Delaware, 1982), 332. Also, the head of the Sisters of St. Mary converted to the Catholic Church in Philadelphia. See "Episcopal Nuns Change," *New York Times*, July 11, 1908. For conversions in a larger context, see Patrick Allitt, *Catholic Converts: British and American Intellectuals to Rome* (Ithaca: Cornell University Press, 1997).

111. "Church Distinctly American Urged: League Adopts Program to Preserve Episcopal Denomination's Protestant Character," *Philadelphia Public Ledger*, February 17, 1927.

112. On relations with the Orthodox churches, see *The Lambeth Conference and the Orthodox in America: A Study of One Path Toward Reunion* (New York: National Council of the Episcopal Church, 1930), available online at http://anglicanhistory.org/orthodoxy/lambeth1930.html; and on Anglican–Roman Catholic relations, see Prichard, *History of the Episcopal Church*, 192.

113. H. Henry Spoer, *An Aid For Churchmen: Episcopal and Orthodox* (New York: AMS Press, 1930); "The Orthodox-Eastern Commission," *JDC 1912*, Appendix T, 444; and "Notes of Recent Visitations," *TCN* (January 1914), 4.

114. "The World Conference on Faith and Order," *TCN* (April 1923), 219. See also Sydney E. Ahlstrom, *A Religious History of the American People*, vol. 2 (Garden City, N.Y.: Image Books, 1975), 396.

115. This dialogue included only the Presbyterian Church, USA, the northern branch of the denomination.

116. Church House (1894) was located at the northeast corner of Twelfth and Walnut streets until it moved to Rittenhouse Square in 1921; the Witherspoon Building (1895–97) was located at Thirteenth and Walnut.

117. For early discussions, see "Correspondence on Church Unity" (Philadelphia, 1896), Presbyterian Historical Society, Philadelphia. On the later proposal, which declared that "unity would be 'organic' in the same way as churches of separate geographic areas, yet of variant organization and worship, were one in the early Church," see "Basic Principles Proposed for the Union of the Presbyterian Church in the United States of America and the Protestant Episcopal Church in the United States of America" (1943), ibid. Talks in the early 1930s had also included the Methodist Church, but its full participation was delayed by its ongoing efforts to foster unity among the various branches of Methodism.

118. "Reunion with the Presbyterians," *TCN* (March 1939), 10; and David Hein and Gardiner H. Shattuck Jr., *The Episcopalians* (Westport, Conn.: Praeger, 2004), 114–15.

119. Edward Hawks, *William McGarvey and the Open Pulpit: An Intimate History of a Celibate Movement in the Episcopal Church and of Its Collapse, 1870–1908* (Philadelphia: Dolphin Press, 1935), 187.

120. Quoted in "Upward of Thirty Parishes of Diocese Are Represented in First Communion Service in New Cathedral Chapel," *TCN* (December 1934), 83. The report was also reprinted in *Cathedral Church of Christ.*

121. In 1942, for instance, more than seven hundred men from the diocese were serving in the armed forces. See "The Church of God Goes Forth to War," *TCN* (April 1942), 11. Even though the Brotherhood of St. Andrew, through its central office in Philadelphia, maintained records of Episcopalians serving in World War I, diocesan reports do not provide clear figures. On the lack of an exact number, see "The Bishop's Annual Address," Part II, *TCN* (May–June 1918), 249. On the work of the Brotherhood of St. Andrew, see Philadelphia War History Commission, *Philadelphia in the World War, 1914–1919* (New York: Wynkoop Hallenbeck Crawford Co., 1922), 625.

122. "From a Nurse at a Base Hospital," and "How the Soldiers' and Sailors' Prayer Book Helped," *TCN* (February 1919), 144.

123. Quoted in Emma E. Brehm, "Diocesan War Commission," *TCN* (November 1942), 10. Bearing the words "For Thee Christ Died," the war cross consisted of a central cross and four smaller crosses, each inscribed in a circle. According to the report, "The circle around the central cross is the symbol of Eternal Life, without beginning and without end. The four small circles with the cross in each represent the four corners of the earth."

124. "Clergy in War Work," *TCN* (October 1918), 9; and "Letters from Chaplains and Soldiers," *TCN* (February 1919), 142–43. The *Living Church Annual* also listed clergy serving with the armed forces. The 1946 edition, for instance, named twenty serving from the diocese.

125. See "Appeal of the War Commission," *TCN* (December 1917), 70–71; "Notes of the Diocesan War Commission," *TCN* (January 1918), 113–14; and the appeal from the diocesan altar guild that appeared in *TCN* (March 1941), 26.

126. See "Report of the War Commission of the Diocese," *JDC 1919*, Appendix W; "Bishop's Address," *JDC 1942;* and "War Service Day Feb. 13th: A Day of Special Remembrance," *TCN* (February 1944), 8–9.

127. Gina Kolata, *Flu: The Story of the Great Influenza Pandemic of 1918 and the Search for the Virus That Caused It* (New York: Farrar, Straus and Giroux, 1999), 18–20.

128. The Episcopal Hospital reported that all sixty nurses who contracted influenza recovered. See "The Church's Ministry of Healing: How Our Hospital Served During the Recent Scourge," *TCN* (December 1918), 86–87. On the condition at St. Timothy's Hospital, Roxborough, see John Charles Manton, *A Splendid Legacy: St. Timothy's, Roxborough, 1859–1984* (Philadelphia: St. Timothy's Church, 1984), 80–81.

129. On Christ Church, see "News Department," *TCN* (April 1917), 24–25; and on St. Mark, Frankford, see "Church of the Colors," *TCN* (December 1943), 17.

130. "Lent and the Nation's Need," *TCN* (February 1918), 137–38; and St. Mark's, *Yearbook* (1913), St. Mark's Church (Locust Street) Archives.

131. Knowles, *Reminiscences of a Parish Priest*, 106.

132. Deborah Mathias Gough, *Christ Church, Philadelphia: The Nation's Church in a Changing City* (Philadelphia: University of Pennsylvania Press, 1995), 328–29. For comments on the need to strengthen ties to the "world community," see "Bishop Hart's Victory Statement," *TCN* (May–June 1945), 5.

133. On parish missionary work, see, for instance, news of the missionary society at St. Thomas's Church, Whitemarsh, in *St. Thomas' Messenger,* January 16, 1914, STCA; on the history of the United Thank Offering, see http://www.episcopalchurch.org/uto_8674_ENG _HTM.htm; and for a graph of missionary budgetary divisions, see *TCN* (December 1928), 84–85.

134. "A Call to Sacrifice," *TCN* (January 1941), 7; "Pennsylvania Leads in Aid to British," *TCN* (April 1941), 6; "How English Church Is Using $300,000 Aid from America," *TCN* (November 1941), 44; and "The China Emergency Fund," *TCN* (January 1938), 111–12.

135. Bishop Garland, "A Campaign for Personal Service," *TCN* (November 1918), 37.

136. On the campaign, see Twelves, *History of the Diocese of Pennsylvania,* 37; "For the Glory of God in the Diocese of Pennsylvania" (published for the diocese's Campaign for Missions and Institutions, November 26–December 6, 1926), Religious Institution Collection, HSP; "Bishop's Address," *JDC 1927,* 70; "Campaign for Missions and Institutions," special issue of *TCN* (November 1926); and "Diocesan Campaign Fund Passes $2,000,000 Mark," *TCN* (March 1927), 193.

137. On the earlier system of apportionments, see "Parochial Shares of the Apportionment, 1917–1918," *TCN* (October 1917), 18–21.

138. Reynolds D. Brown, "Report of the Executive Secretary as to the Present Status of the Nation-Wide Campaign in the Diocese of Pennsylvania," *TCN* (April 1920), 174–76.

139. See ibid.; Rev. Gilbert Pember, "Some Lessons of the Nation-Wide Campaign"; and "Mr. George Wharton Pepper's View of the Campaign," *TCN* (April 1920). The entire issue was devoted to this campaign.

140. "Some Statistics," *St. Thomas' Messenger,* May 1921; and "Explanations," *St. Thomas' Messenger,* February 1925, STCA.

141. *TCN* published annual reports on the budget that included the status of individual parishes in meeting expectations. The listings in the April 1934 issue reflect the challenges of the Depression.

142. "Bishops Say Church Will Meet Crisis," *New York Times,* April 29, 1932; and "A $35,000 Deficit Confronts This Diocese for 1933!" *TCN* (December 1933), 79.

143. "Matters Calling for Action by Diocesan Convention," *TCN* (March 1934), 212.

144. William H. Jefferys, MD, "Our City Mission and the Work It Is Doing as Your Representative," *TCN* (October 1936), 16; "The Completing Improvement at Christ Church," *TCN* (October 1932), 21; and Gough, *Christ Church, Philadelphia,* 300–301.

145. Clinton Rodgers Woodruff, "Department of Christian Social Service," *TCN* (October 1932), 20; "The Thanksgiving Day Offering for Your Episcopal Hospital," *TCN* (November 1938), 18–19; and "Episcopal Hospital—and What It's Doing," *TCN* (November 1941), 11.

146. [Rev. Nathanael Groton], "Rector's Letter," *St. Thomas' Messenger,* October 1922, STCA.

147. A list of the trustees of the Welfare Federation appears on its letterhead. A copy of an appeal letter from the federation from 1924, with a list of the trustees on the letterhead, can be found in box 237, folder W, Pew Family Papers, Collection 1862, Hagley Museum and Library, Wilmington, Delaware. On the 1940 campaign, see "Sharing with Us: United Charities Campaign for 1940 Lists Nine Episcopal Institutions Among Its Many Beneficiaries," *TCN* (February 1940), 8–9.

148. Manton, *Splendid Legacy,* 84.

149. On financial support, see "Thanksgiving Day Offering for Your Episcopal Hospital"; Laurence H. Eldredge, "It's Our Episcopal Hospital," *TCN* (November 1944), 1–3. In honor of his eightieth birthday, Bishop Taitt requested that the diocese conduct a drive for the hospital. See "$100,000 for Episcopal Hospital," *TCN* (September 1941), 11; and "The Bishop's Wish Came True—$100,000," *TCN* (January 1942), 7. On severed ties, see "University to Administer Hospital," *TCN* (December 1948), 7; and Twelves, *History of the Diocese of Pennsylvania,* 42.

8

A Church on Wheels, 1945–1963

WILLIAM W. CUTLER III

In the fall of 1957 Henry C. Gibson was nearing the end of his second year as rector's warden at the Church of Our Saviour in Jenkintown. Once recognized as one of the fastest-growing parishes in the Diocese of Pennsylvania, it still ranked among the largest and most prosperous. That spring, the vestry at Our Saviour had decided to confront an old dilemma. Stored in the church basement was a large and ornate altar. Acquired from St. James's, Philadelphia (Twenty-second and Walnut) after it dissolved in 1945, the altar and its reredos had been a memorial to Mr. Gibson's mother. But these artifacts were too big to fit into the sanctuary at Our Saviour. Either the church would have to be remodeled, or the altar and its accoutrements would have to be made smaller. Painful as it must have been for the rector's warden, he and his colleagues decided not to spend the many thousands of dollars it would have taken to install the Gibson altar. But it did not end up being forgotten or discarded. In November, the Church of the Redeemer, Springfield, bought it for $5,000. Achieving parish status in 1947, Redeemer grew rapidly in the 1950s, just as Our Saviour had done two decades earlier.[1] The story of the Gibson altar is, in effect, metaphorical. The Diocese of Pennsylvania was on the move, and in keeping with this transformation a religious artifact whose home had once been in the heart of the city would now come to rest in a distant suburb.

The Episcopal Church in the 1940s and '50s

Organized religion deeply affected American life in the years that followed World War II. It shaped what many people thought and did as they struggled to reconcile the democratic values for which they had just fought overseas with the blatant injustices that were still so much a part of everyday life at home. In this unsettled climate, thousands sought reassurance from inspirational books like *The Power of Positive Thinking*, by Norman Vincent Peale. Millions looked to the Most Reverend Fulton J. Sheen for guidance through his weekly television program, *Life Is Worth Living*. Even the president, Dwight David Eisenhower, made piety a part of his leadership, demonstrating an approach to faith that was both personal and pragmatic. In so doing, he was in concert with most of those he led. In 1954 a Gallup poll attributed a belief in God to 96 percent of all Americans. Three years later the U.S. Census Bureau estimated that 96.4 percent of all adults identified with a religious tradition. Some scholars tried to explain this trend in material rather than spiritual terms. "The trend toward religious identification and church affiliation may . . . be a reflection of the growing need for conformity and sociability," the social philosopher Will Herberg observed.[2] Such cynicism notwithstanding, many Americans were more than ready to put their finances where their faith was. In fact, such a boom in church construction occurred in the 1950s that a priest and theologian of the Episcopal Church, Bernard Iddings Bell, was prompted to warn against confusing the building itself with the worship it sheltered.[3]

After World War II the national Episcopal Church experienced significant growth. Starting from a base of about 1,500,000 communicants in 1945, the denomination surged, climbing to a near-record high of 2,300,000 in 1965 before leveling off in the 1970s and then declining thereafter. The number of baptized persons affiliated with the church increased commensurately, rising from 2,270,000 in 1945 to 3,616,000 twenty years later.[4] Such growth may have occurred because the Episcopal Church resisted change until the 1960s. In keeping with the political and cultural climate of the times, it stuck with familiar ideas about theology and well-established rituals. Episcopalians worshipped using a prayer book adopted by the previous generation and maintained their long-standing commitment to governance by localism. According to historian David Hein, "the diocese was the real center of church life, or, more accurately, the diocese and the parish together, for this denomination always had a strong congregationalist streak in its make-up."[5]

Episcopalians resisted change in the postwar era in many other respects. Despite or perhaps because of the presence of nuclear weapons in their midst, they were inclined to think that the power of science was limited. They moved cautiously on such touchy matters as divorce and remarriage, reaffirming their faith in matrimony as a lifelong commitment.

Of course, there were exceptions. War brides who no longer found themselves attracted to the GI of their dreams called upon both secular and religious leaders to reexamine their views on the sanctity of marriage and the primacy of the family. In response, the Episcopal Church liberalized its marriage canon in 1946, abandoning a divorce policy that had allowed only the "innocent" party to remarry in the church. Undaunted, conservatives regrouped and three years later beat back an attempt to allow bishops to recognize divorces granted for causes arising after the wedding day as well as for those known to have preceded it.[6] On the subject of gender, it seemed that there might be real reform right away. In 1946 a housewife and mother from St. Louis, Mrs. Randolph H. Dyer, was seated as the first woman deputy to the Episcopal Church's General Convention. This breakthrough was short-lived, however. Although three dioceses elected a woman to represent them at the next General Convention (1949), those in attendance, once assembled, decided not to seat them. Their admission, it was felt, might cause men to lose interest. This convention did appoint a joint commission to study the issue, and it eventually recommended having women deputies. But this proposal also went nowhere, apparently because the national church did not want to get too far out in front of rank-and-file members. In two-thirds of its dioceses women were still excluded from their local conventions, and at least as often from service on vestries. The National Council of the Episcopal Church took the symbolic step of creating a General Division of Women's Work in 1958. But for the most part women remained on the outside looking in throughout the 1950s.[7]

Black Americans also did not find the Episcopal Church to be particularly welcoming. In 1940 the General Convention did establish the post of secretary for Negro work. This post was to be filled by a black man who was to report to a Joint Commission on African Americans. But this was done with the understanding that black Episcopalians were to be kept apart from the rest of the church. Despite calls during World War II for fellowship in worship and church administration, most Episcopalians accepted the widespread existence of separate facilities and congregations. However, changes in the church's racial climate began to occur soon after World War II ended. In 1950 Virginia Theological Seminary broke the color line, formally admitting "a resident Negro student." The School of Theology at the University of the South took a similar step three years later, but only after overcoming serious opposition. Nevertheless, a new day was coming; in 1954 the Diocese of South Carolina became the last in the church to remove race as a barrier to representation at its diocesan convention.[8]

At the national level, the House of Bishops endorsed protests against discrimination at the General Convention in 1952; at this same meeting the church as a whole decided that there would be no segregation at its next general convention. But by choosing Houston, Texas, as the place for this meeting, it almost guaranteed that satisfactory local arrangements could not be made, and, as a result, Honolulu became the last-minute choice as the site for this meeting. Far from the mainland, Episcopalian leaders urged their peers to follow the Supreme Court's recent lead on desegregation, affirming that the Episcopal Church should welcome people of all races. The creation of the Episcopal Society for Cultural and Racial Unity in 1959 was another step in this direction. A largely white organization with no official ties to the church itself, it tried to generate broad support for racial inclusiveness. It attacked segregation in education, housing, and employment as well as organized religion.[9]

The cold war may have strengthened the hand of civil rights activists within the Episcopal Church. Reacting to conflict in the Middle East and to what it called Soviet "tyranny" in Hungary, the House of Bishops issued a pastoral letter in November 1956 calling for reconciliation among all Christians. Such ecumenical thinking was not unprecedented among Episcopalians. Discussions with both the Presbyterians and the Methodists about the possibility of merger had taken place in the 1930s, but ultimately these discussions met a dead end. The full acceptance of each other's clergy stood in the way, especially for Episcopalians.[10] In the mid-1950s the church's bishops reached out to others in a different way. We should remember, they said, "that our own racial divisions and misunderstandings at home are part of the same sad story of division which we see on the international scene." Their introspection on this occasion was a far cry from previous complaints about the materialism and atheism of communism. Hesitant to criticize American capitalism and foreign policy in the early 1950s, the Protestant establishment would gradually overcome such fears over the next fifteen years. In 1962 the Episcopal House of Bishops condemned "total war" and called for a reconsideration of the American policy of massive retaliation. But racism in the Episcopal Church refused to disappear, prompting the famed columnist and editor Ralph McGill to complain in 1962 that the church was losing membership because it was still afflicted with "gruesome persons" who refused to worship with black Americans.[11] It cannot be known whether he had the Diocese of Pennsylvania in mind when he made this observation, but it can said with some assurance that the diocese was by no means immune to these unjust national trends.

The Right Reverend Oliver James Hart and the Suburbanization of the Diocese of Pennsylvania

It must have felt right to the lay and clerical delegates who assembled in Holy Trinity Church, Philadelphia, on May 12, 1942, when they chose Captain Oliver James Hart to be their bishop coadjutor. After all, the Diocese of Pennsylvania was almost as old as the nation itself, and the nation was at war at the time. Born in 1892, Hart, a native South Carolinian, was a military veteran. Sent overseas in 1918, he served in Europe as an army chaplain and was holding down a similar post at New Jersey's Fort Dix when he was called to be coadjutor. Between the wars Father Hart had ministered to congregations in South Carolina, Georgia, Tennessee, Washington, D.C., and Massachusetts. His move to Philadelphia came while he was on leave from the other Trinity Church, the one in Copley Square in Boston, where he had been named rector in 1940. He, too, must have felt right about accepting a call to the post of coadjutor in the Diocese of Pennsylvania, because he had declined similar offers on three previous occasions.[12]

Bishop Hart did not remain long as the diocese's coadjutor. Because his predecessor, the Right Reverend Francis Marion Taitt, died barely a year after his arrival, Hart was installed as the tenth bishop of the Diocese of Pennsylvania in a ceremony that occurred on September 21, 1943, at the Cathedral Church of Christ in Roxborough. That this ceremony took place on land once owned by the family of Henry Howard Houston was certainly fitting. Having made his fortune in railroads, land, and oil, Houston became one of the chief developers of Chestnut Hill, an elite residential neighborhood at the northwestern edge of the city. During his twenty years at the helm of the Diocese of Pennsylvania, Hart saw its center of gravity move from the city to the suburbs. In fact, his first assignment in the diocese had been to direct missionary work at the confluence of the city and its suburbs in the Convocations of North, West, and South Philadelphia. But the demands of the war got in the way of this effort, and by the time conditions were right, Hart had become the diocesan bishop.[13] In 1946 he addressed the missionary question in a speech to the delegates at the diocese's 162nd annual convention. Taking a cautious approach, he recommended against the construction of new churches in areas of demographic expansion unless it could be shown that their congregations had strong leadership. "The quality of our missions is more important than the quantity," the bishop counseled. "It is better to have a few strong missions, commanding respect and support, than to have more than can be properly

FIGURE 8.1 Bishop Oliver Hart

manned." Less than two years later, however, his actions spoke louder than these words. Breaking with a tradition dating back to 1784, the bishop did not preside over the Easter service at Christ Church, Philadelphia. Instead, he spent the day at Trinity, Solebury, a mission church in Bucks County that would not become a full-fledged parish for another six years.[14]

What accounts for this sudden break with the past? Numbers explain a lot. In 1948 the region in which the diocese operated was on the cusp of a historic demographic shift. For those who could choose, the suburbs were becoming the place to live. Between 1940 and 1960 the number of people residing in the four Pennsylvania counties surrounding Philadelphia nearly doubled, while the city's population increased by less than 4 percent.[15] Even within the city itself, there was a significant population drift. Replacing the streetcar as the method of choice by which to commute, the automobile made it possible for more and more Philadelphians to reside in what had once been underdeveloped neighborhoods on the city's edge, especially in the far northeast. Reformers and business leaders responded by attempting to revitalize the city in the 1950s. Mayors Joseph Clark and Richardson Dilworth focused their energies on the downtown and the historic neighborhoods contiguous to it. They relied heavily on Edmund Bacon, the director of the Philadelphia Planning Commission, who put together a comprehensive blueprint for the city that emphasized the renewal of the central business district. Encouraged by Clark and Dilworth, private developers built Penn Center, an office tower complex that replaced the Pennsylvania Railroad's antiquated terminal at Broad and Market streets. An upscale residential neighborhood known as Society Hill emerged from the scramble of factories and tenements south and east of Independence Hall. Traffic congestion on area roadways, coupled with the Philadelphia business community's strong desire to keep workers and shoppers coming into the city, brought about the construction of the Schuylkill Expressway. But this undersized superhighway did not fulfill its backers' social and economic expectations. Connecting the central business district with the Pennsylvania Turnpike at King of Prussia, it actually fostered suburban development as much as, or perhaps even more than, the renewal of the city.[16]

The suburbanization of Episcopalians in the Diocese of Pennsylvania began before the 1950s. Organized by order of the 1933 diocesan convention, the Committee on the Problem of City Churches reported the following year that "churches in growing sections must be prepared to see other parishes come in," while "churches whose people are migrating should seriously plan either to migrate with them . . . or readjust their work to new conditions." Urban parishes whose members had moved away presented a special problem. They possessed legal and financial assets that needed to be conserved and/or reallocated. Faced with this reality, the leaders of the diocese had to find answers to some very tough questions. Could the endowments of such churches be transferred to new or existing congregations in different locations, or did these assets have to become the sole property of the diocese? Such matters took on greater significance in the 1940s, when it became clear that although the Episcopal population

TABLE 8.1 Metropolitan Philadelphia population by county, 1940–1960

County	1940 Total	%	1950 Total	%	1960 Total	%
Bucks	107,715	3.88	144,620	4.60	308,567	8.59
Chester	135,626	4.89	159,141	5.06	210,608	5.86
Delaware	310,756	11.20	414,234	13.18	553,154	15.40
Montgomery	289,247	10.42	353,068	11.24	516,682	14.39
Total Suburban	843,344	30.39	1,071,063	34.08	1,589,011	44.24
Philadelphia	1,931,334	69.61	2,071,605	65.92	2,002,512	55.76
Metropolitan Philadelphia (five-county total)	2,774,678	100.00	3,142,668	100.00	3,591,523	100.00

Source: Geostat Center, Collections, Historical Census Browser, University of Virginia Library, http://fisher.lib.virginia.edu/collections/stats/histcensus/.

TABLE 8.2 Population distribution in Philadelphia, 1940–1960

Region	1940	Percentage of city in 1940	1950	Percentage of city in 1950	1960	Percentage of city in 1960
Central	1,654,042	85.6	1,710,335	82.6	1,532,475	76.5
Northwest	56,207	2.9	60,778	2.9	69,183	3.5
Northeast	221,085	11.5	300,492	14.5	400,851	20.0
Total	1,931,334	100.0	2,071,605	100.0	2,002,509	100.0

Source: John S. Adams, William C. Block, Mark Lindberg, Robert McMaster, Steven Ruggles, and Wendy Thomas, *National Historical Geographic Information System Pre-Release Version 0.1* (Minneapolis: Minnesota Population Center, University of Minnesota, 2004). See http://www.nhgis.org. As reported by NHGIS, the total population for Philadelphia in 1960 is slightly less than that reported by the Historical Census Browser, but the difference is so small (three people) as to be completely insignificant.

Note: For the purposes of this table, the Northwest is defined as Mt. Airy and Chestnut Hill, while the Northeast includes those neighborhoods lying east of Broad Street and north of Godfrey Avenue. Its southern boundary extends from East Oak Lane to Tacony. The census tracts for the Northwest are 11, 15, 17, 19, 21, 23, 25, 28, 29, 33, 35, 41, 51–54, 61, 79, 89, 98, 100, 101, 109, 115, 120, 124, 136, 143, and 150. The census tracts for the Northeast are 1–10, 12–14, 16, 18, 20, 27, 30–32, 37, 38, 40, 43, 48, 50, 56, 57, 60, 62, 64, 70, 72–75, 77, 80, 81, 85, 91–93, 96, 97, 99, 103, 104, 106, 108, 111, 112, 114, 117, 118, 121, 129–33, 135, 137, 139, 140, 147–49, 151, 153, 155, 160, 162, 163, 165–67, 173, 176, 181, 372, and 373.

was growing rapidly in many parts of Chester, Delaware, and Montgomery counties, the diocese lagged behind the demographic curve in the region's less affluent suburbs. This discrepancy raised new concerns about the old image of the Episcopal Church as upper crust. If this is true, said the editors of the diocesan newsletter, *The Church News* (*TCN*), then "something is wrong—with human nature and the Episcopal Church; and we should get busy on both."[17]

Whatever the reason, the suburbanization of the Diocese of Pennsylvania would accelerate after World War II, transforming it in the process. Of course, the diocese as a whole was growing, climbing from 73,782 communicants in 1946 to 84,849 in 1962. But the percentage of communicants attending a church with a Philadelphia address dropped by 16 percent during this period. These numbers look even more dramatic if such low-density, residential areas within the city limits as Mt. Airy and Chestnut Hill, in the northwest, and Lawndale, Mayfair, Tacony, and Bustleton, in the northeast, are excluded. By this accounting, the proportion of communicants who worshipped in "the city" had fallen 18 percent by the early 1960s. Not surprisingly, revenue followed population to the suburbs. In 1956 congregations outside the city were taking in more money than all their urban counterparts, including those in the city's suburban neighborhoods, a trend that would prove just as irreversible as the concomitant population shift.

Episcopalians were not alone in making a move to the suburbs. For example, many Jews abandoned Philadelphia after World War II, and their synagogues soon followed them out of the city.[18] Like other Philadelphia religious and secular leaders, Bishop Hart struggled with this population shift. In a message to those assembled for the diocese's 163rd annual convention in the spring of 1947, he acknowledged it, but his words were reminiscent of what the Committee on the Problem of City Churches had said more than a decade before. "Every parish," the bishop advised, "should carefully evaluate its work and either plan for vigorous continuance of the work at the present location or move to another part of the diocese where constructive work can be done." It was up to each parish to make such decisions, as far as the bishop was concerned, but the rush out of Philadelphia soon forced his hesitant hand. In the winter of 1949 he called a special convention to elect a suffragan bishop whose "primary" responsibility would be "missionary work within the diocese." It chose the Right Reverend J. Gillespie (Gil) Armstrong, the rector of St. Mary's, Ardmore, who was, like the bishop, a World War I veteran.[19] Later that same year Bishop Hart took a bigger step, putting in motion a fund-raising

TABLE 8.3 Communicants in the Diocese of Pennsylvania, 1946–1962

Communicants	1946 Total	%	1949 Total	%	1952 Total	%	1956 Total	%	1959 Total	%	1962 Total	%
Central Philadelphia	37,646	51	37,987	50	34,276	46	31,827	40	30,203	37	28,155	33
Northwest and Northeast Philadelphia	7,855	11	7,615	10	7,998	11	9,030	11	9,052	11	10,596	13
Non-Philadelphia	28,281	38	30,310	40	32,372	43	38,360	49	42,447	52	46,098	54
Total	73,782	100	75,912	100	74,646	100	79,217	100	81,702	100	84,849	100

Source: *Journals of the Protestant Episcopal Church, Diocese of Pennsylvania* (Philadelphia: Diocese of Pennsylvania, 1946, 1949, 1952, 1956, 1959, 1962).

TABLE 8.4 Parish receipts by region in the Diocese of Pennsylvania, 1946–1962 (in dollars)

Receipts	1946 Total	%	1949 Total	%	1952 Total	%	1956 Total	%	1959 Total	%	1962 Total	%
Central Philadelphia	1,873,319	52	1,811,868	47	2,102,255	44	2,595,302	38	2,841,807	34	3,002,339	33
Northwest and Northeast Philadelphia	360,051	10	379,799	10	544,607	11	789,638	11	857,314	10	1,144,421	12
Non-Philadelphia	1,367,355	38	1,693,517	43	2,155,360	45	3,452,842	51	4,769,795	56	5,012,137	55
Total	3,600,725	100	3,885,184	100	4,802,222	100	6,837,782	100	8,468,916	100	9,158,897	100

Source: *Journals of the Protestant Episcopal Church, Diocese of Pennsylvania* (Philadelphia: Diocese of Pennsylvania, 1946, 1949, 1952, 1956, 1959, 1962).

effort designed to respond to the diocese's demographic growth and shift. The Diocesan Advancement Campaign set a goal of $400,000, to be used for church extension ($150,000), a conference center ($125,000), and the Philadelphia Divinity School ($125,000). It was the diocese's first appeal for capital funds in more than twenty years. The extension money was earmarked for the purchase of land and the construction of new facilities, but the bishop soon recognized that $150,000 would not come close to meeting even the existing need, let alone the anticipated demand.

The Diocesan Advancement Campaign almost reached its stated goal. By 1952, $389,200 had been raised. But contributions to the fund were not evenly distributed among the designated recipients. The Philadelphia Divinity School was oversubscribed—perhaps because the school was already well established and the need for priests widely recognized. With the limited dollars at their disposal, those in charge of parish extension looked especially to the suburban northeast, designating $55,000 for St. Andrew's-in-the-Field, Somerton, and $66,500 for new facilities in Bucks County.[20] When the Levitt Corporation donated a tract of land on the condition that an Episcopal church be erected in its new development near the Fairless Hills Steel Plant, the diocese moved quickly. St. Paul's, Levittown, was up and running within a year, but now the extension cupboard was bare. As the man in charge of development, the suffragan, Gillespie Armstrong, pointed out in 1954 that there were still many suburban congregations in need. A case in point was Trinity, Gulph Mills, located at the bustling intersection of the Pennsylvania Turnpike and the yet to be finished Schuylkill Expressway, where attendance had doubled in just three years. Similar situations existed in Eddington (Bucks County), Coatesville (Chester County), and Academy Gardens in the city's far northeast.[21]

In 1955 the Diocese of Pennsylvania took steps to address these needs. At its 171st annual convention it made plans to study the problems presented by population growth and shift. A special committee, to be organized by Bishop Hart, was given the assignment of determining how to build new churches, enlarge existing ones, and eliminate those that were obsolete. Two years later the results of this planning became apparent when the diocese opened a $1.25 million capital campaign whose principal goals were the enhancement of the Philadelphia Divinity School and the development of both existing and new congregations. More than half of this money was earmarked for suburban expansion. When pledges totaling $300,000 quickly came in, Bishop Hart committed the diocese to building a new church in Gulph Mills, moving the Church of the Redemption from West Philadelphia to Southampton (Bucks County), and buying land for a new mission in King of Prussia near the terminus of the Schuylkill Expressway.[22] However, these ambitious plans were only partially fulfilled. By the end of 1959, fund-raising had stalled. Pledges amounted to less than $900,000, and not even two-thirds of that had actually come in. Three years later the diocese terminated its capital campaign with $775,000 in the till—a substantial sum, to be sure, but one that fell far short of the original goal.[23]

The shortcomings of the capital campaign notwithstanding, the diocese remade itself during Bishop Hart's two decades as its leader. It followed the region's population, closing churches in the city, opening them in the suburbs, and merging parishes where demand was declining. Unlike some of his predecessors, such as the Right Reverend Alonzo Potter (1845–65) and the Right Reverend Philip Mercer Rhinelander (1911–23), who had presided over the development and construction of many new churches, Bishop Hart could point to only seven that were both founded as missions and elevated to parish status during his administration. None of these were in the city. However, the promotion of existing mission churches to parish status took a giant leap forward while Hart was the diocesan bishop, and most of these were in the suburbs. Only nine of thirty-four such churches were in Philadelphia County, and two of them were in residential neighborhoods that were still under development and essentially suburban. Twenty were in Delaware and Montgomery counties, where the Episcopal Church had put down roots before 1940 but was now rapidly and significantly expanding. This demographic shift forced thirteen churches to close. Twelve of them were not only inside the city but also in sections affected by such economic and social changes as urban redevelopment, ethnic succession, and the construction of superhighways. St. James's, Philadelphia, shut its doors in 1945, the victim of changing demographics in the Rittenhouse neighborhood. The construction of Interstate 95 along the Delaware River nearly twenty years later forced St. Stephen's, Bridesburg, to close altogether in 1962 and Christ Church, Eddington, to abandon its home on Bristol Pike for a new location on Street Road in nearby Cornwells Heights. In Southwest Philadelphia, St. Titus's closed, and St. Cyprian's merged with St. Barnabas's at Sixty-fifth Street and Haverford Avenue because of the city's decision to redevelop Elmwood in the area known as Eastwick.[24]

The Church of the Resurrection in North Philadelphia and St. Paul's, Levittown, typify the changes that were taking place. Founded in 1850, Resurrection started life in the village of Rising Sun on the outskirts of what was then the developed city. By 1960 it was housed in a stately building on

TABLE 8.5 Changes in parish status in the Diocese of Pennsylvania, 1942–1962

Location	Churches founded and admitted to parish status	Missions admitted to parish status	Closed
Central Philadelphia	0	7	10
Northwest and Northeast Philadelphia	0	2	2
Non-Philadelphia	7	25	1
Montgomery County	3	8	0
Delaware County	1	12	0
Bucks County	2	4	0
Chester County	1	1	1

Source: *Journals of the Protestant Episcopal Church, Diocese of Pennsylvania* (Philadelphia: Diocese of Pennsylvania, 1942, 1946, 1949, 1952, 1956, 1959, 1962); J. Wesley Twelves, *A History of the Diocese of Pennsylvania of the Protestant Episcopal Church in the U.S.A., 1784–1968* (Philadelphia: Diocese of Pennsylvania, 1969).

North Broad Street, but it was not the church it once had been; its congregation was old, and its neighborhood was different. More than 45 percent of its members were at least sixty years of age. They were almost entirely white, but their neighbors were mostly African American. Because the health sciences campus of Temple University was nearby, along with numerous businesses, the church's natural population was shrinking. Many members had to make at least a thirty-minute commute every Sunday morning. These circumstances notwithstanding, the rector and his congregation resisted change. Researchers from the diocese concluded in 1964 that for Resurrection "to survive there must be new methods of ministry, fresh approaches to communication, the setting aside of pre-conceived thought patterns, and different methods of operations."[25]

By contrast, St. Paul's, Levittown, was new, young, and evolving. In existence for less than a decade, its congregation was constantly changing. Many had been in the parish for fewer than five years. More than 31 percent were between the ages of thirty and forty-five. Nearly 40 percent were teenagers and children. In keeping with the residential development of which it was a part, St. Paul's was a family church. But there was something missing. Unlike Resurrection, the congregation at St. Paul's was not a family. It lacked a strong sense of spiritual community. "One problem to be met at St. Paul's," said a research report prepared by the diocese, is "maintaining a feeling of neighborliness even though the congregation is growing beyond the point where an individual member can know more than a small portion of his fellow parishioners."[26]

There was precedent in the diocese for this concern about the importance of belonging to a spiritual community. In December 1951 the diocese had focused on the Bryan Green Mission, which brought to Philadelphia a charismatic evangelist from the United Kingdom. The rector of St. Martin's Church in Birmingham, England, Bryan Green was no amateur when he came to Philadelphia for ten days at the end of 1951; he had conducted revivals all over the world by then. In the United States he was known to churchgoers in New York, Washington, Houston, Los Angeles, and San Francisco. The Philadelphia Council of Churches endorsed his visit, which was organized by more than fifteen hundred volunteers led by the diocesan suffragan bishop, Gillespie Armstrong. "When many people are gathered together looking to God," Armstrong said, "His Holy Spirit speaks to us and fills us with understanding."[27]

The Bryan Green Mission was the first of its kind in Philadelphia in more than fifteen years. Speaking to more than seventy thousand people in mass meetings at the Philadelphia Convention Hall and thirty thousand more at several other locations, Green sought to energize the faithful by strengthening their religious convictions. According to newspaper reports, there were often young people in the large crowds that attended, many looking for answers to questions that were troubling them. But Green did not necessarily accommodate them. "There is no short-cut out of the [spiritual] mess we are in," he said at the revival's end. "We have forgotten our Father. . . . We need world wide education, concerns for the underprivileged, for disease, for suffering and for a religious revival."[28] Regardless of its long-term effect, Green's was a message that reflected the times in which he and his audiences lived.

Bishop Hart believed that the mission revitalized the diocese and prompted many confirmations by clarifying "the basic facts of our salvation." It also taught him the importance of spiritual relationships. "We gain our most important learning almost apart from the language of words," he said in the wake of the mission. "We acquire most of our habits and attitudes and consequent character through relationships."[29] The same theme reappeared six years later in a *TCN* editorial, not long after the appearance of what was probably the most influential book on religion of its time, Will Herberg's *Protestant-Catholic-Jew.* Instead of applauding the rising tide of membership in suburban churches, this editorial questioned the motives of those in the diocese who were flocking to them. Attributing to Herberg the idea that the enormous growth of church membership in the 1950s had resulted from the alienation felt by those relocating to the suburbs, it asked whether new people were joining the Episcopal Church not out of religious conviction but from "a desire to belong to some recognizable group." Perhaps, it said, we have made "church membership too easy; . . . we have talked too much about what the church can do for the individual rather than what the church will require of the individual."[30]

Sentiments like these found a national voice at the same time through the words of an Episcopal priest named Gibson Winter. Writing for the *Christian Century* in 1955, Winter complained that too many suburban churches had lost sight of their true mission. Preoccupied with buildings and budget, they made parish prosperity an end in itself. Six years later Winter took this argument one step further. In a book titled *The Suburban Captivity of the Churches*, he explored the ethics of what he perceived to be a growing divide between Protestants in the cities and the suburbs. Isolated in white, middle-class enclaves, too many suburban churches had lost touch "with the people and problems of the central cities." They depended upon congregational and parochial life for their sense of belonging, thereby becoming captives of their local communities.[31] The problem was not the absence of a communal sense but rather the presence of one that was selfish and shallow.

Bishop Hart certainly believed that the Episcopal Church had an important role to play in making the world a better place, but his articulation of that belief could be vague and general. If his words are any indication of the depth and character of local sentiment, the Diocese of Pennsylvania was far behind Gibson Winter. "The greatest service which a Church can render to the nation and the world," Hart maintained in 1956, "is to develop Christian, public spirited citizens, men and women whose conduct in all matters—home, social life, politics, and industry—is dominated by the conviction that Jesus Christ is the Lord of Life." Leaders at the parish level could be just as circumspect. The rector of the largest and most prosperous African Episcopal church in the city urged his vestry "to think of projecting itself out into the field of service." The rector of Holy Trinity, Philadelphia (located on the still upscale Rittenhouse Square), acknowledged that his church had an obligation to meet the needs of "problem" people—the "proud and the poor," he called them—in its neighborhood. His bishop would not have disagreed. In his 1959 convention message, Hart encouraged parishes, like Holy Trinity, that "were once in residential areas, but are now in business districts," to "move or else revise their programs"—a challenge to which, according to Hart, some inner-city parishes were responding splendidly.[32]

It was not until the Right Reverend Robert DeWitt became the bishop in 1964 that social justice and civil rights would take center stage in the

Diocese of Pennsylvania. But there is at least some evidence to suggest that DeWitt's priorities and values were anticipated. Paraphrasing an article by Truman B. Douglass published in *Harper's Magazine* in 1958, the editors of *TCN* urged their readers not to shy away from the vitality, creativity, and diversity of the city. Our most conspicuous failing as Protestants, they said, has been our inability to become more metropolitan. Before we can serve the city, we must learn to love it. The suffragan bishop, Gillespie Armstrong, may have been the driving force behind this moral reorientation. In his messages to the faithful over the years, he sometimes spoke about the urgency of human need. But at the diocesan convention in 1961, he confronted the so-called urban church problem. A lot has been written about it, he said, some of it "vastly over-simplified." Nevertheless, the urban church had an obligation to seek out and serve the "'little people of God,'" those without resources of any kind, "who have great aching voids, bewilderments, and a gnawing sense of loneliness." The editors of *TCN* now began to echo such liberal thinking. "We believe 'the problem' of the urban church, should be the concern of the suburban church and the suburban Christian," they soon said. Giving to foreign or remote missions may be commendable, but suburban Episcopalians must not fail to recognize "a far more, or at least equally important mission right in their own back (or front) yard."[33] Clearly, change was in the wind.

The Parish and the Diocese: At Peace or at Odds?

In January 1961 the Diocese of Pennsylvania changed the format of *The Church News.* In an effort to increase readership, the diocesan Department of Communications transformed it from a magazine to a tabloid. In its original format, which had lasted for nearly fifty years, *TCN* had never had a press run greater than sixteen thousand. But as a tabloid, its circulation rapidly and greatly expanded. In less than six months there were fifty-four thousand paid subscriptions, and its editorial board decided to publish a September issue for the first time in more than twenty years. Since its inception in 1912, one of *TCN*'s main objectives had been to promote diocesan "unity." Suburbanization may have made this a much greater challenge, but given the importance of the church's work, it was one that the editor-in-chief, Walter N. Connors, readily accepted. *TCN* "should interpret and properly mirror the image of the Church," he said. "Its aim should be to provide a greater understanding of the magnitude and scope of the work of the Church and to create a desire for individuals to become involved."[34]

But what exactly was "the Church"? For most Episcopalians, the parish and its priest were almost always their first and often their only points of contact with their church, and most had no trouble deciding where their loyalties lay if local resources were stretched thin. After all, the bishop was only needed occasionally for such functions as installing a rector or administering confirmation. But while this was a common point of view, not everyone in the diocese shared it. *TCN* regularly touted the importance of both the diocese and the national church. They "make possible the continuance of the Christian work of your parish by supplying administration, guidance and direction," it said, "as well as the 'tools' without which your work would be small and ineffective." Episcopal Hospital, the Seamen's Church Institute, the Church Farm School, and St. John's Settlement were among the many educational, health, and welfare institutions whose essential work the diocese helped. Such holistic thinking was not confined to those who worked closely with the bishop and his staff. "A parish that is concerned only with its fabric and only with its own parishioners . . . is not worthy of its Lord," said the rector of Christ Church, Philadelphia, in 1963. "A vital and alive parish is one that uses its building as a generating plant and its members as conductors and transmitters, sending currents of God's power to encircle the earth."[35]

As the diocesan bishop, Oliver Hart might have been expected to agree wholeheartedly with this sentiment. From time to time he spoke about the importance of local support for the work of the diocese. Even as coadjutor, he urged every parish to meet all its financial obligations, both parochial and diocesan. Liturgical unity was also something that concerned him. Made aware that the greatest variation in the practice of worship among Episcopalians nationwide could be found in the Diocese of Pennsylvania, he urged his parishes not to operate in isolation. To be an Episcopalian, after all, meant being part of a larger spiritual community. Hart had some pragmatic advice for those who needed more convincing. "It has been proven again and again," he once said, "that the parishes which are the most concerned about the work beyond their borders, are the parishes which are doing the best work at home."[36] Reciprocity marked the relationship between the parochial and the ecumenical in successful dioceses. A healthy parish contributes its full measure to its diocese, he said in 1948, while a healthy diocese "is one whose plans and work are designed to strengthen parishes."[37]

These pronouncements notwithstanding, Bishop Hart was essentially a parish man. He fervently believed that fellowship was central to Christian living. As the diocese expanded into its suburban hinterlands, he became more and more convinced that fellowship began at home. "Each parish should strive to make of itself a real community united within itself for the spread of Christ's Kingdom," he told the delegates to the diocese's 168th annual convention. Even as the white middle class was streaming out of Philadelphia in ever increasing numbers, Hart counseled that the parish was the best answer to racial, class, and cultural divisions. The church as a whole might serve as a means by which Christians could communicate across such social and economic barriers. "But if this is to done," he said, "it must be done in the local parish or it will not be done at all," because the church's job was "to take men where they live and help them become the persons God intended them to be."[38] He called upon all his priests to join him in keeping parishes strong. When communicants moved—an increasingly common occurrence in the early 1950s—a new parish home had to be found unless they were going to remain active in their old congregation. The bishop's lead may have moved the Reverend James G. Ludwig and the Reverend H. Lawrence Whittemore to organize a series of intensive weekend conferences at St. Martin's, Radnor, and Trinity, Swarthmore, respectively. Designed to revitalize parish life through spiritual renewal, these small-group retreats carried the endorsement of the national church's Department of Christian Education.[39]

Not everyone in the diocese shared Bishop Hart's parochial orientation, and over time a more corporate perspective would attract a large following. Of course, centralized leadership was far from unprecedented, even within memory. As Thomas Rzeznik shows in chapter 7, both Philip Rhinelander, a patrician educated at St. Paul's School and Harvard College, and Thomas J. Garland (1924–31), an executive with a Pittsburgh steel company before he became a priest, maintained firm control in their respective tours of duty as diocesan bishop. Social and political conditions also played an important role in the making of church management style, especially after 1930. The tag team of depression and war put togetherness and discipline at a premium. In April 1941 the Reverend Granville Taylor, vicar of the Chapel of the Mediator, responded positively to a call from the presiding bishop for church unity. A leader in the diocese, having served on the bishop's Standing Committee and as a delegate to national conventions, he commanded attention when he said, "If the Church is to rise and adequately meet the call of the world, there must be brought into being a much higher degree of loyalty on the part of church men and women to their parish churches, of the parishes to their bishops and dioceses, [and] of the diocese to their Presiding Bishop and the whole Church." Such sentiments seemed less apropos after the war ended, but as critics of suburban parochialism like Gibson Winter began to attract attention, even Bishop Hart had to rethink his position. Should a parish be "a little club," he asked in 1958, or an organization whose purpose was to minister to the whole community?[40] But while such sentiments may have been in the wind in the late 1950s, the Diocese of Pennsylvania did not really embrace them until Gillespie Armstrong became the diocesan bishop, a post to which he ascended in July 1963 upon Bishop Hart's retirement.

Held just before Father Armstrong's formal installation the following fall, a Bishop's Conference on Urban Culture brought 227 priests from the diocese together in Atlantic City, where they engaged in some frank conversation. The conference had three objectives: to awaken those in attendance to the complex social revolution taking place around them; to make them realize that they were not yet equipped to deal with it; and to encourage them to develop some ideas and plans to change the attitudes and structure of the diocese, "so that we might minister effectively in this explosive situation." Not surprisingly, many of the conference participants had difficulty coming to grips with the problem. They shied away from making race the center of their attention, but when parish frustrations with the diocese became the chief topic of conversation, the Reverend Stanley Johnson of the University of Pennsylvania could no longer hold his tongue. Instead of focusing on what we want for ourselves, he complained, we should be talking about the needs of others.[41] Making a Christian value like this into diocesan policy would turn out to be easier said than done.

The Diocese and Civil Rights

In May 1956 the Diocese of Pennsylvania met in annual convention for the 172nd time. It was an eventful meeting, for both what was accomplished and what was not. The Department of Christian Social Relations introduced a strongly worded resolution condemning recent incidents of racial violence in the South and repudiating "the racial superiority doctrine" upon which southern resistance to desegregation was based. However, this resolution did not pass. Instead, the delegates adopted a more temperate declaration that urged churches and their members "to oppose by word and deed any type of racial discrimination and to use in their own communities every available means to make their fellowship representative of the

FIGURE 8.2 Bishop J. Gillespie Armstrong

ideals of Christian worship and action." Just two years after the Supreme Court's historic decision in *Brown v. Board of Education*, the diocese had blinked when confronted with a difference of opinion over race and civil rights. At the same meeting, however, the assembled clergymen and laymen took a step that would ultimately change the diocese forever. By a vote of 216 to 183, they decided to extend convention rights and privileges to women. As required by canon, this decision had to be confirmed at the next convention, and the diocese did just that, making Pennsylvania the forty-fourth diocese in the Episcopal Church (out of eighty-seven) to so empower women.[42]

In the 1950s American attitudes about race and gender were in transition. In the Diocese of Pennsylvania both lay and clergy struggled with the new ideas swirling around them. Translating them into diocesan policy and practice proved to be no small task. In the absence of strong leadership on these issues, there were more than a few missteps and false starts. The history of a woman's right to participate in the councils of the diocese illustrates this point. Beginning in 1952, delegates to the diocesan convention deliberated about admitting women. Considerable ambivalence can be inferred from the fact that a motion to admit them as delegates was approved in 1953 but defeated by both the preceding and the following conventions. By then, women were serving on a few parish vestries or on auxiliary vestries created to give them an unofficial voice. The policy adopted by the African Episcopal Church of St. Thomas is a good example. A parish where sensitivity to discrimination naturally ran high, St. Thomas's formed an auxiliary vestry composed of fifteen men and fifteen women in 1949. But the auxiliary's influence was limited from the start and could easily be further abridged. The "suggestive motions" it was permitted to make could not deal with matters having to do with law or finance, and either the rector or the regular vestry could require the members of the auxiliary to remain silent or to absent themselves if deliberations became too intense.[43]

At issue here, at least in part, were the prerogatives of men. When the diocesan convention debated the wisdom of admitting women in 1953, the Reverend Thorne Sparkman put into words what many of his colleagues may have been thinking. "This may point the way," he said, "to the time when we will have 'clergy persons' instead of clergymen." Little did he know that in fewer than twenty-five years his prophecy would be realized. Meanwhile, even Bishop Hart had difficulty adjusting to the baby steps that the diocese was already taking. At the sight of Mrs. T. Truxton Hare rising to become the first woman delegate ever to speak at a diocesan convention, the bishop, as presiding officer, asked whether she "had the right."[44] Her response has been lost to history, but by speaking out in 1958 Mrs. Hare broke new ground in an institutional setting not known for its openness to women. In the Diocese of Pennsylvania, not to mention in the Episcopal Church as a whole, the rector's wife still set the standard, despite the fact that American women were now reaching for parity with men in higher education, and some were even opening doors in the workplace that had long been closed to them.[45] Nonetheless, by admitting women to its convention the diocese had at least joined those in the church who were moving in a new direction.

The diocese struggled with race as well as gender in the 1940s and '50s. Most blacks in Philadelphia were not Episcopalians, but those who were often worshipped in isolation, many in one of nine historically black churches. Between 1946 and 1962 six previously all-white parishes became predominantly black, more than half of them in North and West Philadelphia.[46] As the population of black Episcopalians grew and moved, the diocese took notice. It facilitated an occasional merger or relocation that helped keep some blacks in the fold. But parishes—regardless of color—had to take the initiative on such matters, and not every historically black parish was able to respond to changes in the city's population. The African Episcopal Church of St. Thomas reacted in a timely fashion to the migration of blacks from South to West Philadelphia in the late 1930s, moving from Twelfth and Walnut streets to Fifty-seventh and Pearl. Relocating again in 1941, this time to a larger facility at Fifty-second and Parrish, the congregation suffered a serious setback a decade later when a fire destroyed its sanctuary. But with the help of other churches, St. Thomas's was back on its feet within two years.[47] By then, it had moved ahead of Holy Apostles and the Mediator to become the largest congregation (black or white) in the diocese. The Church of the Crucifixion was a different matter. Organized in 1847 to serve the black poor in the district of Moyamensing, Crucifixion was prosperous enough by 1884 to build a permanent home at Eighth and Bainbridge. Not long thereafter its vestry founded a mission that later became the Church of St. Simon the Cyrenian. But Crucifixion itself began a slow decline after World War I, as the black population in its area gradually departed. By 1950 the St. Thomas's vestry considered Crucifixion distressed enough to be a candidate for merger. Researchers for the diocese found so few families worshipping there in 1964 that they doubted its viability. However, Crucifixion refused to die, attempting to survive by welcoming people regardless of color.[48]

TABLE 8.6 Historically black churches in the Diocese of Pennsylvania: Number of communicants in selected years, 1946–1962

Church	1946	1949	1952	1956	1959	1962
AE Church of St. Thomas						
52nd and Parrish	1,012	1,366	1,476	1,655	1,734	2,269
St. Augustine's, Philadelphia						
20th and Columbia						
27th and Girard (1955)	820	961	821	NA	1,060	1,035
St. Barnabas, Germantown						
W. Rittenhouse St.	395	428	475	536	384	467
Crucifixion						
8th and Bainbridge	477	492	210	168	173	93
St. Cyprian Mission						
85th and Lindbergh	169	155	128	119	105	229
St. Mary's, Chester	67	71	54	88	101	104
St. Monica's Mission						
Woodland Ave. and						
St. Mark's St.	235	299	280	380	441	575
St. Paul's Mission						
22nd and Cumberland	25	33	31	closed	closed	closed
St. Simon the Cyrenian						
22nd and Reed	1,175	1,238	1,255	1,358	1,367	1,524
Total	4,375	5,043	4,730	4,304	5,365	6,296

Source: "Negro Congregations Honor Their Vicar," *TCN* (October 1940), 31. See also *TCN* (March 1941), 30, and *TCN* (June 1941), 19. For numbers of congregants, see the *Journals of the Protestant Episcopal Church, Diocese of Pennsylvania* (Philadelphia: Diocese of Pennsylvania, 1946, 1949, 1952, 1956, 1959, 1962). St. Paul's Mission merged with the Church of the Advocate in 1953. J. Wesley Twelves, *A History of the Diocese of Pennsylvania of the Protestant Episcopal Church in the U.S.A., 1784–1968* (Philadelphia: Diocese of Pennsylvania, 1969), 256.

FIGURE 8.3 Members of the confirmation class at the African Episcopal Church of St. Thomas, Fifty-second and Parrish streets, ca. 1955. Bishop Hart and the rector of St. Thomas's, the Reverend Jesse F. Anderson Sr., appear in the foreground.

For a long time the diocese pretended that racial discrimination was not a problem in either the church itself or the city as a whole. Its leaders, both lay and clerical, accepted the well-established legal doctrine of separate but equal, taking for granted the existence of segregated parishes and treating blacks as a discrete constituent group. In the 1940s the task of overseeing those blacks who worshipped in the diocese was assigned to the Woman's Auxiliary as part of a general reorganization that divided responsibility for work among blacks between local leaders and the national church.[49] Signs of change began to appear after the *Brown* decision and the Soviet invasion of Hungary two years later. The pastoral letter issued by the church's bishops in 1956 not only condemned racial divisions at home and abroad but also called upon "every member of the Church [to] exercise his reconciling ministry in the community in which he lives."[50] At its annual convention the Diocese of Pennsylvania passed resolutions opposing racial discrimination in both 1952 and 1956. But years of complacency on the subject of race were not easy to overcome. The delegates to the diocesan convention in 1956 could not bring themselves to denounce the systematic resistance that arose in many states after the *Brown* decision. Instead, they commended "all those in the states most involved who are working for a just and Christian solution" to the segregation problem. Only after the national church called upon its members in General Convention to work toward equal opportunity in such fields as education, employment, and housing did the diocese take a similar position, calling for the elimination of "any legal and other restrictions which prevent an end to racial discrimination" by those organizations or institutions that were in any way related to it.[51]

Even as the diocese was beginning to address the problem of discrimination, racism persisted among its members and within its congregations. No Episcopalians knew this better than the priests in its black churches. The most prominent among them was the Reverend Jesse Anderson, the rector of St. Thomas's, Philadelphia.

* * * * *

Jesse Fosset Anderson (1910–1975)

Born in Plainfield, New Jersey, Jesse Fosset Anderson became one of the most prominent black leaders in Philadelphia after World War II. A graduate of Lincoln University (1932) and the General Theological Seminary (1935), he held church posts in New York, Michigan, and Delaware before becoming rector of the African Episcopal Church of St. Thomas in April 1944. In his first ten years at St. Thomas's, more than one thousand persons joined the congregation, and 983 were confirmed. Anderson was willing to do whatever it took to help his church. When a fire destroyed the sanctuary in 1951, Anderson and several of his parishioners appeared on the television game show *Strike It Rich* to raise money for the rebuilding effort. But Anderson was much more than an Episcopal priest and a parish rector. He was a community leader and, toward the end of his life, a candidate for political office, too.

Anderson was a civil rights pioneer in both his church and his city. When demonstrations against segregation were still a rarity, he participated in a program called Silent March, organized to protest segregation in the military. After such demonstrations had become much more common, he joined fifteen hundred picketers from the NAACP protesting discrimination at five-and-ten-cent stores in the city. He was a founder of the Union of Black Episcopalians. Long before his own congregation chose to do so, he urged his vestry to "think seriously in terms of inviting persons of other racial groups to become members of our parish." This kind of thinking won him a place in the leadership councils of many nonsectarian civil rights organizations. He served on the boards of both the Urban League and the Fellowship Commission of Philadelphia, rising to board chairman of the former and vice president of the latter. In 1963 the Fellowship Commission nominated him for a seat on the Philadelphia Board of Education. This appointment was never made, and Anderson subsequently became an outspoken critic of the board for its failure to address the problem of segregation. In 1967 he even accused board chairman and former mayor Richardson Dilworth of being a racist, charging him with wanting to keep the city "white [and] middle class."

Anderson ran for a seat in the Pennsylvania state senate in 1972. True to his calling, he told the voters that if elected he would attack immorality in public life, but this message fell on deaf ears. In politics as well as religion he was consistent, if not always successful, in fighting for the positions he took.

SOURCES: "Evening Bulletin Biographical Sketch," January 16, 1947, and "Rev. Jess[e] F. Anderson Dies; Pastor, Civic Leader Was 65, BCC," both in envelope marked "Reverend Jesse Anderson and Mrs., Dead, June 11, 1975"; Minutes of the Vestry of the African Episcopal Church of St. Thomas, May 12, 1950, and September 20, 1954; Maury Fagan, "A Eulogy for Rev. Jesse Anderson"; "Six Nominated for Vacancy on School Board"; "Rector Calls Phila. Racist"; and "Episcopal Priest Running for Senate; Advocates No-Fault Divorce Law," all in BCC; Matthew Countryman, *Up South: Civil Rights and Black Power in Philadelphia* (Philadelphia: University of Pennsylvania Press, 2006), 100.

* * * * *

In charge at St. Thomas's since 1944, Anderson was a charter member of a national group known as the Episcopal Society for Cultural and Racial Unity. But any satisfaction that Anderson may have felt about this group's expressed commitment to the enhancement of racial unity and understanding must have been at least partially offset by the decidedly unprogressive actions of others. As Anderson reported to his vestry in April 1960, the Diocesan Church Women voted that spring to suspend donations to the NAACP and other liberal organizations. In response, the St. Thomas's vestry decided to keep the contributions of its church women under its control, donating directly to these organizations.[52] Another black priest in the diocese, the Reverend Paul M. Washington, must have understood how his colleague felt. After doing missionary work in Liberia for more than six years, he took the post of vicar at St. Cyprian's, a historically black mission church in Eastwick, one of Philadelphia's only integrated neighborhoods. But when the suffragan bishop, Gillespie Armstrong, recommended that Washington also be named vicar at nearby St. Titus's, Bishop Hart demurred because this white congregation felt squeamish about having a black man for its pastor.[53] Washington encountered a similar problem at the Church of the Advocate, to which he was called in 1962. Located in a part of North Philadelphia that was rapidly becoming exclusively black, it still had about one hundred white parishioners when Washington arrived, some of whom were uncomfortable with their new rector's political views. But unless they chose to worship elsewhere, which most of them eventually did, they could not escape the effects of the burgeoning civil rights movement. Named a "pilot parish in urban work" by the National Council of the Protestant Episcopal Church, Advocate received a large grant from the diocese to help it with this outreach effort. The grant may have prompted some of the white parishioners still at Advocate to abandon ship, but it also turned out to be a mixed blessing for the new rector himself, and perhaps for many other black Episcopalians, because it brought out some latent prejudices. Black men, after all, could not be trusted to manage money. Acting on this stereotype, Bishop Armstrong appointed a special committee to help Father Washington administer the grant.[54]

By the time Paul Washington moved from St. Titus's to the Church of the Advocate, Bishop Armstrong had become the diocese's coadjutor. But his promotion did not take place by acclamation. When Bishop Hart reached age sixty-eight—four years shy of the age at which he would have been forced to retire—he decided that the diocese needed to name his successor. In the spring of 1960, he called for the election of a coadjutor. As suffragan, Bishop Armstrong had the inside track, but, as it turned out, a special convention, held the following November for the sole purpose of electing a coadjutor, cast twelve ballots before settling on him. Opposition came openly from those who preferred someone whose churchmanship was less elevated. It probably came covertly from at least some of those uncomfortable with his actions on race in the diocese. At the 1959 diocesan convention Armstrong sponsored a resolution that called for the allocation of $50,000 to the Church of the Advocate in support of "its mission to Negroes"—a resolution that was sent to die in committee.[55]

It was the Philadelphia City Council's decision to redevelop Eastwick that brought the suffragan bishop's ideas on race sharply into focus. Abandoned by many of their parishioners whose homes were being razed, the two Episcopal churches in the area, St. Cyprian's and St. Titus's, had to decide where to go and what to do. It occurred to some in the diocese that these two congregations might be better off proceeding as one, not two. But even under such difficult circumstances, the people of St. Titus's were not inclined to merge with a historically black church. As the St. Thomas's vestry could have told its Eastwick counterpart, such feelings were not unique or such actions unprecedented. Having been suffragan bishop since 1949, Armstrong knew this, too. But by the time St. Titus's and St. Cyprian's were forced to decide about their futures, he was no longer willing to sit by while his fellow Episcopalians acted on their prejudices. He took public exception at the same diocesan convention that received Bishop Hart's request for the election of a coadjutor. If the diocese was to be "consistent" in its support for integration, he said, it could no longer tolerate the creation of churches with a "racial label." After all, there was only one label that really mattered—Episcopalian.[56]

That the diocese was of two minds on the subject of race would have been apparent to anyone who paid attention at this convention. Despite passing a resolution in support of students demonstrating for civil rights in the United States, and of Anglican churchmen speaking out against apartheid in South Africa, the delegates overwhelmingly rejected an attempt by the Reverend William Vaughn Ischie Jr. to have the diocese conduct a study that would determine "how various geographical areas and racial minorities" could be better represented in its councils and among its officials. Three years later the bishop himself was still conflicted. Reflecting on his leadership as he prepared to step down, Bishop Hart could not admit to others (and perhaps not even to himself) that prejudice had delayed integration in the diocese. "It's not just a question of Negro and white," he told the *Philadelphia Bulletin*. "It's a problem of people moving from one place to another. . . . If you could just put your churches on wheels it would be much easier."[57]

The bishop was absolutely correct in at least one respect. The Diocese of Pennsylvania had redistributed itself. Having once been mainly urban, it was now predominantly suburban, a transformation that Bishop Hart had not just witnessed but facilitated. The installation of J. Gillespie Armstrong as the diocesan bishop opened the door to additional change, especially with regard to race and gender. His sudden and unexpected death not eighteen months later denied him the chance to lead the diocese through that door. It fell instead to his successor, the Right Reverend Robert DeWitt, and it soon became quite apparent that DeWitt would seize that opportunity. If the diocese was now not the one Bishop Hart had inherited twenty-one years before, it was about to become something to which he might not even have felt related. He would not have been alone in this regard.

NOTES

I wish to thank the Right Reverend Charles Bennison, David Contosta, David Watt, David Ford, Glenn Colliver, Margaret Jerrido, the Reverend James Morris, and Mary Sewell-Smith for their invaluable assistance in the preparation of this chapter.

1. Minutes of the Vestry of the Church of Our Saviour, Jenkintown, Pa., January 9, October 7, and November 6, 1945, and May 7 and November 6, 1957. The estimated cost of installing the altar in November 1945 was $15,000, a number that would no doubt have been far larger twelve years later. "The Census, the Suburbs, and the Church," *TCN* (September 1940), 8; *JDC 1956*, parochial reports.

2. James Hudnut-Beumler, *Looking for God in the Suburbs: The Religion of the American Dream and Its Critics, 1945–1965* (New Brunswick: Rutgers University Press, 1994), 33, 41–42, 51–52, 60–64; Will Herberg, *Protestant-Catholic-Jew: An Essay in American Religious Sociology* (Chicago: University of Chicago Press, 1983), 59. Religion was of such significance to Americans in the 1950s that the U.S. Census Bureau seriously considered (but ultimately decided against) adding a question about religious affiliation to the 1960 census. See Kevin M. Schultz, "Religion as Identity in Postwar America: The Last Serious Attempt to Put a Question on Religion in the United States Census," *Journal of American History* 93 (September 2006): 359–84.

3. Hudnut-Beumler, *Looking for God in the Suburbs*, 36–39.

4. Louie Crew, "Communicants in the ECUSA, 1880–2000," in "Historical Statistics Regarding the Episcopal Church," http://newark.rutgers.edu/~lcrew/ecusa_history.html. According to David Sumner, membership in the Episcopal Church reached an all-time high in 1966 of 3,647,267. Sumner, *The Episcopal Church's History, 1945–1985* (Wilton, Conn.: Morehouse, 1987), 161. See also U.S. Bureau of the Census, *Historical Statistics of the United States: Colonial Times to 1970* (Washington, D.C.: U.S. Department of Commerce, Bureau of the Census, 1975), 391–92; and the website of Adherents.com, which provides statistics on national and world religions and churches, at http://www.adherents.com/Na/Na_268.html. Among all Protestants, church affiliation increased by 23.53 percent in the 1950s, compared to 30.94 percent for religious groups in general. At the same time, the U.S. population increased by 19 percent. Hudnut-Beumler, *Looking for God in the Suburbs*, 32.

5. David Hein, *Noble Powell and the Episcopal Establishment in the Twentieth Century* (Urbana: University of Illinois Press, 2001), 82.

6. Ibid., 81; "Much Accomplished in Short Time: A Picture of General Convention," *TCN* (October 1946), 2; "New P.E. Marriage Canon Enacted," "Protestant Episcopal Church, Marriage and Divorce," and "Episcopal Church Defeats Move to Ease Divorce Rules," Protestant Episcopal Church (hereafter PEC), Triennial Conventions, 1940–1949, all in Bulletin Clippings Collection, Urban Archives, Paley Library, Temple University, Philadelphia (hereafter BCC). The marriage canon adopted in 1946 gave diocesan bishops the authority to decide whether a divorced Episcopalian could be remarried in the church, provided that at least one year had elapsed between the civil judgment ending one union and the religious ceremony beginning another. *Journal of the General Convention of the Protestant Episcopal Church in the United States of America Held in Philadelphia from September Tenth to Twentieth, Inclusive, in the Year of Our Lord 1946, with Appendices* (1947), Constitutions and Canons Appendix, 46–47.

7. "Miscellaneous News from the General Convention," *TCN* (November 1949), 5; George E. DeMille, *The Episcopal Church Since 1900: A Brief History* (New York: Morehouse-Gorham, 1955),

190; "Episcopalian Women Want Rights Defined," and "Equal Rights Urged for Women in the Episcopal Church," PEC, Triennial Conventions, 1940–1949; "Episcopal Church Breaks 161-Year Old Precedents," PEC, Triennial Conventions, 1952–1955; "Episcopal Church Defeats Plan for Women Deputies," PEC, Triennial General Conventions, 1958 and 1961, all in BCC. At the 1961 General Convention in Houston, one layman said that while women often had the "best minds," he wouldn't want "them in this house where they would likely be confused." The General Division of Woman's Work replaced the National Executive Board of the Woman's Auxiliary. Margaret M. Sherman, *True to Their Heritage: A Brief History of the Woman's Auxiliary, 1871–1958* (New York: National Council of the Episcopal Church, 1959), 35.

8. Harold T. Lewis, *Yet with a Steady Beat: The African American Struggle for Recognition in the Episcopal Church* (Valley Forge: Trinity International Press, 1996), 135, 141–42; John E. Booty, *Mission and Ministry: A History of Virginia Theological Seminary* (Harrisburg: Morehouse, 1995), 280. The black student admitted to VTS was John Thomas Walker, who eventually became the diocesan bishop of Washington, D.C.

9. Lewis, *Yet with a Steady Beat,* 141–42, 150–51; "Episcopalians Close Session with Plea to Combat Injustice," PEC, Triennial General Conventions, 1952–1955, BCC.

10. In 1937 the General Convention appointed a Joint Commission on Approaches to Unity that was charged with studying a merger with the Presbyterian Church. But at the General Convention in 1946 it became apparent that many Episcopalians were not ready to accept clergy ordained in another denomination, and throughout the 1950s the topic of merger did not progress past the conversation stage. *JDC 1943,* 333–37; DeMille, *Episcopal Church Since 1900,* 150–60; and "Episcopalians End Parley with an Appeal for Unity," PEC, Triennial General Conventions, 1958 and 1961, BCC.

11. "House of Bishops 1956 Pastoral Letter," *TCN* (January 1957), 12; "Protestant Episcopal Bishops Fear U.S. Is Losing Confidence," and "Bishops Take Moral Stand Against War," PEC, House of Bishops, BCC; Ralph McGill, "The Negro Episcopalian," *Episcopalian,* April 1962, quoted in "Church Faces Loss Because of Members Who Resent Worshipping with Colored," *TCN* (April 1962), 15. See also William King, "The Reform Establishment and the Ambiguities of Influence," in *Between the Times: The Travail of the Protestant Establishment in America, 1900–1960,* ed. William R. Hutchinson (New York: Cambridge University Press, 1989), 138.

12. J. Wesley Twelves, *A History of the Diocese of Pennsylvania of the Protestant Episcopal Church in the U.S.A., 1784–1968* (Philadelphia: Diocese of Pennsylvania, 1969), 41; "Captain Hart Chosen Bishop Coadjutor," and "P.E. Bishop Elect Considers Offer," PEC, Oliver J. Hart Biography, BCC. Hart declined offers to be coadjutor from the Diocese of Tennessee (1936), the Diocese of Central New York (1936), and the Diocese of Delaware (1937).

13. Twelves, *History of the Diocese of Pennsylvania,* 41, 253; E. Digby Baltzell, *Philadelphia Gentlemen: The Making of a National Upper Class* (Chicago: Quadrangle Books, 1971), 206.

14. "Strong Episcopal Missions Urged," PEC, Triennial Conventions, 1925–1949, and "Bishop Hart Breaks 164-Year Custom," PEC, Oliver J. Hart Biography, both in BCC; Twelves, *History of the Diocese of Pennsylvania,* 200–201.

15. Across the Delaware River, the three New Jersey counties closest to Philadelphia also grew rapidly, experiencing a 76.8 percent population increase.

16. William W. Cutler III, "The Persistent Dualism: Centralization and Decentralization in Philadelphia, 1854–1975," in *The Divided Metropolis: Social and Spatial Dimensions of Philadelphia, 1800–1975,* ed. William W. Cutler III and Howard Gillette Jr. (Westport, Conn.: Greenwood Press, 1980), 264–65; John F. Bauman, "The Expressway 'Motorists Loved to Hate': Philadelphia and the First Era of Postwar Highway Planning, 1943–1956," *PMHB* 115 (1991): 503–33.

17. "The Report of the Committee on [the] Problem of City Churches," *JDC 1934,* 357–60; "The Census, the Suburbs and the Church," *TCN* (September 1940), 8; "Old City Churches Are P.E. Problem," PEC, Diopa, Miscellaneous 1954 and Before, BCC.

18. Congregations Adath Jeshurun, Beth Sholom, and Keneseth Israel moved out of Philadelphia into eastern Montgomery County between 1952 and 1964. Simeon J. Maslin, *One God, Sixteen Houses: An Illustrated Introduction to the Churches and Synagogues of the Old York Road Corridor* (Elkins Park, Pa: KI Press, 1990), 36, 65, 77.

19. "Convention Meets for the 163rd Time," *TCN* (May–June 1947), 3; "Plan for Second Suffragan Bishop Approved by Special Diocesan Convention," *TCN* (March 1949), 10; Twelves, *History of the Diocese of Pennsylvania*, 42–43.

20. "Bishop Hart Advocates Expansion in Diocesan Facilities," *TCN* (May–June 1950), 2–3; "Bishop's Annual Address," *JDC 1952*, 47–48.

21. "Levittown Church Under Construction," *TCN* (October 1953), 8; "The New Church in Levittown Is Now Occupied," *TCN* (May–June 1954), 15; Rt. Rev. J. Gillespie Armstrong, "Missionary Needs Resulting from Population Movements in the Diocese of Pennsylvania," *TCN* (November 1954), 7–8. The Schuylkill Expressway was not open, end to end, until November 1958. Bauman, "Expressway 'Motorists Loved to Hate,'" 503.

22. "Episcopalians Act to Meet Challenge in Area's Growth," PEC, Diopa, Diocesan Conventions, 1950–1960, BCC; "Episcopal Diocese Plans $660,000 Building Program," PEC, Diopa, Oliver J. Hart, 1956 to Death, BCC; "Campaign for Capital Funds," *TCN* (December 1957), 4; "Campaign for Capital Funds," *TCN* (March 1958), 2; "The Bishop of Pennsylvania Addresses Diocesan Convention," *TCN* (May–June 1958), 1–2.

23. "Report of the Diocesan Campaign for Capital Funds Showing Pledges and Total Payments Received Up to and Including December 1, 1959," *TCN* (January 1960), 14–15; Twelves, *History of the Diocese of Pennsylvania*, 44. On January 7, 1962, the *Philadelphia Bulletin* reported that $822,000 had been raised, but whether the final number was more or less than $800,000, it had to have been a disappointment.

24. Twelves, *History of the Diocese of Pennsylvania*, 127, 156, 19, 225, 243–44; *JDC 1962*, 114–15, 136.

25. "The Church of the Resurrection, Philadelphia" (PH-36), Survey of the Diocese of Pennsylvania, 1964–65, Diopa Archives, Lutheran Theological Seminary, Mount Airy (Philadelphia).

26. "St. Paul's Church, Levittown, Bucks County" (BU-10), ibid.; Twelves, *History of the Diocese of Pennsylvania*, 46, 166–67, 259. These reports were part of a comprehensive self-study commissioned by the diocese. Its purpose was to place every church in its social and economic context. Planning began during the summer of 1963; data were collected during Lent of the following year. "Self-Study by Diocese to Aid Research and Planning," *TCN* (September 1963), 1–2.

27. "The Bryan Green Mission Begins on December 2 and Continues Ten Days," *TCN* (October 1951), 1; "Churches Back Nine-Day Mission," PEC, Diopa, Miscellaneous 1954 and Before, BCC.

28. "5,000 Attend Two Mission Meetings," and "Church Must Show It's More Than Club, Canon Green Says," PEC, Diopa, Miscellaneous 1954 and Before, BCC.

29. "Bishop's Message," *JDC 1952*, 53.

30. Editorial, *TCN* (November 1958), 3.

31. Hudnut-Beumler, *Looking for God in the Suburbs*, 132–36; Gibson Winter, *The Suburban Captivity of the Churches: An Analysis of Protestant Responsibility in the Expanding Metropolis* (New York: Doubleday, 1961), 31–35.

32. "Bishop Hart's Message," *TCN* (October 1956), 5; Minutes of the Vestry of the African Episcopal Church of St. Thomas, January 8, 1948, Archives of the African Episcopal Church of St. Thomas, Philadelphia; Rev. Harry S. Langley Jr., "A Center City Church Exercises Its Ministry," *TCN* (May–June 1959), 7; "Bishop's Message," *JDC 1959*, 53–54.

33. J. Gillespie Armstrong, "Bishop Coadjutor's Address," *JDC 1961*, 59–60. Armstrong became coadjutor in 1961 after twelve years as suffragan. "The Job That Protestants Shirk," *TCN* (April 1959), 5; "Is There an Urban Problem?" *TCN* (May 1962), 4. See also Truman B. Douglass, "The Job Protestants Shirk," *Harper's Magazine*, November 1958, 45–49.

34. Diocese of Pennsylvania, Press Release, July 1961, PEC, Diopa, Church News, BCC.

35. Clarence E. Hall, "Why a Diocese?" *TCN* (October 1953), 4–5; "Many Important Institutions," ibid., 6; "From the Rector to His People," *TCN* (April 1963), 4.

36. Rt. Rev. Oliver J. Hart, "Bishop Coadjutor's Address," *JDC 1943*, 62–63; "Bishop's Report," *JDC 1956*, 48; "Bishop Hart's Message," *TCN* (November 1946), 3. See also "Bishop Hart's Convention Address," *TCN* (May–June 1956), 5.

37. "Bishop Hart's Message," *TCN* (February 1948), 5.

38. *JDC 1952*, 53; "Bishop Hart's Message: On the Occasion of the Tenth Anniversary of His Consecration," *TCN* (November 1952), 1; "Convention Address of Bishop Hart Stresses Importance of the Life of the Christian in the Parish," *TCN* (May–June 1953), 3.

39. "Bishop Hart's Message," *TCN* (December 1953), 5; Rev. James G. Ludwig, "The Christian Living Conference Comes to the Parish," *TCN* (March 1953), 14–15; Rev. H. Lawrence Whittemore, "Description of an Intensive Weekend Conference," *TCN* (February 1954), 3. Bishop Hart succinctly pulled these threads together in a message to the faithful that *TCN* published in March 1954. "The parish is where the church's ministry all comes together," he said; "the spiritual and the institutional coalesce at the parish level." "Bishop Hart's Message," *TCN* (March 1954), 7.

40. Twelves, *History of the Diocese of Pennsylvania*, 33, 36–37; Rev. Granville Taylor, "Forward in Service: As I See It," *TCN* (April 1941), 9; "Bishop Hart's Message," *TCN* (November 1958), 7.

41. Rev. Herbert H. Beardsley, "Bishop's Conference on Urban Culture Had Three Objectives," *TCN* (November 1963), 1, 3. Armstrong succeeded Hart in July 1963; his official installation, which took place at the Church of the Redeemer, Bryn Mawr, occurred on October 26, 1963. Twelves, *History of the Diocese of Pennsylvania*, 47.

42. *JDC 1956*, 36–39; *JDC 1957*, 38; "Women Welcomed to Convention as Delegates," *TCN* (May–June 1958), 3; "Episcopal State Convention Approves Women Delegates," and "Episcopal Parley Okays Women as Delegates," PEC, Diopa, Diocesan Conventions, 1950–1960, BCC.

43. "Eight Penna. Delegates Named to Episcopal Church Parley," PEC, Triennial Conventions, 1952–1955, BCC; "Three New Parishes Admitted to Convention; Women Excluded as Deputies," *TCN* (May–June 1954), 4–5; Minutes of the Vestry of the African Episcopal Church of St. Thomas, September 8 and November 10, 1949. St. Peter's, Philadelphia, at Third and Pine allowed women to serve on its vestry. Because the Church of the Advocate's charter called for an all-male vestry, its rector, the Reverend Paul Washington, created an auxiliary, made up entirely of women, in the early 1960s. "Episcopalians Reverse Stand," PEC, Diopa, Diocesan Conventions, 1950–1960, BCC. Paul M. Washington, with David McI. Gracie, *"Other Sheep I Have": The Autobiography of Father Paul M. Washington* (Philadelphia: Temple University Press, 1994), 54.

44. "Episcopal Convention Votes to Admit Women Delegates," and "Episcopal Diocese Votes 3–1 to Back South India Church," PEC, Diopa, Diocesan Conventions 1950–1960, BCC.

45. In 1960 women represented 37.9 percent of all students enrolled in institutions of higher education. That number would finally exceed 50 percent in 1980. Barbara Miller Solomon, *In the Company of Educated Women: A History of Women and Higher Education in America* (New Haven: Yale University Press, 1985), 63; Alice Kessler-Harris, *Out to Work: A History of Wage-Earning Women in the United States* (New York: Oxford University Press, 1982), 311.

46. Those parishes were Annunciation (Twelfth and Diamond), Church of the Advocate (Eighteenth and Diamond), St. Barnabas, Haddington (Sixty-fourth and Haverford Avenue), St. Luke's, Germantown (Germantown Avenue), St. Matthias (West Oak Lane), and St. Michael and All Angels (Forty-first and Brown). A mission of St. Mark's, at Sixteenth and Locust, St. Mary's, Philadelphia (Eighteenth and Bainbridge), was a black church with white oversight until its neighborhood changed owing to gentrification. Episcopal Church, Diocese of Pennsylvania, *Spanning Four Centuries: Pages of Parish Histories of the Episcopal Diocese of Pennsylvania* (Philadelphia: Episcopal Diocese of Pennsylvania, 1997), sec. 3, pp. 47–48.

47. Minutes of the Vestry of the African Episcopal Church of St. Thomas, December 15, 1937, and May 11 and May 23, 1938. Before the first move, St. Thomas's merged with the Beloved Disciple Mission, and together they both relocated to Fifty-seventh and Pearl streets in 1938. "Venerable Congregation Loses Its Church Through the Ravages of Fire," *TCN* (February 1952), 1–2; "Whitsunday Offering Suggested for St. Thomas Church," *TCN* (March 1952), 1; "St. Thomas Church Occupies New Building," *TCN* (February 1953), 2.

48. In 1951 Mediator reported 1,640 communicants, compared to 1,430 for St. Thomas's. One year later Mediator had fallen to second place, with 1,246, while St. Thomas's had advanced to first with 1,476. See the parochial reports in *JDC 1952*, 114, 170; Diopa, *Spanning Four Centuries*, sec. 3, pp. 5–6; Minutes of the Vestry of the African Episcopal Church of St. Thomas, July 9, 1950; "Church of the Crucifixion, Philadelphia" (PH-16), Survey of the Diocese of Pennsylvania, 1964–65.

49. [Report of the] Diocesan Committee of the Woman's Auxiliary, in Mrs. Oliver Hart, ed., "Woman's Auxiliary," *TCN* (March 1948), 5.

50. "House of Bishops Pastoral Letter," *TCN* (January 1957), 12.

51. "Navy Chaplain and Educator from Japan Address Convention," *TCN* (May–June 1956), 3–4; *JDC 1959*, 34, 47. Christ Church was out in front of the diocese on these matters. After it called E. A. deBordenave to be its rector, the vestry decided to do whatever it could to promote church unity, interracial understanding, and spiritualism. Begun in 1951, its United Spiritual Action Campaign was directed at counteracting communism in particular and moral degeneracy in general by reaffirming America's commitment to the Judeo-Christian tradition. Deborah Mathias Gough, *Christ Church, Philadelphia: The Nation's Church in a Changing City* (Philadelphia: University of Pennsylvania Press, 1995), 334–35.

52. Minutes of the Vestry of the African Episcopal Church of St. Thomas, April 8, 1960. Almost two months later, the St. Thomas's vestry reaffirmed this decision; the church would continue to withhold the funds of its women's group "until the Diocesan Women's Executive Committee clears up the matter of donations to worthy organizations." Ibid., May 30, 1960.

53. Washington, *"Other Sheep I Have,"* 19. According to Washington, a delegation from St. Titus's told Bishop Hart that they knew and liked Father Washington, "but as a vicar he would have to be our pastor, and we have *daughters*." Emphasis in the original.

54. Ibid., 28, 54–55.

55. Twelves, *History of the Diocese of Pennsylvania*, 45–46; "Episcopalians Name Bishop Armstrong as Coadjutor of Diocese," PEC, Bishop J. Gillespie Armstrong, BCC; "Diocese Holds 175th Annual Convention," *TCN* (May–June 1959), 3; *JDC 1959*, 36.

56. Washington, *"Other Sheep I Have,"* 22; *JDC 1960*, 47; "The 176th Diocesan Convention," *TCN* (May–June 1960), 2–3. The Church of the Redemption, a white congregation at Fifty-sixth and Market streets, rejected overtures by St. Thomas's to share space or merge. Struggling to survive, Redemption closed four years later, following a disastrous fire. Both its name and its assets were then transferred to a new church in Bucks County. It should be noted, however, that St. Thomas's did not officially open its own doors to whites until 1965. Minutes of the Vestry of the African Episcopal Church of St. Thomas, November 30, 1950, January 5, October 5, and October 25, 1951, and March 12, 1965; Twelves, *History of the Diocese of Pennsylvania*, 158.

57. *JDC 1960*, 36–38. A similar resolution introduced by the Reverend Ischie in 1959 had been referred to the Committee on the Dispatch of Business, whence it never emerged. *JDC 1959*, 34. See also "Avoid Church Racial Labels, Episcopalian Meeting Told," PEC, Diopa, Diocesan Conventions, 1950–1960; and "Bishop Retires," PEC, Diopa, Oliver J. Hart Retirement, both in BCC.

9

Social Justice, the Church, and the Counterculture, 1963–1979

SHELDON HACKNEY

Bishop Robert L. DeWitt looked out at the delegates to the diocesan convention in May 1965 and intoned, "We live in apocalyptic times." When he made that statement, it was metaphorically true in two senses. At the personal level, it must have seemed like the end time had arrived. After only three weeks on the job as bishop coadjutor, DeWitt was forced to assume the chair of the diocesan bishop when Bishop Gillespie Armstrong died unexpectedly in his sleep on April 24, 1964. DeWitt was superbly prepared by training and experience to grapple with the challenges of the Philadelphia metropolitan area, but he had barely begun to explore the contours of his new diocese when he found himself shouldering the full responsibility.

On a broader level, these were particularly testing times for Philadelphia and the nation. The "second Reconstruction" known as the civil rights movement was expanding out of the South and igniting the tinder box of resentments among African Americans in northern urban centers. The second wave of feminism was just gathering momentum, having been given voice by Betty Friedan's book *The Feminine Mystique* in 1963, and was to be given form by the founding of the National Organization for Women in 1966. The war in Vietnam was on the verge of being widened by President Lyndon Johnson after his election in 1964, leading to the "teach-ins" of the spring of 1965 and an expanding antiwar movement that would soon spill over into the streets and public squares of the nation. At an even more fundamental level, society was being reshaped by the suburbanization made possible by the postwar, federally funded interstate highway system, and by the parallel migration of poor blacks and whites out of the South and into the smoldering cauldron of northern urban centers. Religious denominations therefore were wrestling with demographic problems of great magnitude—thinning and increasingly poor populations in cities where many churches were underpopulated, while the more affluent

FIGURE 9.1 Bishop Robert L. DeWitt

members were moving to culturally homogeneous suburbs, where there were not enough congregations to satisfy the need.

Bishop Robert L. DeWitt

Robert L. DeWitt (1916–2003) was born in Jamaica Plain, Massachusetts, attended high school in Auburn, New York, and received his undergraduate education at Amherst College, graduating in 1937 in the midst of the Great Depression. His was hardly a rags-to-riches story. After earning his bachelor of divinity degree from Episcopal Theological Seminary in 1940, he went to the Diocese of Michigan, where he rose from curate in 1940 to suffragan bishop in 1960. Then, on December 12, 1963, on the sixth ballot, he was elected coadjutor of the Diocese of Pennsylvania.[1] That he was committed to the quest for social justice was already well known from his record in a diocese that was experimenting with innovative programs to bring urban and suburban parishes into supportive contact with one another. It may have been this combination of genteel upbringing and experience in the trenches that made him attractive to a diocese that was struggling to come to terms with the changing realities of modern metropolitan life.

DeWitt had already attracted attention nationally, as one can infer from his being named to membership on the Chapter, the governing board of the National Cathedral in Washington, where Dean Frank Sayre was busy building an influential institution. DeWitt was also elected by the General Convention in October 1964 to the Executive Council, and then was quickly elevated to the chairmanship of that group.[2] The big news of that convention was the election of Bishop John Hines of Texas to become presiding bishop of the national church. Hines was thought to be "liberal" on matters of race. On the other hand, he was born, raised, and educated in the South; therefore he came under some suspicion. Possibly to dispel that suspicion, but certainly because race was a burning question in the public arena, Bishop Hines told the 1964 convention that the church should endorse the goal of racial justice. Although there were vigorous efforts in the House of Deputies by delegates from the South to condemn civil disobedience, the chief tool of the civil rights movement, a resolution was brought forward by the appropriate committee declaring that acts of civil disobedience under the proper circumstances were consonant with Christian conscience. That resolution failed to pass, leading to a dramatic walkout of the New York delegation, led by Thurgood Marshall.

In response, the House of Bishops, almost unanimously, affirmed a "Mind of the House" resolution stating that civil disobedience was consistent with Christian principles. Echoing this theme on the floor of the convention, Bishop DeWitt noted that Philadelphia had just suffered a "deplorable" race riot. He was referring to the events of August 28, 29, and 30, 1964, in North Philadelphia. Sparked by a police incident, African American citizens acted out their smoldering resentments in the streets. More than five hundred businesses were broken into and looted. A total of 461 arrests were made, and 75 percent of those arrested had no previous police record.[3] Nevertheless, as DeWitt argued at the national convention, "Let us not be blind to the fact that it resulted from oppression of Negroes, but show that the church is aware of the situation. This is what I want to take back to my 18,000 Negro communicants and to all of the city's Negroes."[4]

Chester

The August riot in North Philadelphia had deep roots in the local movement for black rights that had been growing in strength and assertiveness since the end of World War II. It had taken a more militant turn in 1963 with the election of Cecil Moore to the presidency of the NAACP, representing a shift from elite maneuvering to mass mobilization.[5] In addition, the dramatic events of the civil rights movement in the South brought racial justice to the forefront of everyone's consciousness. Then, events in Chester, a blue-collar town in the midst of suburban Delaware County, brought these two rivers of change into confluence. Demonstrations against de facto segregation in the schools had been organized by the Chester branch of the NAACP and a group called the Chester Committee for Freedom Now. The use of the slogan of the southern civil rights movement in the name of this local protest group reflected the national impact of events in the South.

Beginning on Good Friday, March 27, 1964, the nearly nightly series of protests in Chester unsettled the community and worried officials. The demonstrations were briefly suspended at the request of state education officials to allow them to seek a solution with the local school board. On April 21, with no solution in sight, the protests resumed. On the following day, a Wednesday, the activities included a rally at Temple Baptist Church, a march to the home of former state senator John McClure, the power in the Delaware County Republican machine, and sit-ins at several schools. The school superintendent ordered all sixteen Chester public schools closed, "pending the return to normal conditions." One hundred sixty-five protestors were arrested.[6]

Among those arrested was Reverend Clayton K. Hewett, one of the leaders of the effort, who was serving on the bishop's staff as the urban missioner. The demonstrations had gotten out of hand. Rocks were thrown at police cars. Then, when police started arresting the most aggressive of the demonstrators, some of them resisted violently—one with a knife. Insults were hurled. Violence escalated. The police used what onlookers described as excessive force. Hewett was seized by the police, even though he was urging the demonstrators to avoid violence: "We must show the city of Chester that we have dignity."[7] In jail, Hewett began a fast, a hunger strike that went on for eighteen days, requiring that he be hospitalized for intravenous feeding and hydration. Bishop DeWitt then intervened, helping to get Hewett released from jail and arranging for him to fly to Michigan so that, while recovering from his ordeal, he could attend an Episcopal training program in Parishfield, just outside Detroit, that would make him even more effective in his pursuit of justice in the streets of Mantua, where Bishop DeWitt assigned him upon his return.[8]

DeWitt received considerable criticism within the diocese, and in the Philadelphia area in general, for his support of the several Episcopal clergymen who were involved in Chester in addition to Clayton Hewett. He explained himself in a lengthy newspaper interview in June, setting forth his understanding of the religious requirement to seek justice for all of God's people. One can proclaim the Gospel from the pulpit, he told the *Philadelphia Evening Bulletin*, but that is an empty effort if it is not also proclaimed by action in the real world. "I see what our clergy were doing and are doing in Chester as a way of proclaiming the Gospel," he said. "I am convinced this is a right way because it calls attention to the injustices which the Church must help correct if it is to be Christian." DeWitt went on to make his support for the dissident clergy clear: "I will, however, support any of my priests, who in good conscience participate in demonstrations. If the demonstrations happen to be breaking a civil law to point out its injustice and my priests believe the law is truly in violation of God's divine law, I will support them. Christ, let us remember, did his teaching in the streets."[9]

This was the same message DeWitt had given to the diocesan convention when it met in May at the Valley Forge Military Academy, while Hewett was still in jail in the midst of his hunger strike. As DeWitt put it there, "The night I arrived in Philadelphia to begin my work here one of our clergy was jailed in Chester. And since then there has been daily unrest and frequent violence." He spoke of the "racial tensions which brood over our country, and over our community, like a thunderhead." The situation was dire because black citizens had lost patience with the slow pace of justice, and "uncounted white citizens are losing patience with Negroes' impatience. This is where we are."[10]

The problem of white flight and urban blight was not new to the Diocese of Pennsylvania. As suffragan, coadjutor, and diocesan bishop, Bishop Armstrong had worked hard to get the diocese to confront the many-sided social revolution going on in urban America. As a prelude to his joyful installation as diocesan bishop, he staged the Bishop's Conference on Urban Culture in October 1963. Reverend Herbert Beardsley attested to the seriousness and intensity of the discussions at the conference. At the same time, he noted a flaw. "We talked about the suburban church's relation to the urban church," he wrote in *The Church News*. "We should have been talking about 'white' and 'Negro.' We failed to comprehend the true nature of the 'revolution' we had been asked to consider."[11] Beardsley's insight into the thinking of the time may explain why the explicitly racial troubles that were beginning to surface were such a shock to so many members of the diocese.

Despite apparently divided public opinion, DeWitt was clear about where the church should be and what the duty of Christians was. The prayer book was not ambiguous "on the fundamental issue involved in the cause of civil rights," De Witt observed. "Nor is that American tradition ambiguous on this principle. 'All men are endowed by their creator with certain unalienable rights. Among these are life, liberty, and the pursuit of happiness.' . . . With one of our brother clergy now on a hunger strike in jail because of his concern and compassion for his fellows, I feel it is laid upon the conscience of each of us to decide how he, too, can best express that same concern and compassion in his own way."[12]

DeWitt's decision was unequivocal. On June 5 he joined a large group of Catholic, Protestant, and Jewish clergy in a public ceremony pledging their commitment to an ecumenical crusade for racial harmony. It was the first such broad, interfaith effort in Philadelphia's history. At the very public worship service, banquet, and rally at the Basilica of SS Peter and Paul, the mayor was present, as was the president of the city council. The Cardinal Dougherty High School band marched around Logan Circle and played in concert while the signers and other dignitaries dined. Bishop DeWitt was much in evidence. His message could not be missed.

As if to emphasize the point, DeWitt staged his installation service on October 31, 1964, at the Church of the Advocate, at Eighteenth and Diamond streets, in the heart of the black community. The rector there since 1962 was Paul Washington, an increasingly visible leader in both the local and national church, and a man who played a significant role as an ally of Bishop DeWitt in the events of the next fifteen years. At DeWitt's installation, a fiery sermon was delivered by liberal activist Paul Moore, then suffragan bishop of Washington, D.C., and later bishop of New York.[13] The man and the cause had come together, and the Diocese of Pennsylvania was at the center of things.

The Girard College Case

It was not surprising, therefore, that when pickets appeared on May 1, 1965, outside Girard College, on Philadelphia's near north side, Episcopal clergy and laymen were among them. The demonstrations were organized by Cecil B. Moore, the president of the Philadelphia chapter of the NAACP and a legendary figure in the long and unheralded struggle of African Americans in the North for equal rights. Despite its name, Girard College was a school for children in grades 1 through 12. It had been founded in 1848 as a boarding school for orphan boys, and it was handsomely endowed through the will of Philadelphia entrepreneur Stephen Girard. The problem was that Girard's will specified that it serve white boys only, as it had been doing for more than a century. The target at this juncture was racial discrimination; gender justice came later. The demonstrations were in support of a suit brought on behalf of seven black orphan boys.

Efforts to break down the barrier of racial exclusion at Girard College had begun in 1954, when two different lawsuits asked the Philadelphia Court of Common Pleas, Orphans' Division, known as the Orphans' Court, to require the board of directors, on which the mayor and the president of the city council served ex officio, to change school policy and admit African Americans. One suit was brought on behalf of several black students seeking admission; the other was brought by the City of Philadelphia as directed by the city council. The court ruled that the school was a completely private operation, using no governmental resources, so the Board of Directors of City Trusts could follow whatever admissions policy it chose. This ruling was upheld by the Pennsylvania Supreme Court. When the case reached the U.S. Supreme Court, however, the decision was unanimously reversed. The Court pointed out that the Board of Directors of City Trusts was in effect a state agency, so the reasoning of *Brown v. Board of Education* should apply. The Court remanded the case to the Pennsylvania Supreme Court to fashion a remedy, and that court sent it back to the Orphans' Court. Instead of simply requiring the Board of Directors of City Trusts to change the admissions policy, the Orphans' Court replaced the board of directors with a completely private board. The U.S. Supreme Court refused to hear the appeal of that ruling. Things had changed, however, by 1965.

The demonstrations continued through the summer and fall of 1965, an amazing feat of organization and persistence. The Diocesan Council, at its meeting on June 11, unanimously passed a resolution in support of the integration of Girard College.[14] Finally, on December 17, the demonstrations were called off. Governor William Scranton had stepped forward. He promised publicly that he would have the matter reviewed by a court, and he hired two prominent attorneys to argue the state's case. On September 2, 1966, the U.S. District Court for Eastern Pennsylvania ruled that Girard College was inextricably tied to the state. Furthermore, under the

Pennsylvania Public Accommodations Act, Girard College was forbidden to discriminate. The protestors had won![15]

Or so it momentarily seemed. When the trustees of the Board of Directors of City Trusts announced that they intended to continue the fight to abide by Stephen Girard's will, Cecil B. Moore announced that the picketing of Girard College would resume on October 8, 1966. The case then followed a rather circuitous and confusing route. On December 6, 1966, the Pennsylvania Supreme Court refused the trustees' petition for a clarification of the Pennsylvania Public Accommodations Act. The court declined to act, declaring that it would be inappropriate inasmuch as the case was under consideration by the U.S. Court of Appeals for the Third Circuit. This kept the case under federal jurisdiction.[16]

On February 28, 1967, the court of appeals ruled that Girard College was not in violation of the state's Accommodations Act of 1939, a conclusion based on various court precedents. On the other hand, the court pointed out that the lower court had based its ruling on the state statute and had not considered Girard College's practices in light of the Fourteenth Amendment. It sent the case back to Judge Lord in the district court to consider the constitutional questions raised by the case.[17]

On July 5, 1967, Judge Lord ruled again on the case in district court, this time finding that Girard College's racially exclusive admission policy violated the Fourteenth Amendment. He issued an injunction requiring Girard to cease racial discrimination in its admissions practices.[18] The next spring, the circuit court affirmed Judge Lord's decision, pointing out that the trustees were appointed by the state and that Girard College was tax exempt.[19] The trustees appealed to the Pennsylvania Supreme Court, but that court, on May 20, 1968, refused certiorari, leaving the circuit court decision standing.[20] Finally, the protestors had won.

Staffing for the Revolution

When Governor Scranton intervened in the Girard College case in December 1965, Bishop DeWitt had heaped praise upon him. "Although the Governor has now given us good reason to cease our active demonstrations outside the wall of the college itself," Bishop DeWitt wrote to the diocese, "he has also given us encouragement to sustain and increase our reconciling ministry to the basic needs of the people of Philadelphia."[21]

Here we have articulated the psychology behind one of the ironic truths of social movements: success breeds dissatisfaction! As goals are achieved, ambitions rise, and they tend to rise faster than they can be satisfied in the real world. The result is a growing gap between reality and desire, rather than a narrowing one, and therefore growing frustration. This phenomenon was already gnawing at the civil rights movement in 1966, both in the South and nationally.

When the diocesan convention convened on May 3 and 4, 1965, at Holy Trinity Church, Rittenhouse Square, the Girard College demonstrations had just begun. Events in Chester were fresh in everyone's memory. "The Diocese of Pennsylvania," the bishop told the delegates, "lives its life today in a world of Selma and Saigon, of moon shots and Telstar, of the stretching and shrinking of space and time. It has come to pass that every day is the Last Judgment."[22]

Among the things that DeWitt reported to the convention was the appointment of the Reverend Layton Zimmer to his staff on a permanent basis to work on problems of intergroup and interracial tensions. Among the last things that Bishop Armstrong had done, with the strong support of the coadjutor, was to make Zimmer the "urban missioner" on an experimental basis, for which Zimmer took a six-month leave of absence from his position as rector of Trinity Church, Swarthmore. The trial period expired at the end of October 1964, and Zimmer returned to Trinity. DeWitt, sensing the deepening of racial conflict, called Zimmer to the bishop's staff on a permanent basis in April 1965. He served in that position until 1967, when he resigned to become the deputy director of the Peace Corps in Fiji.

By 1965 Zimmer was a civil rights veteran. He had worked in Mississippi during the 1964 "freedom summer," worked in the streets of North Philadelphia during the August riot that summer, and demonstrated in Washington for federal intervention in the Selma voting rights confrontations the following March.[23] Then, with hundreds of other clergy and laypeople, including scores of Episcopalians, he joined the march from Selma to Montgomery. It was this set of events in the black belt of Alabama that yielded the notorious scene of Alabama state troopers and sheriff's deputies attacking the nonviolent marchers on the Edmund Pettus Bridge. In the aftermath of the Selma march and the continuing efforts to register blacks to vote in that hostile territory, an Episcopal seminarian, Jonathan Daniels, was murdered in cold blood in nearby Hayneville in August 1965. The chief assailant, a deputy sheriff, was found not guilty in a quick September trial by an all-white Alabama jury, causing a ripple of revulsion across the nation, an incredulous story and angry cartoon in *The Church News* of the

Diocese of Pennsylvania, and a scathing denunciation by John Hines, the presiding bishop.[24]

Financial Stringency

One interesting aspect of the addition of Layton Zimmer to the bishop's staff was that the bishop was at the same time taking major actions to avoid expenses. The Committee on Structure and Organization was not yet ready to report to the convention that met on May 3 and 4, 1965, but the convention nevertheless authorized a search for a suffragan bishop, a new position. Instead, DeWitt announced that Bishop Ervine Swift, retiring from his position in the Virgin Islands, would spend a year in the Diocese of Pennsylvania performing chiefly ceremonial functions in order to release Bishop DeWitt for work on other matters. Now was not a good time to commit to a long-term expense, DeWitt argued. The same reasoning caused DeWitt to agree with the committee studying the feasibility of completing St. Mary's Church in Roxborough to serve as the cathedral. That project was postponed. The budget for the 191-parish diocese nevertheless was a record, but this was chiefly because of the increase in the minimum salaries for clergy. Money was tight and getting tighter.

More evidence of the same problem soon appeared. Church House, at 202 West Rittenhouse Square, adjacent to Holy Trinity, did not have adequate space for the needs of the diocesan administration, and also needed substantial renovation. A committee of clergy and laymen studied the problem and concluded that it would be better to sell Church House and the property at 204 West Rittenhouse Square, which the diocese also owned, and lease space for the bishop and his staff until the financial situation improved. The bishop agreed. The property was sold to a developer in late 1968 with a proviso in the contract that would allow the diocese to lease space at very favorable rates in the high-rise office building the developer then contemplated for that location. Actual ownership finally shifted to the new owner in 1972, and the diocese leased space in the office building at 1700 Market Place.

In another economical move, publication of *The Church News* was suspended. From 1968 to 1972 the diocese had no medium of communication other than recorded messages that one could access by telephone. The *Episcopalian* was circulated, but that did nothing to weld the diocese together. For four years, there was no mechanism to alleviate one of the problems that the national Episcopal self-study emphasized.

Self-Study

The self-study had been started in the fall of 1963, carried out by the Division of Research and Field Study of the Executive Council in New York. It was completed a year later. By the fall of 1965, the data had been organized and analyzed, and the results were ready to be reported and discussed. Six regional briefings and discussion sessions were scheduled for late 1965. Parishioners were encouraged to attend the most convenient one. Following these, the self-study was the principal business of the diocesan convention that met in January 1966.

The self-study was about people rather than property or finances, though the need for money is evident in the report.[25] It was also focused at the parish level and did not look at the diocesan organization or budget. In many ways, the picture that emerged was one of which to be proud. The Diocese of Pennsylvania not only had a fascinating history; it had an unusually diverse mix of races and ethnicities, and it was facing rapid changes. Its members accounted for 2.9 percent of the total population, as compared to the national figure of 1.77 percent. The city of Philadelphia was not only losing population to the surrounding suburbs, but it was disproportionately losing Episcopalians. The percentage of the population that was Episcopalian by county was as follows: Bucks County, 2.5 percent; Chester County, 4.9 percent; Delaware County, 3.9 percent; Montgomery County, 4.7 percent, and Philadelphia Country—still home to the largest number of Episcopalians—2.1 percent. Among the eighty-nine dioceses nationally, the Diocese of Pennsylvania ranked third in the number of parishes and missions; fourth in the number of pupils attending Sunday schools; fifth in membership numbers; forty-eighth in average Sunday attendance; and sixty-ninth in the amount pledged per communicant.

The professional analysts estimated that there was a need for ten to fifteen additional congregations in the growing suburbs, but there were also "discouraged congregations" that needed revitalization or abolition, mostly in the city. Episcopalians in this diocese, as nationally, tended to be better educated and wealthier than their neighbors, but it was also true that in the Diocese of Pennsylvania the average pledge of financial support was well below the national average, as was the expenditure per communicant, hinting at the fact that not all Philadelphia Episcopalians were wealthy.

The most depressing findings, however, had to do with the low state of morale and the weakness of the lines of communication among members of different parishes. Too many divisions existed. Race and class were the unspoken dividers here. Lay leadership did not seem especially strong to the study group, nor were the Convocations, or regional groupings, very effective. Furthermore, the number of communicants was flat, while the population in the metropolitan area was growing.[26]

In his "state-of-the-diocese" report, a direct response to the self-study, DeWitt squarely faced the finding of low morale. This should not be surprising, he argued, given the tumultuous events of the previous nineteen months in the diocese, the rapid changes in leadership in particular. No wonder there was a feeling of disarray in diocesan life, and a feeling of poor communications between bishop and clergy. Underlying it all, DeWitt argued, was the sense that the church was shrinking while the population was growing. This trend, of course, was not of recent origin and was linked to the general deterioration of American cities. "No," DeWitt wrote, "to me the most impressive thing about this Diocese is the evidence of new life. The movement of the spirit is reflected in many facets of our diocesan life. This Diocese is on the move!" To lend some weight to his claim, he announced to the convention a generous gift of $50,000 per year for three years, to initiate a program of adult Christian education.[27]

One of the questions that the self-study did not ask was posed by Scottie Lanahan, the journalist daughter of F. Scott and Zelda Fitzgerald. Writing in the *Philadelphia Inquirer* and the *Washington Post*, she wondered how it could be that the Episcopal Church, the "white glove set," had taken the lead in the new "blue jeans revolution." As evidence, she pointed to the fact that Bishop Paul Moore allowed rock 'n' roll music in the Bethlehem Chapel of the National Cathedral.[28] When Malcolm Boyd, "the espresso priest," visited La Salle College, he was a media sensation.[29] Boyd was the field secretary of the Episcopal Society for Cultural and Racial Unity and the author of popular books and even records. He had rock-star status—he was as comfortable in coffeehouses and bars as he was behind the pulpit—though there are those who point out that he did not test his skills at Smokey Joe's. His ministry recognized that "age" had to be included with the barriers of race and class that were undermining Christian community. The Diocese of Pennsylvania was consciously struggling to make the church receptive to the youth culture of the time, which meant flirting with the counterculture. As Bob Dylan sang, "the times they are a-changing."

The civil rights movement was changing also, spurred by a number of impulses: the frustrations that result from runaway expectations, the psychological fatigue of civil rights workers who lived with the threat of death every day, the ironic fact that young black men and women who demonstrated for racial integration were made to feel increasingly black by the hostile response of the white community, and in part by the rational calculation that the civil rights movement had achieved all that it could achieve through legislation with the passage of the Civil Rights Act of 1964 and the Voting Rights Act of 1965. The more militant of the young black leaders began to think and to say that it was demeaning to have to ask whites to grant the rights to which blacks were entitled by citizenship and humanity. It was much more satisfying to demand one's rights, to act like a "real man."

In the long struggle of African Americans for justice in the United States, there were always two major strands in tension with each other: assimilation and black nationalism. The balance between those two themes changed from time to time, and the latter half of the 1960s contained such a flex point. In 1966 James Meredith, the young man who had integrated the University of Mississippi, thus becoming the target of a white riot, decided to demonstrate that blacks were not going to be intimidated anymore. He intended to do this by walking from the Tennessee border to Jackson, Mississippi. On the second day of his journey, a white man appeared in the bushes at the roadside and shot Meredith with a shotgun. The leaders of the five major civil rights organizations rushed to Meredith's bedside in a Memphis hospital. There they decided that they had to finish the march or white racists would believe that the movement could be intimidated.

Their "March Against Fear" was the last great march of the civil rights movement. Hundreds of volunteers, black and white, assembled and set forth on foot, under the watchful eyes of Mississippi highway police and the national press. Stokely Carmichael, soon to be known as Kwame Ture, the new chairman of the Student Nonviolent Coordinating Committee, used the occasion to introduce the new slogan of the movement: Black Power! No longer would the movement ask for freedom now; it would demand black power. Whatever the term meant, and divergent leaders offered multiple definitions, it implied at least four things: nonviolence was no longer a guiding principle of the movement; there would be a new emphasis on the notion that "black is beautiful"; white allies should go work in white communities to convert racists there, leaving the organizing of the black community to blacks; and blacks should control black communities.

This important turning point occurred in a deteriorating social context. There were uprisings in urban black communities every summer from 1964 through 1968. The Watts riot in Los Angeles in 1965 was the most destructive, but the whole country was affected. When Martin Luther King Jr. was assassinated in Memphis on April 4, 1968, destructive riots exploded in more than a hundred cities across the country, including the nation's capital. In a parallel development, the antiwar movement was also growing and getting more militant, resulting in major episodes of civil unrest as well as constant low-grade dissidence. The response of the public was curious. The agitation in the streets made white Americans more aware of problems that needed solving, and they became more supportive of civil rights for blacks and less supportive of the war in Vietnam. At the same time, the public became increasingly intolerant of social disorder; people became antiwar at the same time that they were becoming anti-antiwar. "Law and order" became a potent political slogan in the presidential election of 1968.

The Black Manifesto

The polarization that flowed from the increasing radicalization of the civil rights and antiwar activists, including delusions of revolution, and an increasingly resistant public was the context for the next chapter of the social gospel drama that was rending the calm of the Diocese of Pennsylvania. On April 26, 1969, the Black Economic Development Conference (BEDC, pronounced "Betsy") met in Detroit and issued the Black Manifesto. It was signed by twenty-three people, including such civil rights heroes as James Forman, Fannie Lou Hamer, Vince Harding, and Julian Bond. The head of the Greater Philadelphia branch of BEDC was a young man born and reared in Chester. He had taken the name Muhammad Kenyatta, with a nod to Jomo Kenyatta, the founding father and longtime president of the decolonized, independent state of Kenya. Muhammad Kenyatta and Bishop DeWitt soon developed a friendly relationship.

The Black Manifesto was a group project, but the introduction to the document was apparently the work of Jim Forman. Forman was also the person who presented the whole document to the Detroit meeting of BEDC. This is important because the four-page introduction was a revolutionary document, reminiscent of the Communist Manifesto, while the body of the manifesto was given over to advocacy for a lot of very practical, reformist proposals, such as education and job development programs. In retrospect, it is easy to see why so many white Americans had trouble getting beyond the introduction.

That introduction explained that it wanted to separate "Negroes and Black Capitalist pimps from the true Vanguard Force." "But while we talk of revolution which will be an armed confrontation and long years of sustained guerrilla warfare inside this country, we must also talk of the type of world we want to live in. We must commit ourselves to a society where the total means of production are taken from the rich people and placed into the hands of the state for the welfare of all the people. That is what we mean when we say total control. And we mean that black people who have suffered the most from exploitation and racism must move to protect their black interest by assuming leadership inside of the United States of everything that exists. The time has passed when we are second in command and white boy stands on top."[30]

The purpose of the Black Manifesto itself was simple: "We are demanding $500,000,000 from Christian white churches and Jewish synagogues. This total comes to $15 per nigger." There follow ten possible uses of such funds, all rather practical and nonrevolutionary, and then eleven ways in which BEDC planned to get massive support for the effort.[31] The amazing thing is that Bishop Hines and Bishop DeWitt took the demand seriously, raising in a more fundamental way the question of why "the white glove set" was leading the revolution. Other denominations began rejecting the demand, using the term "reparations" to describe what was being asked of them. The two Episcopal leaders began maneuvering to encourage a sympathetic response at the national level as well as at the diocesan level.

DeWitt, for instance, met with Kenyatta and Forman in his office at Church House on June 26, 1969. He scheduled a meeting of the Diocesan Council for July 10 and invited the two representatives of BEDC to attend. He even asked them to give him an outline of what they might say so that he could coach them a bit on how to be effective. BEDC wanted the diocese to assume a portion of the costs of the campaign to secure the "reparations." In effect, the diocese would be a partner in the enterprise, footing a major part of the bill. At the same time, Forman and Kenyatta made it clear to DeWitt that such cooperation would not absolve the diocese of paying its share of the reparations.[32]

At the same time, with the help of the Reverend David Gracie, who had replaced Zimmer as urban missioner on the staff, DeWitt sent a bulletin to the clergy of the diocese asking them to prepare for possible disruptions, such as occurred at Riverside Church in New York on May 4, when James Forman interrupted the worship service and presented the demands of the Black Manifesto.[33] "Only if we take these demands seriously can we engage in creative dialogue and avoid internal division and separation from social reality," DeWitt maintained. In particular, DeWitt cautioned his clergy not to call the police unless there was "an absolutely clear and present danger to life and limb." Instead, he advised that clergy engage BEDC activists in a discussion. For such an effort to be successful, the clergy and the parishioners needed to be well informed, so DeWitt recommended that they read and circulate the Black Manifesto right away.[34] DeWitt was

FIGURE 9.2 The Reverend David Gracie, urban missioner

also engaged with members of his cabinet in trying to fashion the terms of an appropriate response to the manifesto.

The meeting of Kenyatta with the Diocesan Council on July 10 did not go well. DeWitt sent a letter the next day to each of the members of the council saying that he thought the church had not been at its best in that meeting and apologizing for not having intervened more forcefully. The black community of America was crying out for recognition, and DeWitt wanted some sort of positive response. The official "indifference," he said, was tantamount to rejection. DeWitt also pointed out that the Union of Black Clergy and Laity (the national Episcopal organization) had gone on record as being in favor of the BEDC program.[35] Nevertheless, Reverend Theodore F. Jones, the council's executive secretary, wrote to Kenyatta saying that the council had "determined to study the matter at greater depth at a subsequent meeting, to be called soon."[36] This was the "official indifference" that DeWitt had feared.

While the council was "cooling out" Kenyatta, DeWitt was going out of his way to help. He sent a telegram to John Mitchell, the U.S. attorney general, protesting in strong terms the grand jury investigation of BEDC that was going on in Detroit. The grand jury was looking into the involvement of churches in the organizing activities of BEDC in black communities. Free expression was being stifled, DeWitt maintained, and "the freedom of the church to make its own decisions are at stake. Urge an immediate end to the proceedings in Detroit."[37]

At a special meeting of the General Convention at the University of Notre Dame held August 31–September 3, 1969, the Episcopal Church became the first denomination to appropriate funds, $200,000, in response to the Black Manifesto. The discussions were heated. There was strong opposition from southern delegates, especially southern laymen, to such an appropriation. In a clever parliamentary move, the southerners insisted that the voting be done "by orders," meaning that each diocese had two votes, one decided upon by the lay delegates and the other determined by the clerical delegates.

* * * * *

Father Washington

The Reverend Paul M. Washington (1921–2002) was a highly visible leader of Christian progressivism in the Diocese of Pennsylvania, as well as a widely respected presence in the affairs of the Episcopal

Church nationally. He was born in Charleston, South Carolina, and raised as a Baptist, pointed by his mother toward the ministry. His quiet dignity seemed less suited to the pulpit performers of the Baptist tradition than to the restrained emotions of the Episcopal liturgy. After graduating from Lincoln University, he completed his transition to the Episcopal Church at the Philadelphia Divinity School. As deacon, he served as assistant rector at the Church of the Crucifixion at Eighth and Bainbridge streets, a historically black church. He was ordained a priest in 1947. Then came a six-year stint teaching at Cuttington College in Liberia, after which he returned to Philadelphia as vicar of St. Cyprian's in Elmwood. In 1962 he became rector of Church of the Advocate at Eighteenth and Diamond streets, where he was a commanding presence for twenty-five years.

In word and deed, Father Washington urged blacks to "stand up! Become what God made you." At the same time, he demanded that whites cease their racial oppression. He served for seven years, from 1964 to 1971, on the city's Human Relations Commission, all the while making sure that the Church of the Advocate was at the center of the civil rights movement. In 1968 the Church of the Advocate was the site of the first national Black Power convention. He was a vigorous advocate in 1969 and thereafter for the Black Economic Development Conference and its demands, serving on the diocesan restitution commission that disbursed the funds appropriated for black development by the Diocese of Pennsylvania. With the city gripped by racial tension in 1970, the Church of the Advocate hosted the national convention of the Black Panther party. In 1974 the Church of the Advocate was the site of the unauthorized ordination of eleven women as priests of the Episcopal Church, a controversial act that hurried the national church to its decisions in 1976 and 1979 to permit the ordination of women priests. Barbara Harris, a native of Philadelphia and the first woman to be consecrated a bishop, was a protégé of Father Washington.

Though many people in the church disagreed with Washington about many things, everyone respected him. No one ever impugned his integrity or questioned his motives. In his long service at the Church of the Advocate, he was always to be found on the front lines in the battle for social justice.

* * * * *

FIGURE 9.3 The Reverend Paul Washington, rector of the Church of the Advocate

Paul Washington was a delegate from the Diocese of Pennsylvania and a member of BEDC. He played a prominent role in the deliberations and maneuvering at the convention. When Muhammad Kenyatta, now the vice chairman of BEDC, seized the microphone from Bishop Hines at the beginning of the convention in order to make the BEDC demands clear—an act of preemptive intimidation that was completely in tune with the psychology of black power—Paul Washington stood at his side as a sort of guardian.[38] The Pennsylvania delegation as a whole was strongly in favor of the appropriation.[39] The solidarity and visibility of the Union of Black Clergy and Laity of the Episcopal Church also played an important role.

On one issue the conservatives won. BEDC wanted the money to go directly to itself, but there were many at the convention deeply suspicious of any organization that was associated with such a revolutionary document as the introduction to the Black Manifesto. DeWitt tried on every occasion and in every way to urge whites not to be diverted by the rhetoric of the introduction but to look at the practicality of the actual proposals, while keeping in mind that justice cried out for some effort to help the black community. DeWitt made that argument also at the General Convention. In addition, the Union of Black Clergy and Laity said early and clearly that the money should go directly to BEDC. The House of Bishops was not convinced. It adopted a resolution insisting on a middleman, despite DeWitt's best efforts. That resolution probably exerted an influence on the vote of many delegates. Observers also noted that "voting by orders" made the difference in the floor vote.[40] The appropriated funds would go to the National Committee of Black Churchmen, an ecumenical group that had indicated its intention to direct the funds to BEDC projects.[41]

Providing "reparations" in response to the Black Manifesto set off a storm of protest within the Episcopal Church nationally.[42] Critics argued that the church's action appeared to reward threats and legitimize revolution. "Blackmail" was the descriptive term of choice. Supporters of the action, black and white, replied that BEDC was a responsible organization with strong support in the black community and among black Episcopalians. Some even pointed out that James Forman had been eased out of his leadership position. As Bishop William F. Creighton of Washington, D.C. put it as he rhetorically addressed BEDC, "We've tried to minister to hurt humanity in the name of Christ and we haven't done very well; you may know better; take this in trust."[43]

With the national church embroiled in controversy, the convention of the Pennsylvania diocese met in May 1970 to try to sort things out for itself. Wisely, it chose the old "appoint-a-committee" option. The Task Force for Reconciliation was to consult widely and think deeply and then make recommendations to a special diocesan convention later that month.

In order to set the stage for those promising deliberations, Muhammad Kenyatta appeared at the 11:00 A.M. service at Holy Trinity on Rittenhouse Square on Sunday, May 17, 1970. He and the two men who were with him stood at the front of the church until the service was over. The woman who arrived with them sat in the rear. The minister, unflustered because forewarned, then introduced Kenyatta to the seventy-five communicants in the pews. Kenyatta spoke for about twenty minutes, demanding that the diocese turn over to the Greater Philadelphia BEDC an amount equal to the combined market value of Holy Trinity and Church House. "We of the BEDC must reject as domestic neo-colonialism any scheme that would have the Diocese of Pennsylvania creating a heavily-funded buffer group to further divide the Black community," he said.[44] He then overturned the collection plates, spilling money on the floor, and stalked out of the church with his three companions.[45]

This was not helpful to Bishop DeWitt. The council had been meeting to try to generate a consensus in advance of the special convention. The group was closely divided between those who wanted to do something in response to the Black Manifesto and those who thought the demand for reparations was simply illegitimate.[46]

Nevertheless, when the one-day special convention met in Irvine Auditorium on the Penn campus on Saturday, May 23, the Task Force for Reconciliation recommended, and the convention approved, a plan for the diocese to set up a fund of $500,000 to be used for projects that would benefit the black community. The money was to come partly from the $30,000 that had been raised specially by the task force but primarily from the sale of assets, the most obvious candidate being the proceeds from the sale of Church House itself, which was under contract but had not yet closed. The funds would be controlled by a Restitution Fund Commission, to consist of all the black clergy in the diocese, matched by an equal number of black laity (both men and women) to be chosen from the majority-black congregations. This was an extraordinary act because it came at a time of financial stringency. The 1970 budget of $1,157,000 represented a 23 percent reduction from the budget of 1969![47]

As Bishop DeWitt explained to the delegates, "This is a first in terms of a Diocese doing something like this . . . for an amount of this magnitude, and that the money would be dispersed with no controls." He also pointed out that "the key to this was the principle of self-determination." The money was to be spent by black people for their own purposes.[48] As it turned out, the selection procedure produced a commission of forty members, including one nonresident, Reverend James E. P. Woodruff, the executive director of the Union of Black Clergy and Laity.[49]

Before the special convention, DeWitt had gotten a letter from Leon Sullivan, written on the letterhead of his church, Zion Baptist, but signed by Sullivan, Herman Wrice, and Muhammad Kenyatta. Herman Wrice was a thoroughly admirable community activist in West Philadelphia who spent his life developing programs for poor kids. Their message was simple: the black community is united, so don't try to divide it. After the convention, DeWitt responded to Sullivan, thanking him for his letter and saying that it had been read to the convention to good effect. "Our Convention," DeWitt wrote, "turned something of a corner, and took only a little step. But even turning that corner is a pretty big step for us, and we appreciate your help."[50]

The controversy did not abate. Instead, it grew more acrimonious and complex.[51] There were numerous Episcopalians, mostly white, who considered the idea of reparations a faulty principle and an unfortunate precedent. They did not go away. Among black Episcopalians, there were supporters of BEDC who saw the Restitution Fund Commission as an insult to the true voice of the black community, just as Kenyatta and Sullivan had warned. Father Washington was their voice on the commission itself, making the functioning of the commission rancorous. Washington and the commission chairman, Harold Pilgrim of Northern Liberties, had a particularly testy relationship. A year after the commission started operating, BEDC still had not been successful in getting a grant from it, so Kenyatta denounced the commission.[52] Dark glasses and all, Kenyatta was busy interrupting meetings of various kinds in the Philadelphia area, but without much positive effect. The Philadelphia Presbytery, for instance, survived his disruption and decided subsequently not to meet any of the demands of BEDC.[53]

DeWitt's friendly, supportive relationship with Kenyatta endured these tensions. Just before Christmas in 1970, DeWitt sent Kenyatta a check for $200, which was the beginning of a monthly stipend. Just a month later, DeWitt sent another check from the bishop's discretionary fund for $4,000, which he told Kenyatta was to be used "for the general purposes of the Black Economic Development Conference."[54] Then, when Kenyatta and his associates were in trouble with the district attorney for the disruption of the Presbytery meeting in the summer of 1970, DeWitt provided a character reference.[55] Kenyatta also became something of a protégé of Paul Washington's, using the facilities of the Church of the Advocate for BEDC programs. Soon DeWitt was addressing Kenyatta as "Dear Mo," but he warned that he could not continue the stipend beyond June 1972.[56] More seriously, Kenyatta confessed to DeWitt in March 1972 that BEDC was not going to be able to repay the loan it had gotten from the diocese, and that it was in trouble with the IRS and owed $1,200 in taxes. DeWitt arranged for money to go to BEDC from diocesan funds, $1,500 for immediate emergency needs and $1,500 to be available for needs over the next six months. DeWitt also forgave the loan. In this way, BEDC limped forward and was still operating in 1976.[57]

The Ordination of Women

While race was roiling the Diocese of Pennsylvania, and the backlash against Dewitt was growing, gender had begun to assert its claim on the attention of Episcopalians. This was not a new issue. The demand that women be allowed to serve as delegates to the General Convention had been made during the first wave of feminism in the second and third decades of the twentieth century, but it had always been turned down. The diocese had wrestled with the question repeatedly, finally voting in 1956 to allow women to serve as delegates to the diocesan convention. That vote was repeated, as required by the constitution, in 1957. So the Diocese of Pennsylvania was considerably more progressive than the church nationally.

At the triennial General Convention of 1970, held in Houston, the first at which women served as delegates, there was much discussion of the need to purge the church of racism, but an argument was also made for the ordination of women. There is, in the reports of the deliberations, a sense of crisis. The convention approved the ordination of women to the diaconate but voted down the measure that would have authorized ordination of women into the priesthood.[58] This, however, was an issue that was not going away.

The House of Bishops took up the question of the ordination of women in the fall of 1971. Rather than take action, it appointed yet another study commission. When, on October 30, 1971, the gathering of professional laywomen and deacons heard what the bishops had done, they constituted themselves as the Episcopal Women's Caucus (EWC) and notified the presiding bishop that they would refuse to cooperate further. An organizing effort soon produced chapters in various parts of the country, and the lobbying began. The EWC is the feminist voice of the church, but it should be understood that its definition of "feminist" is very broad and includes "anyone who believes that God created males and females equally human."[59]

When a task force studying the status of women in the diocese proposed in May 1973 the ordination of women, the measure failed to pass the Diocesan Council on a 10–10 vote.[60] The House of Bishops, meeting in Houston the previous year, had also narrowly defeated a similar measure. It was not a surprise, therefore, when the triennial General Convention in Louisville in October 1973 also rejected a bid to change the canon law to permit women to become priests.[61] Not only were opinions divided nationally and locally on this crucial issue, but patience was wearing increasingly thin.

Lyman C. Ogilby

A key character in the next act of this drama, Lyman C. Ogilby, arrived in the Diocese of Pennsylvania in June 1971, having been appointed assistant bishop (functionally archdeacon) by Bishop DeWitt.[62] Ogilby came to the priesthood naturally. His father was an Episcopal priest and was also the president of Trinity College in Hartford, Connecticut. Lyman Ogilby had been born in 1922, attended Loomis prep school and Hamilton College in Clinton, New York, and then trained at the Episcopal Theological School in Cambridge. His blood line was pure blue. After his ordination in 1950, he served in the Philippines, racing from chaplain to bishop at the age of only thirty-six. His most recent position had been as missionary bishop of the Episcopal District of South Dakota. Although their family backgrounds in New England seem similar, Ogilby and DeWitt had very different experiences as priests in preparation for service in the Diocese of Pennsylvania, and they possessed very different personalities. Perhaps for this reason, they worked very well together.

DeWitt needed help. Not only was he overworked, but his progressive stance on race and gender questions had created considerable opposition in the diocese. Fortunately, DeWitt was also charming and gregarious, so he was well liked even by many who had fundamental differences with him. Ogilby could help shoulder the burden of pastoral care and sacerdotal duties, and his judicious temperament helped to balance DeWitt's more single-minded approach to issues. The political and moral commitments of the two men were similar; their leadership styles were vastly different. Ogilby might be seen as the model of "the leader as servant," drawing people together and helping them develop a consensus about the issue at hand. Though he was an extrovert, he did not lead by giving orders from on high.

At the annual convention in October 1972, DeWitt announced that he would not serve beyond June 1974. This gave the diocese time to select a coadjutor, so that that person could be comfortably in place for an orderly transition.

To accomplish this task, the reconvened session of the annual convention took place in Irvine Auditorium on the Penn campus on May 5, 1973. Six candidates had been screened by a special nominating panel from a list of roughly seventy-five possibilities. The short list of six included Ogilby, Paul Washington, Charles M. Long of St. Peter's Church in Glenside, and Tom Turney Edwards, rector of St. Paul's Church in Chestnut Hill. The other two were from outside the diocese. Though Ogilby had been in the diocese less than two years, he had made a very good impression and many friends. He had also caused a little stir by celebrating Mass on the steps of the Capitol in Harrisburg as part of an antiwar vigil. After much discussion and some maneuvering, Ogilby emerged on the sixth ballot with a majority of both the lay and clerical delegates, as required by diocesan rules. Washington, Long, and Edwards threw their support to Ogilby on the last ballot, when it was clear that their chances were slim and decreasing. Ogilby was gracious in victory. When invited afterward by a newspaper reporter to comment on the hot issues of the day, such as the ordination of women, he declined. Until he became the diocesan bishop, he said, his role was to support Bishop DeWitt, and he would do nothing that might get in the way of that.[63]

Something of the mutual respect between DeWitt and Ogilby is revealed in DeWitt's announcement in September that he would step down on January 1, 1974. Since Ogilby was already familiar with the workings of the diocese, there was no need to wait longer. In a letter to clergy and lay leaders, DeWitt said that he planned to spend his time working on issues concerning the relationship between the church and society. "For centuries the church has ministered to a troubled world," he wrote, "offering consolation and help; but the church has not provided enough assistance to the world in helping it to understand why it is in trouble. Human justice, freedom and dignity are jeopardized as never before. I am interested in finding ways to encourage both the church and society to ask why this is so, and also to seek possible solutions."[64]

DeWitt's ten years of service as bishop were deservedly celebrated as he presided over his final diocesan convention in Irvine Auditorium on October 25 and 26. Part of his appeal to the delegates was to give more support to the Restitution Fund. Harold Pilgrim reported that the diocese had provided $675,308 since 1970. To date, a third of those funds had been dispensed. On the less political agenda, the convention heard encouraging reports about the twenty-eight missions and aided parishes, tools in the effort to solve the problems of suburbanization and demographic drift.[65]

Ogilby's investiture as diocesan bishop occurred on February 2, 1974, in an impressive ceremony at the Church of the Advocate, Paul Washington's church. The investiture proper was conducted by Ernest Harding, rector of Christ Church and president of the diocesan Standing Committee. Reconciliation, appropriately enough, was the theme of Ogilby's sermon. "The world is our field of action," he told the congregation, "the world where people, persons, men and women, the youth and the aged, the oppressed and the opulent, of every condition, strive and live." He went on to say that he was committed to action along three avenues: proclaiming the Gospel; witnessing to the Gospel through involvement in the solution of social problems; and governing the diocese in a way that was faithful to parishioners' responsibilities to the Episcopal Church in the United States, to the Anglican Communion worldwide, and to the members of the church within the Pennsylvania diocese.

FIGURE 9.4 Bishop Lyman Ogilby

Forcing the Issue

Ogilby's diplomatic skills were soon tested. Robert DeWitt, two other bishops from outside the diocese, Paul Washington, and a small group of clergy planned and announced a ceremony to be held at Church of the Advocate on July 29, 1974, at which eleven women were to be ordained priests. Only one of the eleven—Suzanne Hiatt of Chestnut Hill—was from the Diocese of Pennsylvania. Though he reiterated his personal position in favor of the ordination of women as priests, Bishop Ogilby declined to participate because, as he put it, "I do not believe this is the way God would have me proceed with this cause at this time." He also withheld his consent and approval. The problem was that the traditions of the church had prohibited women from ordination as priests.

It was precisely the silence of the canons on which DeWitt and his associates, by contrast, leaned. If the ordination of women was not prohibited, they argued, then it must be permissible. Ogilby, however, saw that in explicit tests of the question, the church had always turned down legislation that would have authorized women's ordination. In 1970, as noted above, the General Convention had explicitly authorized women to serve as deacons of the church, but not as priests. All of the eleven women candidates for priesthood were deacons. In 1973, when the matter had last been tested, the House of Deputies had turned it down at the General Convention. Ogilby adopted a tortured but perhaps brilliant position. He said that the ordination would be "theologically valid, though irregular in terms of the current ecclesiastical policy and structures of the church."[66] On this, Ogilby had the support of the Standing Committee.[67]

The proposed ordination may have been renegade, but it was scarcely a stealth ceremony. It was widely known and debated nationally before it happened. Ogilby was in close touch with the presiding bishop, John M. Allin, who was opposed to the ordination of women in general and who had "requested" that no such ceremony take place. Ogilby also informed clergy in the diocese that they would be in violation of the constitution and canons of the national church if they participated in the ordination, or if they subsequently allowed any of the women to perform priestly functions.

A large group of clergy and laypeople antagonistic to the idea of women priests, or to the irregular ordination, met in Rosemont at the Church of the Good Shepherd to plan a protest at the ceremony itself.[68] The American Church Union, a national organization of Episcopalian traditionalists, planned to seek a court injunction against the use of the Church of the Advocate but at the last moment decided not to do so because Ogilby had warned the three bishops leading the noncanonical ordination that they would be in violation of the constitution and canons of the national church if they proceeded.[69] The world was watching.

Despite official disapproval and vigorous criticism from all over the country, the ceremony went forward. A joyous mood was exuded by the fifteen hundred to two thousand people crowded into the cavernous sanctuary of the Church of the Advocate. About ten minutes into the service, four clergymen stepped forward, were allowed to take the microphone, and began to explain why they thought the ceremony was in error. Among the four was Canon Charles Osbourne, head of the American Church Union, and Reverend George Rutler, rector of Church of the Good Shepherd in Rosemont, site of the opposition meeting. A chorus of boos began to swell. Father Washington raised his arms in admonition and asked the audience to respect the four priests and to listen to their remarks. The audience complied. The four spoke briefly. Rutler was the most vehement. "I declare this ordination void," he said. "You may break the laws, sirs," he told the bishops, "but you break today a law He did not break. God should be called Father and so shall his priests." Rutler eventually, in 1978, resigned from Good Shepherd and took a position in the dissident Anglican Church of North America.[70] Soon thereafter, he went to Rome to become a Catholic priest, thus prompting Bishop Ogilby and the Standing Committee to depose (defrock) him.[71] On the other side of the ideological spectrum, at the ceremony on July 29, 1974, some thirty priests joined the three bishops in the ritual gesture of the laying on of hands, a gesture they made in direct defiance of their bishop.[72]

Bishop Ogilby quickly repeated his inhibition of Suzanne Hiatt. If she were to try to carry out the functions of a priest in the Diocese of Pennsylvania, he said, he would initiate action to suspend her. By contrast, David Gracie, the urban missioner on the bishop's staff, said, "I hope the action today will hasten the day when ordination of women is a common and accepted thing throughout the church."[73] Gracie left the staff the following year. Ogilby also quickly placed official inhibitions on his predecessor, phoning him as well as sending a letter. DeWitt responded by saying, "I consider this is a very appropriate action. If our roles were reversed, it is exactly what I would do."[74]

Presiding Bishop Allin called a special meeting of the House of Bishops for August 14 in Chicago. At that meeting, the bishops voted to invalidate the Philadelphia ordination. The backlash was strong, national, and multidirectional. DeWitt, with characteristic candor, told the press that the bishops were insensitive and sexist.[75] The layman who was vice president of the House of Deputies of the General Convention announced that he was thinking of resigning to protest the action of the bishops. The Committee to Plan for and Promote the Ordination of Women to the Priesthood, a group operating across the diocese, began to hold meetings and communicate their feelings to the bishop. At the same time, thirty clergymen from the Diocese of Pennsylvania filed a complaint with Bishop Ogilby against thirteen of their brother clergy whom they could identify as having participated in the ceremony at the Church of the Advocate.

Emotions were clearly aroused by the situation. When the Diocesan Council met in September, it went through its regular agenda with no difficulty. Then Richardson Blair, a lawyer, confronted Paul Washington and suggested that he take a leave of absence from the council because he had defied the rules and procedures of the church. By doing so, Blair maintained, Washington had removed himself from the discipline of the church. Father Edward Chinn agreed with Blair and added, "I doubted that I'd get through this meeting without speaking about that painful event." Ogilby, chairing the meeting, said that he was unsure which council procedures covered the current situation. One member pointed out that it would not be fair to punish Washington but not others who were involved. Still others sought some middle ground. Jim Trimble, who had been chaplain of the Episcopal Academy since 1963 and would become rector of Christ Church, Philadelphia, in 1978, observed that it would be terrible if they were to let legalistic methods get in the way of the humane treatment of individuals. Washington then defused the situation a bit by replying without rancor that he could understand Blair's feelings. On the other hand, Washington argued, the ordination of women had been defeated at the General Convention by unjust voting procedures, and he could not respect that decision. "I would choose to stay on the Diocesan Council," he said, "because in the Body of Christ there must be room for those who hold different opinions. If there is not room, then indeed I weep for the church." Blair withdrew his motion, receiving the thanks of several members for having raised the issue.[76]

Meeting in September 1975, the House of Bishops formally censured the three bishops who had participated in the now-invalidated ordination ceremony.[77] At their regular annual meeting in October, however, held in Mexico, the House of Bishops voted 97 to 35 in favor of the ordination of women. Keep in mind, though, that the bishops had adopted a similar resolution in 1972, yet the General Convention in 1973 did not approve the ordination of women.[78]

The irregular ordination had raised the issue of women in the priesthood in a way that could not be ignored. Whether it advanced the chances of success in the General Convention of 1976 was the question on everyone's mind. So much of the opposition was procedural, or at least was explained in procedural terms, that it was difficult to measure the depth of the sort of theological conservatism expressed by Father Rutler. But it was certain that the question would be the centerpiece of convention deliberations in 1976.[79]

The eleven newly ordained women priests at first declined to do anything further to exacerbate the situation. By September 1975, however, they had begun to test the limits of tolerance. Suzanne Hiatt, who had joined the faculty of the Episcopal Divinity School in Cambridge, announced that she planned to preside at celebrations of the Eucharist in late September. Six churches in the diocese scheduled services in which women priests would participate. This brought forth from Bishop Ogilby another of his wonderfully conflicted positions. In a pastoral letter written to the diocese on September 17, he explained that the proposed celebrations of Communion by the women were "valid as were the ordinations of the celebrants, though certainly uncanonical and irregular."[80] He also stated that he would "allow" but not "approve" of their performing priestly functions.[81]

The General Convention, which met in Minneapolis for thirteen days in September 1976, approved the ordination of women, a resolution supporting abortion rights, one supporting nondiscrimination against gays and lesbians, and the revised draft of the Book of Common Prayer. The mood of the church had changed dramatically since 1973. Bishop Ogilby, characteristically, hid his pleasure by saying there were no winners or losers, just unity in Christ.[82]

Bishop Ogilby began officiating at the ordination of women to the priesthood right away—for instance, at St. Asaph's Church in Bala Cynwyd on January 5, 1977, with the ordination of Alice B. Mann. Paul Washington was in attendance, undoubtedly feeling vindicated for the role he had played in helping the church take such an important, yet difficult, step forward.[83]

The bitter dispute about the ordination of women left the national church divided, which was true of the Diocese of Pennsylvania as well. Undoubtedly, the self-effacing style of Bishop Ogilby, and his evenhandedness, minimized the friction. He was, after all, a bishop who described himself not as the leader of the diocese but as the pastoral priest for pastoral priests. With the question of the ordination of gays and lesbians just beginning to appear on meeting agendas throughout the country, the church could not pause to pursue reconciliation. The Diocese of Pennsylvania remained engaged in social issues, each of which had the potential to fracture the diocese. For instance, Bishop Ogilby joined seventeen other Philadelphia religious leaders in 1978 in calling for an end to racial polarization. This came in response to the campaign for charter reform, a measure that would have revised the city charter to allow Mayor Frank Rizzo to run for a third term. Rizzo had shown his true colors by calling on Philadelphians to "vote white."

The Philadelphia Divinity School

This period also saw the loss of one of the jewels in the diocesan crown, the Philadelphia Divinity School (PDS). Founded in 1858, PDS thrived until the Great Depression, when it suffered serious financial difficulties. The stringency meant that it limped through the 1940s and 1950s until new leadership in the late 1950s and early 1960s brought a renaissance. Nevertheless, there was worry within the Episcopal Church nationally about the sustainability of its seminaries, given the falling numbers of students nationwide. Indeed, this was a worry in all the Protestant denominations. For several years in the 1960s, faculty committees from the Philadelphia area theological schools were in serious conversation with one another about consolidating their operations somehow to achieve efficiencies and to borrow strengths from one another. This approach was thwarted by loyalties to location as well as to denomination. At the national level, the Episcopal Church created a group called the Episcopal Consortium of Theological Consolidation in the Northeast. This effort led eventually to the merger of the Episcopal Theological School in Cambridge, Massachusetts, and the Philadelphia Divinity School, a merger completed in 1974 after very complicated negotiations about programs, student status, and faculty appointments. The location of the combined schools, to be called the Episcopal Divinity School, was to be Cambridge. A significant number of diocesan clergy had trained at PDS, and they were sorry to see it go. Because bishops DeWitt and Ogilvie had supported the merger, this was yet another irritant in the human relationships within the diocese.[84]

* * * * *

The 1979 Book of Common Prayer

Several broad forces lay behind the movement for an extensive revision of the prayer book: the growing ecumenical movement, a revival of biblical theology, and an interdenominational belief that the liturgy should be grounded in the practices of the early church rather than in forms that had come down from the Middle Ages. As early as 1950 the Standing Liturgical Commission of the national church began a detailed review of the 1928 book, and in 1963 the Anglican Congress issued broad liturgical guidelines based on early Christian practice. Just a year later, the General Convention of the American church instructed its liturgical commission to submit a plan to the next convention for the trial use of a proposed prayer book revision that would emphasize more modern language and make the services more relevant to the church's "present ministry and life."

Recognizing that the task of revision required the best knowledge, talent, and experience, the liturgical commission selected three hundred consultants. Some of them worked on the various drafting committees and others served as reader-consultants. There were separate committees for each section of the prayer book. In 1967 the General Convention authorized a three-year trial use for the new "Liturgy of the Lord's Supper." Feedback about this service convinced the liturgical commission that no single form would serve all needs, and this led to the decision to create both traditional and contemporary language for the most regularly used services—morning prayer, evening prayer, Holy Eucharist, and burial of the dead.

Although the Rite I forms used traditional language, they were not verbatim copies from the 1928 book but were carefully edited to reflect the forms of the early church and to eliminate excess verbiage and confusing or incorrect translations. The two rites were also the same length and were organized in the same way. The only difference was the language, and here the principal variation was the use of the once familiar second person singular in Rite I services (thou, thee, thine), along with seventeenth-century verb forms, compared to the Rite II use of the contemporary you and your, along with twentieth-century verb forms.

The commission added some new services to the prayer book, such as the blessing of a civil marriage and thanksgiving for the adoption of a child. Finally, the contemporary language of the various services purposely drew from the same sources as many other Christian denominations in the English-speaking world, including the Roman Catholic Church. This commonality of language was particularly evident in such things as the Lord's Prayer and the Nicene and Apostles' creeds, which had been worked out by the International Consultation of English Texts and published in 1970 as *Prayers We Have in Common*. This is one important reason why the contemporary Catholic Mass and the Episcopalian Eucharist seem so similar to anyone who experiences both.

In 1970 the General Convention authorized a series of rites to be used over the next three years, known officially as Services for Trial Use and more familiarly as the "green book" because of its green cover. Three years later, in response to many comments about the trial services, the liturgical commission came out with a revised version called the Authorized Services. Taking into consideration a further round of criticisms and suggestions, the commission produced a Draft Proposed Book of Common Prayer (dubbed "the blue book" because of its sky-blue cover) in time for the 1976 General Convention to approve it.

As the reality of the new prayer book approached, opponents organized the Society for the Preservation of the Book of Common Prayer, which claimed to have a hundred thousand members by 1976. The opponents failed to sway the General Convention, and the new prayer book appeared, with only minor editorial adjustments, in 1979.

It became evident that a new hymnal was needed to harmonize with the 1979 prayer book. The 1982 hymnal, the first since 1940, introduced much more service music. It also deleted a number of outdated Victorian hymns and added about a hundred new hymns.

SOURCE: This discussion of the 1979 prayer book is based largely on William Sydnor, *The Real Prayer Book: 1549 to the Present* (Wilton, Conn.: Morehouse-Barlow, 1978), 84–106.

* * * * *

The 1928 prayer book, beloved by many, nevertheless had almost from the first failed to satisfy a wide swath of Episcopalians. As early as the 1950s, the Standing Liturgical Commission of the national church had begun a careful review. The process was lengthy and tortured, with versions of different revisions being given trials in the 1960s and 1970s. Finally, a proposed new edition was ready (see above). It was adopted at its first reading at the 1976 General Convention, and it repeated that triumph in 1979. Episcopalians were learning that language is important. Dissatisfaction with the archaic language of the 1928 prayer book had led to the long and meticulous process of revision. Even the inclusion of two rites, with different language styles, did not resolve the differences of taste. This was yet another issue of the 1960s and 1970s that fractured the church. Reactions to the new prayer book would be played out over the next couple of decades. For the moment, however, the successful modernizers of the prayer book joined a long line of modernizers in gender and racial justice who had been victorious but who left the battlefield littered with metaphorical carcasses and the ruins of battle.

NOTES

1. "Rt. Rev. Robert L. DeWitt Elected Coadjutor," *TCN* (January 1964), 1.
2. "Bishop DeWitt Chairman of Home Department," *TCN* (January 1965), 1.
3. "Bishop DeWitt Tells Convention, Negroes Want Church 'Aware,'" *TCN* (November 1964), 8; "Highlights—61st Convention of the Episcopal Church," ibid., 8–9.
4. Quoted in George Riley, "Episcopal Bishops Disagree with Laity, Uphold Civil Disobedience Principle," *Philadelphia Evening Bulletin*, October 23, 1964.
5. See Matthew J. Countryman, *Up South: Civil Rights and Black Power in Philadelphia* (Philadelphia: University of Pennsylvania Press, 2005), chapter 4.
6. Dennis M. Higgins and Eric D. Blanchard, "Truce Ends, All Chester Schools Shut," *Philadelphia Inquirer*, April 23, 1964.
7. Quoted in "Hail of Rocks at Chester Hurts Two Policemen," *Philadelphia Inquirer*, April 24, 1964.
8. Joseph F. Lowry, "Hewett Leaves for Detroit to Take Civil Rights Training," *Philadelphia Evening Bulletin*, May 13, 1964.
9. Quoted in the *Philadelphia Evening Bulletin*, June 28, 1964.
10. "Bishop DeWitt's Convention Message Points to 5 Concerns," *TCN* (June 1964), 3.
11. Rev. Herbert Beardsley, "Bishop's Conference on Urban Culture Had Three Objectives," *TCN* (November 1963), 1.
12. "Bishop DeWitt's Convention Message Points to 5 Concerns," 3.
13. "Speaker Lauds DeWitt for Lack of Anxious Timidity," *TCN* (December 1964), 8; "Colorful Ceremony Marks Induction of 12th Bishop," ibid., 9.
14. "Diocese Supports Integration of Girard College by Resolution of Diocesan Council," *TCN* (September 1965), 1.
15. Ralph Knowles Jr., "The Girard College Trust: Past, Present, and Future," *Alabama Law Review* 20, no. 308 (1968): 308–25.
16. "Girard Case Plea Refused by Court," *New York Times*, December 7, 1966.
17. "Girard Is Upheld by Court on Race," *New York Times*, March 1, 1967.
18. "U.S. Judge Widens Ruling on Girard," *New York Times*, July 6, 1967.
19. "Girard Loses Appeal to Exclude Negroes," *New York Times*, March 8, 1968.
20. "Racial Case Lost by Girard College," *New York Times*, May 21, 1968.
21. "Demonstrations Outside Girard College Wall Terminated," *TCN* (November 1965).
22. "Bishop DeWitt Speaks Out on His Concerns and Hopes for the Diocese," *TCN* (June 1965), 8.
23. "Swarthmore Rector Accepts Call as General Missioner in Urban Areas," *TCN* (April 1965), 3.

24. For the cartoon, see "Alabama Justice," *TCN* (December 1965), 3; for the denunciation, see "Acquittal of Alabama Deputy Is 'Verdict Heard Around the World,'" *TCN* (November 1965), 1. Bishop Arthur Walmsley reminds me that Ruby Sales, the woman whose life was saved when Jonathan Daniels pushed her out of the way during the fatal confrontation on the Edmund Pettus Bridge, subsequently went to seminary and was ordained. For his heroism and self-sacrifice, Daniels was added to the calendar of lesser feasts and fasts of the Episcopal Church.

25. General Division of Research and Field Study, Executive Council, New York, "Discussion and Recommendations on the Self-Study of the Diocese," *TCN* (January 1966), 6.

26. Ibid.

27. "'State of the Diocese' Reflected by Self-Study Forms Basis of Bishop's Address," *TCN* (February 1966), 6–7.

28. Scottie Lanahan, "Episcopal Churches Take the Lead in New 'Blue-Jeans Religion,'" *Philadelphia Inquirer*, July 5, 1967.

29. Marta Robinet, "The Young Want Sex to Make Sense," *Philadelphia Evening Bulletin*, March 14, 1967.

30. Introduction to the Black Manifesto, copy in Records of the Episcopate, Robert L. DeWitt (1916–2003), Twelfth Diocesan Bishop, 1964–1974, box 3, folder 9, Diopa Archives, Lutheran Theological Seminary, Mount Airy (Philadelphia). Hereafter cited as DeWitt Papers.

31. Ibid.

32. Kenyatta to DeWitt, July 1, 1969, ibid., folder 6.

33. Emanuel Perlmutter, "'Reparations' Are Asked—Lindsay Is 'Shocked,'" *New York Times*, May 5, 1969.

34. Box 3, folder 10, DeWitt Papers. See also Betty Medsger, "Black Militant Says Church Is 'White Racism,'" *Philadelphia Evening Bulletin*, June 19, 1969.

35. DeWitt to Council, July 11, 1969, box 3, folder 11, DeWitt Papers.

36. Jones to Kenyatta, July 16, 1969, ibid., folder 6.

37. DeWitt to John M. Mitchell, telegram, July 11, 1969, ibid.

38. Louis Cassels, "'Black Manifesto' Grant Ignites White Backlash," *Philadelphia Evening Bulletin*, September 20, 1969.

39. Betty Medsger, "Unity Helped Negroes Win Church Funds," *Philadelphia Evening Bulletin*, September 7, 1969.

40. Ibid.

41. Cassels, "'Black Manifesto' Grant Ignites White Backlash."

42. George Dugan, "'Manifesto' Fund Is Proving Vexing: Churchgoers Fear Money Will Be Spent Unwisely," *New York Times*, September 21, 1969.

43. Quoted in Cassels, "'Black Manifesto' Grant Ignites White Backlash."

44. "Statement of the Greater Philadelphia Black Economic Development Conference," May 17, 1970, box 3, folder 6, DeWitt Papers.

45. William Lovejoy, "Collection Dumped in Church by Kenyatta," *Philadelphia Evening Bulletin*, May 18, 1970.

46. See response to Urban Research Council questionnaire, March 9, 1970, box 3, folder 6, DeWitt Papers.

47. James C. Young, "Episcopalians Set $500,000 Fund for Use by Negroes," *Philadelphia Inquirer*, May 24, 1970.

48. Ibid.

49. J. Rupert Picott and Walter N. Ridley, *History of the Restitution Fund Commission of the Episcopal Diocese of Pennsylvania: A Challenge* (Washington, D.C.: Restitution Fund Commission, 1976), 73–75.

50. Sullivan, Wrice, and Kenyatta to DeWitt, May 20, 1970, box 3, folder 6, DeWitt Papers.

51. For an excellent discussion of the Black Manifesto, see Gardiner Shattuck, "Episcopalians and Race: The Philadelphia Story," address at the Church of the Advocate, Philadelphia, November 3, 2000.

52. "Kenyatta Assails Episcopal Diocese Black Fund Group," *Philadelphia Evening Bulletin*, June 8, 1971.

53. Andrew Wallace, "Presbytery Votes to Reject Demands by Blacks," *Philadelphia Inquirer*, July 1, 1970.

54. DeWitt to Kenyatta, January 6, 1971, box 3, folder 7, DeWitt Papers.

55. DeWitt to Michael Rotko, Deputy Assistant District Attorney, January 26, 1971, ibid.

56. DeWitt to Kenyatta, January 21, 1972, ibid.

57. Kenyatta to DeWitt, March 14, 1972; Kenyatta to Charles L. Ritchie Jr. (of Bishop DeWitt's staff), March 20, 1872; Paul Washington to Lyman Ogilby, November 7, 1975, all in ibid.

58. "A Summary of General Convention Actions," *Episcopalian*, December 1970.

59. See http://episcopalwomenscaucus.org/history.html.

60. "Episcopalians Reject Bid for Women Priests," *Philadelphia Evening Bulletin*, May 19, 1973.

61. Eleanor Blau, "Five Are Nominated by Episcopalians: Disclosure of Bishops' Names Is Break with Precedent," *New York Times*, October 3, 1973.

62. "Episcopal Diocese Appoints New Aide," *Philadelphia Inquirer*, March 13, 1971.

63. Andrew Wallace, "Six Names Are in Running to Head Episcopal Diocese," *Philadelphia Inquirer*, April 5, 1973; Andrew Wallace, "Episcopal Bishop Was Three-Letter Man in College," *Philadelphia Inquirer*, May 12, 1973; Raymond C. Brecht, "Clerical Duty All in Family," *Philadelphia Evening Bulletin*, May 8, 1973; Henry R. Darling, "Bishop Ogilby Elected to Succeed DeWitt," *Philadelphia Sunday Bulletin*, May 6, 1973.

64. Quoted in Andrew Wallace, "Bishop DeWitt to Quit Jan. 1," *Philadelphia Inquirer*, September 29, 1973.

65. Carol Innerst, "Episcopalians to Honor Retiring Bishop DeWitt," *Philadelphia Evening Bulletin*, October 25, 1973.

66. Quoted in Carole Rich, "Balloonist Piccard's Wife to Be Priest," *Philadelphia Evening Bulletin*, July 21, 1974.

67. Marci Shatzman, "Pa. Episcopal Body Hits Plan to Ordain Women," *Philadelphia Evening Bulletin*, July 25, 1974.

68. "Ogilby Warns Bishops on Ordaining 11 Women," *Philadelphia Evening Bulletin*, July 26, 1974.

69. Marci Shotzman [*sic*], "Episcopal Group Cancels Action Against Church," *Philadelphia Evening Bulletin*, July 27, 1974.

70. Paula Herbut, "Pa. Episcopal Diocese Restrains Leader in Dissident Movement," *Philadelphia Evening Bulletin*, March 24, 1979.

71. "Priest Is Defrocked After Switching Faith," *Philadelphia Evening Bulletin*,, November 28, 1979.

72. Marci Shatzman and Carole Rich, "Women Named Episcopal Priests," *Philadelphia Evening Bulletin*, July 29, 1974.

73. Quoted in Marci Shatzman, "Eleven Women Celebrate Unmarred Ordination," *Philadelphia Evening Bulletin*, July 30, 1974.

74. Quoted in "Bishop Is Restricted Because of Ordination," *Philadelphia Evening Bulletin*, August 2, 1974.

75. Marci Shatzman, "DeWitt Raps Bishops for Voiding Ordination," *Philadelphia Evening Bulletin*, August 16, 1974.

76. "Council Debates July 29 Action," *Diocesan News*, November 1974, 1.

77. "Bishop DeWitt, 2 Others Censured," *Philadelphia Inquirer*, September 24, 1975; "Bishops Unit Avoids Women Priest Issue," *Philadelphia Evening Bulletin*, September 25, 1975.

78. "Episcopal Unit Is for Ordaining Women," *New York Times*, October 19, 1974.

79. Marci Shatzman, "Church Faces Uncertain Future on Women Priests," *Philadelphia Evening Bulletin*, August 18, 1974; Carol Innerst, "Thirty File Complaints over 11 Female Priests," *Philadelphia Evening Bulletin*, September 13, 1974.

80. Margaret A. Pala, "New Round: Female Clergy; 'Something I Had to Do,' New Priest Says," *Philadelphia Evening Bulletin*, September 29, 1975.

81. Chapin Day, "Bishop Acquiesces in Rites by Women Priests," *Philadelphia Inquirer*, September 18, 1975.

82. "Episcopalians Unresolved on Women Priests Issue," *Philadelphia Evening Bulletin*, September 29, 1976.

83. Paula Herbut, "'Give Your Holy Spirit to Alice' . . . A Priest," *Philadelphia Evening Bulletin*, January 6, 1977.

84. Dan Stevick, a professor at Episcopal Divinity School in Cambridge from 1974 to 1990 and a participant in the merger, interview by author, July 25, 2008.

10

A Perfect Storm, 1979–2010

DAVID R. CONTOSTA

The upheavals of the 1960s and '70s seemed far away in May 1984, a festive time for the Diocese of Pennsylvania. After months of planning, the diocese was celebrating the two-hundredth anniversary of its founding with a host of events. Beginning on May 5, the entire ground floor of the First Bank of the United States was given over to a comprehensive exhibit of diocesan history called Our Common Prayer. Featured were historic altar settings and portraits of all thirteen bishops to date. There were also numerous photographs and documents that chronicled the life of the church. On May 16 there was a huge celebration at the Philadelphia Civic Center, with banners from every parish in the diocese. The exhibit was co-chaired by the Reverend Frank T. Griswold, then rector of St. Martin-in-the Fields in Chestnut Hill, and his wife, Phoebe. The Griswolds worked with curator Bruce Gill and a number of volunteers.[1]

Four years later, in October 1989, the national church observed the two-hundredth anniversary of its founding in Philadelphia. There was a historical conference at Christ Church on October 18–20. The Most Reverend Robert A. K. Runcie, archbishop of Canterbury, celebrated a convention Eucharist at 5:00 P.M. on Friday evening, October 20, and preached the sermon at the 11:00 A.M. service at Christ Church on Sunday, October 22. The night before, the diocese had hosted a banquet at Fairmount Park's Memorial Hall in honor of the archbishop.[2]

In fact, the divisions and frictions of the previous quarter-century, focusing on racial cleavages, gender equality, urban/suburban population shifts, the new Book of Common Prayer, and scriptural interpretation, had not gone away. Adding to and exacerbating these tensions were disputes over human sexuality and ongoing financial strains. Most of these difficulties would have surfaced regardless of who was leading the diocese and could be considered signs of the times, locally and beyond.

FIGURE 10.1 Two-hundredth anniversary exhibit of the diocese in 1984, housed in the First Bank of the United States in Philadelphia

Together, these forces produced what might be called a perfect storm in the diocese. This term has become well known, thanks to the book *The Perfect Storm* (1997) by Sebastian Junger and a movie (2000) by the same name, adapted from the book. Both dramatized the disappearance at sea of six fishermen from Gloucester, Massachusetts, in October 1991 during an unusually powerful nor'easter. Although the troubles besetting the Diocese of Pennsylvania did not threaten to end any lives, a broader understanding of the term "perfect storm" seems appropriate in summing up the difficulties in which the diocese found itself, defined by one source as "the simultaneous occurrence of events which, taken individually, would be far less powerful than the result of their chance combination."[3]

City and Suburbs

Since the end of World War II, Philadelphia had been experiencing an economic and demographic decline, as thousands of its residents left the city for the surrounding suburbs, or left the metropolitan area altogether for better opportunities outside the region. After reaching an all-time high of nearly 2.1 million people in 1950, Philadelphia had fewer than 1.5 million half a century later. In order to keep urban parishes afloat, the diocese agreed to subsidize a number of them. In February 1981, for example, the Standing Committee voted $5,000 a year to fund the Reverend Geralyn "Gerry" Wolf as vicar at St. Mary's, Bainbridge. Wolf became the first woman to have a full-time position as a priest in the diocese, and before going to St. Mary's she had been the first woman assistant at St. Mary's, Ardmore, and then at St. Martin-in-the-Fields, Chestnut Hill.[4]

Helping to fund the hardest-pressed urban parishes was the Diocesan Coalition for Mission and Ministry (DCMM), established in 1984 to replace the Coalition of Aided Congregations, formed thirteen years before. In addition to administering grants to parishes, the new coalition emphasized the sharing of concerns, solutions, resources, and mutual support. In 1985, thirty-two parishes belonged to the DCMM, under the direction of the Reverend Franklin D. Turner. Twenty of these received financial support from the diocese, ranging from $72,000 for Christ Church in Old City and St. Ambrose in Kensington, to $2,200 for St. James the Less in the East Falls section of Philadelphia.[5]

In 1989, after Turner's election as suffragan bishop, the Reverend John Midwood was appointed archdeacon and worked closely with the DCMM. Six congregations in key locations essential for missionary work were named diocesan missions, and their clergy were funded by the diocese: Advocate, Christ and St. Ambrose, Free Church of St. John, St. Mary's, Chester (coupled with Mision San Pablo), All Souls Church for the Deaf, and St. Gabriel's.[6]

For some parishes, subsidies were not enough, and eighteen of them were closed between 1980 and 2006. Eight other struggling parishes merged, hoping that they could stay afloat by combining resources. During the same period, only four new parishes were founded, with the result that the total number of parishes declined from 170 in 1980 to 153 a quarter-century later. Meanwhile, total diocesan membership slipped during the same period from around 90,000 to approximately 55,000.[7] This more than one-third decline was alarming, but it was very much in line with what was happening in the national Episcopal Church as a whole, which went from 3.3 million members in 1960 to around 2 million forty years later.[8]

What growth there was in the diocese took place mainly in the suburbs, where several new parishes were created and some of the older outlying churches expanded their physical plants to serve new residents, though this growth did not begin to make up for the steep declines elsewhere. In July 1989 the *Diocesan News* featured Holy Spirit, a mission in the Harleysville area of Montgomery County, where the population growth had been 41 percent in the 1970s and 63 percent in the 1980s. Holy Spirit was admitted to the diocese as a parish in 1995.[9]

At St. Mary's, Warwick, some 112 members of the parish, led by a forty-one-year-old cabinet maker named Charles "Rocky" Stone, had built a new church structure and saved themselves about $400,000 in labor costs. At the Church of the Advent in suburban Hatboro, the parish broke ground for a new and larger building in November 1990.[10] The old church was a century old and was simply too small for a growing congregation. In fact, 123 of the 166 churches then in the diocese were more than a hundred years old, forcing even prosperous parishes to undertake capital campaigns for restoration and repair. As of June 2002, thirty parishes, roughly 20 percent of them, were in the process of conducting capital campaigns for that purpose.[11]

Facing Urban Problems

Diocesan conventions attempted to deal with urban problems beyond providing subsidies to needy parishes. At the 1981 convention, delegates approved a resolution urging each congregation to participate in making interest-free loans to the Philadelphia Urban Finance Corporation through the bishop's task force on housing, the first of several initiatives over the past quarter-century to address urban needs. During the preceding year, twelve parishes had contributed a total of $100,000 to this fund.[12] At the same convention, delegates urged the church "to reclaim its ancient tradition of service through a vigorous and creative effort on behalf of our Lord for the poor, the hungry, the sick, and the imprisoned."[13] A decade later, in 1990, the convention urged parishes to invest in the Delaware Valley Community Reinvestment Fund, which made low-interest loans for both housing and new businesses.[14]

The diocese directed its outreach efforts toward specific populations, such as the elderly, the homeless, and those living in depressed neighborhoods. In 1982 the convention endorsed the concept of shared housing for the elderly, "defined as a situation in which two or more related individuals, at least one of whom is 60 years of age or over, live in the same dwelling unit and share kitchen, bathroom, and living areas."[15] In early 1983 the *Diocesan News* reported that food cupboards established in individual parishes to collect canned, dried, and other nonperishable items had assisted 247 families in recent months.[16] The April issue informed readers that the Center for Human Services, the social division of Episcopal Community

Services, had opened a branch office on North Broad Street to serve the neighborhoods of lower Germantown, Logan, Olney, and Nicetown.[17]

In 1984 the convention resolved to "urge and exhort the people of this diocese prayerfully to consider, study, and seek ways and means to help and respond to the needs of the homeless."[18] A resolution on urban ministry in 1989 affirmed the "special warrant for the presence of the church wherever there is an urban concentration of minority peoples and poor."[19]

The *Pennsylvania Episcopalian* highlighted a variety of activities in the city that fulfilled these and other resolutions. One was Winter Shelter, located in the basement of Trinity Memorial Church at Twenty-second and Spruce streets. The facility provided meals, clean clothes, and sleeping quarters for twenty-two homeless men. Staffing it were members of Trinity Memorial, along with volunteers from the First Presbyterian Church, Holy Trinity, Rittenhouse Square, and Temple Beth Zion.[20]

The diocese also acted in 1993 to help finance the construction of 160 new homes for low-income people in North Philadelphia when it lent $1 million for this purpose to Philadelphia Interfaith Action.[21] Meanwhile, individual parishes had contributed some $2.5 million to the Episcopal Community Reinvestment Program, which made loans to various community projects.[22] A dozen years earlier, the Standing Committee of the diocese had invested a quarter of a million dollars in the very similar Philadelphia Urban Finance Corporation.[23]

There were also initiatives on education. The St. Barnabas School had been founded in 1969 following a merger, in Germantown, of St. Luke's and St. Barnabas's (formerly St. Luke's Mission Church to African Americans). The school provided education for kindergarten through sixth grade, mainly for black children whose parents could not afford quality private education. St. Luke's donated the space, and volunteers assisted the teachers in a variety of ways. Unlike a public school, St. Barnabas's could teach "spiritual and ethical development."[24] Unfortunately, owing to financial difficulties, the school had to close in 2006.

The diocese continued to reach out to Philadelphia's Hispanic community. At various times in the past, a rector who could speak at least some Spanish had ministered to the Spanish-speaking residents of a surrounding neighborhood, but when he or she left, these outreach efforts would come to an end. Then, in 1976, Mision San Pablo in Chester, where there was a growing Puerto Rican population, engaged a native Spanish speaker as vicar. He was the Reverend Elias Penalosa, a Peruvian-born priest who was then a chaplain at the University of Puerto Rico. In 1978 Penalosa became director of the Diocesan Hispanic Mission, and in 1980 he also became

FIGURE 10.2 The Reverend Elias Penalosa and children at Mision San Pablo, Chester, Pennsylvania

FIGURE 10.3 Bishop Hart confirming inmates at Graterford Prison, Philadelphia

rector of Christ Church and St. Ambrose at Sixth and Venango streets in Philadelphia, an area with a large Puerto Rican population. Later, the Reverend Carlos Santos-Rivera became rector of this growing parish.[25]

To minister to those in prison, the diocese established, in 1995, a congregation at Philadelphia's Graterford Prison, which had been a diocesan mission for many years. With some forty inmate members, it took the name of Mission Congregation of St. Dismas. The following year, St. Dismas's was "yoked" with St. Mary's, Bainbridge Street, whose vicar, the Reverend Julius W. Jackson, served both congregations, which were added to the roster of diocesan missions.[26]

Addressing Racism

The diocese attempted to deal with the question of race in a variety of ways. In 1984 the Standing Committee appropriated $10,000 to aid the victims of the bombing of MOVE headquarters on Philadelphia's Osage Avenue.[27] In an effort to break a standoff with this radical African American commune, police had dropped explosives on a fortified section of the roof of the MOVE row houses. The fire soon got out of control and destroyed sixty-two neighborhood homes. Six adults and five children in the MOVE houses were also killed.

At the 1989 convention, a resolution called on the entire diocese to adopt an affirmative action program for hiring, based on the Equal Employment Policy and Affirmative Action Program passed by the General Convention of the national church in 1982 and 1988.[28] Three years later, the African Episcopal Church of St. Thomas in West Philadelphia, a historically black congregation founded by Absalom Jones in 1792, hosted the kickoff for the national bicentennial celebration of black presence in the Episcopal Church. Held on November 4–8, the celebration included the installation of Jones's portrait in the State Capitol at Harrisburg, and a play based on Jones's life. There was also a conference on the challenges faced by black Episcopalians in the 1990s. The climax was a service of celebration and thanksgiving at the Church of the Advocate in North Philadelphia. The Right Reverend Barbara Harris, suffragan bishop of Massachusetts, preached, and officiating was the Right Reverend Franklin D. Turner, suffragan bishop of Pennsylvania, the first African American bishop in the diocese. Bishop Harris was also an African American, and in 1989 had become the first woman in the Anglican Church to become a bishop. She challenged the whole church "to get into the forefront of the struggle for justice locally and globally."[29]

In 1995 racism was the Lenten study focus in the diocese. An article in the *Pennsylvania Episcopalian* stated that although racism was less overt than in the past, it was "no less virulent." "Barely recognized prejudices," it added, "and ingrained habits on the part of the privileged can create an exclusive atmosphere where any strangers—especially persons of a different color or ethnic background—end up feeling marginalized." To combat these subtler forms of racism, the diocese sent copies of a study guide on racism to all parishes. There was also a diocesan conference on racism held on Saturday, March 4, at the Church of the Saviour. The principal speaker at the conference was David Booth Beers, chancellor to the presiding bishop, who focused on what the House of Bishops had called "the sin of racism" in their recent pastoral letter.[30] Six years later, in January, April, and October 2001, the diocese held a series of two-day workshops at St. Luke's and the Epiphany for parish staff and members of committees and commissions that explored the reality of personal and institutional racism. These workshops were mandated by resolutions at the 1999 diocesan convention and the 2000 General Convention. Altogether, the diocese spent $250,000 on these workshops, which were mandatory for all clergy, as well as for those seeking ordination.[31]

To combat racism in South Africa, the diocesan convention had passed resolutions in 1985 and 1986 urging all congregations and institutions in the diocese to protest apartheid in South Africa by divesting themselves of corporations doing business in that country. The 1986 resolution spoke about the "evil of apartheid" and expressed "solidarity with Archbishop Desmond Tutu and other courageous leaders in South Africa and Namibia working for non-violent change." Bishop Tutu had been one of the featured speakers at the diocesan bicentennial celebrations the year before.[32] The tactic of divestiture was based on the Sullivan principles, developed in 1977 by the Reverend Leon Sullivan (1922–2001), pastor of the Zion Baptist Church in Philadelphia. These principles became widely recognized as one of the most effective contributions to dismantling apartheid in South Africa.

The Diocese and International Affairs

Diocesan concerns also extended far beyond the local area. In 1981 the convention endorsed a freeze on the development of nuclear weapons and nuclear weapons systems. This resolution was part of a national nuclear freeze movement that emerged in direct reaction to a 1979 decision by the United States and its NATO allies to deploy nearly six hundred nuclear weapons in western Europe, as well as to the Reagan administration's criticisms of the Strategic Arms Limitations Treaties, which had substantially slowed the nuclear arms race.[33]

The convention's 1981 resolution directed the bishop to appoint a committee "to establish a peace initiative by providing clergy and laity . . . with peace-oriented education programs and opportunities for action," and to designate a staff person to coordinate such a program. There was a follow-up resolution the next year, which the convention sent to the president and vice president of the United States, members of the U.S. Congress representing districts within the diocese, the secretary-general of the United Nations, and the chairman of the Presidium of the Soviet Union.

In March 1982, at the invitation of the Philadelphia yearly meeting of the Society of Friends, approximately 750 Episcopalians joined a crowd of about fifteen thousand on Independence Mall for a candlelight interfaith vigil against the nuclear arms race, as part of a massive nationwide demonstration.[34] John Cardinal Krol, head of the local Catholic archdiocese, gave the principal address. He concluded by saying, "I pray that we may speak with one voice, the voice of human conscience, in persuading our political leaders and decision makers to change directions, to make a moral about-face."[35] In January of that year, a group had assembled to reestablish a chapter of the Episcopal Peace Fellowship, which had been active during the Vietnam War. Its organizers were Mary Austin, Margaret Sheets, the Reverend Thomas McClellan, and the Reverend Charles Pickett.[36]

In 1985 the diocesan convention passed a resolution in support of the Episcopal Diocese of Nicaragua, which had called on all nations to "refrain from economic and military interference in Nicaragua, . . . and that the entire Anglican Communion influence its members, their communities and governments to help in fostering peace in Central America." The following year the convention specifically called on the U.S. government to stop all aid to the Contras or any other military forces in Nicaragua and to seek a negotiated settlement.[37]

In defiance of specific congressional legislation, the Reagan administration had been illegally and surreptitiously selling arms to Iran and using the money from these sales to aid the Contras in Nicaragua, a right-wing group that fought against and ultimately overthrew the legally elected, left-wing Sandinista Party under Daniel Ortega, president of the country. Revelations of these actions resulted in the Iran-Contra Affair, though the very popular Ronald Reagan remained largely unscathed, and no one in his administration was punished.

Iraq's invasion of Kuwait in 1990 prompted the convention to condemn this act of aggression under Iraqi leader Saddam Hussein, but it also urged the United States to work for a peaceful solution to this crisis in the Persian Gulf region. The resolution quoted Archbishop of Canterbury Robert Runcie's call for prayer: "No matter how turbulent the world or how painful the choices, it is through the grace of God that we are made instruments of peace in the ambiguities of a world made dangerous by human folly and wickedness." When the United States did enter what would later be called the First Gulf War, in February 1991, Bishop Allen Bartlett issued a statement through the *Pennsylvania Episcopalian:* "We must give support to our courageous men and women in the armed forces. . . .

At the same time, we must do all we can to see that the cause of long-term peace and justice in the Middle East, in the name of which this was undertaken, is not lost. As Christians, we have a special responsibility to see that this does not become a religious war." On Ash Wednesday, February 17, churches throughout the diocese began an around-the-clock prayer vigil for peace in the Persian Gulf. Parishes volunteered to cover a particular day, with individuals offering continuous prayers. "At every moment, day and night," Bartlett wrote, "someone will be holding up before God all the persons and issues in this complex and tangled web of violence, seeking God's reign of peace with justice."[38] The diocese also repeatedly adopted resolutions urging peace and justice in the Israeli-Palestinian struggle, and a Middle East study group brought in speakers from the region.[39]

Additional forms of outreach beyond national boundaries included the alliances between the Diocese of Pennsylvania and Anglican dioceses abroad. In 1993 the diocese allied with the companion Diocese of Mityana, Uganda, and in 1996 with the Diocese of Guatemala. Many parishes became very active in the Guatemalan pairing. By 2007 the Diocese of Guatemala had grown so large that two suffragan bishops had to be appointed.[40]

* * * * *

The Right Reverend Allen L. Bartlett Jr.

Allen Bartlett became bishop coadjutor in early 1986 and diocesan bishop a year later. Before coming to Philadelphia, he served parishes in his native Alabama and in West Virginia, and was dean of the Episcopal Cathedral in Louisville, Kentucky. Because, unlike his recent predecessors, Bartlett did not come as a bishop from another diocese, he became the first person since Gillespie Armstrong (see chapter 8) to be consecrated by the Episcopal Church in Philadelphia. The ceremony making him bishop coadjutor took place on February 15, 1986, at the city's old convention hall, with sixty-five hundred persons in attendance, including the presiding bishop, Edmond Browning.

SOURCE: *Diocesan News*, January, February, and March, 1985.

* * * * *

Mission Strategy

Shortly after becoming bishop, Bartlett formed the Diocesan Mission Strategy Commission, which reported to the diocesan convention in October 1987. Among other things, the commission called for the development of two to four new congregations, an expanded ministry to Hispanics, the creation of an Asian congregation, new ministries of peace, justice, and love, a more permanent location for Church House, a cathedral, and a conference center. A bishop's mission campaign raised $1.9 million to assist in reaching these goals, and most of them were accomplished over the next decade.[41]

Cathedral and Church House

Clearly, one of Bartlett's most significant accomplishments was naming the Church of the Saviour a cathedral for the diocese.[42] The idea of building a cathedral in Roxborough (see chapter 7) had long since been abandoned, and for a number of years the diocese had used this spacious Italian Romanesque-style church (rebuilt in 1906), in West Philadelphia at Thirty-eighth and Chestnut streets, for large meetings and assemblages, including the annual diocesan conventions. The Church of the Saviour could seat eight hundred people, was near bus and subway stops, could utilize several public parking lots, had a significant endowment, and was located in a multicultural neighborhood close to University City (the campuses of Drexel University and the University of Pennsylvania). Bartlett believed that the cathedral would become an "instrument of unity for the whole diocese" and would "magnify" the diocesan voice when it chose to speak to the wider public.[43] In the presence of a large congregation, it was dedicated on January 1, 1992, as the Cathedral Church of the Saviour.

Bartlett's successor, the Right Reverend Charles E. Bennison Jr., and the cathedral's dean, Richard Giles, had the interior of the Church of the Saviour extensively renovated. The renovations were completed in 2002 and provoked some criticism. The Preservation Alliance of Greater Philadelphia complained that they created "an atmosphere that never existed [in the past]." Giles responded that the simplification of the church's once elaborate interior decoration would allow the liturgy to speak more clearly, thus putting the focus on the "Word." What's more, the renovations made it possible to rearrange the interior of the building for many different kinds of functions.[44]

FIGURE 10.4 Cathedral Church of the Saviour, Philadelphia

FIGURE 10.5 Church House

Several months after the renovations were completed, in September 2002, Elizabeth Doering, the artist in residence at the cathedral, conceived and crafted a unique memorial to the victims of the September 11, 2001, terrorists attacks, who included 40 persons in western Pennsylvania on Flight 93, some of whom had bravely wrested control of their plane from the terrorists and deliberately crashed it into a field. Calling it *Initiation*, Doering created her memorial by melting pewter and lowering drops of it into cold water. Some of the drops, each of them uniquely shaped, came out looking like buds, others like angel wings. It was blessed and installed in the cathedral on the one-year anniversary of the 9/11 tragedy.[45]

In April 1986 the diocese had established a Christian Education Resources Center at the Church of the Saviour, after eighteen months of planning coordinated by Phoebe Griswold and Helen White of St. Martin-in-the-Fields.[46] The center had begun with an ad hoc committee in 1983, chaired by Ruth Fiesel. The center, with its curriculum resources, was later transferred to Church House in center city.[47]

Bishop Bartlett succeeded in moving the diocesan headquarters from the twenty-sixth floor of a large office building at 1700 Market Street, where they had been located since moving out of Rittenhouse Square in 1974. The new facility, Church House, consisted of two connected historic residences, the four-story Shippen-Wistar House and the five-story Morris-Cadwallader House. The purchase price of $2.1 million, as well as the $500,000 cost of renovations, came mainly from the sale of the leasehold on the Rittenhouse Square property fifteen years before.[48]

Plans to open new parishes bore fruit with the establishment of St. Dismas's at Philadelphia's Graterford Prison in 1995, St. Martin's Episcopal Korean Congregation in 1990, and Holy Spirit, Harleysville, in 1995. Another goal achieved was the School for the Diaconate, initiated under the Reverend Peyton Craighill in 1988. More than twenty vocational deacons were eventually ordained in this program of outreach and servant ministry. A much revitalized youth ministry initiated an annual bishop's ball, acolyte festival, "happening retreat," and summer camp, among other activities.[49]

The Challenges of Sexuality

Official diocesan pronouncements on race relations and foreign affairs did not appear to provoke any widespread criticism or dissatisfaction among Episcopalians in the Philadelphia area. The situation was very different with the diocese's evolving position on homosexuality and gay and lesbian rights. In 1981 the General Convention had passed a resolution condemning campaigns against homosexuals by individuals and institutions calling themselves Christian. The resolution called upon "Christians and all people of conscience to refrain from participating in or supporting campaigns intended to foster ill-will toward homosexual persons and to join us in recommitting ourselves to the cause of full civil rights for members of the gay community and an end to discrimination against homosexual persons within the church."[50] This call for justice toward the gay community was repeated at the 1986 convention and was coupled with a condemnation of discrimination against individuals suffering from AIDS, a disease particularly prevalent within the gay community.[51] In December of that year the diocese held a full-day teaching conference on the AIDS crisis at the Church of the Saviour, attended by more than a hundred clergy and laypeople. In 1989 the convention proclaimed November 8 as "a day of prayer and intercession for the AIDS crisis," and a year later it called upon employers not to discriminate against persons with AIDS and to grant them the same rights and benefits as other employees.[52]

John Harrison, the chancellor of the diocese and a member of St. Paul's, Chestnut Hill, proposed a resolution for the 1988 General Convention of the national church that would have the denomination "affirm stable, loving and committed relationships . . . regardless of whether or not their relationship was sexual."[53] Learning of Harrison's plans, the vestry of All Saints, Wynnewood, a conservative parish on the Philadelphia Main Line, protested it with an advertisement in the *Episcopalian.* In response to this and other expressions of opposition, Harrison resigned as chancellor, and in July the national church's Commission on Human Affairs and Health voted not to bring the resolution before the convention.[54]

In the spring of 1989 Bishop Bartlett appointed a fourteen-member commission on human sexuality, chaired by the Reverend Richard Kirk of Advent, Kennett Square, made up of seven clergy and an equal number of laypersons.[55] A little more than two years later, in the fall of 1991, the diocese launched a dialogue about sexuality, as directed by the General Convention of the national church the previous summer. This mandate was partly in response to the highly publicized ordination of an openly gay man, Robert Williams, by Bishop John Spong in Hoboken, New Jersey, and the ordination a year later, by Bishop Walter Righter of Newark, New Jersey, of a gay man to the diaconate.[56] By the summer of 1993, sixty-eight of the 166 parishes in the diocese had held dialogues. Although the participants generally approved of the church's being a "safe place" in which to talk about sexuality, their conclusions were otherwise mixed. The *Pennsylvania Episcopalian* reported that "while some found evidence in the Bible for a liberal view of matters of faith and morals, others affirmed traditional standards of morality and decried what was seen as the increasingly permissive stance of the Church."[57]

Bishop Bartlett's decision in 1993 to ordain, as a deacon, James B. Robertson, a gay man in a committed relationship of twenty years, stirred further opposition from conservative parishes in the diocese. In a letter to diocesan clergy, Bartlett explained that he had decided to go ahead with the ordination after Robertson had met all the qualifications for the diaconate, including psychological examinations and approvals by the commission on ministry and the Standing Committee. He added that the ordination did not violate any canon of the diocese or of the national church.[58]

Those who took a more conservative view of sexuality formed a group called Concerned Episcopalians, led by Hartley S. Connett and

Mary E. Walmsley of Good Samaritan, Paoli, and the Reverend Gary L'Hommedieu, rector of Atonement in Morton, Delaware County. When Bishop Bartlett ordained to the priesthood David J. Morris, a gay man in a committed relationship, Concerned Episcopalians brought official charges in 1996 against the bishop, maintaining that he had "violated his ordination vows, the Constitution and Canons of the Episcopal Church, and the rubrics of the Book of Common Prayer." In declining to take any action on the charges, Presiding Bishop Edmond Browning referred to the decision in the recent trial of Bishop Walter Righter. Righter had been brought up on similar charges but had been acquitted in May of that year, according to the ecclesiastical court, because there was no church doctrine forbidding the ordination of "non-celibate homosexuals."[59]

Good Shepherd, Rosemont, which also opposed the church's stance on homosexuality, refused to pay its diocesan assessment in 1993 because of "theological disagreements."[60] David Moyer, the rector of Good Shepherd, also refused to allow visitations by any of the bishops from the diocese. The immediate catalyst for this action was Bishop Bartlett's ordination of James Robertson to the diaconate that year. But Good Shepherd and other conservative parishes had also been offended in 1989 when Bartlett served as one of the co-consecrators of Barbara Harris, the first woman bishop in the worldwide Anglican Communion, as suffragan bishop of Massachusetts.[61]

Good Shepherd and other members of Concerned Episcopalians in the local diocese were not alone in the national church. Meeting in Denver in April 1990, a "traditionalist" group called the Episcopal Synod of America (ESA) voted to seek the creation of a tenth "non-geographical province" in the national church as "the only way for keeping together people of diametrically opposed theological outlooks."[62] By 1997 nine parishes in the Diocese of Pennsylvania had affiliated with the ESA: All Saints, Wynnewood; Atonement, Morton; Good Shepherd, Rosemont; Redemption, Southampton; St. James the Less in East Falls, Philadelphia; St. John's, Huntington Valley; St. John's, Norristown; St. Luke's, Newtown; and St. Paul's, Chester. These parishes ranged widely in socioeconomic makeup and in churchmanship, some describing themselves as Anglo-Catholic and others as low church. However, most of them (six of nine) either continued to use the 1928 prayer book or preferred the more traditional language of the Rite I Eucharist from the 1979 book. The same six parishes emphasized that their understanding of faith and worship was grounded in the Bible. In three cases, the parishes emphasized their devotion to both scripture and traditional liturgies. In brief parish histories, compiled for a 1997 diocesan publication, these ESA parishes tended to use the words "tradition" and "traditional" to describe themselves, probably code words to express their opposition to women clergy and the ordination of homosexuals.

In the summer of 1997, about a hundred delegates from the ESA met at Good Shepherd, where they again voted to seek a tenth province for "dioceses and parishes unhappy with . . . the liberal agenda of the Episcopal Church." In an open letter to the wider Anglican Communion, the synod charged that the General Convention of the national church, which had recently met in Philadelphia, had "refused to uphold orthodox doctrine and restore godly discipline, while acting to persecute the faithful." The letter went on to condemn the General Convention for passing resolutions to study the blessing of same-sex unions and to allow dioceses to provide insurance coverage for the domestic partners of both clergy and lay gay and lesbian employees. It also reiterated the ESA's opposition to the ordination of women, which the 1997 General Convention had voted to mandate in the national canons.

Between 1994 and 1997, as a temporary measure, Bishop Bartlett agreed to allow local parishes to be visited by an ESA bishop, in exchange for their agreeing to pay their assessments to the diocese. Conducting these visitations, at Bartlett's official invitation, was the Right Reverend Donald Parsons, a retired Anglo-Catholic from the Diocese of Quincy, Illinois.[63]

* * * * *

Sexuality and the Episcopal Church

> The Episcopal Church began addressing sexuality at its 1973 General Convention, and at the 1976 convention it declared that "homosexual persons are children of God" entitled to pastoral care and legal protection in the larger society. The following year, Paul Moore, the diocesan bishop of New York, ordained Ellen Barrett to the diaconate, knowing that she was a lesbian. This unleashed a howl of protest from dozens of bishops around the country and forced delegates to the 1979 General Convention to speak more directly to the issue. The result was a compromise resolution, which stated that a homosexual orientation was acceptable but that homosexual activity was not, and forbade the ordination of anyone, gay or straight, engaging in sexual relations outside marriage.
>
> Liberal bishops objected to this compromise, and when Walter Righter, assistant bishop of the Diocese of Newark, New Jersey,

ordained an openly gay man to the diaconate in September 1990, a group of conservative bishops brought formal charges of heresy against him. After a long, drawn-out judicial process, a church court made up of eight bishops exonerated Righter. In their majority opinion the "judges" distinguished between core doctrines of the church, defined as "essential, unchangeable Christian truths that were expressed in ancient documents such as the Nicene Creed," and mere "doctrinal teachings" that changed over time, such as teachings that had once upheld slavery or condemned divorce and contraception. For a doctrinal teaching to be binding, they added, it had to be a canon or in the Book of Common Prayer, and since there was no doctrinal teaching that clearly forbade the ordination of homosexuals, Righter and others who ordained gay men and lesbians could not be held in violation of church law.

Anglicans in the Third World, and especially in Africa, where the greatest growth has occurred in the church in recent years, were generally opposed to these views. This divide became very apparent at the eighteenth Lambeth Conference of the worldwide Anglican Communion, held in England from July 18 to August 9, 1998. While there was agreement that homosexuals were "full members of the Body of Christ," the conference's final resolution on sexuality declared that homosexual practice is incompatible with scripture, that abstinence is the proper state for those not called to marriage, and that the conference could not advise "the legitimizing or blessing of same-sex unions, nor the ordination of those involved in such unions." The resolution passed overwhelmingly by a vote of 526 to 70, with forty-five abstentions. The breach between the Americans and other delegates was exacerbated further when the General Convention of the Episcopal Church USA, meeting in Minneapolis, Minnesota, in August 2003, voted to confirm the election of V. Gene Robinson, a gay man living in a committed relationship, as bishop of New Hampshire. Presiding Bishop Frank T. Griswold was among those voting to confirm.

Three years later, in Columbus, Ohio, the General Convention, in response to a request by the archbishop of Canterbury and other Anglican leaders to declare a moratorium on the ordination of gay bishops, arrived at a consensus to call for restraint in electing gay bishops in the future. At this 2006 meeting the national church also elected its first woman as presiding bishop, Katharine Jefferts

Schori, then bishop of Nevada. Schori's election seemed sure to widen the breach within the worldwide Anglican Communion and to further exacerbate rifts within the American church.

SOURCES: See David Hein and Gardiner H. Shattuck Jr., *The Episcopalians* (Westport, Conn.: Praeger, 2004), 143–46.

* * * * *

A New Bishop

Bartlett's successor would most assuredly have to cope with the ongoing controversy over homosexuality and the church, and with the larger debate between liberals and conservatives within the diocese. In 1995 Bartlett called for the election of a bishop coadjutor, who would succeed him as diocesan bishop.

* * * * *

The Right Reverend Charles E. Bennison Jr.

In November 1996 the diocesan convention selected Charles E. Bennison Jr. as bishop coadjutor. The favorite-son candidate was John E. Midwood, archdeacon of the diocese, who had had considerable support at the convention.

Bennison, who was fifty-two years old when elected coadjutor, came from Episcopal Divinity School in Cambridge, Massachusetts, where he was director of congregational studies and associate professor of pastoral theology. Previous to that he had been a rector in Atlanta, Georgia, and in Upland, California. Bennison became diocesan bishop upon Bishop Bartlett's retirement in May 1998.

SOURCE: *Pennsylvania Episcopalian*, October 1995, November 1996.

* * * * *

When Charles Bennison heard that he was among the final candidates for bishop coadjutor, he launched a thorough study of the diocese by reading convention journals and various diocesan reports. He also visited the

FIGURE 10.6 Bishop Allen L. Bartlett Jr., Suffragan Bishop Franklin D. Turner, and Bishop Charles E. Bennison Jr.

Philadelphia area and drove around to see as many of the churches as he could find. This self-guided tour gave him an initial sense of the tremendous variety among the 166 parishes then in the diocese—urban, suburban, and rural; white, African American, Hispanic; large and small; poor and affluent; high and low church; with "seemingly an Episcopal Church in every neighborhood," as he put it later.[64] Superimposed on these impressions—and reinforcing them—was the fact that the Diocese of Pennsylvania was the smallest in land area in the United States, even though it was the fifth-largest in membership, meaning that it was extraordinarily well populated with Episcopal parishes.

Bennison believed that the large number and diverse nature of local parishes stemmed from several factors. One was the lack of a religious monopoly in early Pennsylvania, where all religions were tolerated, in contrast to New England, with its Puritan establishment, and to most of the South, with its Anglican establishment. Another factor was Quaker individualism in southeastern Pennsylvania, which may have engendered a lack of respect for hierarchy and a belief in institutional fragmentation. As a consequence, Bennison reflected, "The diocese is more an association of individual parishes than it is a unit itself."[65] Yet another explanation was the intense consciousness of neighborhood in a city that in 1854 had annexed, but never really digested, several dozen formerly independent communities.

These local trends, Bennison thought, were both positive and negative. In a city where people hesitated to leave their own neighborhoods to worship, the large number of Episcopal parishes had facilitated evangelism. But to Bennison's way of thinking, this proliferation of churches was inefficient when it came to finances and utilization of clergy. Thus, when certain neighborhoods in center city began to lose population after 1950, and large parts of North and West Philadelphia underwent shifts in their ethnic, racial, or socioeconomic composition, many parishes lost so many members that they had no choice but to close.

Divisions and Schisms

The large number of Episcopal parishes, many of them relatively close together, had also produced an intense competition for members, Bennison believed, and the creation of "niche churches" that went out of their way to differentiate themselves from those nearby. As a result, there were high churches that were liberal and high churches that were conservative; upscale African American parishes and less affluent African American churches; and parishes that welcomed homosexuals and those openly opposed to homosexuality.

The threat of schism extended well beyond the local diocese to the national church. Heading the national church as presiding bishop, beginning in 1998, was Frank Tracy Griswold III, who had been bishop of Chicago since 1984. Griswold had grown up in suburban Radnor, Pennsylvania. Before going to Chicago, he had been rector of St. Martin-in-the-Fields, Chestnut Hill, and before that, rector of St. Andrew's, Yardley. He was well known in the diocese, having served as chair of its liturgical commission, and as such he had spoken to a number of parishes about liturgical reform. Griswold was also one of the authors of Eucharistic Prayer B in the 1979 Book of Common Prayer.[66]

* * * * *

The 1997 General Convention in Philadelphia

The Diocese of Pennsylvania enthusiastically hosted the General Convention at the Pennsylvania Convention Center in the summer of 1997, which elected native son Frank Griswold as presiding bishop of the national church. Eighteen hundred volunteers turned out, astonishing the national church's New York staff. "Pennsylvania Night," ending at the Museum of Art, showed the delegates the best side of Philadelphia. One factor in selecting Philadelphia for the General Convention had been the very successful meeting of the House of Bishops hosted by the diocese eight years before, in 1989.

SOURCE: Allen L. Bartlett Jr. to author, January 27, 2007.

* * * * *

Both Griswold and Bennison had first experienced divisions in the worldwide Anglican Communion while attending the thirteenth Lambeth Conference in 1998, held every ten years by the archbishop of Canterbury at Lambeth Palace in London. Bennison worked with a subgroup on the sexuality report. Although this group labored to come up with a compromise that recognized different positions on sexuality, in a plenary session several conservative bishops succeeded in changing the wording of the resolution to read, "Homosexual practice is incompatible with Scripture." Bennison was disappointed with this change as well as with another Lambeth resolution that opposed the ordination of women.[67]

Back home, Bennison had to deal with continuing problems at St. James the Less in the East Falls section of Philadelphia, a superb architectural example of the early Gothic Revival in the United States. On April 25, 1999, the vestry of this Anglo-Catholic parish voted unanimously to disaffiliate from the Episcopal Church USA. Although the parish had belonged to the ESA, St. James's (and the ESA itself) had remained within the Episcopal Church. But now the St. James's vestry cited the General Convention's passage of a resolution mandating the ordination of women as among the several events that "led us to believe that there really is no longer a place for us in the Episcopal Church." The refusal of the diocesan convention in 1998 to seat their delegates because of nonpayment of the diocesan assessment was another justification cited by the St. James's vestry. Bishop Bennison responded by requesting a parish meeting to express his sadness over the decision and to hold out the possibility of reconciliation.[68] The following year, however, St. James's voted to disaffiliate from the Episcopal Church and acted illegally to establish a "dummy" corporation and to merge the parish corporation into it so that they could claim to own the parish property independently of the diocese. In 2001 the diocese filed suit to seize its property, and the case eventually went to the Pennsylvania Supreme Court, which ruled in favor of the diocese in early 2006.[69]

Meanwhile, the diocesan policy of allowing an outside, or "flying," bishop to make visitations to the ESA parishes in the diocese expired in 1997. Bennison did not renew it because he believed that the policy had caused the disaffected parishes to become "more distant, alienated, [and] estranged" instead of drawing them closer to the diocese.[70] When Good Shepherd, Rosemont, refused to allow Bennison to visit or to pay its diocesan assessments, he informed the Standing Committee. Invoking diocesan canon IV.10, he formally deposed from the ministry its rector, David Moyer, on September 4, 2002, in the presence of two priests, as required by the canon. In response, the vestry of Good Shepherd passed a unanimous resolution stating that Moyer remained their rector.[71]

Anglican-Lutheran Concordat

At the same time that internal schisms threatened the Anglican Communion, the Episcopal Church and the Evangelical Lutheran Church in America agreed to full communion, a culmination of discussions that had begun three decades earlier.[72] Following this historic decision, the Diocese of Pennsylvania joined with the Southeast Pennsylvania Synod of the Evangelical Lutheran Church in America in several cooperative ventures. In 2000, even before the concordat between the two denominations became official the following year, the diocese joined with the local Lutheran synod to address issues in Philadelphia's public schools that had arisen from unequal school funding in Pennsylvania, as wealthier school districts were able to supplement state funding with their larger property tax revenues.[73] In 2003 a chair of Anglican studies was established at the Lutheran Theological Seminary in the Mt. Airy section of Philadelphia. This was made possible by a bequest of $1.2 million from the estate of Anna Werner, who had lived in a modest home in the working-class Rhawnhurst section of Philadelphia.[74] Three years later the diocese leased space for its archives in a newly built Lutheran archive at the Mt. Airy seminary. Facilitating these cooperative ventures was the Reverend Claire Burkat, a Lutheran pastor and mission director for the two denominations, who spent half her time working with the Episcopal diocese and half with the Lutheran Synod of Southeastern Pennsylvania. In October 2006 Burkat became the synod's bishop.

Stormy Waters

Although the cooperation with Lutherans was a very happy and positive turn of events for the diocese, it was counterbalanced by continuing disagreements over the budget, which in turn reflected disagreements over program priorities. One of these issues concerned the decision to purchase Camp Wapiti, a 618-acre waterfront tract along Chesapeake Bay in Maryland. The diocese purchased the property in early 2003 for $6 million. Half the amount came from the diocese and the other half from a grant from the Conservation Fund in Washington, D.C.[75]

The search for a suitable diocesan camp that could be used by individuals and groups of all ages, but especially by youth, went back to 1954, when the diocese acquired, through donation, the fifty-four-acre Denbigh Estate in Radnor Township. Because of mounting maintenance costs, the diocese sold Denbigh in 1972 for $800,000, and the proceeds were placed in the Denbigh Fund, which was worth about $2 million by 2003. It was this money, along with an additional $1 million from unrestricted diocesan endowment funds, that the diocese used to come up with the $3 million for Camp Wapiti. In a memorandum to the diocesan council, Chandler Joyner, the diocese's chief financial officer, wrote that the purchase of the camp "should pose no significant hazard to the financial health of the diocese."[76] In case of financial difficulties, he added, the diocese could always sell part of the land at tremendous financial gain. The camp dedication took place on October 16, 2004.[77]

The decision to purchase Wapiti was part of a larger strategic plan approved by the 2003 diocesan convention and called "our holy experiment," a term borrowed from Pennsylvania's founder, William Penn. In addition to the camp, the plan called for the strengthening of congregations through the creation of new parishes, and the expansion and upgrading of some older parishes. The recently acquired cathedral site would be developed further by acquiring adjacent properties and by constructing a high-rise office building that could house the diocesan headquarters, while the rest of the building could be rented as office space and provide steady income. Finally, the plan called for the establishment of campus ministries at a number of colleges and universities in the Philadelphia area.[78]

Although the plan was both bold and forward looking, it did not please all constituencies in the diocese and in fact exacerbated a number of preexisting cleavages. This was especially true of Camp Wapiti, which many of the urban parishes, dependent on diocesan financial support, saw as a facility that would divert funds away from them. Since many of the aided urban parishes had substantial African American congregations, the camp became a racial issue, with claims that it would provide recreation primarily for white, suburban parishioners. The emphasis on diocesan planning also raised old tensions between congregational autonomy and central control. If this were not enough, unhappiness over what more conservative parishes saw as liberal diocesan stances on sexual and gender issues continued to flare. Some dissatisfied individuals reduced or discontinued their pledges to individual parishes, while some parishes withheld their contribution to the diocese.[79] Especially revealing was the decline in the total annual diocesan budget from $3,762,000 in 2000 to $2,832,000 in 2007. Although part of the decline could be attributed to a lower return on endowment funds, income from parish donations was $350,000 lower in 2007 than what had been pledged initially for that year.[80]

Difficulties and disagreements in the diocese came to a head in January 2006, when the ten-member Standing Committee voted unanimously to ask for Bishop Bennison's resignation, alleging that he had repeatedly circumvented the committee's authority and had misused and misappropriated diocesan funds, most especially endowment money. When Bennison declined to resign, the committee asked the presiding bishop to remove him, citing a "total breakdown of trust" between themselves and the bishop. A separate accusation, brought by others in the diocese, charged that Bennison had "engaged in conduct unbecoming a member of the clergy" while rector of a parish in Upland, California, in the early 1970s. They alleged that Bennison had done nothing to stop his brother, John Bennison, a seminarian and youth minister in his parish, from sexually abusing, over a period of several years, a teenage girl in the congregation. Furthermore, they charged, he knew about the abuse at the time and had covered it up to protect both his brother and himself.

A review committee of the national church dismissed the charges brought by the Standing Committee, finding that other officials in the diocese had either approved of or gone along with Bennison's financial decisions, and that he alone could not be held accountable. However, the review committee did decide that Bennison should face charges relating to the sexual misconduct of his brother. In October 2007 Presiding Bishop Katharine Jefferts Schori "inhibited" (suspended) Bennison as bishop, pending an ecclesiastical trial. The trial took place over four days (June 9–12, 2008) at the Philadelphia Marriott Hotel, only the third such trial of a bishop in the history of the Episcopal Church. He faced a panel of nine judges made up of five bishops, two priests, and two laypeople. Five of the judges were women. Testifying in his own defense, Bennison said that he had acted in accordance with the standards of the 1970s and that he had not wanted to shame the girl by confronting her or by telling her parents about the abuse.[81] The nine-judge panel found Bennison guilty.[82] In late July 2010 a church court of appeals, meeting in Wilmington, Delaware, overturned the conviction because the canonical statute of limitations of ten years had long since expired. Bennison returned as bishop the following month.

How this most recent storm would play out was unclear, but there could be some comfort in knowing that Episcopal Diocese of Pennsylvania had survived other grave crises during its more than two-century history. During the colonial period, local Anglicans had struggled with a constant clergy shortage and the lack of an American bishop to provide unity and discipline. The Revolution forced clergy and laity alike to chose between their established church, whose head was the king of England, and the rebel movement. Following independence, the great challenge was how to become a separate American branch of the Anglican Communion. The nineteenth century brought discord over racial prejudice in the church, and over drawn-out, often dramatic disputes between high- and low-church factions. Two world wars and the Great Depression presented serious challenges during the first half of the twentieth century, followed by the cold war and new conflicts in Korea and Vietnam. Postwar suburbanization demanded the creation of new parishes, while older congregations in Philadelphia struggled with declining membership, changing neighborhoods, and aging physical plants. In the latter decades of the twentieth century and the first years of the twenty-first, disagreements flared over race, gender, and sexuality, as well as the continuing tension between the needs of individual congregations and those of the diocese as a whole.

In truth, there have been few periods in the past when the Diocese of Pennsylvania did not face some serious challenge. There was no reason to believe that the present and future would be any different. It is to be hoped that new challenges will be addressed in the spirit of broad toleration and respectful dialogue that has characterized the Anglican tradition at its best.

NOTES

1. See *Diocesan News* (*DN*), April, May, and June 1984.
2. *DN*, September, October, and December 1989.
3. This definition is from the online encyclopedia Wikipedia.
4. Standing Committee Minutes, February 24, 1981, Diopa Archives, Lutheran Theological Seminary, Mount Airy (Philadelphia).

5. *JDC 1984*, 92–94; *DN*, April 1985; DCMM Vital Statistics, 1985, and DCMM Guidelines, 1985, both in Diopa Archives.

6. The Right Reverend Allen L. Bartlett Jr. to author, January 27, 2007.

7. These figures were compiled at the author's request by Glenn Colliver, diocesan archivist. According to the convention journal for 2003, there were sixty thousand baptized members of the diocese at that point (66).

8. David Hein and Gardiner H. Shattuck Jr., *The Episcopalians* (Westport, Conn.: Praeger, 2004), 119, 133, 154.

9. Episcopal Church, Diocese of Pennsylvania, *Spanning Four Centuries: Pages of Parish Histories of the Episcopal Diocese of Pennsylvania* (Philadelphia: Episcopal Diocese of Pennsylvania, 1997), sec. 5, p. 14.

10. *DN*, March 1989; *Pennsylvania Episcopalian* (*PE*), November 1990.

11. *PE*, June 2002.

12. *JDC 1981*, 35.

13. "Convention Urges Diocese to Reclaim Social Ministry," *DN*, December 1981, p. A.

14. *PE*, October 1990.

15. *JDC 1982*, 30.

16. *DN*, February 1983.

17. *DN*, April 1983.

18. *JDC 1984*, 40.

19. *JDC 1989*, 43.

20. *PE*, March 1990.

21. *PE*, April 1993.

22. *PE*, May 1994.

23. Standing Committee Minutes, May 27, 1980, Diopa Archives.

24. *PE*, June 1990.

25. Hispanic Ministries, Report to the Diocesan Convention, 1986; History, in Minutes, Hispanic Ministries, 1981–1999, both in Diopa Archives; Diopa, *Spanning Four Centuries*, sec. 3, p. 37; sec. 5, p. 11; the Right Reverend Allen L. Bartlett Jr., interview by author, January 16, 2007.

26. *PE*, January and July 1991; Diopa, *Spanning Four Centuries*, sec. 5, p. 15.

27. Standing Committee Minutes, May 26, 1984, Diopa Archives.

28. *JDC 1989*, 38.

29. *DN*, August, September, and November 1988; *PE*, November 1991, September, November, and December 1992.

30. "Racism Is Lenten Study Focus," *PE*, February and April 1995.

31. *PE*, March 2001.

32. *JDC 1986*, 42; *DN*, May 1986.

33. For more on this movement, see David Cortright and Ron Pagnucco, "Limits to Transnationalism: The 1980s Freeze Campaign," in *Transnational Social Movements and Global Politics*, ed. Jackie Smith, Charles Chatfield, and Cheryl Chatfield (Syracuse: Syracuse University Press, 1997); and Walter Douglas, *Congress and the Nuclear Freeze* (Amherst: University of Massachusetts Press, 1987).

34. Standing Committee Minutes, January 26, 1982, Diopa Archives.

35. *JDC 1981*, 38; *JDC 1982*, 32; *DN*, May 1982.

36. *DN*, April 1982.

37. *JDC 1985*, 41; *JDC 1986*, 48; *JDC 1990*, 41; *DN*, March 1984, October 1985, April 1986; *PE*, January 1990.

38. *JDC 1990*, 43; *PE*, February and March 1991.

39. *JDC 1991*, 36–39; *JDC 1992*, 36; *JDC 1994*, 77; *JDC 1996*, 43.

40. Bartlett, interview.

41. Report of the Diocesan Mission Strategy Commission, October 23–24, 1987, Diopa Archives; *JDC 1994*, 77; Bartlett, interview.

42. Standing Committee Minutes, June 28, 1988, Diopa Archives; Diopa, *Spanning Four Centuries*, sec. 3, pp. 8–10.

43. *PE*, February 1991; *JDC 1997*, 57; Bartlett, interview.
44. *PE*, January and May 2002.
45. *PE*, September 2002.
46. *DN*, June and July 1986.
47. Lyman C. Ogilby to Members of the Diocese of Pennsylvania, January 26, 1984, Diopa Archives.
48. *DN*, April and June 1989.
49. *JDC 1989*, 92; *JDC 1995*, 98.
50. *JDC 1981*, 37.
51. *DN*, December 1986.
52. *JDC 1986*, 41–42; *JDC 1989*, 44; *JDC 1990*, 44.
53. *DN*, May 1988.
54. *DN*, May and June 1988; John L. Harrison Jr. to the Right Reverend Allen L. Bartlett Jr., April 27, 1988, and Bartlett to Members of the Diocese of Pennsylvania, May 1, 1988, both in Diopa Archives.
55. *DN*, May 1989.
56. *Episcopalian*, February 1990; *PE*, November 1991; Hein and Shattuck, *Episcopalians*, 144.
57. "Sexuality Dialogues Yield Different Views," *PE*, July 1993, 6.
58. Allen L. Bartlett Jr. to "Dear Brothers and Sisters," October 7, 1993, Bartlett Papers, Diopa Archives.
59. *PE*, October 1996. See also the issues of June and September 1996.
60. *PE*, December 1994.
61. Bartlett, interview; *JDC 1997*, 58.
62. "Dissidents Challenge Bishops' Truce," *Episcopal Life*, June 1990, 1.
63. *PE*, September 1997; Bartlett, interview.
64. The Right Reverend Charles E. Bennison Jr., interview by author, February 14, 2006.
65. Ibid.
66. David R. Contosta, *A Venture in Faith: The Church of St. Martin-in-the-Fields* (Philadelphia: St. Martin-in-the-Fields, 1988), 95–96; *DN*, January 1985; *PE*, September 1997, February 1998.
67. "Bishops Build Communion," *PE*, September 1998, p. A.
68. *PE*, June 1999.
69. The *Fallser* (a neighborhood newspaper published in the East Falls section of Philadelphia), February 2006.
70. Bennison to author, January 23, 2007.
71. The *Fallser*, October 2002. See also the issue of March 2000.
72. Hein and Shattuck, *Episcopalians*, 152–53.
73. *PE*, May 2000.
74. *PE*, February and June 2003.
75. *PE*, March 2003.
76. "We've Done It," ibid., p. A.
77. *PE*, November 2004.
78. *JDC 2003*, 98; Diopa, "Our Holy Experiment: A Quest for Renewal, Reconciliation, and Mission," July 2001, Diopa Archives.
79. The Reverend Robert Tate, interview by author, January 5, 2007.
80. Memorandum, Program Budget Committee to Clergy and Delegates of Diocesan Convention, January 2, 2007, and 2000 Diocesan Budget, both in Diopa Archives.
81. The trial was covered in reports dated June 10, 11, 12, and 13, 2008, Diopa Archives. The Diocese of Pennsylvania also put out, by e-mail, daily coverage of the trial. Its reports were written by Jerry Hames, former editor of *Episcopal Life*.
82. Diopa, *Newsletter*, July 2008, Diopa Archives.

CONTRIBUTORS

Charles D. Cashdollar is University Professor Emeritus of History at Indiana University of Pennsylvania. He was president of the Pennsylvania Historical Association in 2007–8. Among his publications is *A Spiritual Home: Life in British and American Reformed Congregations, 1830–1915* (Pennsylvania State University Press, 2000).

Marie Conn is Professor of Religious Studies at Chestnut Hill College in Philadelphia. Her most recent books are *C. S. Lewis and Human Suffering: Light Among the Shadows* (Paulist Press, 2009), and (co-editor with Therese McGuire) *Imaging the Other: Essays on Diversity* (University Press of America, 2010).

David R. Contosta is Professor of History at Chestnut Hill College in Philadelphia. He is the author or editor of some twenty books, including, most recently, *Rebel Giants: The Revolutionary Lives of Abraham Lincoln and Charles Darwin* (Prometheus Books, 2008) and *Metropolitan Paradise: The Struggle for Nature in the City* (St. Joseph's University Press, 2010).

William W. Cutler III is Professor Emeritus of History at Temple University. He is the author of *Parents and Schools: The 150-Year Struggle for Control in American Education* (University of Chicago Press, 2000) and the co-editor of *The Divided Metropolis: Social and Spatial Dimensions of Philadelphia, 1800–1975* (Greenwood Press, 1980). He is a member of the Historical Commission of the Diocese of Pennsylvania.

Deborah Mathias Gough is the Director of Advising and New Student Initiatives at the University of Wisconsin–Eau Claire. She is the author of *Christ Church, Philadelphia, The Nation's Church in a Changing City* (Philadelphia: University of Pennsylvania Press, 1995).

Ann Norton Greene is an Assistant Professor and administrator in the History and Sociology of Science Department at the University of Pennsylvania. She is the author of *Horses at Work: Harnessing Power in Industrial America* (Harvard University Press, 2008), and has also written on various aspects of Philadelphia history.

Sheldon Hackney is Professor Emeritus of U.S. History at the University of Pennsylvania, with a specialty in the history of the American South since the Civil War. His *Populism to Progressivism in Alabama* won the American Historical Association's Albert J. Beveridge Award, and he is currently working on a biography of C. Vann Woodward, the noted historian of the American South. Professor Hackney is the former president of Tulane University (1975–81) and the University of Pennsylvania (1981–93), and the former chairman of the National Endowment for the Humanities (1993–97).

Emma Jones Lapsansky-Werner is Professor Emerita of History at Haverford College. Her recent publications include *Quaker Aesthetics*, with Anne Verplanck (University of Pennsylvania Press, 2003), and *Back to Africa: Benjamin Coates and the American Colonization Movement*, with Margaret Hope Bacon (Pennsylvania State University Press, 2005). She is currently at work on a history of a Bryn Mawr Quaker family; a study of a mid-twentieth-century Philadelphia intentional community; and, with Dee Andrews, a reevaluation of eighteenth-century British abolitionist Thomas Clarkson.

William Pencak is Professor Emeritus of History and Jewish Studies at Penn State University and is currently lecturing at Susquehanna University. He is the current editor of *Pennsylvania History* and is completing a biography of Bishop William White. He has written a more extensive article on Anglican loyalist clergy during the American Revolution that appeared in *Pennsylvania's Revolution*, published by Pennsylvania State University Press in 2010.

Thomas F. Rzeznik is Assistant Professor of History at Seton Hall University. He has published articles in American religious history and has written a book, forthcoming from Penn State Press, that explores the intersection of religion and wealth in industrial-era Philadelphia.

INDEX

Italicized page references indicate photographs. Tables are denoted with "t" following the page number. Endnotes are indicated with "n" between the page and note numbers.